Swing for Jython

Jython UI and Scripts Development using Java Swing and WebSphere Application Server

Robert A. Gibson

Swing for Jython: Graphical Jython UI and Scripts Development using Java Swing and WebSphere Application Server

ISBN-13 (pbk): 978-1-4842-0818-2

ISBN-13 (electronic): 978-1-4842-0817-5

Managing Director: Welmoed Spahr
Lead Editor: Steve Anglin
Development Editor: Tracy Brown Hamilton
Technical Reviewers: Rohan Walia, Dhrubojyoti Kayal, Manuel Jordan Elera, and Frank Wierzbicki
Editorial Board: Steve Anglin, Louise Corrigan, Jonathan Gennick, Robert Hutchinson, Michelle Lowman, James Markham, Matthew Moodie, Jeff Olson, Jeffrey Pepper, Douglas Pundick, Ben Renow-Clarke, Gwenan Spearing, Steve Weiss
Coordinating Editor: Mark Powers
Copy Editor: Kezia Endsley
Compositor: SPi Global
Indexer: SPi Global
Artist: SPi Global
Cover Designer: Anna Ishchenko

Distributed to the book trade worldwide by Springer Science+Business Media New York, 233 Spring Street, 6th Floor, New York, NY 10013. Phone 1-800-SPRINGER, fax (201) 348-4505, e-mail orders-ny@springer-sbm.com, or visit www.springeronline.com. Apress Media, LLC is a California LLC and the sole member (owner) is Springer Science + Business Media Finance Inc (SSBM Finance Inc). SSBM Finance Inc is a Delaware corporation.

For information on translations, please e-mail rights@apress.com, or visit www.apress.com.

Apress and friends of ED books may be purchased in bulk for academic, corporate, or promotional use. eBook versions and licenses are also available for most titles. For more information, reference our Special Bulk Sales–eBook Licensing web page at www.apress.com/bulk-sales.

Any source code or other supplementary material referenced by the author in this text is available to readers at www.apress.com/9781484208182. For detailed information about how to locate your book's source code, go to www.apress.com/source-code/.

I thank God for his countless gifts and blessings and dedicate this work to my bride Linda, and our children. Thank you for loving me, and for putting up with me and my fondness of puns. I'm sorry for all the time that this has required, but I have thought of you all throughout its development. I also thank everyone who helped make this book a reality. I could not have done this without your assistance, nor would it have been anywhere as good as you have helped make it.

Contents at a Glance

Contents

About the Author

Robert A. (Bob) Gibson is an Advisory Software Engineer with decades of experience in numerous software-related roles at IBM, including Architect, Developer, Tester, Instructor, and Technical Support. While providing technical support for the IBM's WebSphere Application Server product, he was the primary author for "WebSphere Application Server Administration Using Jython" which was published by IBM Press. He is currently a member of the IBM technical support team responsible for the IBM MQ product on distributed platforms. He holds both a Bachelor of Science degree in Engineering Science and a Master of Science degree in Computer Science from the University of Virginia.

About the Technical Reviewers

Manuel Jordan Elera is an autodidactic developer and researcher who enjoys learning new technologies for his own experiments and creating new integrations.

Manuel won the 2010 Springy Award – Community Champion and Spring Champion 2013. In his little free time, he reads the Bible and composes music on his guitar. Manuel is known as dr_pompeii. He has tech reviewed numerous books for Apress, including *Pro Spring, 4th Edition* (2014), *Practical Spring LDAP* (2013), *Pro JPA 2, Second Edition* (2013), and *Pro Spring Security* (2013).

Read his 13 detailed tutorials about many Spring technologies, contact him through his blog at http://www.manueljordanelera.blogspot.com, and follow him on his Twitter account, @dr_pompeii

Dhrubojyoti Kayal is a hands-on Java developer and architect. He is an open source evangelist. He has been helping enterprises solve integration challenges and build complex large applications leveraging Java technologies for the past 14 years. His current area of focus is data migration and real-time analytics with Java. Dhrubojyoti is also the author of *Pro Java EE Spring Pattern* (2008) from Apress.

Rohan Walia is a Senior Software Consultant with extensive experience in client/server, web-based, and enterprise application development. He is an Oracle Certified ADF Implementation Specialist and a Sun Certified Java Programmer. Rohan is responsible for designing and developing end-to-end applications consisting of various cutting-edge frameworks and utilities. His areas of expertise are Oracle ADF, Oracle WebCenter, Fusion, Spring, Hibernate, and Java/J2EE. When not working, Rohan loves to play tennis, hike, and travel. Rohan would like to thank his wife, Deepika Walia, for using all her experience and expertise when reviewing this book.

Frank Wierzbicki is the head of the Jython project and a member of the Python Software Foundation. He has over 15 years of experience as a software developer, primarily working in Python and Java. He has been programming since the Commodore 64 was the king of home computers (look it up kids!) and can't imagine why anyone would do anything else for a living. Frank's most enduring hobby is picking up new programming languages, but he has yet to find one that is more fun to work with than Python.

Introduction

A long time ago, in a galaxy far, far away...

Okay, maybe not so long ago, unless you are thinking in terms of "web years." In 1995, Java was introduced into the world. At that time, it included a Graphical User Interface (GUI) framework called the Abstract Window Toolkit (AWT). Unfortunately, the AWT contained many native widgets that depended on the underlying operating system.

It didn't take long to realize that the AWT approach was limited, and unfortunately, unreliable. So, in 1997, the Java Foundation Classes (JFC) was introduced and included the Swing component classes.[1]

Late in 1997, Jython was created to combine the performance provided by the Java Virtual Machine (JVM) with the elegance of Python. In so doing, the entire collection of existing Java classes were added to the ones available from Python. What this means to a software developer is that the rapid prototyping and iteration of Python can be combined with the impressive class hierarchy of Java to provide an amazing software development platform.

In 2002, Samuele Pedroni and Noel Rappin wrote a book titled *Jython Essentials* which, interestingly enough, uses an example similar to the one shown in Listing 1.

Listing 1. Welcome to Jython Swing

```
wsadmin>from javax.swing import JFrame
wsadmin>win = JFrame( "Welcome to Jython Swing" )
wsadmin>win.size = ( 400, 100 )
wsadmin>win.show()
```

The output of this interactive wsadmin code snippet is shown in Figure 1.

Figure 1. *Welcome to Jython Swing application output*

At the time of this writing, the first chapter of Jython Essentials was (still) available on the O'Reilly website.[2]

So, it has been obvious, at least to some people, just how valuable and powerful Jython can be as a Swing development environment.

---

[1] I hadn't realized, at least until I looked at *Java Foundation Classes in a Nutshell* by David Flanagan, just how much of the JFC was composed of Swing classes and components. Most of Part I of that book documents the GUI Application Programming Interfaces (APIs) used in client-side Java programs.

[2] See http://oreilly.com/catalog/jythoness/chapter/ch01.html.

Why Read This Book?

You may ask, if the *Jython Essentials* book has been around for more than a decade and talks about using Swing with Jython, is this book really necessary? The answer to that question is yes, because *Jython Essentials*, as well as the other Jython books, talk a little about using Swing with Jython and provides occasional example programs, but this topic is mentioned only in passing.

There are some other books about Jython, most notably *The Definitive Guide to Jython: Python for the Java Platform* by Jim Baker, Josh Juneau, Frank Wierzbicki, Leo Soto, and Victor Ng (Apress, ISBN 978-1-4302-2527-0). It too has some examples of using Swing with Jython. Unfortunately for the person interested in learning how to write Jython Swing applications, the amount of information is limited.

What Does This Book Cover?

The focus of this book, on the other hand, is to show you how to use Swing to add a GUI to your Jython scripts, with an emphasis on the WebSphere Application Server `wsadmin` utility. In fact, we teach you Swing using Jython and do it in a way that will make your scripts easier for people to use, more robust, more understandable, and therefore easier to maintain.

The Swing hierarchy is a huge beast.

How do you eat an elephant? One bite at a time.

That's what you're going to do with Swing in this book—consume it in a lot of small bytes.

In order to make it more easily consumable, the book uses lots of examples, with most of them building on earlier ones. In fact, by the time you're done, you'll have touched on the almost 300 scripts that were written during the creation of this book.

Additional challenges exist, for example, event handling and threads. These too require some clarifying examples and explanation. We will also be dealing with concurrency, especially in the context of using threads in the applications that are created.

As you progress, you'll see that there are often a number of different ways to do things. We try to point some of these different approaches, depending on the context. Why only some? Well, unfortunately, we are rarely able to identify them all. As I found after reading lots of different programs, there is often yet another way to do something. So, we admit that we don't know everything. In fact, that's one of the things that we find neat and interesting about writing code. We love to learn and hope that you do too.

Swing development is a "target rich" environment.

These days, it's a challenge to find command-line only programs. Wherever you look, programs have a graphical interface and allow the users to use their mouse to make selections. Frequently, you can use the mouse to completely specify the information required by a program to perform the user-desired operations. How many times have you been able to use a mouse to make all of the selections from the displayed information? I bet you don't have to think too hard to come up with a number of examples of this kind of interaction.

Unfortunately, this has not been the case for most WebSphere Application Server (WSAS) administrative scripts. When using `wsadmin` to execute one of these WSAS administrative scripts, developers have been forced to do one of the following:

- Provide command-line options as input.

- Use some kind of input file (such as a properties file, Windows `.ini` file, and so on).

- Have the script prompt the users and wait for them to provide an appropriate response.

This book is going to help you change all that. We're going to cover all of the information that you need to help you add a Graphical User Interface (GUI) to your WSAS Jython scripts. Does that mean that we cover each and every Java Swing class, method, and constant? No, unfortunately not. Take a look at *Java Swing* by Robert Eckstein, Marc Loy, and Dave Wood (ISBN 1-56592-455-X); it's more than 1,000 pages long! And, it's not the only huge book on Java Swing. Unfortunately, this is part of the problem. Many people are intimidated by the amount of information and are unsure of how and where to start.

One thing that you should realize is that we don't have to create a huge tome about each and every aspect on this subject in order to make it useful. For one, we don't duplicate information that is available elsewhere. What we do need to do is show you:

- What is possible

- What is required

- How to make use of existing information

- How to take Java examples and produce equivalent (possibly even better) Jython scripts that do the same kind of thing

And that is what we intend to do with this book. How does that sound?

What You Need

What is required?

This book is all about using the Java Swing classes in your Jython scripts. The fact that a number of examples use the IBM WebSphere Application Server (WSAS) to demonstrate different things does not mean that you must have WSAS in order to use Swing in your Jython scripts. I happen to use the WSAS environment to demonstrate some of the more complete applications. So it is important to note that some, but not all, of the scripts included with this work depend on information that is provided by a WSAS environment. If you are interested in using the information in this book in your own Jython scripts, I encourage you to do so.

All of the book's scripts have been tested using WSAS versions 8.5, 8.0, and 7.0. Some of them are also usable on version 6.1, but there are some things that don't exist in that version of wsadmin.[3] When these issues pop up, they are addressed.

Most contemporary software programs have a graphical user interface. In fact, some people (like my kids) would be stymied by something like a Windows or UNIX command prompt.

They would likely ask something like, "What am I supposed to do now? There's nothing to click on!" That's what this book is all about—helping you create user-friendly Jython scripts using Java Swing classes.

---

[3]Most notably, any scripts that depend on the SwingWorker class won't work on version 6.1 of WSAS since that class is not available in the 6.1 wsadmin class hierarchy.

CHAPTER 1

Components and Containers

Before you begin your exploration of Swing objects and classes, I need to first explain how I am going to describe these things. For the most part, the objects that you use on your graphical applications are called *components*. In some places, they may be referred to as widgets. I'll try to be consistent and stick with components in hope of minimizing confusion.

In this chapter, you get your first exposure to the Swing hierarchy and see how a Jython application can use the Swing classes to create a Graphical User Interface (GUI). You'll begin with top-level container types and see what makes them special. Then you will see how Jython can help you to investigate and understand the class hierarchy. Next, you create a trivial application using an interactive session. You also get your first exposure to some of the challenges associated with the positioning of components on an application when you aren't aware of class default values. Finally, you'll see how users can impact the way that things are displayed should they resize the application window.

Another thing that you need to realize is that the Java Swing classes are not a complete replacement of the AWT. There are a number of places, as you will see, where AWT features continue to be used. For example, the AWT event-handling elements and mechanisms are an integral part of the user interface that most people consider "Java Swing." When AWT features are needed, they are identified accordingly.

As you will soon see, you will be building applications using Swing components placed in a way to convey information to the users. Sometimes the users can interact with these components in order to provide information to the application. At other times, the components are used only to provide information to the users. An example of this kind of component is text placed on the application near an input field to direct users as to what kind of information, or input, is expected.

Sometimes, multiple components or objects are grouped together and associated with one another. An example of this is a list of some sort that's used to make a selection. This grouping of components will be associated with, and contained within, a collection. One of the many concepts explained in this book is how to tell the Swing classes how a collection should be displayed. In fact, in order for a component to be visible, it must be associated with a container of some sort. Because of this, a hierarchy of containers and components exists in every Swing application. At the top of the hierarchy there needs to be a root, or top-level, container that holds the complete collection of application components.[1] This might make a little more sense when you see some examples.

Top-Level Containers

Some Swing containers are special. The main difference between these and other containers in the Swing hierarchy is that none of the top-level containers are descended from the `javax.swing.JComponent` class. In fact, each of them is a descendant of an AWT class. Because of this, these containers may not be placed into any other container. All of these special containers are called "top-level" containers because they are at the top (relatively speaking) of the application hierarchy.

---

[1]The biggest difference between collections and components is that a collection is a kind of component that can hold other components.

What are these container classes, and what does it mean that they aren't descended from `javax.swing.JComponent`?

Take a look at the Java class documentation (i.e., the output of the Javadoc tool that's used to generate API documentation in HTML).[2] In this documentation, you need to locate the top-level containers. Table 1-1 shows the top portion of the class hierarchy for each of the top-level containers.

Table 1-1. *Top-Level Containers*

Container Type	Class Hierarchy
JApplet[3]	java.lang.Object
	java.awt.Component
	java.awt.Container
	java.awt.Panel
	java.applet.Applet
	javax.swing.JApplet
JDialog[4]	java.lang.Object
	java.awt.Component
	java.awt.Container
	java.awt.Window
	java.awt.Dialog
	javax.swing.JDialog
JFrame[5]	java.lang.Object
	java.awt.Component
	java.awt.Container
	java.awt.Window
	java.awt.Frame
	javax.swing.JFrame
JWindow[6]	java.lang.Object
	java.awt.Component
	java.awt.Container
	java.awt.Window
	javax.swing.JWindow

As you can see, each of these classes descends from a `java.awt` class, not from the `javax.swing.JComponent` class. As with all AWT classes, this means that there is a significant portion of the class that is composed of native (i.e., operating system-specific) code.

---

[2]See http://www.oracle.com/technetwork/java/javase/documentation/index-jsp-135444.html.
[3]See http://docs.oracle.com/javase/8/docs/api/javax/swing/JApplet.html.
[4]See http://docs.oracle.com/javase/8/docs/api/javax/swing/JDialog.html.
[5]See http://docs.oracle.com/javase/8/docs/api/javax/swing/JFrame.html.
[6]See http://docs.oracle.com/javase/8/docs/api/javax/swing/JWindow.html.

Looking at these top-level components might make you wonder about the difference between a window (JWindow) and a frame (JFrame). Listing 1-1 shows a trivial interactive wsadmin session[7] that can be used to display a JWindow instance of a specific size.[8]

Listing 1-1. Simple JWindow example

```
wsadmin>from java.awt     import Dimension
wsadmin>from javax.swing import JWindow
wsadmin>win = JWindow()
wsadmin>win.setSize( Dimension( 400, 100 ) )
wsadmin>win.show()
```

Wait a minute. How did I know that I needed to import the Dimension class from the java.awt library and then instantiate one of them in order to invoke the setSize() method?

The answer is I cheated. I first tried to do it without importing the Dimension class, as in Listing 1-2.

Listing 1-2. The setSize() exception

```
wsadmin>from javax.swing import JWindow
wsadmin>win = JWindow()
wsadmin>win.setSize( ( 400, 100 ) )
WASX7015E: Exception running command: "win.setSize( ( 400, 100 ) )";
exception information: com.ibm.bsf.BSFException: exception from Jython:
... setSize(): 1st arg can't be coerced to java.awt.Dimension
```

Did you notice how the exception tells you exactly what you need to use to resolve the issue? This demonstrates just how easy it is to use an interactive wsadmin (or Jython) session to develop and test your applications.[9]

Now, getting back to the JWindow. If you execute the steps shown in Listing 1-1, you'll notice how empty it is. It is a completely blank slate. This provides you with the opportunity to completely define how your application will look. The tradeoff though is that you have to define each and every aspect of the application. For this reason, however, I prefer to use the JFrame as a starting point (at least for now), since it does a lot of the work for me. In fact, the vast majority of scripts in the remainder of the book use the JFrame class.

Getting Help from Jython

You just looked at the Java class documentation for the top-level containers. Do you really have to use the documentation, or is there any way to get to this kind of information from Jython? Let's take a quick look at what Jython can do to help you. Listing 1-3 shows an interactive wsadmin session that includes the definition of a simple Jython class function (called classes) that can display information about the class definition hierarchy. In this case, this function is used to show information about the JFrame class.

---

[7]To start an interactive session, execute either the wsadmin.bat or wsadmin.sh shell script and identify the scripting language to be used as Jython. For example, "./wsadmin.sh -conntype none -lang Jython".
[8]I did not include a figure of the result because it is simply a plain white rectangle displayed in the top-left corner of the screen. Go ahead and try it for yourself, and you'll see what I mean.
[9]You'll find that we often use script and application interchangeably in this book.

Listing 1-3. The **classes** function

```
wsadmin>from javax.swing import JFrame
wsadmin>
wsadmin>def classes( Class, pad = '' ) :
wsadmin>    print pad + str( Class )
wsadmin>    for base in Class.__bases__ :
wsadmin>        classes( base, pad + '| ' )
wsadmin>
wsadmin>classes( JFrame )
javax.swing.JFrame
| java.awt.Frame
| | java.awt.Window
| | | java.awt.Container
| | | | java.awt.Component
| | | | | java.lang.Object
| | | | | java.awt.image.ImageObserver
| | | | | java.awt.MenuContainer
| | | | | java.io.Serializable
| | | javax.accessibility.Accessible
| | java.awt.MenuContainer
| javax.swing.WindowConstants
| javax.accessibility.Accessible
| javax.swing.RootPaneContainer
wsadmin>
```

How does this information compare with what you saw earlier from the Java class documentation? One difference is that the information that is displayed is from the specified class, which in this case is JFrame, down toward its ancestor components. It is also more complete. The really neat thing about this is that you are using the power of Jython to understand what is available from the Java Swing hierarchy.

How and Why Are You Able to Do This?

Java includes some properties that allow objects and classes to be dynamically "queried" to determine information about what the objects and classes can do. These properties are called *reflection* and *introspection*. The classes function in Listing 1-3 illustrates one way to use these properties. I won't get into this too much, at least at this point, but you will be seeing more about how to use some of the properties later.[10]

What's Next?…Starting Simple

After starting with a frame, you need to decide what your application should display. Let's start by adding the ubiquitous "Hello World!" message. How do you go about doing that? First, you have to figure out what kind of object you need to display text.

Swing has a component for that, called a JLabel. (You will soon realize that many of the Java Swing components start with a capital J).

---

[10]One important point to mention is that the output produced by the classes function when Jython (not wsadmin) is used is much harder to read. I chose to use the wsadmin environment for simplicity and readability.

Before you create a JLabel object, you need to tell Jython where it can obtain details about this class, just like you did for the JFrame class. Again, you use a variation of the Jython import statement. Listing 1-4 shows one way to do exactly this.

Listing 1-4. Adding a JLabel to the application

```
wsadmin>from javax.swing import JFrame
wsadmin>from javax.swing import JLabel
wsadmin>
wsadmin>frame = JFrame( 'Hello world' )
wsadmin>label = frame.add( JLabel( 'Hello Swing world' ) )
wsadmin>frame.pack()
wsadmin>frame.setVisible( 1 )
wsadmin>
```

The steps used in this example can be described as follows:

1. Instantiate (create) a JFrame object (supply the title). This is done by calling the JFrame constructor.

2. Instantiate a JLabel object (supply the label text). This is done by calling the JLabel constructor.

3. Add the JLabel object to the JFrame (application) object. This is done by calling the JFrame add() method and passing the JLabel object to it.[11]

The result of executing the code in Listing 1-4 is a small application window located in the top-left corner of the screen. first image in Figure 1-1

Figure 1-1. The "Hello Swing world" window

The shows what this window looks like. It's interesting to note, however, that the application title, which is normally on the title bar, is obscured by the application icons. The second image in Figure 1-1 shows what happens when you grab the right side of the window and drag it to the right, thereby increasing the window width and making the application title visible.

Adding a Second Label

Hopefully, that seems pretty straightforward to you. Let's add another label just to see what happens. Listing 1-5 shows a different interactive wsadmin session that does just that.

---

[11]The program saves the result of calling **frame.add()** into a variable simply to make the interactive session more readable.

Listing 1-5. Adding a second JLabel to the application

```
wsadmin>from javax.swing import JFrame
wsadmin>from javax.swing import JLabel
wsadmin>
wsadmin>frame = JFrame( 'Hello world' )
wsadmin>label = frame.add( JLabel( 'Hello Swing world' ) )
wsadmin>label = frame.add( JLabel( 'Testing, 1, 2, 3' ) )
wsadmin>frame.pack()
wsadmin>frame.setVisible( 1 )
wsadmin>
```

Figure 1-2 shows the output. Unfortunately, it probably doesn't look like you expected it to. What happened? The simple answer is that you didn't tell the frame where to add the second label, so it put both labels in the same place, and Swing can't show both labels in the same place. This chapter isn't the best place get into details about Layout Managers; you'll learn about them in Chapter 5. You'll do just enough to get by here.

Figure 1-2. *After adding the second JLabel*

Is there a something simple that you can do make this example work? Yes there is! Listing 1-6 shows how you can change the default Layout Manager used by the JFrame objects.[12]

Listing 1-6. Changing the default JFrame Layout Manager

```
wsadmin>from java.awt import FlowLayout
wsadmin>
wsadmin>from javax.swing import JFrame
wsadmin>from javax.swing import JLabel
wsadmin>
wsadmin>frame = JFrame( 'Frame title' )
wsadmin>frame.setLayout( FlowLayout() )
wsadmin>label = frame.add( JLabel( 'Hello Swing world' ) )
wsadmin>label = frame.add( JLabel( 'Testing, 1, 2, 3' ) )
wsadmin>frame.pack()
wsadmin>frame.setVisible( 1 )
wsadmin>
```

Unfortunately, as you can see in the image on the left in Figure 1-3, the two labels are side by side on the same line. If you drag the corner of the window to narrow the application window a little bit, you'll get better results. The image on the right in Figure 1-3 shows how the two labels are separate and distinct.

---

[12]In case you are interested, BorderLayout is the default Layout Manager used by JFrame.

Figure 1-3. *Adjacent JLabel objects*

Summary

What has this chapter taught you? For one thing, it shows how easily you can create a trivial graphical application using Jython and Swing. However, these aren't really good examples because they were created using interactive `wsadmin` sessions. In the next chapter, you'll learn about the differences between interactive sessions and script files.

CHAPTER 2

■ ■ ■

Interactive Sessions vs. Scripts

It shouldn't take long for you to realize that you don't want to be using interactive wsadmin sessions for your applications. What does it take? Well, there are some things of which you must be aware.

This chapter begins with some additional interactive scripts to help illustrate some of the important differences between the interactive environment and what is needed for your Jython Swing scripts to be successful. Part of this process includes using the Java compiler to understand that some methods have been deprecated. Unfortunately Jython doesn't warn you about this when the scripts using those methods are executed. Finally, you'll take a look at thread safety and the challenge that it presents to developers.

Running Your First Script from a File

Let's start by putting the trivial script from the previous chapter into a text file and then execute it using wsadmin.[1] Listing 2-1 shows the contents of the Welcome.py script file.

Listing 2-1. The Welcome.py Script File

```
from javax.swing import JFrame
win = JFrame( 'Welcome to Jython Swing' )
win.size = ( 400, 100 )
win.show()
```

What happens when you execute this script using wsadmin?[2] Nothing, that's what. The question is, why don't you see anything? The simple answer is that the call to the show() method returns immediately, and the script exits. There isn't time for the Swing framework to display the instantiated window. To verify this, you can add a statement that causes the script to wait. The easiest and simplest way to do this is to use the raw_input() function to display a message and then wait for user input. Listing 2-2 shows the contents of the modified Welcome1.py script file.

Listing 2-2. The Welcome1.py Script File

```
from javax.swing import JFrame
win = JFrame( 'Welcome to Jython Swing' )
win.size = ( 400, 100 )
win.show()
if 'AdminConfig' in dir() :
    raw_input( '\nPress <Enter> to terminate the application: ' )
```

---

[1]For those using Jython and not wsadmin, you don't need to use raw_input() to pause the script.
[2]The command should look something like wsadmin -conntype none -f Welcome.py.

9

That's better! When you execute this script, the wsadmin utility stays around long enough for the application window to be displayed. Even though the application isn't too exciting, it is interesting enough as a starting point.

The next question you should ask at this point is, "What happens when you use (click on) the application close icon in the top-right corner of the application window?" The application exits, right? No, it doesn't. Look at the interactive wsadmin command prompt window. It continues to show the "Press <Enter> to terminate the application:" message. If you press the Enter key at this point, wsadmin exits and the operating system command prompt is displayed.[3]

How do you fix this behavior? How do you get wsadmin to exit when you use the application's close icon? The simple answer is that you have to tell it to. If you take a moment to think about it, you'll realize that the close icon is part of the JFrame. If you take a look at the JFrame online documentation,[4] you'll find the following:

> *Unlike a Frame, a JFrame has some notion of how to respond when the user attempts to close the window. The default behavior is to simply hide the JFrame when the user closes the window. To change the default behavior, you invoke the setDefaultCloseOperation(int) method.*

Listing 2-3 shows the revised script, Welcome2.py. The only change from the previous script is the addition of a call to the setDefaultCloseOperation() method. What happens when you run this script and click on the close icon? The application window is removed, and the wsadmin utility terminates.

Listing 2-3. The Welcome2.py Script File

```
from javax.swing import JFrame
win = JFrame( 'Welcome to Jython Swing' )
win.setDefaultCloseOperation( JFrame.EXIT_ON_CLOSE )
win.size = ( 400, 100 )
win.show()
if 'AdminConfig' in dir() :
    raw_input( '\nPress <Enter> to terminate the application: ' )
```

This is perfect, right? No, not really. There are a couple of things that aren't as they should be.

Depending "Too Much" on Limited Information

The first problem with the trivial script in Listing 2-3 isn't very obvious. In fact, to figure out this problem, you can either:

- Look closely at the JFrame documentation.

- Write and compile an equivalent Java application.

Listing 2-4 shows an equivalent Java application.

---

[3]For readers who use Jython and not wsadmin, the Java process will still be executing in the background when you execute the script.
[4]See http://docs.oracle.com/javase/8/docs/api/javax/swing/JFrame.html.

Listing 2-4. Welcome3.java

```java
import javax.swing.JFrame;

public class Welcome3 {
    public static void main( String args[] ) {
        JFrame win = new JFrame( "Welcome to Java Swing" );
        win.setDefaultCloseOperation( JFrame.EXIT_ON_CLOSE );
        win.setSize( 400, 100 );
        win.show();
    }
}
```

What happens when you compile this? The warning messages (notes) shown in Figure 2-1 are generated.

```
Note: Welcome3.java uses or overrides a deprecated API.
Note: Recompile with -Xlint:deprecation for details.
```

Figure 2-1. *Welcome3 warning messages*

If you recompile Welcome3 using the specified option, you get a more detailed explanation of the problem, as shown in Figure 2-2.

```
warning: [deprecation] show() in java.awt.Window has been deprecated
```

Figure 2-2. *Welcome3 detailed deprecation message*

Looking at the documentation for this show( ) method,[5] you'll find that you should be using setVisible(boolean) instead.

This shows[6] you a challenge that you'll encounter when using Jython to call Java methods. The Java compiler informs the users when a method has been deprecated, but the Jython environment does not. I'm not suggesting that you should avoid using calls to Java methods in your Jython scripts. Far from it' I'm just letting you know that you should check to see if a method has been deprecated before using it in your scripts. This situation is most likely to occur, at least from my experience, if you obtain an existing Java Swing program and translate, or convert, it to the equivalent Jython without checking for this kind of issue.

---

[5]See http://docs.oracle.com/javase/8/docs/api/java/awt/Window.html#show%28%29.
[6]Pun intended.

Swing Threads

Deprecated methods aren't the only kind of issue of which you need to be aware. One of the most significant differences between simple applications and ones where the developer needs to be able to interact with users and respond to events is related to threads of control (aka threads). Articles have been around for quite some time that discuss issues related to the fact that Swing developers should be aware of the fact that most Swing components are not thread-safe,[7] and techniques exists for performing long-running operations.[8]

One technique is to define the application in a separate class and then wrap the instantiation of this class in a Java Runnable class. The calling of this Runnable class is deferred until the Swing environment is ready for it. This slight delay is performed by the Swing Event Dispatch thread and is initiated by a call to the invokeLater() method call of the SwingUtilities, or EventQueue class. This concept can be hard to follow. Take a look at an example of this technique, as shown in Listing 2-5.

Listing 2-5. Template1.py

```
 1|import java
 2|import sys
 3|from    java.awt    import EventQueue
 4|from    javax.swing import JFrame
 5|class Template1 :
 6|    def __init__( self ) :
 7|        frame = JFrame( 'Title' )
 8|        frame.setDefaultCloseOperation( JFrame.EXIT_ON_CLOSE )
 9|        frame.pack()
10|        frame.setVisible( 1 )
11|class Runnable( java.lang.Runnable ) :
12|    def __init__( self, fun ) :
13|        self.runner = fun
14|    def run( self ) :
15|        self.runner()
16|if __name__ in [ '__main__', 'main' ] :
17|    EventQueue.invokeLater( Runnable( Template1 ) )
18|    if 'AdminConfig' in dir() :
19|        raw_input( '\nPress <Enter> to terminate the application: ' )
20|else :
21|    print '\nError: This script should be executed, not imported.\n'
22|    if 'JYTHON_JAR' in dir( sys ) :
23|        print 'jython %s.py' % __name__
24|    else :
25|        print 'Usage: wsadmin -f %s.py' % __name__
26|    sys.exit()
```

A detailed description for this code can be found in Table 2-1.

---

[7]See http://java.sun.com/products/jfc/tsc/articles/threads/threads1.html.
[8]See http://java.sun.com/products/jfc/tsc/articles/threads/threads2.html.

Table 2-1. *Template1.py Details*

Lines	Detailed Description
1-4	Statements used to add class names to the Jython namespace.
5-10	User-defined application class (i.e., Template1).
11-15	Wrapper class, descended from java.lang.Runnable, that saves a class reference in the constructor and delays the instantiation of the class until the run() method is called (on the Swing Event Dispatch thread).
16-22	This is the (apparent) script-entry point. This code determines if the script was executed or imported. If imported, an error message is displayed and the script exits. If the script was executed, a call to instantiate the user application class is deferred until the Swing Event Dispatch thread is ready to do so.

A roughly equivalent approach is shown in Listing 2-6.

Listing 2-6. Template2.py

```
 1|import java
 2|import sys
 3|from   java.awt    import EventQueue
 4|from   javax.swing import JFrame
 5|class Template2( java.lang.Runnable ) :
 6|    def run( self ) :
 7|        frame = JFrame( 'Title' )
 8|        frame.setDefaultCloseOperation( JFrame.EXIT_ON_CLOSE )
 9|        frame.pack()
10|        frame.setVisible( 1 )
11|if __name__ in [ '__main__', 'main' ] :
12|    EventQueue.invokeLater( Template2() )
13|    if 'AdminConfig' in dir() :
14|        raw_input( '\nPress <Enter> to terminate the application: ' )
15|else :
16|    print '\nError: This script should be executed, not imported.\n'
17|    if 'JYTHON_JAR' in dir( sys ) :
18|        print 'jython %s.py' % __name__
19|    else :
20|        print 'Usage: wsadmin -f %s.py' % __name__
21|    sys.exit()
```

Looking closely at these two listings, you should notice the differences. Instead of defining a separate user application class that creates the Swing application components in the class constructor, this code places all of the Swing component-creation operations in the class run() method.

The example scripts provided and described in this book tend to use the second template since it requires a little less code. It also makes a bit more sense, at least to me. While writing the example scripts in this book I found it extremely easy to start with the Template script and add the code that was required to demonstrate the topic being discussed. One useful feature of this technique is the fact that it should help you focus on the important differences and hopefully spend less time with the script as a whole.

Summary

This chapter shows what happens when you start using script files instead of interactive wsadmin sessions for your applications. The biggest difference is that you have to add a way for the script file to wait for the users to interact with the application. To do so, the script files will often use something like the raw_input() function provided by Jython. Additionally, subsequent script files in this book include an application class that defines the Jython components, containers, and structures used by the applications demonstrating the use of Swing classes and constructs.

CHAPTER 3

■ ■ ■

Building a Simple Global Security Application

In my experience, learning a programming topic is much easier when good examples are included. Throughout this book, you're going to go through the process of building simple Jython Swing applications from scratch. As you do so, you will be learning about some of the available Swing components and using them to make your application useful. In this chapter, you take a quick look at a simple graphical application that displays whether the WebSphere Global Security has been enabled or not. This will lead you to the topics of panes and layers, which are so very important to Swing applications.

Adding Text to the Application Using a JLabel

At this point, you haven't learned how to build a non-trivial, fully functional application. However, you do have information eno ugh to get started. How so? Well, you'll start simple by building a simple application that displays the status of the global security. For those who may be unfamiliar with it, global security is simply a setting that determines whether a username and password is required to administer the application server environment. Listing 3-1 shows a complete Jython script to do just this.

Listing 3-1. SecStatus.py

```
 1|import java
 2|from    java.awt    import EventQueue
 3|from    javax.swing import JFrame
 4|from    javax.swing import JLabel
 5|class SecStatus( java.lang.Runnable ) :
 6|    def run( self ) :
 7|        frame = JFrame( 'Global Security' )
 8|        frame.setDefaultCloseOperation( JFrame.EXIT_ON_CLOSE )
 9|        security = AdminConfig.list( 'Security' )
10|        status = AdminConfig.showAttribute( security, 'enabled' )
11|        frame.add( JLabel( 'Security enabled: ' + status ) )
12|        frame.pack()
13|        frame.setVisible( 1 )
14|if __name__ in [ '__main__', 'main' ] :
15|    EventQueue.invokeLater( SecStatus() )
16|    raw_input( '\nPress <Enter> to terminate the application: ' )
17|else :
18|    print 'Error: This script should be executed, not imported.\n'
19|    print 'Usage: wsadmin -f %s.py' % __name__
```

The statements that make use of wsadmin scripting objects are shown in lines 9 and 10. This application doesn't require a graphical user interface. In fact, it can easily be performed using a single wsadmin command with a print statement to display the status. Listing 3-2 shows a simple wsadmin command line that can be used to display the same security status information.[1]

Listing 3-2. wsadmin Command that Displays the Global Security Status

```
wsadmin -conntype none -lang jython -c "print 'Security enabled: '
+ AdminConfig.showAttribute( AdminConfig.list( 'Security' ), 'enabled' )"
```

However, you will quickly see that scripts that interact with users are often good candidates for graphical user interface, and so that is what you will be learning to do.

No "Pane," No Gain

When your application creates one of the top-level containers (e.g., a JFrame), a number of things are created by that container to help it perform its role. One of the things created by the JFrame constructor is a RootPane (which happens to be of type JRootPane).[2]

What does this RootPane do? It is composed of, and is used to manage, the following panes, each of which will be described in the following sections:

- A glass pane
- A layered pane
- A content pane
- An optional menu bar

When You Live in a Glass House, Everything Is a Pane

The glass pane can be used to intercept events.[3] For most applications, it is a transparent pane that doesn't get in the way of your visible application components. However, there may be a time when you want to have something made visible on the glass pane that covers an existing component on the content pane. There is an interesting example in the *Java Swing Tutorial,* on the :How to Use Root Panes" page,[4] that demonstrates one possible use of the glass pane. A section about the glass pane can be found on that same page.[5]

At this point, I haven't discussed enough of using Swing with Jython for the novice user to understand this particular example. However, someone with some knowledge of Java Swing and Jython might be interested in how an equivalent Jython script would look. For those folks, I have included a translated version of the GlassPaneDemo.py script to read and play with. Figure 3-1 shows some sample images that can be created using this script. The complete script is available in the source code for this chapter.

---

[1]The contents of Listing 3-2 must be entered as a single line / statement.
[2]See http://docs.oracle.com/javase/8/docs/api/javax/swing/JRootPane.html.
[3]Which have not yet been defined. For the time being, you can think of things like mouse clicks as events, the first discussion of which appears in Chapter 4.
[4]See http://docs.oracle.com/javase/tutorial/uiswing/components/rootpane.html.
[5]See http://docs.oracle.com/javase/tutorial/uiswing/components/rootpane.html#glasspane.

Figure 3-1. *GlassPaneDemo.py sample images*

The Layered Look Can Also Be a Pane

I'm certain that you have used an application that includes components that involve different layers. One of the most common instances of layers occurs when a pop-up menu is displayed. It is important that this menu isn't obscured by any of the existing components. The layered pane is used to great effect for component positioning. Right now, you don't have to worry about this pane. It is discussed in Chapter 19.

The Optional MenuBar

Almost every graphical application that you can think of has some kind of menu. The MenuBar is a collection of MenuItems that are displayed to allow users to make selections. The applications that you create are likely to use MenuBars. In fact, many of the complete scripts that are developed in the last few chapters of this book use MenuBars and MenuItems. Since this is an important topic, the book spends all of Chapter 10 on menu-related issues.

The Content Pane Will Contain Most of the Visible Items

All Swing applications have at least one top-level container. Each of these top-level containers is the top, or root, of the application containment hierarchy (i.e., all of the visible components that appear in the container). In this book, almost all of the example applications will have a JFrame as the top-level container.

Additionally, just about every application will place the components to be displayed on the JFrame content pane. So, one of the most common things that needs to be done with a JFrame instance is to obtain a reference to its content pane. This is typically done using syntax like that shown in Listing 3-3.

Listing 3-3. Getting a JFrame Content Pane Reference

```
contentPane = frame.getContentPane()
```

What kind of object is returned by this call? The simple answer is that a java.awt.Container[6] is returned. What, exactly, is a java.awt.Container? It certainly is a lot easier to comprehend than it is to describe. In fact, I described Swing containers as components that can hold a group of zero or more components.

---

[6]See http://docs.oracle.com/javase/8/docs/api/javax/swing/JFrame.html#getContentPane().

Looking at the documentation,[7] you can see that it has six dozen methods. Granted, seven of these have been deprecated and another five are protected, which means that you really shouldn't be using them from your Jython scripts. Another seven have multiple overloaded variations (e.g., there are five different add() methods). These add() methods are shown in Table 3-1.

Table 3-1. *Component add() methods*

Modifier and Type	Method and Description
Component	add(Component comp)
	Appends the specified component to the end of this container.
Component	add(Component comp, int index)
	Adds the specified component to this container at the given position.
void	add(Component comp, Object constraints)
	Adds the specified component to the end of this container.
void	add(Component comp, Object constraints, int index)
	Adds the specified component to this container with the specified constraints at the specified index.
Component	add(String name, Component comp)
	Adds the specified component to this container.

I won't be digging too deeply into these various methods, but I will be making good use of a number of them. In fact, you have already seen some example uses of the add() method (see line 11 of Listing 3-1, for example).

Did you catch that? I snuck one in on you there. If you were watching closely, you may have wondered why Listing 3-1 doesn't include a call to the getContentPane() method, as shown in Listing 3-3. How does this work? Well, the Swing developers realized that some method calls are very common, so they have provided a convenience. Instead of writing a statement like you see in Listing 3-4, you are allowed to leave out the call to the getContentPane() method.

Listing 3-4. Calling getContentPane() to add() Something

```
frame.getContentPane().add( something )
```

Where is this documented? Right on the JFrame documentation,[8] where you'll find the paragraph shown in Figure 3-2.[9]

---

[7]See http://docs.oracle.com/javase/8/docs/api/java/awt/Container.html.
[8]See http://docs.oracle.com/javase/8/docs/api/javax/swing/JFrame.html.
[9]Yes, convenience is misspelled in the documentation.

... As a conveniance add and its variants, remove and setLayout have been overridden to forward to the contentPane as necessary. This means you can write:

frame.add(child);

And the child will be added to the contentPane.

Figure 3-2. *JFrame conveniences from the JFrame documentation*

Can you still include the call to the getContentPane() method in your code? Certainly. You aren't forced to use this convenience. If this makes your code easier and more understandable, that is your choice. Don't be surprised when most of the sample Java Swing code found in the wild[10] uses this convenience.

Summary

In this chapter, you saw a simple Jython Swing application that displays the current WebSphere global security status as the text of a JLabel component. Even though it is trivial in nature, it demonstrates the structure of the applications to be found throughout the book. Additionally, you had your first exposure to the layering that exists in the JFrame class, which will be used in almost every example application found in this book.

---

[10]The "wild" here refers to the wild, wild west, also known as the World Wide Web (WWW).

CHAPTER 4

Button Up! Using Buttons and Labels

Up to this point, the applications you built in this book have been kind of boring.[1] They really haven't done anything except display a message. But now it's time to change that. In this chapter, you're going to add a button to your application and then have it react when the user presses it. How does that sound?

To do this you'll first take a look at the JButton class hierarchy and see the Java way to create a button and add it to the application frame. Then you'll see a verbose way, in Jython, to do the same thing. Then you'll see a more concise way to put a button on the frame and have an event handler update another component when the user presses the button. This technique will allow your applications to react when the users click one of the buttons.

JButton Class Hierarchy

Before you start making buttons, it seems appropriate to take a look at this class. In Chapter 1, you saw a function named classes that displayed the class hierarchy for a given type from the inside out. Listing 4-1 shows this simple function again.[2]

Listing 4-1. classes.py

```
def classes( Class, pad = '' ) :
    print pad + str( Class )
    for base in Class.__bases__ :
        classes( base, pad + '| ' )
```

Using this function, you can display the JButton class hierarchy. Listing 4-2 shows an interactive wsadmin session that does just that.[3]

Listing 4-2. JButton class hierarchy

```
wsadmin>from javax.swing import JButton
wsadmin>
wsadmin>classes( JButton )
javax.swing.JButton
| javax.swing.AbstractButton
| | javax.swing.JComponent
| | | java.awt.Container
| | | | java.awt.Component
```

---

[1]Except, of course, for the GlassPaneDemo.py script mentioned in Chapter 3, which was converted from the original Java. But it doesn't count since I haven't covered the concepts used in that code.

[2]Remember that the output shown in this book is from the wsadmin version of Jython since it's easier to understand.

[3]The command used to start this wsadmin session included the -profile classes.py parameters.

```
| | | | | java.lang.Object
| | | | | java.awt.image.ImageObserver
| | | | | java.awt.MenuContainer
| | | | | java.io.Serializable
| | | java.io.Serializable
| | java.awt.ItemSelectable
| | javax.swing.SwingConstants
| javax.accessibility.Accessible
wsadmin>
```

What are you going to do with this information? Well, the first thing that you need to do is to create, or instantiate, a button instance. Then you'll add it to the frame. To begin, take a quick look at a trivial Java application to do this. Listing 4-3 contains the relevant code snippet.[4]

Listing 4-3. The Java Code to Create a Button and Add It to a Frame

```java
JFrame frame = new JFrame( "ButtonDemo" );
frame.setDefaultCloseOperation( JFrame.EXIT_ON_CLOSE );
JButton button = new JButton( "Press me" );
frame.add( button );
frame.pack();
frame.setVisible( true );
```

What would this look like in Jython? Listing 4-4 shows the equivalent Jython code.

Listing 4-4. The Verbose Jython Way to Do the Same Thing

```
frame = JFrame( 'ButtonDemo_01' )
frame.setDefaultCloseOperation( JFrame.EXIT_ON_CLOSE )
button = frame.add( JButton( 'Press me' ) )
button.addActionListener( ButtonPressed() )
frame.pack()
frame.setVisible( 1 )
```

They certainly do look similar, don't they? What if you use an interactive wsadmin session to execute these steps? Listing 4-5 shows what happens when you try to do this.

Listing 4-5. The wsadmin interactive session to create and add a button

```
wsadmin>from javax.swing import JFrame, JButton
wsadmin>frame = JFrame( 'ButtonDemo_01' )
wsadmin>button = JButton( 'Press me' )
wsadmin>frame.add( button )
javax.swing.JButton[,0,0,0x0,invalid,alignmentX=0.0,alignmentY=...
```

---

[4]The complete application can be found in the code\Chap_04\ButtonDemo_01.java file.

The figure ends when some output is generated by the `frame.add()` method call. What was returned by the `add()` method call? Listing 4-6 shows a slightly different interactive session. This time, the value returned by the `add()` method call is saved into a variable named `result`. Then you determine if the value returned by `add()` is the same one passed in. Why? Well, the `JFrame` class[5] inherits five different `add()` methods from the `java.awt.Container`. This Jython statement is calling the `Container add()` method[6] that returns the same value that was passed in.

Listing 4-6. The `wsadmin` interactive JButton session 2

```
wsadmin>from javax.swing import JFrame, JButton
wsadmin>
wsadmin>frame = JFrame( 'ButtonDemo' )
wsadmin>button = JButton( 'Press me' )
wsadmin>result = frame.add( button )
wsadmin>result == button
1
wsadmin>
```

You can use this fact to simplify your code. Listing 4-7 shows this simplification. Instead of instantiating the JButton instance and saving the returned value in a variable (e.g., `button`), you can combine the `add()` call with the JButton constructor call and save the value returned from the `add()` call.

Listing 4-7. The `wsadmin` interactive JButton session 3

```
wsadmin>from javax.swing import JFrame, JButton
wsadmin>
wsadmin>frame = JFrame( 'ButtonDemo' )
wsadmin>frame.setDefaultCloseOperation( JFrame.EXIT_ON_CLOSE )
wsadmin>button = frame.add( JButton( 'Press me' ) )
wsadmin>...
```

■ **Note** This technique doesn't work for every `Container add()` method call, since not every `add` method returns a value.

The application found in `Button_01.py` contains a button that says "Press me!" that can be pressed. Unfortunately, it doesn't do anything yet, but you'll get there right after a short digression. At this point it is appropriate to address an important question: How does Swing know where to put things on the application?

The Layout of the Land

One of the many parts of a Container is something called the Layout Manager. I touched on this a little in Chapter 1, and I will be going into detail about it in Chapter 5. For the moment, you'll simply take a quick peek "under the covers," so to speak.

For the time being, you're going to use `JFrame` as the top-level container. One way that you can learn more about the `JFrame` class hierarchy is to use the Java documentation. Figure 4-1 shows this relationship, at least the portion covered by the Java documentation.

---

[5]See http://docs.oracle.com/javase/8/docs/api/javax/swing/JFrame.html.
[6]See http://docs.oracle.com/javase/8/docs/api/java/awt/Container.html#add%28java.awt.Component%29.

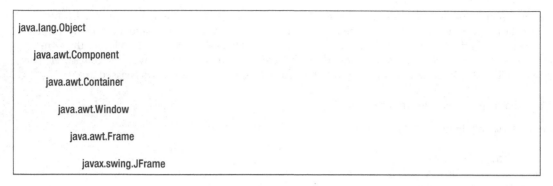

Figure 4-1. *JFrame class hierarchy*

The root of this class hierarchy is an Object, which isn't too surprising. The class hierarchy for the JFrame Swing class can be seen in Listing 4-8. Note, however, that unlike the JFrame Javadoc class hierarchy shown in Figure 4-1, the output of the classes function starts at the JFrame class and works its way up the hierarchy. So this is kind of an inside-out view of the hierarchy. One of the things that I found interesting about this view is the presence of additional classes that don't show up in the Javadoc.

Listing 4-8. Another look at the JFrame class hierarchy

```
wsadmin>from javax.swing import JFrame
wsadmin>
wsadmin>classes( JFrame )
javax.swing.JFrame
| java.awt.Frame
| | java.awt.Window
| | | java.awt.Container
| | | | java.awt.Component
| | | | | java.lang.Object
| | | | | java.awt.image.ImageObserver
| | | | | java.awt.MenuContainer
| | | | | java.io.Serializable
| | | javax.accessibility.Accessible
| | java.awt.MenuContainer
| javax.swing.WindowConstants
| javax.accessibility.Accessible
| javax.swing.RootPaneContainer
wsadmin>
```

This diagram is kind of nice, but it would be more useful if it also allowed you to see the methods and attributes that exist at each level of the hierarchy. Better yet, it would be really nice if you had a way to filter the list of methods and/or attributes based on some text. Listing 4-9 contains a function that includes these additional capabilities.

Listing 4-9. classInfo.py

```
 1|def classInfo( Class, meth = None, attr = None, pad = '' ) :
 2|    print pad + str( Class )
 3|    prefix = pad + '  '
 4|    if type( meth ) == type( '' ) :
 5|        comma, line = '', '' + prefix
 6|        methods = [
 7|            n for n, v in vars( Class ).items()
 8|            if n.lower().find( meth.lower() ) > -1 and callable( v )
 9|        ]
10|        methods.sort()
11|        for m in methods :
12|            if len( line + comma + m ) > 65 :
13|                print line.replace( '|', '>' )
14|                comma, line = '', '' + prefix
15|            line += comma + m
16|            comma = ', '
17|        if not line.endswith( '  ' ) :
18|            print line.replace( '|', '>' )
19|    if type( attr ) == type( '' ) :
20|        comma, line = '', '' + prefix
21|        attribs = [
22|            n for n, v in vars( Class ).items()
23|            if n.lower().find( attr.lower() ) > -1 and not callable( v )
24|        ]
25|        attribs.sort()
26|        for a in attribs :
27|            if len( line + comma + a ) > 65 :
28|                print line.replace( '|', '*' )
29|                comma, line = '', '' + prefix
30|            line += comma + a
31|            comma = ', '
32|        if not line.endswith( '  ' ) :
33|            print line.replace( '|', '*' )
34|    for b in Class.__bases__ :
35|        classInfo( b, meth, attr, pad + '| ' )
```

How do you use it? Well, when you call the classInfo() function, you must specify at least one parameter, which is a class (e.g., JFrame). In addition, you can als provide one or two parameters to show the methods and/or attribute names at each level of the class hierarchy. I find it best to include the parameter keyword (i.e., meth or attr) to indicate which parameter is being provided.

For example, if you want to display all of the methods in the JFrame hierarchy that contain the case-insensitive string "layout", you could call this function a statement, as shown on line 3 in Figure 4-7. Method names that include the specified text (i.e., "layout") are indicated using the > character.

Listing 4-10. JFrame class hierarchy showing the "layout" methods.

```
 1 wsadmin>from javax.swing import JFrame
 2 wsadmin>
 3 wsadmin>classInfo( JFrame, meth = 'layout' )
 4 javax.swing.JFrame
 5 | java.awt.Frame
 6 | | java.awt.Window
 7 | | | java.awt.Container
 8 > > >   getLayout, setLayout
 9 | | | | java.awt.Component
10 > > > >   doLayout
11 | | | | | java.lang.Object
12 | | | | | java.awt.image.ImageObserver
13 | | | | | java.awt.MenuContainer
14 | | | | | java.io.Serializable
15 | | | javax.accessibility.Accessible
16 | | java.awt.MenuContainer
17 | javax.swing.WindowConstants
18 | javax.accessibility.Accessible
19 | javax.swing.RootPaneContainer
```

I wasn't too surprised by the presence of getter and setter methods in the layout (i.e., getLayout and setLayout), but I didn't expect to see the doLayout method in the java.awt.Component class. Looking at the Javadoc for the java.awt.Component class, you'll find the information about the doLayout() method[7] shown in Figure 4-2.

.

---

public void doLayout()Causes this container to lay out its components. Most programs should not call this method directly, but should invoke the validate method instead.

Figure 4-2. *java.awt.Component.doLayout() description*

---

[7]See http://docs.oracle.com/javase/8/docs/api/java/awt/Container.html#doLayout%28%29.

That's kind of neat, but I don't intend to be calling that method in any of my code. Let's stick with the recommendation and avoid using it.

Since you looked for the layout methods, it's wise to take a moment to see if any attributes exist that refer to "layout". Listing 4-11 shows how to specify the attr keyword argument for the classInfo() function. The generated output of the JFrame class hierarchy shows that only one attribute exists in this hierarchy that contains the string "layout". It occurs in the java.awt.Container class.

Listing 4-11. JFrame class hierarchy showing "layout" attributes

```
wsadmin>from javax.swing import JFrame
wsadmin>
wsadmin>classInfo( JFrame, attr = 'layout' )
javax.swing.JFrame
| java.awt.Frame
| | java.awt.Window
| | | java.awt.Container
* * *    layout
| | | | java.awt.Component
| | | | | java.lang.Object
| | | | | java.awt.image.ImageObserver
| | | | | java.awt.MenuContainer
| | | | | java.io.Serializable
| | | | javax.accessibility.Accessible
| | | java.awt.MenuContainer
| javax.swing.WindowConstants
| javax.accessibility.Accessible
| javax.swing.RootPaneContainer
wsadmin>
```

What does this mean? Well, if you look at the Javadoc for java.awt.Container,[8] you might expect to see a "field"[9] called layout. So why isn't one there? Well, you can thank Jython for that. It automatically recognizes a property for which a getter (i.e., getPropertyName or isPropertyName) and a setter (i.e., setPropertyName) method are defined. This allows you to use the PropertyName as an expression or in an assignment statement. You'll use this feature throughout the examples in this book. Let's take a quick look at the example interactive wsadmin session shown in Listing 4-12.

---

[8]See http://docs.oracle.com/javase/8/docs/api/java/awt/Container.html.
[9]Java terminology for what is called an "attribute" in Jython programs.

Listing 4-12. Huh? What's goin' on, Lucy?

```
 1 wsadmin>from java.awt    import FlowLayout
 2 wsadmin>from javax.swing import JFrame
 3 wsadmin>
 4 wsadmin>fLayout = FlowLayout()
 5 wsadmin>frame = JFrame( 'Title' )
 6 wsadmin>frame.layout
 7 java.awt.BorderLayout[hgap=0,vgap=0]
 8 wsadmin>frame.layout = fLayout
 9 wsadmin>frame.layout
10 java.awt.BorderLayout[hgap=0,vgap=0]
11 wsadmin>frame.getLayout()
12 java.awt.BorderLayout[hgap=0,vgap=0]
13 wsadmin>frame.getContentPane().getLayout()
14 java.awt.FlowLayout[hgap=5,vgap=5,align=center]
15 wsadmin>frame.getContentPane().getLayout() == fLayout
16 1
17 wsadmin>
```

Wait a minute! What's going on here? This demonstrates one situation where you have to be mindful of what Jython is trying to do with the "automatic" attribute when it finds getter and setter methods. Table 4-1 describes each line of the wsadmin interactive session shown in Listing 4-12.

Table 4-1. *What's Goin' on Lucy, Explained*

Lines	Detailed Description/Explanation
1-3	Import the AWT and Swing classes that you will be using.
4	Instantiate a FlowLayout Layout Manager object (fLayout).
5	Instantiate a JFrame object and provide a title.
6-7	Use the frame.layout attribute to display information about the default Layout Manager that was created by the JFrame constructor. **Note:** It is a BorderLayout Manager object.
8	Use the frame.layout attribute to assign the kind of Layout Manager you want the frame to use.
9-10	Use the frame.layout attribute to verify the Layout Manager associated with the frame. **Note:** It is *still* a BorderLayout Manager object.
11-12	Use the frame.layout getter method to determine which Layout Manager is associated with the frame. **Note:** It is *still* a BorderLayout Manager object.
13-14	Use the frame.getContentPane() method to obtain a reference to the frame ContentPane, then use its layout getter method to determine the Layout Manager associated with the Content Pane. **Note:** It is a FlowLayout Manager object.
15-16	Verify that the FlowLayout Manager object being used by the Content Pane is, in fact, the same object that was created in line 4. **Note:** The 1 in line 16 means true.

The code you are seeing here is due to a special convenience provided by the JFrame class developers. The sentence from the Javadoc is shown in Figure 4-3.

> As a convenience add and its variants, remove and setLayout have been overridden to forward to the contentPane as necessary.

Figure 4-3. *JFrame "convenience"*

I'm bringing this to your attention now so that you are less likely to be surprised when you stumble upon it while you are developing and maintaining your Jython Swing scripts.

Buttons! Labels! Action!

You've looked at how to create a button and add it to your application. The next thing that you need to figure out is how to make the button do something when it's clicked. When a button is clicked, something called an "event" occurs. A button click is one of many events that can occur in a Swing application. For the time being, I'm going to focus[10] on this specific kind of event. You will learn about other events as they occur in the book.

Listing 4-13 shows a trivial Java application that prints a message (using the System.out.println() method call) when the button is pressed.

Listing 4-13. ButtonDemo_02.java : Reacting to a Button Press

```
 1|import java.awt.event.*;
 2|import javax.swing.*;
 3|public class ButtonDemo_02 {
 4|    public static void main( String[] args ) {
 5|        javax.swing.SwingUtilities.invokeLater( new Runnable() {
 6|            public void run() {
 7|                JFrame frame = new JFrame( "ButtonDemo" );
 8|                frame.setDefaultCloseOperation( JFrame.EXIT_ON_CLOSE );
 9|                JButton button = new JButton( "Press me" );
10|                button.addActionListener( new ActionListener() {
11|                    public void actionPerformed( ActionEvent ae ) {
12|                        System.out.println( "button pressed" );
13|                    };
14|                } );
15|                frame.add( button );
16|                frame.pack();
17|                frame.setVisible( true );
18|            }
19|        });
20|    }
21|}
```

---

[10]Gaining and losing focus are two other kinds of events that can occur.

Listing 4-14 shows the first attempt at implementing this application in Jython. One of the things that Java includes is the concept of anonymous classes. Lines 10–14 of Listing 4-13 show how an anonymous class can be used to define an ActionListener, which contains an `actionPerformed()` method to be invoked when the button-pressed event occurs. Jython doesn't allow anonymous classes. Listing 4-14 shows (in lines 7–9) one way to define a `ButtonPressed` descendent of the `ActionListener` class. In line 15, an instance of this class is instantiated and added as an action listener to the button. Many (most?) programmers, especially those new to Java, find the use of anonymous inner classes cumbersome and hard to read and write.

Listing 4-14. ButtonDemo_01.py: Reacting to a Button Press

```
 1|import java
 2|import sys
 3|from    java.awt        import EventQueue
 4|from    java.awt.event  import ActionListener
 5|from    javax.swing     import JButton
 6|from    javax.swing     import JFrame
 7|class ButtonPressed( ActionListener ) :
 8|    def actionPerformed( self, e ) :
 9|        print 'button pressed'
10|class ButtonDemo_01( java.lang.Runnable ) :
11|    def run( self ) :
12|        frame = JFrame( 'ButtonDemo_01' )
13|        frame.setDefaultCloseOperation( JFrame.EXIT_ON_CLOSE )
14|        button = frame.add( JButton( 'Press me' ) )
15|        button.addActionListener( ButtonPressed() )
16|        frame.pack()
17|        frame.setVisible( 1 )
18|if __name__ in [ '__main__', 'main' ] :
19|    EventQueue.invokeLater( ButtonDemo_01() )
20|    if 'AdminConfig' in dir() :
21|        raw_input( '\nPress <Enter> to terminate the application:\n' )
22|else :
23|    print '\nError: This script should be executed, not imported.\n'
24|    which = [ 'wsadmin -f', 'jython' ][ 'JYTHON_JAR' in dir( sys ) ]
25|    print 'Usage: %s %s.py' % ( which, __name__ )
26|    sys.exit()
```

Another approach is shown in Listing 4-15. This example, instead of defining a separate class, uses multiple inheritance. The class defined in line 8 is a descendent of the java.lang.Runnable and the java.awt.event.ActionListener classes. This means that it includes the run() method from the Runnable class and the actionPerformed() method from the ActionListener class. So all you need to do is identify the current class instance as the ActionListener, as shown in line 13.

Listing 4-15. ButtonDemo_02.py: Using Multiple Inheritance

```
 1|import java
 2|import sys
 3|from    java.awt        import EventQueue
 4|from    java.awt.event  import ActionListener
 5|from    java.lang       import Runnable
 6|from    javax.swing     import JButton
 7|from    javax.swing     import JFrame
```

```
 8|class ButtonDemo_02( Runnable, ActionListener ) :
 9|    def run( self ) :
10|        frame = JFrame( 'ButtonDemo_02' )
11|        frame.setDefaultCloseOperation( JFrame.EXIT_ON_CLOSE )
12|        button = frame.add( JButton( 'Press me' ) )
13|        button.addActionListener( self )
14|        frame.pack()
15|        frame.setVisible( 1 )
16|    def actionPerformed( self, e ) :
17|        print 'button pressed'
18|if __name__ in [ '__main__', 'main' ] :
19|    EventQueue.invokeLater( ButtonDemo_02() )
20|    if 'AdminConfig' in dir() :
21|        raw_input( '\nPress <Enter> to terminate the application:\n' )
22|else :
23|    print '\nError: This script should be executed, not imported.\n'
24|    which = [ 'wsadmin -f', 'jython' ][ 'JYTHON_JAR' in dir( sys ) ]
25|    print 'Usage: %s %s.py' % ( which, __name__ )
26|    sys.exit()
```

Although this is pretty interesting, it's not the only way that this feat can be accomplished. Next, you'll take advantage of another Jython feature called "keyword arguments."

Listing 4-16 shows that you don't even have to declare the class as a descendent of the ActionListener class in order to use it as one (see line 7). You can simply use the implied setter (in line 12) to identify another class method as the ActionListener event handler. The really neat part of this, at least to me, is that you don't have to call the method actionPerformed(); you can call it something more intuitive, like buttonPressed().

Listing 4-16. ButtonDemo_03.py: Multiple Inheritance Isn't Required

```
 1|import java
 2|import sys
 3|from    java.awt      import EventQueue
 4|from    java.lang     import Runnable
 5|from    javax.swing   import JButton
 6|from    javax.swing   import JFrame
 7|class ButtonDemo_03( Runnable ) :
 8|    def run( self ) :
 9|        frame = JFrame( 'ButtonDemo_03' )
10|        frame.setDefaultCloseOperation( JFrame.EXIT_ON_CLOSE )
11|        button = frame.add( JButton( 'Press me' ) )
12|        button.actionPerformed = self.buttonPressed
13|        frame.pack()
14|        frame.setVisible( 1 )
15|    def buttonPressed( self, e ) :
16|        print 'button pressed'
17|if __name__ in [ '__main__', 'main' ] :
18|    EventQueue.invokeLater( ButtonDemo_03() )
19|    if 'AdminConfig' in dir() :
20|        raw_input( '\nPress <Enter> to terminate the application:\n' )
```

```
21|else :
22|    print '\nError: This script should be executed, not imported.\n'
23|    which = [ 'wsadmin -f', 'jython' ][ 'JYTHON_JAR' in dir( sys ) ]
24|    print 'Usage: %s %s.py' % ( which, __name__ )
25|    sys.exit()
```

The biggest difference between using the automatic, or implied, setter call in an assignment statement (e.g., line 12 in Listing 4-16) and using a call to the addActionListener() method (e.g., line 13 in Listing 4-15) is that using the call to the addActionListener() method is necessary when you need to register multiple ActionListener objects.

While you're looking at some Jython techniques for creating a button, adding it to the frame, and adding an ActionListener, let's take a look at some other things that you can do using Jython.

Listing 4-17 contains the run() method from two versions of the ButtonDemo_03 script. Lines 1–7 are from the ButtonDemo_03.py script file and lines 9-21 are from the ButtonDemo_03a.py script file.

Listing 4-17. Another Way to Create a Frame and Add a Button

```
 1|    def run( self ) :
 2|        frame = JFrame( 'ButtonDemo_03' )
 3|        frame.setDefaultCloseOperation( JFrame.EXIT_ON_CLOSE )
 4|        button = frame.add( JButton( 'Press me' ) )
 5|        button.actionPerformed = self.buttonPressed
 6|        frame.pack()
 7|        frame.setVisible( 1 )
 8|...
 9|    def run( self ) :
10|        frame = JFrame(
11|            'ButtonDemo_03a',
12|            defaultCloseOperation = JFrame.EXIT_ON_CLOSE
13|        )
14|        frame.add(
15|            JButton(
16|                'Press me',
17|                actionPerformed = self.buttonPressed
18|            )
19|        )
20|        frame.pack()
21|        frame.setVisible( 1 )
```

In lines 2 and 3 (of Listing 4-17), you can see the technique that has been used up to this point to:

- Create a JFrame instance.

- Provide a title string.

- Set the default close operation to be used when the close icon is selected.

This code corresponds with the commonly used Java style. Lines 10–13, on the other hand, show that you can do these same things with a single Jython statement. Granted, since I don't want the lines to be too long, this statement is being displayed across multiple lines. However, it is still a single statement.

Lines 4 and 5 (again of Listing 4-17) show how you can:

- Create a JButton instance.

- Provide a text string to be displayed on the button.

- Add the button to the frame and save a reference to the button in a variable.

- Define the actionPerformed() method to be called when a button press event occurs.

The code in lines 14–19 does many of these same steps in a single statement. Again, multiple lines are used to make the various parts of the statement easier to read. The only significant thing that this statement doesn't do is save a reference to the button in a variable. This is simply because I didn't see the need to save that information. If you do need to save this value, you can have the code save the result of calling the frame.add() method in a variable.

Updating the Application

It seems kind of silly to have a GUI application display a message to the command prompt window when a button is pressed. This section explains what you need to do in order for the application to make changes to the user display when the button is pressed.

- Add a label to the application, the text of which can be modified by the event handler (the ActionListener actionPerformed()) method.

- Have the actionPerformed (i.e., buttonPressed()) method change the text in the label.

That sounds pretty straightforward, but there's something tricky you need to know about. In order for the buttonPressed() method to access the application label, it needs to be able to identify it and refer to it. So when you create the label, you need to save a reference to it in an instance attribute. Listing 4-18 contains the run() and buttonPressed() methods from the ButtonDemo_04.py application that does these things.

Listing 4-18. Parts of ButtonDemo_04.py

```
11|    def run( self ) :
12|        frame = JFrame( 'ButtonDemo_04' )
13|        frame.setDefaultCloseOperation( JFrame.EXIT_ON_CLOSE )
14|        button = frame.add( JButton( 'Press me' ) )
15|        button.actionPerformed = self.buttonPressed
16|        self.label = JLabel( 'button press pending' )
17|        frame.add( self.label, BorderLayout.SOUTH )
18|        frame.pack()
19|        frame.setVisible( 1 )
20|    def buttonPressed( self, e ) :
21|        self.label.setText( 'button pressed' )
```

Table 4-2 explains, in detail, each of the statements in Listing 4-19. The most important ones are in line 16, where a reference is saved to the label instance, and in line 21, where this reference is used to update the label text field.

Table 4-2. *ButtonDemo_04.py Explained*

Lines	Detailed Description/Explanation
12-13	These are the same steps used previously to create a `JFrame` instance and to define the action to take when the close icon is selected.
14-15	These are the same steps used previously to create a button with some text and to identify the method to call when the button press event occurs.
16	Create a `JLabel` instance and save the reference as an object attribute value (i.e., `self.label`).
17	Add the `JLabel` instance to the frame, using the Layout Manager constant (i.e., `BorderLayout.SOUTH`),[11] to identify where on the application the label should be placed.
18-19	These are the same steps used previously to adjust the application size and to make the application visible.
20-21	ActionListener `actionPerformed` method that is invoked when a button pressed event occurs. Note how the object instance variable (`self.label`) is used to modify the text being displayed in the label field.

What happens when you execute this application? Figure 4-4 shows the application, before (on left) and after (on right) the e. This demonstrates that the technique performs as expected.

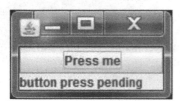 

Figure 4-4. *ButtonDemo_04.py output images.*

Summary

This chapter demonstrates that you can choose to write Jython scripts using syntax that closely matches Java Swing constructs or you can use Jython idioms to make the applications more readable. This means that you should be able to use sample Java Swing applications or code snippets from the Internet to learn how to write and test your Jython Swing applications.

Additionally, you have started looking at some of the many Swing components and learning about how the Swing class hierarchy handles events such as button clicks. Chapter 5 delves into the topic of Layout Managers in great detail; they give you more control over how things are positioned on your application frame.

---

[11]http://docs.oracle.com/javase/8/docs/api/java/awt/BorderLayout.html.

CHAPTER 5

■ ■ ■

Picking a Layout Manager Can Be a Pane

Earlier in this book,[1] you learned a bit about how items are placed, or positioned, on an application. This chapter deals with that topic in more detail and discusses some of the most commonly used Layout Managers. These include some of the more complicated ones, like the Absolute Layout and GridBagLayout Managers, as well as some of the simpler ones like the FlowLayout, BorderLayout, and BoxLayout Managers.

You will also learn about components that aren't exactly Layout Managers, including SplitPane and TabbedPane. You will then be better able to decide how to position the components on the application window in order to best communicate and interact with your users.

The Absolute Layout Manager Does Not Corrupt Absolutely

Designing and creating graphical applications can be frustrating. This is especially true when you have to position every component on the frame that is displayed to the users. Let's take a look at what this entails.

First, you need to remove any Layout Manager that's already on the container. Then, for each child component, you need to define its size and location on the frame content pane. Finally, you need to call the container `repaint()` method to render the components within the container using the current details known about the objects.

This isn't particularly difficult, but it can be tedious and requires a lot of code. Listing 5-1 shows a portion of one way to do this.

Listing 5-1. AbsoluteLayout Example

```
 6|class AbsoluteLayout( java.lang.Runnable ) :
 7|    def run( self ) :
 8|        frame = JFrame(
 9|            'AbsoluteLayout',
10|            defaultCloseOperation = JFrame.EXIT_ON_CLOSE
11|        )
12|        frame.setLayout( None )
```

---

[1]Chapter 1 touched on the subject when you added a second label to the frame, In Chapter 4, you saw the layout-related methods and attributes.

```
13|          data = [
14|                      [ 'A', 20, 10,  0,  0 ],
15|                      [ 'B', 40, 40, 10, 10 ],
16|                      [ 'C', 80, 20, 20, 20 ]
17|                  ]
18|          insets = frame.getInsets()
19|          for item in data :
20|              button = frame.add( JButton( item[ 0 ] ) )
21|              size   = button.getPreferredSize()
22|              button.setBounds(
23|                  insets.left + item[ 1 ],
24|                  insets.top  + item[ 2 ],
25|                  size.width  + item[ 3 ],
26|                  size.height + item[ 4 ]
27|              )
28|          frame.setSize(
29|              300 + insets.left + insets.right,    # frame width
30|              150 + insets.top + insets.bottom     # frame height
31|          )
32|          frame.setVisible( 1 )
```

How does it work? Well, line 12 shows how to remove any existing Layout Manager. Lines 19-27 show one relatively simple way to create some buttons and define their location and size on the containing frame. It's important to remember, though, that the call to frame.add() is, in fact, equivalent to calling frame.getContentPane().add(), as discussed in Chapter 3.

When a component (e.g., a button) is created, its constructor will determine its "preferred" size. This preferred size can be obtained by calling the getPreferredSize() method for the component, as you can see in line 21. Then the component's setBounds() method can be used to locate and possibly resize the component.

The first two parameters of the setBounds() method define the component's position by identifying its top-left point. The next two parameters of the method identify the width and height of the component.

What happens when you run this script? Well, you will see three buttons positioned on the application frame. Figure 5-1 shows how the application frame should look. It also shows how challenging it can be to "do it yourself." Did you anticipate that some of the buttons would be overlaid on the screen? I certainly didn't.

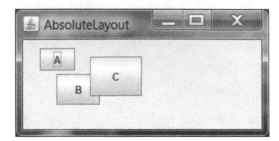

Figure 5-1. *AbsoluteLayout example output*

Are there any advantages to using this technique? Yes, there are. If you resize the application, you will notice that the component's location and size don't change. This is not the case with every Layout Manager, as you will see.

Going with the Flow: The FlowLayout Manager

The next Layout Manager that you're going to investigate is quite simple to use and is called the FlowLayout Layout Manager.[2] This manager attempts to place the components in a row. If there isn't sufficient space in the container to do so, multiple rows will be used. If more than enough space exists, the Layout Manager will, by default, center the components horizontally in the available space.

Listing 5-2 shows part of the FlowLayoutDemo.py sample application, which demonstrates how this works in an application.

Listing 5-2. FlowLayout Example

```
 9|def run( self ) :
10|    frame = JFrame(
11|        'FlowLayout',
12|        defaultCloseOperation = JFrame.EXIT_ON_CLOSE
13|    )
14|    cp = frame.getContentPane()
15|    #----------------------------------------------------------
16|    # The alignment can be one of the following values:
17|    #----------------------------------------------------------
18|#   cp.setLayout( FlowLayout( FlowLayout.LEFT ) )
19|#   cp.setLayout( FlowLayout( FlowLayout.RIGHT ) )
20|    cp.setLayout( FlowLayout() ) # FlowLayout.CENTER = default
21|#   cp.setLayout( FlowLayout( FlowLayout.LEADING ) )
22|#   cp.setLayout( FlowLayout( FlowLayout.TRAILING ) )
23|    for name in '1,two,Now is the time...'.split( ',' ) :
24|        frame.add( JButton( name ) )
25|    #----------------------------------------------------------
26|    # The ComponentOrientation can be either LEFT_TO_RIGHT, or
27|    # RIGHT_TO_LEFT.  The default is based upon system locale
28|    #----------------------------------------------------------
29|#   cp.setComponentOrientation( ... )
30|    frame.setSize( 350, 100 )
31|    frame.setVisible( 1 )
```

Here are some things to note about this code include:

- The FlowLayout class is part of the java.awt hierarchy.

- A default FlowLayout instance centers the components, with a small space between each.

- The component orientation (left-to-right vs. right-to-left) is inherited from the java.awt.Component class.

Figure 5-2 contains some sample outputs generated using this script.

---

[2] See http://docs.oracle.com/javase/8/docs/api/java/awt/FlowLayout.html.

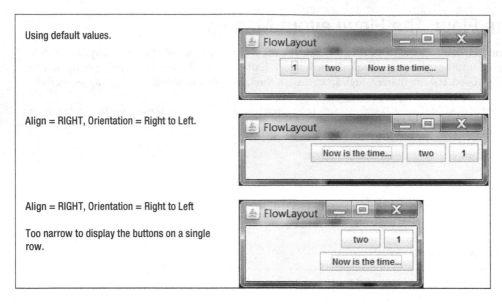

Using default values.	
Align = RIGHT, Orientation = Right to Left.	
Align = RIGHT, Orientation = Right to Left Too narrow to display the buttons on a single row.	

Figure 5-2. *FlowLayout examples*

The description to the left of each image identifies the alignment and orientation values used to produce it.

The FlowLayout Layout Manager is much easier than having to specify exactly where components should be placed. However, you must be mindful of what things will look like should the application change size.

South of the Border: The BorderLayout Manager

Next, take a look at the BorderLayout Layout Manager. What do layouts using this Layout Manager look like? Figure 5-3 shows a simple application using this manager.

Figure 5-3. *BorderLayout examples*

The BorderLayout Layout Manager enables you to easily position the components using some simple constants. The labels for each of the buttons shown in Figure 5-3 contain the names of these BorderLayout constants. Additionally, Listing 5-3 shows a portion of the script that generated this output.

Listing 5-3. BorderLayout Example

```
 9|    def run( self ) :
10|        frame = JFrame(
11|            'BorderLayout',
12|              layout = BorderLayout(),
13|              defaultCloseOperation = JFrame.EXIT_ON_CLOSE
14|        )
15|        data = [
16|                    [ 'PAGE_START', BorderLayout.PAGE_START ],
17|                    [ 'PAGE_END'  , BorderLayout.PAGE_END   ],
18|                    [ 'LINE_START', BorderLayout.LINE_START ],
19|                    [ 'LINE_END'  , BorderLayout.LINE_END   ],
20|             ]
21|        for name, pos in data :
22|            frame.add( JButton( name ), pos )
23|        big = JButton(
24|                    'CENTER',
25|                     preferredSize = Dimension( 256, 128 )
26|                  )
27|        frame.add( big, BorderLayout.CENTER )
28|        frame.pack()
29|        frame.setVisible( 1 )
```

■ **Tip**   I encourage you to execute the script and resize the application frame to see what happens to the buttons. Remember that the results that you are seeing are because you're using the BorderLayout Layout Manager.

The BorderLayout Layout Manager has advantages, (e.g., simplicity of use) and disadvantages (e.g., the results of resizing the application may not be to your liking). Take these issues into account when you choose your application Layout Manager.

In addition to the constants shown on lines 16-27 in Listing 5-3, BorderLayout also includes some common directional constants. Figure 5-4 shows where these constants position components.

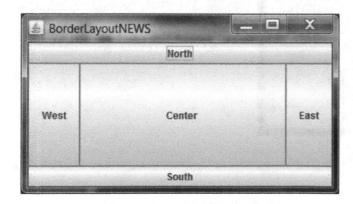

Figure 5-4. *BorderLayout directional constants*

Listing 5-4 shows a portion of the BorderLayoutNEWS.py script that was used to generate this output.

Listing 5-4. BorderLayoutNEWS Example

```
 9|   def run( self ) :
10|       frame = JFrame(
11|          'BorderLayoutNEWS',
12|           layout = BorderLayout(),
13|           defaultCloseOperation = JFrame.EXIT_ON_CLOSE
14|       )
15|       data = [
16|                 BorderLayout.NORTH,
17|                 BorderLayout.SOUTH,
18|                 BorderLayout.EAST,
19|                 BorderLayout.WEST
20|              ]
21|       for pos in data :
22|           frame.add( JButton( pos ), pos )
23|       big = JButton(
24|                      'Center',
25|                       preferredSize = Dimension( 256, 128 )
26|                  )
27|       frame.add( big, BorderLayout.CENTER )
28|       frame.pack()
29|       frame.setVisible( 1 )
```

The only other point worth noting about the BorderLayout class is that you can have the Layout Manager automatically separate components by specifying horizontal and vertical gap values when the Layout Manager is instantiated. You can see what this means by looking at Figure 5-5.

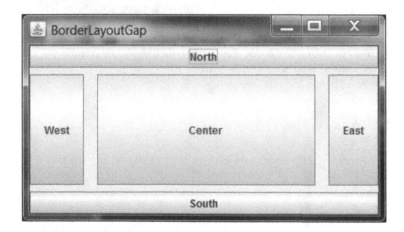

Figure 5-5. *BorderLayout with component separation*

What change was required? All you have to do is specify the gap values on the call to the BorderLayout constructor. The important line from the BorderLayoutGap.py script is shown in Listing 5-5.

Listing 5-5. BorderLayoutGap Example

```
12| layout = BorderLayout( 16, 8 ),
```

The constructor used in Listing 5-5[3] identifies the horizontal and vertical gaps to be used between components.

What's in the Cards? Using the CardLayout Manager

The next Layout Manager you'll learn about is the CardLayout Manager. As with the previously described Layout Managers, this one lets you position the components. The interesting thing about this one is that like a deck of cards in a stack, only the top one is visible. What does this mean? Figure 5-6 shows a simple application using the CardLayout Manager. It uses the top row of buttons to allow users to select one of the cards to be displayed.

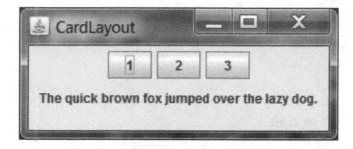

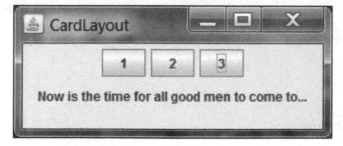

Figure 5-6. *CardLayout examples*

---

[3]See http://docs.oracle.com/javase/8/docs/api/java/awt/BorderLayout.html#BorderLayout%28int,%20int%29.

Before you learn about the CardLayout Manager, I first have to quickly mention another container, specifically a JPanel[4] that is used in a number of places in this CardLayout application.

What is a JPanel? It is best to think of a JPanel as a simple, lightweight container that can be used to hold a group of components. In this example, you will simply create JPanel instances and add some components to each.

Alright, let's dig into the example. If you click on any of the buttons in the top row, you'll see that the top panel doesn't change but the bottom one displays the other components.

How do you do this? Note that the application, (i.e., the JFrame instance) uses one Layout Manager (on its ContentPane). In this case, the application will have two separate parts, or panes. Each pane will be a JPanel instance. The top is used to display the fixed buttons and the bottom is used to display the current CardLayout view.

Listing 5-6 shows the run() method for this example. In it, you can see how:

- The frame layout is configured to use a BorderLayout Manager instance.

- A reference to the frame ContentPane is obtained and the two support routines are called to populate the different parts of the frame panel.

Listing 5-6. CardLayoutDemo run() Method

```
10|class CardLayoutDemo( java.lang.Runnable ) :
11|    def run( self ) :
12|        frame = JFrame(
13|            'CardLayout',
14|            layout = BorderLayout(),
15|            defaultCloseOperation = JFrame.EXIT_ON_CLOSE
16|        )
17|        cp = frame.getContentPane()
18|        self.addButtons( cp, BorderLayout.NORTH )
19|        self.addCards( cp, BorderLayout.CENTER )
20|        frame.setSize( 300, 125 )
21|        frame.setVisible( 1 )
```

Listing 5-7 shows how the addButtons() method uses the default JPanel Layout Manager, i.e., a FlowLayout Manager instance, to add three buttons to the panel. The choice of button labels will become clear shortly. Please note that the ActionListener actionPerformed method for each button is assigned to be the buttonPress() method in this object instance. It is important to realize that each container component in the application has its own, possibly default, Layout Manager. This allows the application designers to position the individual components as they see fit.

Listing 5-7. CardLayoutDemo addButtons() Method

```
22|    def addButtons( self, container, position ) :
23|        panel = JPanel()
24|        for name in '1,2,3'.split( ',' ) :
25|            panel.add(
26|                JButton(
27|                    name,
28|                    actionPerformed = self.buttonPress
29|                )
30|            )
31|        container.add( panel, position )
```

Finally, the addButtons() method adds the button panel to the user-specified container, i.e., the frame ContentPane, using the specified location or position.

___

[4]See http://docs.oracle.com/javase/8/docs/api/javax/swing/JPanel.html.

Listing 5-8 shows how the addCards() method uses a default JPanel instance for each of the card panels. For simplicity's sake, the first and last of these card panels contain only a label, which can be used to verify which card panel is being displayed. The middle card panel contains three more buttons to show how easily a card panel can be populated with components.

Listing 5-8. CardLayoutDemo addCards() Method

```
32|    def addCards( self, container, position ) :
33|        card1 = JPanel()
34|        card1.add(
35|            JLabel(
36|                'The quick brown fox jumped over the lazy dog.'
37|            )
38|        )
39|        card2 = JPanel()
40|        for name in 'A,B,C'.split( ',' ) :
41|            card2.add( JButton( name ) )
42|        card3 = JPanel()
43|        card3.add(
44|            JLabel(
45|                'Now is the time for all good men to come to...'
46|            )
47|        )
48|        cards = self.cards = JPanel( CardLayout() )
49|        cards.add( card1, '1' )
50|        cards.add( card2, '2' )
51|        cards.add( card3, '3' )
52|        container.add( cards, position )
```

Finally, another JPanel is created to hold the various card panels that you just created and populated. Each of these card panels is added to the panel that is using the CardLayout Layout Manager. Note that when a panel is added, you specify an identifier to be used to select this panel. These strings correspond to the button labels used in the addButtons() method shown in Listing 5-7.

Listing 5-9 shows how the buttonPress() event-handling method can obtain a reference to the Layout Manager object instance being used by the panel. Then this Layout Manager's show() method can be used to specify a card panel instance to be displayed. The label of the button that was pressed can be used by calling the event.getActionCommand() method. All in all, this makes for a very clear, concise, and precise event handler.

Listing 5-9. CardLayoutDemo buttonPress() Method

```
53|    def buttonPress( self, event ) :
54|        deck = self.cards.getLayout()
55|        deck.show( self.cards, event.getActionCommand() )
```

Hopefully you can see how easily this can be used to create a really neat application. Next, you will take a look at some of the various components that your applications can use.

Splitting Up Is Easy to Do: Using Split Panes

Unlike splitting the atom, Swing provides for a very easy way to partition all of, or part of, your application into two pieces. Unfortunately, it's not a Layout Manager, but it certainly applies to the topic at hand, so I cover it here anyway.

The JPanel that was mentioned earlier provides you with a lightweight container for keeping a collection of components together. Wouldn't it be neat if you had a simple way of splitting a panel in two, either vertically or horizontally? Well, there is a way, called a JSplitPane.[5] Figure 5-7 shows a very simple application with two buttons, one in each of the two parts of the horizontally split panel.

Figure 5-7. *JSplitPane sample output*

One feature that might not be immediately obvious in Figure 5-7 is that the separator (the divider) between the two parts of the split pane is moveable. The image on the right shows how the application appears after moving the separator as far to the right as possible. The limitation is imposed by the minimum size of each button.

Listing 5-10 shows just how easy it is to create and use one of these split panes in your applications.

Listing 5-10. SplitPane1: Simple Horizontal Separation

```
 7|class SplitPane1( java.lang.Runnable ) :
 8|    def run( self ) :
 9|        frame = JFrame(
10|            'SplitPane1',
11|            defaultCloseOperation = JFrame.EXIT_ON_CLOSE
12|        )
13|        frame.add( JSplitPane(
14|                JSplitPane.HORIZONTAL_SPLIT,
15|                JButton( 'Left' ),
16|                JButton( 'Right' )
17|            )
18|        )
19|        frame.pack()
20|        frame.setVisible( 1 )
```

Vertical Splits: Not as Painful as They Sound

It is just as easy to have a portion of your application window separated vertically. Look at line 14 in Listing 5-10. You can see how the JSplitPane class contains a constant that indicates in which direction (horizontally or vertically) the pane should be split. If, instead of using JSplitPane.HORIZONTAL_SPLIT, you use JSplitPane.VERTICAL_SPLIT, your application will look similar to Figure 5-8.

---

[5]See http://docs.oracle.com/javase/8/docs/api/javax/swing/JSplitPane.html.

Figure 5-8. *JSplitPane2, vertical split*

Unlike in the previous application, this separator doesn't move. Well, that's only partially true. If you resize the window, as shown in Figure 5-9, you can see how the top part remains the same and all of the additional height is given to the bottom part. Then, you can move the separator bar down, resizing the two parts of the split panel. Again, each portion of the split pane is limited by the minimum size restriction of the components.

Figure 5-9. *JSplitPane2, vertical split and resizing*

Limited Resources: Setting Size Attributes

A long time ago, in a galaxy far, far away, I took an economics class that used something called the "Guns versus butter model"[6] to describe the concept of choosing between two limited resources. In the same way, split panes restrict the amount of space that the separator bar can move. How is this determined? Every Swing component has the JComponent[7] and the Component[8] as some of its base classes. Therefore, each Swing component has different size attributes, as you can see in Listing 5-11. These attributes are used to identify things like the minimum, maximum, and preferred size of a component.

Listing 5-11. Component size attributes

```
wsadmin>from javax.swing import JButton
wsadmin>
wsadmin>classInfo( JButton, attr = 'size' )
javax.swing.JButton
| javax.swing.AbstractButton
| | javax.swing.JComponent
| | | java.awt.Container
| | | | java.awt.Component
* * * *    ancestorResized, baselineResizeBehavior
* * * *    componentResized, maximumSize, maximumSizeSet
* * * *    minimumSize, minimumSizeSet, preferredSize
* * * *    preferredSizeSet, size
| | | | | java.lang.Object
| | | | | java.awt.image.ImageObserver
| | | | | java.awt.MenuContainer
| | | | | java.io.Serializable
| | | java.io.Serializable
| | java.awt.ItemSelectable
| | javax.swing.SwingConstants
| javax.accessibility.Accessible
wsadmin>
```

What are all of those "size" attributes in the java.awt.Component class, anyway? Well, the size attribute identifies the current width and height of the component, which shouldn't be too much of a surprise. The others—minimumSize, maximumSize, and preferredSize—are suggestions, or hints,[9] to the Layout Manager about how the particular component should be represented.

The effect of the minimumSize attribute can be the borne out with a little testing. Figure 5-10 shows the initial application image, including the separators between the split panes. Each button in the application uses the same event handler routine to display the button text, the current button size, and the other size attributes mentioned previously. I encourage you to use the application to improve your understanding about the various component size attributes.

---

[6]See http://en.wikipedia.org/wiki/Guns_versus_butter_model.
[7]See http://docs.oracle.com/javase/8/docs/api/javax/swing/JComponent.html.
[8]See http://docs.oracle.com/javase/8/docs/api/java/awt/Component.html.
[9]"…the code is more what you'd call 'guidelines' than actual rules." From http://www.imdb.com/title/tt0325980/quotes.

Figure 5-10. *SplitPane4: initial rendering*

To use the application, you need only click on the buttons to display the button size attributes. Then you can resize the window and use the buttons again to see which attribute values have changed. When the window size increases, you can also move the split pane divider lines by dragging them. Again, you can use the buttons to see the effect on the button size attributes.

Nested Split Panes

The application that illustrates the divider movement seen in Figure 5-10 uses the simple concept of nested split panes. Listing 5-12 shows the part of the SplitPane4.py script that produced this output.

Listing 5-12. Nested Split Panes

The button() method, on lines 17, 20, and 21, is a local reference to a method used to create a JButton with the actionPerformed() method assigned. The actionPerformed() method is the event handler used to display the button component sizes.

One interesting thing from this listing is how the top component (i.e., the second argument to the JSplitPane constructor) in line 17 is a simple call to the JButton constructor. Notice how the next argument, (i.e., the third for the JSplitPane constructor), which is used to specify the bottom component for the vertically split pane, is itself a JSplitPane constructor. This is the nesting to which this section refers.

Imagine how much fun you could have using this technique to create deeply nested split pane components![10] If you search the web, you can find an interesting article, written by Hans Muller entitled "MultiSplitPane: Splitting Without Nesting."[11] If you are really adventurous, you might investigate adding his class files to your environment and using them or converting them to Jython. If you do, please let me know how it goes.

Divider and Conquer

What, exactly, can you do with, and about, the separator (aka divider) bar? As you saw earlier, the Layout Manager decides how to allocate the available space to display the components. Do you have any control over the divider bar, and how it can be used? Sure, there are a number of JSplitPane methods related to the divider.

For example, Figure 5-11 shows how you can easily adjust the size of the divider bar using the setDividerSize() method. The image corresponds to the selected size button (i.e., the top image has a divider size of zero, the middle image has a divider size of 10, and the bottom image has a divider size of 20).

---

[10]This was discussed in Chapter 3.
[11]See http://today.java.net/pub/a/today/2006/03/23/multi-split-pane.html.

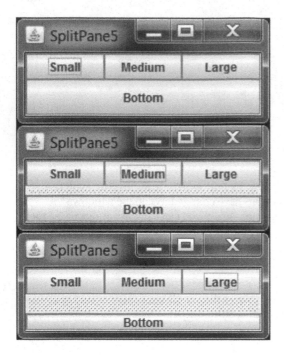

Figure 5-11. *SplitPane5: various divider sizes*

One SplitPane attribute with which you may be unfamiliar is the OneTouchExpandable property. By default, this Boolean attribute is set to false. When it is true, the divider has two little triangles added to it, as shown in Figure 5-12.

Figure 5-12. *SplitPane6 with the OneTouchExpandable divider*

By enabling OneTouchExpandable, you allow the user to minimize one component with a single mouse click, which is really quite cool. Looking at the script used to produce this output, which can be found in the SplitPane6.py script file, you can see that you only needed to specify the oneTouchExpandable keyword argument on the JSplitPane constructor call. Listing 5-13 shows how easily this can be accomplished using Jython.

Listing 5-13. oneTouchExpandable Keyword Argument

```
15|         frame.add(
16|            JSplitPane(
17|                JSplitPane.HORIZONTAL_SPLIT,
18|                JButton( 'Left' ),
19|                JButton( 'Right' ),
20|                oneTouchExpandable = 1
21|            )
22|        )
```

Rules for Using Split Panes

Unlike a during knife fight, there are rules for using a split pane. Most of them deal with how to determine the component sizes, and therefore the divider bar. This can also lead to dealing with the sizes of any nested components, which can be a challenge. In fact, there is a wonderful statement on the Java tutorials page entitled "How to Use Split Panes"[12] that says:

■ **Note**   Choosing which sizes you should set is an art that requires understanding how a split pane's preferred size and divider location are determined.

Immediately after this statement, the page contains a bulleted list of rules for making split panes work well for you and your applications. If you intend to use split panes, I suggest that you bookmark that URL and study it often. I certainly have.

Can I Run a Tab? Using a TabbedPane

This section discusses something else that really isn't a Layout Manager. It seems to be related to the CardLayout Layout Manager you read about earlier. In fact, it's a different kind of panel. The reason I am discussing it here is because of the similarities it has to the CardLayout Manager mentioned in the previous section. Figure 5-13 shows how JTabbedPane can be used to display one of a group of panes based on the user's selection. Unlike the CardLayout Layout Manager, an instance of JTabbedPane has a selectable tab label that can be used to determine the content to be displayed.

---

[12]See http://docs.oracle.com/javase/tutorial/uiswing/components/splitpane.html.

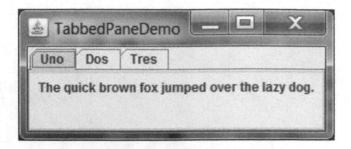

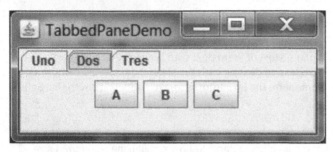

Figure 5-13. *TabbedPaneDemo examples*

To demonstrate the similarities and differences between a panel using the CardLayout Manager and a TabbedPane class, the code shown in Listing 5-14 uses the same child panel contents as those seen in Listing 5-8.

Listing 5-14. TabbedPaneDemo Class

```
10|class TabbedPaneDemo( java.lang.Runnable ) :
11|    def run( self ) :
12|        frame = JFrame(
13|            'TabbedPaneDemo',
14|            defaultCloseOperation = JFrame.EXIT_ON_CLOSE
15|        )
16|        self.addTabs( frame.getContentPane() )
17|        frame.setSize( 300, 125 )
18|        frame.setVisible( 1 )
19|    def addTabs( self, container ) :
20|        tab1 = JPanel()
21|        tab1.add(
22|            JLabel(
```

```
23|              'The quick brown fox jumped over the lazy dog.'
24|          )
25|      )
26|      tab2 = JPanel()
27|      for name in 'A,B,C'.split( ',' ) :
28|          tab2.add( JButton( name ) )
29|      tab3 = JPanel()
30|      tab3.add(
31|          JLabel(
32|              'Now is the time for all good men to come to...'
33|          )
34|      )
35|      tabs = JTabbedPane()
36|      tabs.addTab( 'Uno' , tab1 )
37|      tabs.addTab( 'Dos' , tab2 )
38|      tabs.addTab( 'Tres', tab3 )
39|      container.add( tabs )
```

What's the main difference? Well, in lines 36-38, you can see how the child panes are added to the JTabbedPane instance using the addTab() method instead of the JPanel add() method shown in lines 49-51 of Listing 5-8.

A JTabbedPane instance is also easier because the selection mechanism is built into the class. Take another look at Listings 5-7 and 5-9, where you had to specifically identify how the CardLayout panel instances would be selected by the users.

Are You Boxed In? Using the BoxLayout Manager

Earlier in this chapter, you saw how easy it was to use the FlowLayout Layout Manager to position the components in a row. You also saw that when the application window was resized, the Layout Manager would reposition the components on different rows when the width of the application window would otherwise be too narrow. There are times when you don't want this to occur. This leads to the next Layout Manager, i.e., the one defined in the BoxLayout class.[13]

Figure 5-14 shows the sample output of the BoxLayoutDemo sample application. It uses a JTabbedPane with three tabs. In each tab, you can see three buttons that are layered out along the Y_AXIS (i.e., vertically). The only difference between the tabs is how the buttons are aligned within the pane.

---

[13]See http://docs.oracle.com/javase/8/docs/api/javax/swing/BoxLayout.html.

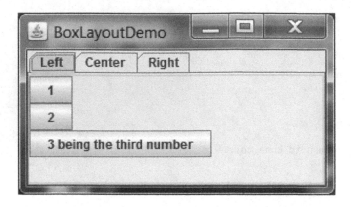

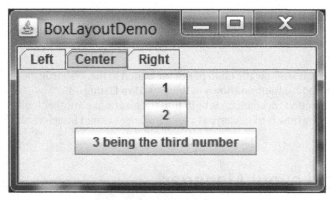

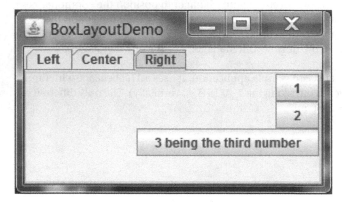

Figure 5-14. *BoxLayout tabs*

Listing 5-15 shows the BoxLayoutDemo class that produces the output shown in Figure 5-14. As you can see, when you instantiate the Layout Manager, as shown in line 29, you tell it how the components should be displayed. Later, in line 31, you see that when you instantiate the buttons, you can use a Component alignment constant to tell the component where the other part should be displayed (i.e., along the x-axis of the panel).

Listing 5-15. BoxLayoutDemo Class

```
10|class BoxLayoutDemo( java.lang.Runnable ) :
11|    def run( self ) :
12|        frame = JFrame(
13|            'BoxLayoutDemo',
14|            defaultCloseOperation = JFrame.EXIT_ON_CLOSE
15|        )
16|        self.addTabs( frame.getContentPane() )
17|        frame.setSize( 300, 175 )
18|        frame.setVisible( 1 )
19|    def addTabs( self, container ) :
20|        align = [
21|                    [ 'Left'  , Component.LEFT_ALIGNMENT   ],
22|                    [ 'Center', Component.CENTER_ALIGNMENT ],
23|                    [ 'Right' , Component.RIGHT_ALIGNMENT  ]
24|                ]
25|        names = '1,2,3 being the third number'.split( ',' )
26|        tabs  = JTabbedPane()
27|        for aName, aConst in align :
28|            tab = JPanel()
29|            tab.setLayout( BoxLayout( tab, BoxLayout.Y_AXIS ) )
30|            for name in names :
31|                tab.add( JButton( name, alignmentX = aConst ) )
32|            tabs.addTab( aName, tab )
33|        container.add( tabs )
```

The constants provided by the BoxLayout class include those listed in Table 5-1.

Table 5-1. *BoxLayout Constants*

Constant	Description
BoxLayout.X_AXIS	Components are laid out horizontally, left to right.
BoxLayout.Y_AXIS	Components are laid out vertically, top to bottom.
BoxLayout.LINE_AXIS	Components are laid out based on the container's ComponentOrientation property, either horizontally or vertically.
BoxLayout.PAGE_AXIS	Components are laid out the way text is displayed on a page, based on the container's ComponentOrientation property, either horizontally or vertically.

The Box Class

Even though this chapter has been focusing mainly on Layout Managers, you have also learned about some container classes to help define how the application components are displayed. The Box class is another of these lightweight containers that helps arrange application components.

If you need to create a single row or column of components, you might want to take a look at the Box class,[14] which works kind of like a JPanel. One significant difference between these two classes is that the Box class can *only* use a BoxLayout Layout Manager,[15] whereas the JPanel allows the developer to choose any kind of Layout Manager.[16]

Building a Box

The Box class has a single constructor, as shown in Figure 5-15. One of the interesting things about this constructor is that it isn't used as often as the createHorizontalBox() and createVerticalBox() methods. I think that calling the Box.createHorizontalBox() method is more understandable than Box(BoxLayout.X_AXIS), don't you? Can you think of a reason that you might prefer the constructor to the createHorizontalBox() method?

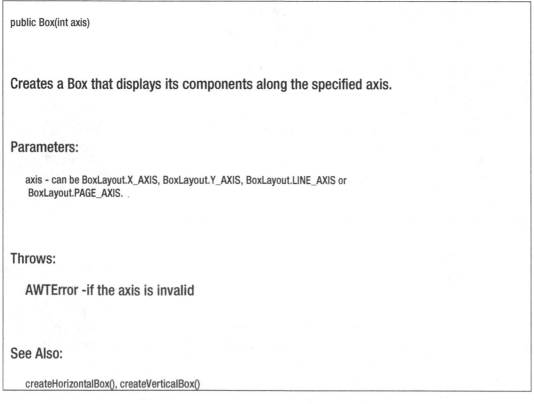

```
public Box(int axis)
```

Creates a Box that displays its components along the specified axis.

Parameters:

axis - can be BoxLayout.X_AXIS, BoxLayout.Y_AXIS, BoxLayout.LINE_AXIS or
BoxLayout.PAGE_AXIS.

Throws:

AWTError -if the axis is invalid

See Also:

createHorizontalBox(), createVerticalBox()

Figure 5-15. *Box constructor*

If nothing comes to mind, you might want to take another look at Table 5-1. The important thing to note is that the createHorizontalBox() class is equivalent to using the Box(BoxLayout.X_AXIS) constructor call, which will position the components left to right, regardless of the user locale. This might not be what you intend. You have to be the judge.

---

[14]See http://docs.oracle.com/javase/8/docs/api/javax/swing/Box.html.
[15]See http://docs.oracle.com/javase/8/docs/api/javax/swing/Box.html#setLayout%28java.awt.LayoutManager%29.
[16]By default, a JPanel instance will use a FlowLayout Layout Manager.

Invisible Box Components

One of the challenges with using a Box instance to hold your components is the fact that they are, by default, adjacent to one another. Figure 5-16 shows what happens when three fixed-size components (i.e., JLabel instances) are added to a horizontal box container. The left image shows how the application looks when the application is first made visible. The right image shows what happens to the components when the application is widened.

Figure 5-16. *Horizontal (fixed-size) components*

If you were expecting the components to be centered or right-aligned, you aren't going to be pleased with the results. To help adjust this kind of alignment, the Box class includes the following "filler" components:

- Glue

- Struts

- Rigid areas

Your choice of filler component will depend upon the initial appearance of your box, as well as on how you want it to look when it is resized.

Glue

If you research Java Swing glue components, most of the references mention the fact that glue is not a very good description for this type of component. This is true because most people think of glue as a kind of adhesive. Instances of this invisible Swing component will start out with a width or height of zero. This attribute then increases in size as the container size increases.

Three Box methods exist that can be used to create glue components. These methods are listed and described in Table 5-2.

Table 5-2. *Box Class Glue Methods*

Method Name	Description/Details
createGlue()	Used to create a component that can be used between horizontal or vertical components.
createHorizontalGlue()	Used to create a component that is oriented horizontally.
createVerticalGlue()	Used to create a component that is oriented vertically.

Glue components have a minimum size (horizontal width or vertical height) of zero. This means that it shouldn't be obvious when a glue component is between other components on the box container. When the container becomes larger, the Layout Manager will increase the size of all of the resizable components (i.e., the ones smaller than their maximum size). When multiple fixed-size components are positioned between glue components, the available space will be allocated equally to the glue components.

It may help to see an example to better understand what this means. Table 5-3 shows what happens when glue components are positioned around some fixed-size components (i.e., JLabel instances), and the application frame containing the horizontal box is widened.

Table 5-3. *Using Glue Components in a Horizontal Box*

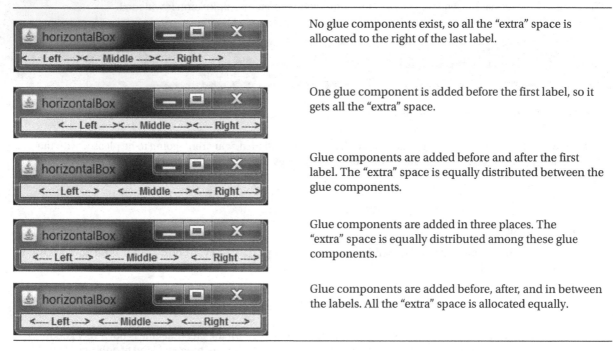

	No glue components exist, so all the "extra" space is allocated to the right of the last label.
	One glue component is added before the first label, so it gets all the "extra" space.
	Glue components are added before and after the first label. The "extra" space is equally distributed between the glue components.
	Glue components are added in three places. The "extra" space is equally distributed among these glue components.
	Glue components are added before, after, and in between the labels. All the "extra" space is allocated equally.

When a vertical box is used to hold components, glue components act in a similar fashion.

Strut Components

There are times when it is appropriate to have some minimum distance between components. For those times, consider using horizontal or vertical struts. Table 5-4 shows two methods that you can use to create these strut components.

Table 5-4. *Box Class Strut Methods*

Method Name	Description/Details
createHorizontalStrut(int width)	Create a filler component of the specified width (in pixels).
createVerticalStrut(int height)	Create a filler component of the specified height (in pixels).

Is there any problem related to using strut components? Well, I have found some references that indicate that horizontal strut components have an unlimited height, and vertical strut components have an unlimited width, which can be a problem. Apparently, if you use strut components with nested vertical and horizontal box containers, alignment issues can arise. Take a look at this example to see what they are talking about. Figure 5-17 shows an application that has five buttons (all of which have the same text) aligned in a plus pattern. The issue isn't obvious until you drag the bottom-right corner of the application down to increase the size and width. As you can see from the image on the right, the results are unexpected. The glue components are placed before the leftmost button, after the rightmost one, above the top one, and beneath the bottom one. When the frame becomes larger, the strut component before the rightmost button has extra space.

Figure 5-17. *Alignment issues with strut components*

Rigid Area Components

The final invisible component—called a rigid area—is created using specific, fixed dimensions. This means that the component size should not change even if its container is resized. This would seem to make it the preferred filler component if your application is best rendered with some space between visible components. Table 5-5 shows the Box method that you can use to create this type of invisible component.

Table 5-5. *Rigid Area Creation Method*

Method Name	Description/Details
createRigidArea(Dimension d)	Creates an invisible component that's always the specified size.

Boxes and Resizable Components

Up to this point, you have been using fixed-size components when dealing with box containers (e.g., labels and buttons). It is important to note, however, that some components have a maximum size that isn't the same as the minimum and preferred size. What happens when that occurs?

Based on what I have already discussed, you probably realize that the Layout Manager will also allocate available space to these components as space becomes available. The distribution of the available size depends on a number of factors, including:

- The maximum size attribute of the resizable components

- The current size of the container

- The size of the screen

I don't know about you, but I was a little surprised about this last one. In fact, I had to try it out, so I played around with the fBox.py script, which displays information about the text field width when the button is pressed. When the maximum width of the text field is less than or near the screen width, the amount of space allocated to the text field as the application width increases is relatively small. As the maximum width of the text field is increased, you'll see that the amount of space allocated to the text field as the application is widened increases accordingly. If the maximum width of the text field is not limited (i.e., if the default maximum width is used), the text field will receive all of the available extra width.

Gridlock, Anyone? Using the GridLayout Manager

Another common layout configuration is when the components are laid out in a grid. The GridLayout Layout Manager provides this configuration. Figure 5-18 shows a simple example where the application has two panes, each of which contains a group of buttons displayed in a grid. Each grid has three columns and enough rows to display all of the buttons.

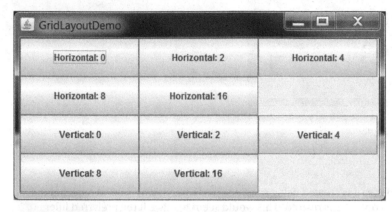

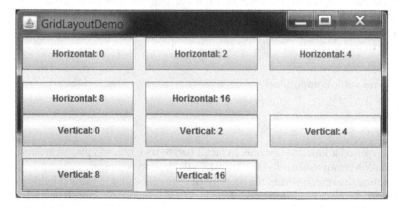

Figure 5-18. *GridLayoutDemo examples*

The interesting thing about this application is that the buttons allow you to dynamically change the horizontal or vertical gap between the buttons on each pane that is using the GridLayout Layout Manager.

Listing 5-16 shows the run() method in the GridLayoutDemo application. In this method, you can see how the main panel uses a BoxLayout Layout Manager to position two inner panes along the Y_AXIS (i.e., vertically). Then, the addButtons() method is called to add another inner pane, which uses a GridLayout Layout Manager to position a group of buttons.

Listing 5-16. GridLayoutDemo run() Method

```
def run( self ) :
    frame = JFrame(
        'GridLayoutDemo',
        defaultCloseOperation = JFrame.EXIT_ON_CLOSE
    )
    main = JPanel()
    main.setLayout( BoxLayout( main, BoxLayout.Y_AXIS ) )
    self.panes = []
    self.addButtons( main, 'Horizontal:' )
    self.addButtons( main, 'Vertical:' )
    frame.add( main )
    frame.setSize( 500, 250 )
    frame.setVisible( 1 )
```

Listing 5-17 shows how the addButtons() method creates a new panel, populates it with buttons, and then adds it to the specified container. A reference to the new panel is saved in the self.panes list, created in the run() method, for use by the button event handler.

Listing 5-17. GridLayoutDemo addButtons() Method

```
def addButtons( self, container, prefix ) :
    pane = JPanel( GridLayout( 0, 3 ) )
    self.panes.append( pane )
    for size in '0,2,4,8,16'.split( ',' ) :
        pane.add(
            JButton(
                '%s %s' % ( prefix, size ),
                actionPerformed = self.buttonPress
            )
        )
    container.add( pane )
```

Listing 5-18 shows how the button label is retrieved using the event.getActionCommand() method. The program then uses the space that exists between the direction (i.e., Horizontal or Vertical) and the size (i.e., the number of pixels) for the inner component gap.

Listing 5-18. GridLayoutDemo buttonPress() Method

```
def buttonPress( self, event ) :
    dir, size = event.getActionCommand().split( ' ' )
    if dir[ 0 ] == 'H' :
        for pane in self.panes :
            layout = pane.getLayout()
            layout.setHgap( int( size ) )
            layout.layoutContainer( pane )
```

```
    else :
        for pane in self.panes :
            layout = pane.getLayout()
            layout.setVgap( int( size ) )
            layout.layoutContainer( pane )
```

This is where you need to process each of the panes using a GridLayout Layout Manager. Given a pane, you can obtain a reference to the Layout Manager used by that pane using the pane.getLayout() method call. You can use this reference to adjust the horizontal or vertical gap used by this Layout Manager (i.e., by calling the setHgap() or setVgap() method).

Once the gap has been changed, a call is made to the layoutContainer() method to force the Layout Manager to adjust how the components are displayed.

Shaking Things Up: The GridBagLayout Manager

One of the problems with the GridLayout Manager is that sometimes you'll want there to be some differences between the size and placement of the components. For example, you might want things to be arrayed in rows, but not use the regular column arrangement provided by GridLayout. You can use the GridBagLayout Layout Manager for these purposes. Unfortunately, it comes with a price. Specifically, in order for you to have more control over the size and placement of components in a grid, you must provide a greater level of detail to each component. Therefore, the GridBagLayout Manager is a bit more complicated than the others.

Figure 5-19 shows sample output of the GridBagLayout applications found in the code\Chap_05 directory. These are just examples of the kind of control that the GridBagLayout Layout Manager provides for component placement.

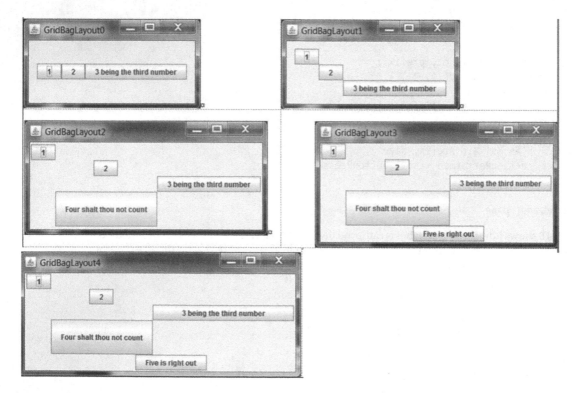

Figure 5-19. GridBagLayout examples

Listing 5-19 shows the addComponents() method from the GridBagLayout4 script, which was used to generate the output shown in Figure 5-19. There are some important points about this method to note. For example, a new GridBagConstraints instance is created for each component. Why is this considered a "best" practice? This is recommended because the reuse of existing GridBagConstraints objects can easily lead to subtle, and therefore difficult-to-diagnose, problems. It is all too easy to forget that one of the many constraint fields has a non-default value.

Listing 5-19: GridBagLayout4 addComponents() Method

```
def addComponents( self, container ) :
    container.setLayout( GridBagLayout() )
    c = GridBagConstraints()
    c.gridx = 0          # first column
    c.gridy = 0          # first row
    container.add( JButton( '1' ), c )
    c = GridBagConstraints()
    c.gridx = 1          # second column
    c.gridy = 1          # second row
    container.add( JButton( '2' ), c )
    c = GridBagConstraints()
    c.fill = GridBagConstraints.HORIZONTAL
    c.gridx = 2          # third column
    c.gridy = 2          # third row
    c.weightx = 0.0
    c.gridwidth = 3
    container.add( JButton( '3 being the third number' ), c )
    c = GridBagConstraints()
    c.gridx = 1          # second column
    c.gridy = 3          # forth  row
    c.ipady = 32         # make this one taller
    container.add( JButton( 'Four shalt thou not count' ), c )
    c = GridBagConstraints()
    c.gridx = 1          # second column
    c.gridy = 4          # fifth  row
    c.gridwidth = 3      # make this one 3 columns wide
    container.add( JButton( 'Five is right out' ), c )
```

This provides me with another opportunity to highlight some of the features and strengths of Jython. If you take a look at the Javadoc for the GridBagConstraints class,[17] you will see that two constructors exist. The first constructor has no parameters and creates a GridBagConstraints instance using all of the default values. The other has 11 parameters and requires that all of the values be provided.

Jython, on the other hand, lets you use keyword arguments to selectively provide only those values of interest. Listing 5-20 shows an interactive session that uses a displayConstraints() function[18] to show any non-default constraint values that exist in the specified object. In lines 8, 14, and 19, you can see how keyword arguments can be provided when the object is instantiated.

[17]See http://docs.oracle.com/javase/8/docs/api/java/awt/GridBagConstraints.html.
[18]The complete source for which can be found in code\Chap_05\displayConstraints.py script file.

Listing 5-20. Specifying GridBagConstraints parameters using keywords

```
wsadmin>from java.awt import GridBagConstraints
wsadmin>from java.awt import Insets
wsadmin>
wsadmin>c = GridBagConstraints()
wsadmin>displayConstraints( c )
All constraint values match defaults
wsadmin>
wsadmin>c = GridBagConstraints( gridx = 1, gridy = 2 )
wsadmin>displayConstraints( c )
Non-default constraint values:
    gridx: 1
    gridy: 2
wsadmin>
wsadmin>c = GridBagConstraints( insets = Insets( 1, 2, 3, 4 ) )
wsadmin>displayConstraints( c )
Non-default constraint values:
    insets: java.awt.Insets[top=1,left=2,bottom=3,right=4]
wsadmin>
wsadmin>c = GridBagConstraints( fill = GridBagConstraints.CENTER )
wsadmin>displayConstraints( c )
Non-default constraint values:
    fill: CENTER
wsadmin>
```

Looking at Other Layout Managers

In addition to the Layout Managers you already read about, there is the SpringLayout class[19]. I'm not going to cover it here because of its complexity, as well as because it's most often used by GUI builders. At this time, I am unaware of any GUI builder that generates Jython code, so it would seem that your best bet is to find one that generates Java code and translate it to the corresponding Jython code. Unfortunately, I don't know how many people would invest the time to do this, especially if the application's "look and feel" changes frequently.

Another Layout Manager, called GroupLayout,[20] exists, and is also used by GUI builders. It too is beyond the scope of this book due to its complexity. If you are interested in learning more about it, read the section in the Java Swing tutorials called "How to Use GroupLayout."[21]

The other alternative that isn't covered here is the "roll your own" option. There is good information about this approach at your fingertips; see the section in the Java Swing tutorials entitled "Creating a Custom Layout Manager."[22] This, too, is beyond the scope of this book, and I don't have enough experience with it to feel comfortable trying to tackle this topic here.

---

[19]See http://docs.oracle.com/javase/8/docs/api/javax/swing/SpringLayout.html.
[20]See http://docs.oracle.com/javase/8/docs/api/javax/swing/GroupLayout.html.
[21]See http://docs.oracle.com/javase/tutorial/uiswing/layout/group.html.
[22]See http://docs.oracle.com/javase/tutorial/uiswing/layout/custom.html.

Summary

This chapter is all about providing you with information to help you understand how you can use Layout Managers or containers to position your application components. As you can see, there are a number of options open to you and your applications. It's all about how you want the application components to be arranged. One of the aspects discussed in each section is how the components change when the container is resized. This is an important topic to consider when you are designing and developing your application, so keep that in mind.

CHAPTER 6

■ ■ ■

Using Text Input Fields

Up to this point, you've been limited in the kinds of applications that you can build because of the lack of ways of getting information (i.e., input) into the application. You will now start to remedy that deficiency by learning to create an input field that lets the users enter text.

This chapter discusses a couple of input-related fields such as JTextField and JTextArea. Additionally, you will take a look at how the data is displayed e.g., using alignment and fonts. The chapter also covers creating a simple Swing application that allows you to display and modify a value in the WebSphere Application Server (WSAS) environment. One reason to do this is so that you can see how to perform "long-running" operations on a separate thread using instances of the SwingWorker class.

What Does It Take to Get Data Into an Application?

To start, you'll create a fairly simple value that you want to be able to view and possibly modify. How about the WebSphere Administrative Console inactivity timeout? Well, unfortunately, the WebSphere documentation only contains one sample Jacl script that shows how this can be done.[1] You'll start by creating two Jython functions, one to get the current inactivity timeout value and the other to set it.

Listing 6-1 shows an interactive wsadmin session where these functions are used to get and set the timeout value. The complete functions can be found in code\Chap_06 directory.[2] They've been tested, as shown in Listing 6-1, so you should be all set to use them, right?

Listing 6-1. Getting and setting the admin console inactivity timeout

```
wsadmin>print getTimeout()
30
wsadmin>print setTimeout( '123' )
Successfully modified.
wsadmin>print getTimeout()
123
wsadmin>print setTimeout( '30' )
Successfully modified.
wsadmin>
```

---

[1]See http://www14.software.ibm.com/webapp/wsbroker/redirect?version=compass&product=was-nd-dist&topic=cons_sessionto.
[2]In files named getTimeout.py and setTimeout.py, respectively.

JTextField: Getting Data Into the Application

To make things easy, you will start with a simple text field that solicits information from the users. What is required and how does it work? You start by creating a JTextField instance, which provides a simple, lightweight input field that allows users to enter a small amount of text. When the user input is complete, which is generally indicated by the user pressing the Enter key, any associated ActionListener will receive an action event.[3]

If you look at the Java documentation for the JTextField class,[4] you'll see that a number of constructors exist. The simplest of these requires no parameters. One of those enables you to provide an initial string value to be displayed, one allows the field width in number of columns, and another allows the initial string value to be specified as well as the number of columns to be displayed. This application will use something simple—the one that allows you to specify the number of columns to be displayed. Since you are unlikely to need more than three digits, you can use a value of three for the number of columns.

To provide the users with visual indications of what the input field contains, you need to surround it with some labels. And to be a little more complete, you can have a message label field on a separate line to display a message indicating the success or failure of the requested action.

■ **Note**   Do you remember how you were able to use the actionPerformed keyword assignment as part of the constructor call when you created a JButton? If not, have a look at Chapter 4.[5]

You can use the same technique to specify the ActionListener routine to be called when an actionEvent occurs. In the case of JTextField, this is when the user presses the Enter key.

Your First, Almost Real, Application

What does it take to use one or more existing routines and turn them into a graphical wsadmin application? Well, after a bit of work, you're likely to take what you have learned, including the information about the JTextField, and build an application, the output of which might look something like Figure 6-1.

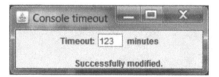

Figure 6-1.   *consoleTimeout1 sample output*

---

[3]I haven't covered action events in great detail, at least not yet. They are covered in Chapter 14. However, you have used the actionPerformed() method when you learned about buttons earlier.
[4]See http://docs.oracle.com/javase/8/docs/api/javax/swing/JTextField.html.
[5]For example, take a look at Listing 4-8.

What code do you need to do this? Listing 6-2 shows the consoleTimeout1 class from the sample application script file. Note how it calls the getTimeout() and setTimeout() routines, just like the interactive session shown in Listing 6-1. This makes it look pretty simple, doesn't it?

Listing 6-2. consoleTimeout1 Class

```
class consoleTimeout1( java.lang.Runnable ) :
    def run( self ) :
        frame = JFrame(
            'Console timeout',
            defaultCloseOperation = JFrame.EXIT_ON_CLOSE
        )

        cp = frame.getContentPane()
        cp.setLayout( BoxLayout( cp, BoxLayout.Y_AXIS ) )

        input = JPanel( layout = FlowLayout() )
        input.add( JLabel( 'Timeout:' ) )
        self.text = JTextField( 3, actionPerformed = self.update )
        input.add( self.text )
        self.text.setText( getTimeout() )
        input.add( JLabel( 'minutes' ) )
        cp.add( input )

        self.msg  = cp.add( JLabel() )

        frame.setSize( 290, 100 )
        frame.setVisible( 1 )

    def update( self, event ) :
        value = self.text.getText().strip()
        if re.search( '^\d+$', value ) :
            self.msg.setText( setTimeout( value ) )
        else :
            msg = 'Invalid value "%s" ignored.' % value
            self.msg.setText( msg )
            self.text.setText( getTimeout() )
```

Unfortunately, it isn't as simple as it looks. If you test the application and watch closely, you are likely to notice a delay between the time that you type a value and press Enter, and the message being displayed. What's happening?

Welcome to the world of event-driven applications. What you are seeing is the fact that a non-trivial delay is occurring between the time that the setTimeout() routine is being called and when it returns. In the meantime, the entire application is hung. This is a really bad thing, and exhibits a terrible practice.

Help Me SwingWorker, You're My Only Hope!

A first attempt at fixing this might involve changing the message field to show some kind of message. You might even want to disable the input field before calling the setTimeout() routine. So, how might you do this? Well, you could replace the call to the setTimeout() routine in Listing 6-1 with something like what's shown in Listing 6-3.

Listing 6-3. Attempt to Fix the update( ) Method

```
self.msg.setText( 'working...' )
self.text.setEnabled( 0 )
self.msg.setText( setTimeout( value ) )
self.text.setEnabled( 1 )
```

What do the calls to the setEnabled( ) method associated with the JTextField do? The first one attempts to disable it by specifying 0, which is interpreted as false, and the second call attempts to enable it by specifying 1, which is interpreted as true.[6]

If it worked, this would disable the input field so that the AdminConfig scripting object could locate and modify the inactivity timeout value associated with the appropriate configuration object.

Unfortunately, this doesn't work because the part of the Swing framework that updates the screen never has a chance to gain control to update the display. How do you fix this? How do you force the application to perform some separate action while the Swing framework displays the GUI and allows the user to generate events like button clicks?

Well, to do this, I need to take a trip down the rabbit hole and talk about something called *concurrency*.[7] It's similar to when you have multiple separate programs running on your computer at the same time. In this case, you need the application to have multiple things going on. The challenge is that all of this needs to be happening within one program, the wsadmin Jython script.

When multiple programs execute at the same time, the operating system and the program developer are responsible for keeping things straight, so that two or more programs don't try to manipulate the same piece of information (e.g., an object or variable) at the same, or nearly the same time.

How do you have separate things going on at the same time in your Jython scripts? Well, you are going to have to make use of a concurrent programming concept called *threads*. You need to identify operations that may require a "long" time to complete and have these executed on a separate thread. A *thread* is a short form of, or nickname for, a thread of control. Each thread operates separately and distinctly.

Since I don't have the time or space to completely cover this topic, I am going to try to provide just enough so that you can resolve the common issues that you'll likely encounter when using the applications discussed.

The really good news is that Jython scripts are executing on a Java Virtual Machine, and Java was created with concurrency in mind. This means that your scripts can make use of classes and techniques that have been part of Java for years.

The primary class that you need to use is called SwingWorker. The Javadoc for the SwingWorker class[8] includes a simple case example that translates to Listing 6-4.

---

[6]Just like you do with the call to frame.setVisible(1) in the application run( ) method.

[7]Concurrent programming is a large topic all by itself. I don't have the time or space to cover it here completely. You will, however, learn enough to be able to develop graphical Jython applications. There are lots of good articles available on the topic. I encourage you to search for "threads and concurrent programming."

[8]See http://docs.oracle.com/javase/8/docs/api/javax/swing/SwingWorker.html.

Listing 6-4. Simple SwingWorker Subclass

```
class InTheSwing( SwingWorker ) :
    def __init__( self, labelField = None ) :
        self.label = labelField
    def doInBackground( self ) :
        try :
            self.result = longRunningRoutine()
        except :
            self.result = 'Exception encountered.'
    def done( self ) :
        self.label.setText( self.result )
...
label = frame.add( JLabel() )
InTheSwing( label ).excecute()
```

How well does this work? The images shown in Figure 6-2 can answer this question. You can see that when there's an invalid value entered (in this case "x"), the bad value is replaced with the original value and an appropriate error message is displayed. The next image shows what happens when a valid value is entered. The input field has been disabled and a "working..." message is displayed, at least until the update is complete. The last image shows that the input field has been enabled; the "Update successful" message is displayed.

Figure 6-2. consoleTimeout2 Sample Output

What code do you need to do this? Listing 6-5 shows the WSAStask class, which is a SwingWorker descendent class. How does it work?

Listing 6-5. WSAStask Class

```
58|class WSAStask( SwingWorker ) :
59|    def __init__( self, textField, labelField ) :
60|        self.text = textField                # Save the References
61|        self.label = labelField
62|        SwingWorker __init__( self )
63|    def doInBackground( self ) :
64|        self.text.setEnabled( 0 )            # Disable input field
65|        self.label.setText( 'working...' )   # Inform user of status
66|        value = self.text.getText().strip()
```

```
67|         if not re.search( re.compile( '^\d+$' ), value ) :
68|             msg = "Invalid numeric value "%s",' % value
69|             self.label.setText( msg )
70|             self.text.setText( getTimeout() )
71|         else :
72|             self.label.setText( setTimeout( value ) )
73|     def done( self ) :
74|         self.text.setEnabled( 1 )             # Enable input field
```

The explanation of how this class works can be found in Table 6-1. Fortunately, the code that needs to be executed on a separate thread of control is quite easy to understand.

Table 6-1. *WSAStask Class, Explained*

Lines	Description/Explanation
59–62	Class constructor used to save references to the necessary component fields and call the SwingWorker (i.e., base class) constructor (i.e., the SwingWorker.__init__() method).
63–72	Method called by the SwingWorker execute() method that does the actual, possibly long, running work. It is interesting to note how calls to global functions (i.e., getTimeout() and setTimeout()) are made here. Note also how the field references saved by the constructor method (i.e., the __init__() method) are used here to access and manipulate the actual components.
73–74	The done() method is also called by the SwingWorker execute() method when the doInBackground() method completes.

What does that do for your consoleTimeout class? In Listing 6-2, the update() method required half a dozen steps. Listing 6-6 shows how you only need to instantiate a WSAStask object and call its execute method to do the work. Remember that all of the stuff that was previously done in the update() method has been moved to the WSAStask doInBackground() method. So the code to perform the work is now performed on the separate thread of control.

Listing 6-6. consoleTimeout2's update() Method

```
def update( self, event ) :
    WSAStask( self.text, self.msg ).execute()
```

■ **Warning**   It's important to note that SwingWorker objects cannot be reused. Additional work, even if it is identical to what was done previously, must be done using a completely new instance of the SwingWorker descendant class.

Back to the JTextField

Up to this point, I haven't provided many details about the JTextField component. The reason for this was to allow you to quickly use a simple kind of input field for the sample application. Now, however, it's appropriate to revisit the JTextField class, so you can garner a more complete understanding of its capabilities, limitations, and uses.

If you look into the Java Swing Tutorial, you'll can find a section entitled, "How to Use Text Fields".[9] Let's start by describing and using the JTextField, which is the simplest of the text input fields.

Looking at the JTextField Javadoc shows that it includes a number of methods. Unfortunately, I don't have the time or space to completely describe each and every method. However, there are some that warrant investigation. One getter/setter pair that is likely to catch your eye is the one dealing with horizontal alignment. Figure 6-3 shows the output of the TextAlignment.py[10] script, which illustrates the various JTextField alignment values and how they affect text display in a JTextField.

Figure 6-3. *TextAlignment output*

Listing 6-7 shows the TextAlignment class from the script used to display this output. It is interesting to note how easily you can display this information using a GridLayout. You don't even have to tell the Layout Manager how many rows will be displayed. By initializing the number of rows as 0, as shown on line 12, you let the Layout Manager keep track of how many rows are provided.

Listing 6-7. TextAlignment Class

```
 8|class TextAlignment( java.lang.Runnable ) :
 9|   def run( self ) :
10|        frame = JFrame(
11|            'TextAlignment',
12|            layout = GridLayout( 0, 2 ),
13|            defaultCloseOperation = JFrame.EXIT_ON_CLOSE
14|        )
15|        data = [
16|            [ 'Left'    , JTextField.LEFT     ],
17|            [ 'Center'  , JTextField.CENTER   ],
18|            [ 'Right'   , JTextField.RIGHT    ],
19|            [ 'Leading' , JTextField.LEADING  ],
20|            [ 'Trailing', JTextField.TRAILING ]
21|        ]
```

---

[9]See http://docs.oracle.com/javase/tutorial/uiswing/components/textfield.html.
[10]The complete script is in the Code\Chap_06\TextAlignment.py file.

```
22|        for label, align in data :
23|            frame.add( JLabel( label ) )
24|            text = frame.add(
25|                JTextField(
26|                    5,
27|                    text = str( align ),
28|                    horizontalAlignment = align
29|                )
30|            )
31|        frame.pack()
32|        frame.setVisible( 1 )
```

The other thing to note here is how you can use the Jython keyword parameter assignments (lines 12, 13, 27, and 28) to greatly simplify the code.

Consider the difference between the Left and Leading alignments. Remember that you might be building applications that are used in a variety of locations across the world. Left and Right are absolute direction indicators, whereas the Leading and Trailing alignments are related to the locale and the direction that text should be displayed, based on the locale setting.

Size Matters: Looking at Text Font Attributes

While you're looking at the JTextField documentation, it's smart to consider also the setFont() method. Can you change the font used by the JTextField components? With a tiny bit of work, I was able to change the TextAlignment.py example to use a different font for each of the JTextField values. The output of this modification is shown in Figure 6-4.

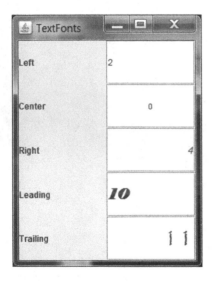

Figure 6-4. *TextFonts output*

The changes you need to make to generate this output are shown in Listing 6-8. This isn't anything nearing a complete discussion about fonts; it's just a glimpse as to how easy they are to change.

Listing 6-8. TextFonts Changes

```
data = [
    [ 'Left'    , JTextField.LEFT     , None ],
    [ 'Center'  , JTextField.CENTER   , Font( 'Courier' , Font.BOLD, 12 ) ],
    [ 'Right'   , JTextField.RIGHT    , Font( 'Ariel'   , Font.ITALIC, 14 ) ],
    [ 'Leading' , JTextField.LEADING  , Font( 'Elephant', Font.BOLD | Font.ITALIC, 20 ) ],
    [ 'Trailing', JTextField.TRAILING, Font( 'Papyrus'  , Font.PLAIN, 36 ) ]
]
for label, align, font in data :
    frame.add( JLabel( label ) )
    text = frame.add(
        JTextField(
            5,
            text = str( align ),
            horizontalAlignment = align,
        )
    )
    if font :
        text.setFont( font )
```

This code adds an additional column for each row in the data array. The value of this column is None or a font instance. If a font instance is present, it is used to define the font to be used for the associated JTextField instance. The test and associated assignment are performed in the last two lines of Listing 6-6.

The Elephant (Font) in the Room

One of the questions that might come to you as you are looking at this code is, "Is there really a font named 'Elephant'"? I was a little surprised by that one as well. This made me wonder what it would take to create a simple application that displays the list of available font names.

First, you need some kind of data area that can be used to hold a bunch of information. For this purpose, you're going to use the next kind of input field, called a JTextArea. One of the things to note about this particular application is that it uses an output field, not an input field.

How do you do that? The Java documentation for this component[11] includes half a dozen constructors, half of which allow you to provide a string to be used to initialize the text. Listing 6-9 shows how you can obtain the list of available fonts from a local graphics environment instance. One thing that you have to note, however, is that you have to convert this list of strings into a single string, with newline characters delimiting each line of text. Fortunately, a simple Jython idiom exists to do exactly this, as you can see in line 19.

---

[11]See http://docs.oracle.com/javase/8/docs/api/javax/swing/JTextArea.html.

Listing 6-9. AvailableFonts Class

```
 8|class AvailableFonts( java.lang.Runnable ) :
 9|    def run( self ) :
10|        frame = JFrame(
11|            'Available Fonts',
12|            defaultCloseOperation = JFrame.EXIT_ON_CLOSE
13|        )
14|        lge = GraphicsEnvironment.getLocalGraphicsEnvironment()
15|        fontNames = lge.getAvailableFontFamilyNames()
16|        frame.add(
17|            JScrollPane(
18|                JTextArea(
19|                    '\n'.join( fontNames ),
20|                    editable = 0,
21|                    rows = 8,
22|                    columns = 32
23|                )
24|            )
25|        )
26|        frame.pack()
27|        frame.setVisible( 1 )
```

The other important thing to notice is that this text area is likely to contain more lines of text than will comfortably fit on the application screen. Therefore, you need to put the text area instance in a container that will automatically provide vertical and horizontal scroll bars, as needed, to comfortably display a reasonable application window. You do this using an instance of the JScrollPane class.[12]

Is it always this simple and easy? Well, it all depends. In this case, you can use almost all of the default settings. The other really good thing about Jython is that you can also use keyword arguments to help document what the parameters mean. So, all in all, you benefit from the well-designed Swing classes hierarchy.

Take a moment and comment out lines 21 and 22. Don't forget to remove or comment out the trailing comma on line 20 as well.[13] Before you execute the script, what do you expect it to display? When I ran the modified script, it didn't match my expectations. I don't know about you, but I think that the use of the keyword arguments on the JTextArea constructor call certainly made the application better looking. This just to point out to you that not all of the Swing default values will match your expectations or needs. Try to keep this in mind.

Using JTextArea for Input

Let's talk for a moment about the editable keyword assignment in line 20 of Listing 6-7. By now, you should be able to recognize it as equivalent to a call to the setEditable() method with a value of false. All this so the area of text can't be modified by the user. All you have to do to make this input component editable is remove this keyword assignment or change the value from 0 (false) to 1 (true).

What happens if you execute the script after making this change? Well, you can select, modify, remove, or add text. And all it really takes is a JTextArea instance. With the JTextField, as you saw earlier in the chapter, you can add an ActionListener in order for an event handler routine of your choice to be invoked when the user presses Enter.

---

[12]See http://docs.oracle.com/javase/8/docs/api/javax/swing/JScrollPane.html.
[13]You could replace lines 16–25 with the following statement, which I find much easier to read:
`frame.add( JScrollPane( JTextArea( '\n'.join( fontNames ), editable = 0 ) ) )`

Which listeners make sense for a JTextArea? I don't know. Let's use the classInfo() routine, seen earlier, to find out what kind of listeners can be added. Oops. That's one of the problems about asking questions. You may not want to see the answer you get. What are all of these things? Table 6-2 briefly explains the kinds of listeners that can be added.

Table 6-2. *JTextArea Listeners*

Listener Name	Listener Description
AncestorListener	Support notification when changes occur to a JComponent or one of its ancestors.
CaretListener	Listens for changes in the caret position of a text component.
ComponentListener	The listener interface for receiving component events.
ContainerListener	The listener interface for receiving container events.
FocusListener	The listener interface for receiving keyboard focus events on a component.
HierarchyBoundsListener	The listener interface for receiving ancestor moved and resized events.
HierarchyListener	The listener interface for receiving hierarchy changed events.
InputMethodListener	The listener interface for receiving input method events.
KeyListener	The listener interface for receiving keyboard events (keystrokes).
MouseListener	The listener interface for receiving "interesting" mouse events (press, release, click, enter, and exit) on a component.
MouseMotionListener	The listener interface for receiving mouse motion events on a component.
MouseWheelListener	The listener interface for receiving mouse wheel events on a component.
PropertyChangeListener	A PropertyChange event gets fired whenever a bean changes a "bound" property.
VetoableChangeListener	A VetoableChange event gets fired whenever a bean changes a "constrained" property.

If you chose to have a listener for each kind of event, you would be able to micromanage the JTextArea instance. I'm not even going to investigate all of these listeners. I am, however, going to take a look at the CaretListener, since it can be used to monitor changes to the current position in the JTextArea portion of your application.

What does that require? Well, looking at the CaretListener Javadoc,[14] you see that only one method, caretUpdate(), needs to be implemented.

You can see that as you type into the input area, the label at the bottom of the application is updated to reflect the number of words and lines that exist. Figure 6-5 shows the sample output after pasting some text into the input area.

---

[14]See http://docs.oracle.com/javase/8/docs/api/javax/swing/event/CaretListener.html.

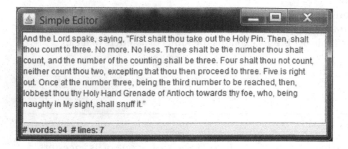

Figure 6-5. *SimpleEditor output*

Listing 6-10 shows just how easy it is to use a TextArea and a CaretListener to create a very simple text editor.

Listing 6-10. SimpleEditor Class

```
class SimpleEditor( java.lang.Runnable ) :
    def run( self ) :
        frame = JFrame(
            'Simple Editor',
            layout = BorderLayout(),
            defaultCloseOperation = JFrame.EXIT_ON_CLOSE
        )
        self.area = JTextArea(
            rows = 8,
            columns = 32,
            caretUpdate = self.caretUpdate
        )
        frame.add( JScrollPane( self.area ), BorderLayout.CENTER )
        self.words = JLabel( '# words: 0  # lines: 0' )
        frame.add( self.words, BorderLayout.SOUTH )
        frame.pack()
        frame.setVisible( 1 )

    def caretUpdate( self, event, regexp = None ) :
        if not regexp :
            regexp = re.compile( '\W+', re.MULTILINE )
        pos = event.getDot()
        text = self.area.getText()
        if text.strip() == '' :
            words = lines = 0
        else :
            words = len( re.split( regexp, text ) )
            lines = len( text.splitlines() )
        msg = '# words: %d  # lines: %d' % ( words, lines )
        self.words.setText( msg )
```

■ **Warning**   This `caretUpdate()` method does not work well with large amounts of data. Each time the caret (cursor) moves, the method is invoked, and it retrieves the entire text area and uses a regular expression to separate the data into "words." The `splitlines()` method then separates the data into "lines." This is very inefficient and suitable only for a trivial example such as this one.

Summary

This chapter is the first one to discuss the use of text input fields for your application scripts. It also introduced the important topic of threads, and the use of SwingWorker class instances to perform potentially long-running operations on a separate thread to keep the application from hanging. In the next chapter, you'll take a look at some other components that allow the users to provide input.

CHAPTER 7

■ ■ ■

Other Input Components

This chapter presents other input components available in the Swing class hierarchy. Specifically, it deals with some specialized text input fields, such as JPassword, three types of ComboBoxes (static, editable, and dynamic), and formatted text fields. Additionally, I combine some of these while discussing the JSpinner class at the end of the chapter.

Password Fields

One common reason for having a fairly small input field is to allow the users to enter a password. The good news is that the Swing class hierarchy includes an input component specifically for this purpose. Having recently seen the JTextField component, you shouldn't be too surprised to learn that a descendent component exists, called JPasswordField.[1] The bad news is that working with passwords, especially within a scripting language such as Jython, includes the possibility of security exposures, especially if the script writer doesn't think in terms of potential vulnerabilities.

Fortunately, the Swing developers did keep security in mind when designing Java as well as this input component.[2] For example, you may not realize it, but unlike a normal text input field, the text in a JPasswordField can't be cut or copied. If you try to do so, a little bell sound is played to indicate that the requested action cannot be performed.

JPasswordField is a descendent of JTextField, which was discussed in Chapter 6. What happens when text is entered into JPasswordField? Figure 7-1 shows that as you enter text, each character is replaced by a user-configurable echo character. Each instance of this component can, if you choose, have a unique echo character. To identify the character to be displayed for this input field, you use the setEchoChar() method.

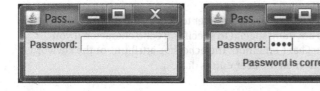

Figure 7-1. *PasswordDemo sample output*

---

[1]See http://docs.oracle.com/javase/8/docs/api/javax/swing/JPasswordField.html.
[2]Unfortunately, there are lots of ways for script writers to overlook good security practices, so be careful.

What does it take to use `JPasswordField`? Listing 7-1 contains the `PasswordDemo` class used to generate the output shown in Figure 7-1. There are some things I need to mention about this code though. Notice how, on line 13, the `size` keyword attribute is used to define the size of the frame to be displayed. This is especially useful in an example like this, which includes an initially empty `JLabel` component that will be used on the application window to display a message.

Listing 7-1. PasswordDemo Class

```
 9|class PasswordDemo( java.lang.Runnable ) :
10|   def run( self ) :
11|        frame = JFrame(
12|            'PasswordDemo',
13|            size = ( 215, 100 ),
14|            layout = FlowLayout(),
15|            defaultCloseOperation = JFrame.EXIT_ON_CLOSE
16|        )
17|        frame.add( JLabel( 'Password:' ) )
18|        self.pwd = frame.add(
19|            JPasswordField(
20|                10,
21|                actionPerformed = self.enter
22|            )
23|        )
24|        self.msg = frame.add( JLabel() )
25|        frame.setVisible( 1 )
26|   def enter( self, event ) :
27|        print 'ActionCommand: "%s"' % event.getActionCommand()
28|        pwd = self.pwd.getPassword()
29|        if pwd == jarray.array( 'test', 'c' ) :
30|            result = 'correct'
31|        else :
32|            result = 'wrong!'
33|        self.msg.setText( 'Password is %s' % result ) .
```

If the frame size isn't specified, and a call to the `frame.pack()` method is used to determine the initial size of the application, space won't be allocated for the message field. This choice would require the `ActionListener` method (i.e., the `enter()` method on lines 26-33) to adjust the size of the application frame so the message text is visible. It's much easier to specify the frame size when the frame is constructed.

The `JPasswordField` instance, as shown on lines 19-22, uses the first parameter to specify the number of characters that are allowed. Notice that you don't have to do anything special to specify an echo character. If you don't like the default echo character, you can use the `setEchoChar()` method, the `echoChar` attribute, or the keyword constructor argument to specify the character to be displayed when the user enters data.

Is There an Echo in Here? Using the Character-Obfuscation Property

Sometimes it might be convenient to allow the users to "turn off" the character-obfuscation property of a password field. If this is the case, you can change the `echoChar` property of the field to have a value of zero (i.e., `\x00` or `chr(0)`). When this is the case, any text in the field will be displayed "in the clear." To enable obfuscation, you simply specify a non-zero `echoChar` value. The `PasswordDemo2.py` script file uses a button to demonstrate one way that this might be performed.

The important part of this script is the showHide() method, which acts as the event handler for the application button. Initially, this button has a value of Show and can be used to display the user input in the clear. Listing 7-2 shows that when the button is activated, the method uses the current text associated with the button to determine how to proceed. When the button text is Show, the password field echoChar attribute is set to zero and the text of the button changes to Hide. When the button text is Hide, the password field echoChar attribute is set to its original value and the text of the button is reset to Show.

Listing 7-2. showHide() Method from PasswordDemo2.py

```
def showHide( self, event ) :
    button = event.getSource()
    if button.getText() == 'Show' :
        self.pwd.setEchoChar( chr( 0 ) )
        button.setText( 'Hide' )
    else :
        self.pwd.setEchoChar( self.echoChar )
        button.setText( 'Show' )
```

Figure 7-2 shows some sample images from the PasswordDemo2.py script. The first image shows what happens when text is entered. The next image shows the result of using the Show button. Notice how the button value has been changed and the password input field is now "in the clear."[3] The next image shows the result of using the Submit button to verify the user input, and the final image shows how the Hide button can be used to obfuscate the password text field again.

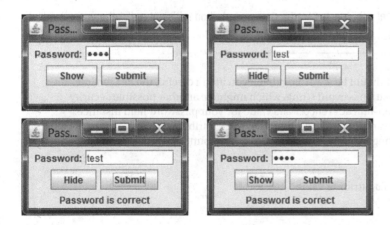

Figure 7-2. PasswordDemo2.py *sample output*

---

[3]It is interesting to note that even though the password text is visible, you still can't copy its value to the system's clipboard.

The getPassword() Method

Reading the Javadoc for the JPassword class should help you understand that even though two getText() methods exist for the underlying text field, they have been deprecated and shouldn't be used. Each getText() method description includes the following statement:

■ **Note** For security reasons, this method is deprecated. Use the getPassword method instead.

Some interesting things should be noted about the differences between the getText() methods and the getPassword() method. One of the most obvious differences is that the return type of the getText() methods is String, whereas the return type of the getPassword() method is a character array. The primary reason for this is security. Strings are immutable and will stick around in memory until a garbage collection cycle can free the storage. A character array, on the other hand, can be replaced or overwritten immediately.

The event.getActionCommand() Method

What's so important about the event handler that it warrants a separate section? JPasswordField has JTextField as its base class. Because of this, it inherits some properties from that class that could be possible security concerns. The following statement comes from the JTextField Javadoc page:

■   JTextField will use the command string set with the setActionCommand method if it's not null; otherwise, it will use the text of the field as a compatibility with java.awt.TextField.

What does it mean for your application? It should be a warning that if you aren't careful, the actionCommand attribute of the JPasswordField instance may be a password string, which might be another possible security exposure. So it is a best practice to provide a non-null actionCommand value for your password field instance. Listing 7-3 shows how easily this can be done using the actionCommand keyword attribute on the constructor call. When this is done, using the Enter key is indistinguishable from using the Submit button as far as the event handler is concerned.

Listing 7-3. Defining a Non-Null actionCommand Attribute Value

```
self.pwd = frame.add(
    JPasswordField(
        10,
        actionCommand = 'Submit',
        actionPerformed = self.enter
    )
)
```

The JPasswordField Event Handler

You finally get to the ActionListener event handler method that is used to process the user-supplied password. You can see an example of this routine in lines 26-33 of Listing 7-1. As mentioned earlier, the data type returned by calling the getPassword() method is a Java array.

The simplest way to check the user-supplied password against the required password value is to create a Java array of the appropriate type and value and compare it with the value returned by the getPassword() method. To do so, you can use the jarray module. If you are unfamiliar with the array method in the jarray module,[4] it exports two functions for the creation of Java arrays for Jython scripts.[5] The exported functions are explained in Table 7-1.

Table 7-1. *The jarray Module Functions*

Function Signature	Description
array(sequence, typeCode)	Returns a Java array containing the values initialized using the specified sequence.
zeros(length, typeCode)	Returns a Java array containing zero (or null) values of the specified length.

The possible values for the typeCode argument of these functions are listed in Table 7-2.

Table 7-2. *typeCode Values Used by the jarray Module*

typeCode Character Value	**Data Type of the Returned Array**
'b'	byte
'c'	char
'd'	double
'f'	float
'h'	short
'i'	int
'l'	long
'z'	Boolean

Using this information allows you to better understand the expression on line 29 in Listing 7-1. Listing 7-4 demonstrates this even more clearly. From this image, you can see just how easy it is to create a Java array using a string value to initialize the array.

Listing 7-4. Creating a Java array

```
wsadmin>import jarray
wsadmin>
wsadmin>jarray.array( 'test', 'c' )
array(['t', 'e', 's', 't'], char)
wsadmin>
```

Using functions from the jarray module allows you to simplify the testing of the value returned by the JPasswordField getPassword() method call. So, you need to be able to compare the value entered by the users against the appropriate password value. Unfortunately, you also need to be able to view the user password in this simple application. Please don't use this kind of technique—i.e., hard-coded passwords—in your applications.

---

[4]See http://www.jython.org/javadoc/org/python/modules/jarray.html.
[5]Table 7-2 only lists the function signatures that have a typeCode argument for simplicity's sake.

Converting jarray Values to Strings

What if you need a Jython string in your script? Can't you use the toString() method to convert the array value to a string? Unfortunately, the data types returned by the jarray array() function and the JPasswordField getPassword() method are, in fact, of type org.python.core.PyArray. Listing 7-5 demonstrates this.

Listing 7-5. Java array type

```
wsadmin>import jarray
wsadmin>from   javax.swing import JPasswordField
wsadmin>
wsadmin>result = jarray.array( 'test', 'c' )
wsadmin>type( result )
<jclass org.python.core.PyArray at 1926329041>
wsadmin>
wsadmin>pwd = JPasswordField( 'test' )
wsadmin>type( pwd.getPassword() )
<jclass org.python.core.PyArray at 1926329041>
wsadmin>
```

So how do you convert this Java array of characters into a string that can be passed to one of the wsadmin scripting object methods? Listing 7-6 shows a couple of ways to do this. The first builds a simple array of the individual characters, and then uses the string join() method to return a string formed by concatenating the characters of the array with an empty string between each. The second shows how simple this operation can be when list comprehension is used instead.

Listing 7-6. Converting a Java array of characters to a string

```
wsadmin>result = []
wsadmin>for ch in pwd.getPassword() :
wsadmin>    result.append( ch )
wsadmin>
wsadmin>str( result )
"['t', 'e', 's', 't']"
wsadmin>''.join( result )
'test'
wsadmin>
wsadmin>
wsadmin>result = []
wsadmin>for ch in pwd.getPassword() :
wsadmin>    result.append( ch )
wsadmin>
wsadmin>''.join( result )
'test'
wsadmin>
wsadmin>result = ''.join( [ ch for ch in pwd.getPassword() ] )
wsadmin>result
'test'
wsadmin>
```

Why do you need to worry about this? All you have to do is not set the `ActionCommand` string, and you will be able to retrieve the password as a string when the users press Enter, right? Not really. What happens when your application has multiple input fields, such as a user ID as well as a password? What about when you want to have two password fields for verification purposes? What happens when you also need or want to have a button? Then your script will have to use the `JPasswordField getPassword()` method to retrieve the Java array of characters. Then, before you can pass it to a WebSphere scripting object, you need some way to easily convert it from a Java array of characters into a Jython string. All this really means is that you need to know how to perform this type of conversion.

Choosing from a List

One nice technique for allowing users to provide input in your application is to provide a list of values and allow the users to select one. The Swing component that provides this kind of choice is the `JComboBox`. If you are interested in what that looks like, take a look at the sample output shown in Figure 7-3.

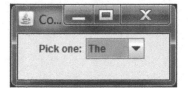

Figure 7-3. *ComboBoxDemo sample output*

There are some things that you should know about a `JComboBox` instance:

- The `JComboBox` class doesn't include an `actionPerformed` attribute that can be used as keyword argument in the constructor call. So you must either use the `addActionListener()` method call or the `actionListener` keyword argument to identify the `ActionListener` instance to be used.

- One of the side effects of this decision is that the application class has to be a descendent of the `ActionListener` class, and it must have an event handler method named `actionPerformed()`. An example of this can be seen on lines 9, 21, and 24 in Listing 7-7.

- It is important to realize that only one ComboBox item can be selected at a time. Multiple items cannot be selected using this component.

- The `ActionListener` event handler code can use the `event.getSource()` method to obtain a reference to the `JComboBox` instance. This technique allows you to access the ComboBox object easily, an example of which is shown on lines 25 and 26 in Listing 7-7. An alternative is to have the application keep an object instance reference to the `JComboBox` object.

Listing 7-7. ComboBox Class

```
 9|class ComboBoxDemo( java.lang.Runnable, ActionListener ) :
10|    def run( self ) :
11|        frame = JFrame(
12|            'ComboBoxDemo',
13|            size = ( 200, 100 ),
14|            layout = FlowLayout(),
15|            defaultCloseOperation = JFrame.EXIT_ON_CLOSE
16|        )
17|        frame.add( JLabel( 'Pick one:' ) )
18|        choices = 'The,quick,brown,fox,jumped'.split( ',' )
19|        choices.extend( 'over,the,lazy,spam'.split( ',' ) )
20|        ComboBox = frame.add( JComboBox( choices ) )
21|        ComboBox.addActionListener( self )
22|        self.msg = frame.add( JLabel() )
23|        frame.setVisible( 1 )
24|    def actionPerformed( self, event ) :
25|        ComboBox = event.getSource()
26|        msg = 'Selection: ' + ComboBox.getSelectedItem()
27|        self.msg.setText( msg )
```

Editing a ComboBox

One of the questions that can come up when you are looking at the JComboBox class is whether it can be edited. The simple answer is yes. There is an editable attribute that you can set to allow users to enter a value that isn't on the list.

Figure 7-4 shows some sample output of the EditableComboBox.py script.

Figure 7-4. *EditableComboBox sample output*

What do you need to do to allow users to enter off-list values? Interestingly enough, you only have to set the editable attribute on the JComboBox instance. Listing 7-8 shows just how simple it is to do so.

Listing 7-8. Making a ComboBox Editable

```
ComboBox = frame.add(
    JComboBox(
        self.choices,
        editable = 1
    )
)
```

There is one important thing to note, however. Even though the event handler method can obtain a user value that isn't in the original list, the list of items doesn't change. So, if the users want to use the same value again, they will have to re-enter it. This should make you wonder if there is a way to add and remove items from the list.

Using the DynamicComboBox

There is also a DynamicComboBox, but it requires a bit more effort and code to use it well. First, take a quick look at some sample output from this sample application, and then you can take a look at and learn about the instructions required to generate the desired results.

Figure 7-5 shows how the list of items in the ComboBox can be removed and added to completely replace the list. What does it take to completely replace the items in the list? The next three listings show methods from the DynamicComboBox.py script.

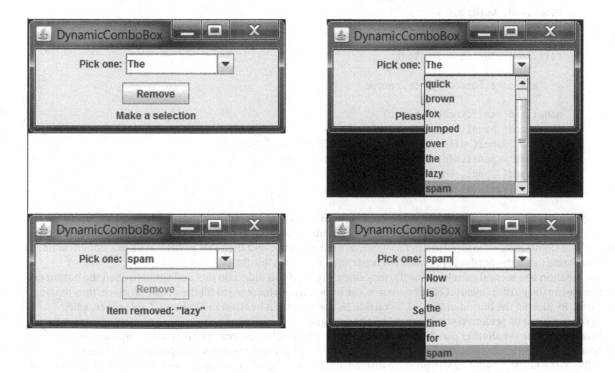

Figure 7-5. *DynamicComboBox sample output*

Listing 7-9 shows the run() method, which creates the various Swing components, places them on the application, and assigns the appropriate ActionListener event handler for the JComboBox and the new Remove button. This is where you'll see the initial list of nine ComboBox items (i.e., lines 22 and 23).

Listing 7-9. DynamicComboBox run() Method

```
12|class DynamicComboBox( java.lang.Runnable, ActionListener ) :
13|    def run( self ) :
14|        self.frame = frame = JFrame(
15|            'DynamicComboBox',
16|            size = ( 310, 137 ),
17|            layout = BorderLayout(),
18|            defaultCloseOperation = JFrame.EXIT_ON_CLOSE
19|        )
20|        panel = JPanel()
21|        panel.add( JLabel( 'Pick one:' ) )
22|        self.choices = 'The,quick,brown,fox,jumped'.split( ',' )
23|        self.choices.extend( 'over,the,lazy,spam'.split( ',' ) )
24|        self.ComboBox = ComboBox = JComboBox(
25|            self.choices,
26|            editable = 1
27|        )
28|        ComboBox.addActionListener( self )
29|        panel.add( ComboBox )
30|        frame.add( panel, BorderLayout.NORTH )
31|        panel = JPanel()
32|        self.RemoveButton = JButton(
33|            'Remove',
34|            actionPerformed = self.remove
35|        )
36|        panel.add( self.RemoveButton )
37|        frame.add( panel, BorderLayout.CENTER )
38|        panel = JPanel( alignmentX = Component.CENTER_ALIGNMENT )
39|        self.msg = panel.add( JLabel( 'Make a selection' ) )
40|        frame.add( panel, BorderLayout.SOUTH )
41|        frame.setVisible( 1 ) .
```

One thing that might surprise you is the use of JPanel instances. The first is created on line 20. Then, you add a label (line 21) and a ComboBox (line 29) to it. Finally, this panel is added to the frame on line 30. This allows both the label and the ComboBox to be kept together as a group of components, and then this panel can be positioned on the top of the frame using the BorderLayout.NORTH constant, as shown on line 30.

The creation of a second panel, on line 31, may surprise you. If you didn't do this and simply added the button to the frame using the BorderLayout.CENTER constant, the button would increase to fill the available space, thus making it too large. By placing the button in a panel, as on line 36, the panel can be sized to fill the available space, while leaving the button at its preferred size in the middle of the panel.

Then you create yet another panel, on line 38. This time you use the alignmentX keyword assignment to configure the horizontal alignment accordingly. If you chose to simply add the message label (e.g., self.msg on line 39) to the BorderLayout.SOUTH position instead, the message label would be aligned to left and would look out of place.

The `actionPerformed()` method, shown in Listing 7-10, is the `ActionListener` event handler that is associated with the ComboBox by the statement on line 28 in Listing 7-9. This method is invoked when someone uses a mouse button or a keyboard event to make a selection on the ComboBox. It is especially interesting to note that the item returned by the call to the `getSelectedItem()` method, as shown on line 44, might in fact return a value that doesn't currently exist in the list of items currently associated with the ComboBox. This is only possible when the `ComboBox` editable attribute is `true`, as you can see on line 26 in Listing 7-9.

Listing 7-10. DynamicComboBox `actionPerformed()` Method

```
42|    def actionPerformed( self, event ) :
43|        cb = self.ComboBox
44|        item = cb.getSelectedItem().strip()
45|        items = [
46|            cb.getItemAt( i )
47|            for i in range( cb.getItemCount() )
48|        ]
49|        if item :
50|            if item not in items :
51|                cb.addItem( item )
52|                self.RemoveButton.setEnabled( 1 )
53|            msg = 'Selection: "%s"' % item
54|            self.msg.setText( msg )
55|        else :
56|            cb.setSelectedIndex( 0 )
```

This event handler is responsible for determining if the specified item is valid, and whether or not it currently exists on the list. If it doesn't exist, a call is made to the `addItem()` method (line 51) to add it to the list of items currently associated with the ComboBox. Why do you call the `setEnabled()` method when an item is added? Because it is possible for the remove method, shown in Listing 7-11, to reduce the number of items on the ComboBox to one. At this point, the Remove button should be disabled.

Listing 7-11. DynamicComboBox `remove()` Method

```
57|    def remove( self, event ) :
58|        cb = self.ComboBox
59|        index = cb.getSelectedIndex()
60|        item = cb.getSelectedItem()
61|        try :
62|            cb.removeItem( item )
63|            self.msg.setText( 'Item removed: "%s"' % item )
64|        except :
65|            self.msg.setText( 'Remove request failed' )
66|        self.RemoveButton.setEnabled( cb.getItemCount() > 1 )
```

The `remove()` method, shown in Listing 7-11, is associated with the button, as shown on line 34 in Listing 7-9. This method is invoked only when the user selects the Remove button, and the event handler routine is responsible for removing the current ComboBox item. It is also responsible for disabling the button when the number of items on the ComboBox list is reduced to one.[6]

---

[6]The expression (i.e., `cb.getItemCount() > 1`) will be `true` (i.e., 1) when more than one item is present on the list; this keeps the button enabled. When the list only has one item, the expression is `false` (i.e., 0) and the button is disabled.

Formatted Text Fields

There are times when it is important to control the way information is displayed by a text field. For situations such as this, Swing provides the JFormattedTextField class[7] and the Format class hierarchy.[8]

A formatted text field allows you to specify the kinds of values that are appropriate for a specific field and determine how these values are displayed. What kind of formatting can you apply? Well, you can format a text field as a number (e.g., as an integer, a floating point, or as currency). You can also specify a pattern to identify how a value should appear (e.g., a date, Social Security Number, or even a telephone number).

Take a quick look at a sample application that uses the various instances of formatted numbers.[9] Figure 7-6 shows the output of this simple application.

getInstance()	12,345.679
getCurrencyInstance()	$12,345.68
getIntegerInstance()	12,346
getNumberInstance()	12,345.679
getPercentInstance()	1,234,568%

Figure 7-6. *FormattedTextFieldDemo sample output*

What does it take to generate the output? You might be surprised to see just how easy it is. Listing 7-12 contains the code from the FormattedTextFieldDemo.py script used to produce the output shown in Figure 7-6.[10]

Listing 7-12. FormattedTextFieldDemo Class

```
class FormattedTextFieldDemo( java.lang.Runnable ) :
    def addFTF( self, name ) :
        pane = self.frame.getContentPane()
        pane.add( JLabel( name ) )
        pane.add(
            JFormattedTextField(
                eval( 'NumberFormat.' + name ),
                value = 12345.67890,
                columns = 10
            )
        )
    def run( self ) :
        self.frame = frame = JFrame(
            'FormattedTextFieldDemo',
            layout = GridLayout( 0, 2 ),
            defaultCloseOperation = JFrame.EXIT_ON_CLOSE
        )
```

---

[7]See http://docs.oracle.com/javase/8/docs/api/javax/swing/JFormattedTextField.html.

[8]See http://docs.oracle.com/javase/8/docs/api/java/text/Format.html.

[9]Note: You'll revisit the JFormattedTextField class in Chapter 14.

[10]Note: The eval() function, as shown in line 15, is normally discouraged. However, using it in this example allowed the addFTF() method call to be greatly simplified and much shorter.

```
self.addFTF( 'getInstance()'          )
self.addFTF( 'getCurrencyInstance()' )
self.addFTF( 'getIntegerInstance()'  )
self.addFTF( 'getNumberInstance()'    )
self.addFTF( 'getPercentInstance()'  )
frame.pack()
frame.setVisible( 1 )
```

Looking closely at this script, you can see that the format of the value to be displayed in each field is defined by the NumberFormat instance that is used to instantiate each formatted text field.

The generated output may make you wonder about the kind of control that is provided by the NumberFormat class. Looking at the NumberFormat Javadoc,[11] you see that you can modify the attributes in Table 7-3. By the way, this table shows the initial/default settings for each of these attributes for the specified NumberFormat instance type.

Table 7-3. *NumberFormat Instance Type Attributes*

NumberFormat Instance Type	Integer Part		Fraction Part	
	Minimum Digits	Maximum Digits	Minimum Digits	Maximum Digits
getInstance()	1	MAXINT	0	3
getCurrencyInstance()	1	MAXINT	2	2
getIntegerInstance()	1	MAXINT	0	0
getNumberInstance()	1	MAXINT	0	3
getPercentInstance()	1	MAXINT	0	0

How are you supposed to understand this information? Well, take a look at a row in the table, e.g., the one for the currency instances. It differs from the others in that these kinds of values have a minimum and maximum of two fractional digits. That's why the value in the currency row of Figure 7-6 appears as $12,345.68. If you execute that script and enter a value of $0 in the input field, it will be reformatted as $0.00, which makes sense when you look at the row in Table 7-3 specifying currency values. There will be a minimum of one digit before and exactly two digits after the decimal point.

One important point to note about these types of constructors for the NumberFormat class is that the instance attributes are specific to the locale of the operating system on which the wsadmin script is being executed. If your application requires a specific locale formatting, it might be specified as a parameter on the instance constructor:

```
format = NumberFormat.getCurrencyInstance( Locale.FRENCH )
```

---

[11] See http://docs.oracle.com/javase/8/docs/api/java/text/NumberFormat.html.

Using a JSpinner Text Field

The last of the text input fields to be discussed here makes use of the `javax.swing.JSpinner` class. What does the `JSpinner` object look like? Each `JSpinner` field has a text input field and two small buttons. Figure 7-7 shows a trivial `JSpinner` field displaying the days of the week.

It should be obvious that the text field in this particular example isn't wide enough to display all of the characters in the longest weekdays. First, take a look at the class used to display this sample output. Listing 7-13 shows the `Spinner1` class from this script file.[12]

Figure 7-7. *Sample JSpinner text field*

Listing 7-13. `Spinner1` Class

```
from    java.text    import DateFormatSymbols as DFS
...
class Spinner1( java.lang.Runnable ) :
    def run( self ) :
        frame = JFrame(
            'Spinner1',
            layout = FlowLayout(),
            defaultCloseOperation = JFrame.EXIT_ON_CLOSE
        )
        daysOfWeek = [ dow for dow in DFS().getWeekdays() if dow ]
        frame.add( JSpinner( SpinnerListModel( daysOfWeek ) ) )
        frame.pack()
        frame.setVisible( 1 )
```

Some DateFormatSymbols Methods

To understand this example, you need to understand a few concepts. Let's begin with the `getWeekdays()` method of the `DateFormatSymbols` module.[13] Listing 7-14 shows an interactive `wsadmin` session showing what is returned by the `DateFormatSymbols`' `getWeekdays()` and `getMonths()` methods.[14]

---

[12]Line 5 is included to show how an alias for the `DateFormatSymbols` was defined. This allowed line 17 to be short enough to be fit easily in the available space.

[13]See http://docs.oracle.com/javase/8/docs/api/java/text/DateFormatSymbols.html.

[14]There are many more methods provided by the `DateFormatSymbols` class that aren't covered in this book. Feel free to experiment with and use these other methods.

Listing 7-14. DateFormatSymbols methods

```
wsadmin>from java.text import DateFormatSymbols as DFS
wsadmin>
wsadmin>DFS().getWeekdays()
array(['', 'Sunday', 'Monday', 'Tuesday', 'Wednesday', 'Thursday', 'Friday', 'Saturday'], java.lang.
String)
wsadmin>
wsadmin>len( DFS().getWeekdays() )
8
wsadmin>DFS().getMonths()
wsadmin>array(['January', 'February', 'March', 'April', 'May', 'June', 'July', 'August',
'September', 'October', 'November', 'December', ''], java.lang.String)
```

It should be no surprise to you that the getWeekdays() and getMonths() methods return Java arrays. What might be a surprise to you—it certainly was to me—was the fact that the getWeekdays() method returns eight values and the getMonths() method returns 13 values.[15] That's why the Spinner1 class, as shown in Listing 7-13, uses list comprehension to process the results of calling the getWeekdays() method and returns the non-empty values that exist.

The JSpinner Class

Unlike the JComboBox, JSpinner instances do not display any kind of drop-down list of values. Only the current value is visible. The buttons on the field can be used to display the next or previous values. Why would you use a spinner instead of a ComboBox? Spinners are normally used when the number of valid items is too large to display. Does the use of the JSpinner class force the users to use the buttons? No, it doesn't.

Figure 7-8 shows the same Spinner1 application after various actions. You can see that the text portion of the spinner can be selected and user input (i.e., from the keyboard) can be used to filter or select the value to be displayed.

Figure 7-8. *Spinner value selections*

---

[15] This is *not* a bug, as is explained in the bug report found here: http://bugs.sun.com/bugdatabase/view_bug.do?bug_id=4146173. It's a feature. Personally, I kind of like the explanation that exists in various places on the web that these eight-day weeks and 13-month years were created for managers and product planners to explain and justify the development schedules. But that's just a guess.

The various actions shown in Figure 7-9 are explained in Table 7-4.

Figure 7-9. *Default (numeric) spinner examples*

Table 7-4. *Spinner Value Selection, Explained*

Image	Description
1	Shows the application output after the window is slightly widened.
2	Shows how the text in the input field can be selected.
3	After typing W (and clicking on the window edge to cause the text input field to be widened), you can see that the first value matching the specified text has been selected. It is interesting to note how the W has been deselected.
4	After selecting the entire text in the field again.
5	After typing T, notice that Tuesday has been selected, even though it precedes Wednesday in the list of values.
6	After typing h, notice how Thursday has been selected. This tells you that the value that you typed is used to match the selected portion of the text field.

This raises a number of questions in my mind. What kinds of values can be displayed in a spinner field? Do they have to be alphabetic strings? Let's take a look at the JSpinner Javadoc[16] to find out.

According to that page, there are only two JSpinner constructors—the default (i.e., empty) and one that uses something called a SpinnerModel argument. The default spinner constructor shows that it can be used to display numeric (i.e., integer). The images in Figure 7-9 show how numeric spinner values can be selected.

From left, the first image shows the initial, or default, value of 0. The second shows how a million is displayed. The third shows the maximum integer value (i.e., java.lang.Integer.MAX_VALUE of 2,147,483,647). The final image shows the value shown when the button is used to display the next value. Hopefully, you aren't too surprised by the fact that a wraparound occurs, and the value that is displayed is the smallest integer value (i.e., java.lang.Integer.MIN_VALUE of -2,147,483,648).

One of the interesting things to note about this output is how the numeric values are formatted. From this output, you should quickly come to the realization that the text field portion of the spinner instance is a formatted text field.

The SpinnerModel Class

The SpinnerModel Javadoc[17] explains that this class is used for potentially unbounded values, which makes sense, especially looking back at the default spinner that you saw in Figure 7-9.

---

[16]See http://docs.oracle.com/javase/8/docs/api/javax/swing/JSpinner.html.
[17]See http://docs.oracle.com/javase/8/docs/api/javax/swing/SpinnerModel.html.

One of the important points to note about the `SpinnerModel` is that it is an interface. Your applications can use one of your own classes based upon this interface class or one of the implementations provided by the Swing API, specifically `SpinnerDateModel`, `SpinnerListModel`, or `SpinnerNumberModel`. Looking back at Listing 7-13, you can see that the `Spinner1` class uses the `SpinnerListModel` class. The constructor for this class was passed an array of strings. This particular example contains a short list of values, so a ComboBox may be a better choice in this type of situation. But it's your decision.

The `SpinnerNumberModel` class constructors have either zero or four parameters. The zero parameters constructor was used by the default `JSpinner()` constructor shown on line 15 of Listing 7-15.

Listing 7-15. Spinner2 Class

```
 8|class Spinner2( java.lang.Runnable ) :
 9|    def run( self ) :
10|        frame = JFrame(
11|            'Spinner2',
12|            layout = FlowLayout(),
13|            defaultCloseOperation = JFrame.EXIT_ON_CLOSE
14|        )
15|        frame.add( JSpinner() )
16|        frame.pack()
17|        frame.setVisible( 1 )
```

This is the one that was used to display a selection of four billion values, as shown in Figure 7-9. The four-parameter variant of the `SpinnerNumberModel` class constructor identifies:

- The initial value to be displayed
- The minimum valid value
- The maximum valid value
- The `stepSize`, or increment value, to be used

The `Spinner3` class that shows how this might be used is demonstrated in Listing 7-16.

Listing 7-16. Spinner3 Class

```
class Spinner3( java.lang.Runnable ) :
    def run( self ) :
        frame = JFrame(
            'Spinner3',
            layout = FlowLayout(),
            defaultCloseOperation = JFrame.EXIT_ON_CLOSE
        )
        frame.add(
            JSpinner(
                SpinnerNumberModel(
                    0,          # Initial value
                    -3141.59,   # Minimum value
                    +3141.59,   # Maximum value
                    3.14159     # stepSize
                )
            )
        )
        frame.pack()
        frame.setVisible( 1 )
```

One of the interesting points to note about this application is that no value exists above the maximum or below the minimum specified values. This differs from the `Spinner2` class, which uses a wraparound effect.

Figure 7-10 shows what the default `SpinnerDateModel` looks like, at least for my locale. The multiple images show that you can select different portions of the date in the text field and then use either the spinner buttons or the up and down keys on your keyboard to change the date.

Figure 7-10. *Default SpinnerDateModel examples*

For example, I set the current date to 3/1/00 and selected the day of the month part (i.e., the 1). Pressing the down key changes the date to 2/29/00 (i.e., Leap Day). How do you specify March 1, 2000 as the starting date for the spinner? Listing 7-17 shows one way to do this and is part of the `Spinner5.py` script.

Listing 7-17. Sample Use of SpinnerDateModel

```
frame.add(
    JSpinner(
        SpinnerDateModel(
            Date( 2000,  2,  1 ),    # zero origin month
            None,                    # minimum
            None,                    # maximum
            Calendar.DAY_OF_MONTH    # Ignored by GUI
        )
    )
)
```

One of the things to remember about this example is that even though a `calendarField` argument is specified, this does not automatically cause the specified field to be selected on the application window. You might be surprised to see the cursor located at the beginning or end of your input field, depending on your locale.

The JSpinner Editor

What if you don't like the way that the value (e.g., `Date`) is shown in the spinner text field? To change it, you need to change the default spinner editor, which is based on the kind of `SpinnerModel` being used. Four spinner editors are provided by Swing:

- `JSpinner.DateEditor`—Used for `SpinnerDateModel` instances

- `JSpinner.ListEditor`—Used for `SpinnerListModel` instances

- `JSpinner.NumberEditor`—Used for `SpinnerNumberModel` instances

- `JSpinner.DefaultEditor`—A simple base class for more specialized editors

Figure 7-11 shows the sample output that is generated using a different date pattern used by the `Spinner6` class shown in Listing 7-18.

Figure 7-11. *The Spinner6 output using a different date pattern*

Lines 27-30 show how you can specify a different date display pattern[18] for the formatted text field used by the spinner instance.

Listing 7-18. Spinner6 Class

```
10|from    javax.swing import SpinnerDateModel
11|class Spinner6( java.lang.Runnable ) :
12|    def run( self ) :
13|        frame = JFrame(
14|            'Spinner6',
15|            layout = FlowLayout(),
16|            defaultCloseOperation = JFrame.EXIT_ON_CLOSE
17|        )
18|        spinner = JSpinner(
19|            SpinnerDateModel(
20|                Date( 2000,  2,  1 ),   # zero origin month
21|                None,                   # minimum
22|                None,                   # maximum
23|                Calendar.DAY_OF_MONTH   # Ignored by GUI
24|            )
25|        )
26|        spinner.setEditor(
27|            JSpinner.DateEditor(
28|                spinner,
29|                'dd MMM yy'
30|            )
31|        )
32|        frame.add( spinner )
33|        frame.pack()
34|        frame.setVisible( 1 )
```

This is just a simple example that should provide you with enough of a start for your applications.

Summary

This chapter explained many new input components that you can now utilize. By now, you should be getting a better feel for how Swing components can be used to provide user-friendly input choices for the users of your applications. In the next chapter, you will turn your attention to selectable input components.

---

[18] See http://docs.oracle.com/javase/8/docs/api/java/text/SimpleDateFormat.html.

CHAPTER 8

■ ■ ■

Selectable Input Components

So far, you have learned how to use simple buttons and a variety of text input fields. In this chapter, you'll take a look at using some other input components, ones that can be selected. All of the components in this chapter have two possible states, they are either selected or not. I'll start by describing toggle buttons, proceed to check boxes, and then to radio buttons. I will also discuss how to group these fields in order to make interesting user presentations.

Toggle Buttons

Simple push buttons are used to initiate an event of some kind. Occasionally, it can be useful for a button to have an associated state to convey additional information to the users. Toggle buttons perform this role. Thinking of this obvious difference makes me think of when I was little. The radio in my parents' car had buttons that you would press to select a station. It was quite obvious which of the buttons had been selected. You will learn how to group toggle buttons together so that only one button can be selected at a time.

Before you do that, though, you need to better understand toggle buttons and their states. The toggle button state can indicate whether the button has been selected/clicked or not. What does a toggle button look like? Figure 8-1 shows a simple application window containing a single toggle button, before and after it is pressed. In order to accentuate the button's state, this application also changes the button's text based on its selected attribute.

Figure 8-1. *Sample toggle button application output*

What does it take to create a **JToggleButton**?[1] Listing 8-1 shows the **ToggleButton** class that instantiates a toggle button using the specified text and identifies the event handler to be invoked when the button state changes. The most significant difference between simple buttons and toggle buttons is the presence of the selected state. A push button, on the other hand, initiates an action when the button is clicked. Because of this, the event handler of the toggle button invokes the **itemStateChanged()** method of the **ItemListener** interface.[2] By comparison, the event handler for a **JButton** will invoke the **actionPerformed()** method of the **ActionListener** interface.[3] You can see this difference in the **itemStateChanged** keyword argument of the JToggleButton constructor in Listing 8-1.

---

[1]See http://docs.oracle.com/javase/8/docs/api/javax/swing/JToggleButton.html.
[2]See http://docs.oracle.com/javase/8/docs/api/java/awt/event/ItemListener.html.
[3]See http://docs.oracle.com/javase/8/docs/api/java/awt/event/ActionListener.html.

Listing 8-1. ToggleButton Class

```
 8|class ToggleButton( java.lang.Runnable ) :
 9|    def run( self ) :
10|        frame = JFrame(
11|            'Toggle Button',
12|            layout = FlowLayout(),
13|            size   = ( 275, 85 ),
14|            defaultCloseOperation = JFrame.EXIT_ON_CLOSE
15|        )
16|        button  = JToggleButton(              # Make a toggle button
17|            'Off' ,                           # Initial button text
18|            itemStateChanged = self.toggle    # Event handler
19|        )
20|        frame.add( button  )
21|        frame.setVisible( 1 )
22|    def toggle( self, event ) :
23|        button = event.getItem()
24|        button.setText( [ 'Off', 'On' ][ button.isSelected() ] )
```

The **toggle** method, shown in lines 22-24 of Listing 8-1, uses the getItem() method of the event that caused the method to be called in order to determine which component had a state change. It wasn't necessary to do this in this simple application, because there is only one component that has this property. However, this example is useful when you have multiple components that share an event handler. In fact, you'll see this scenario in the next example.

Check Boxes

While reviewing the Javadoc for the **JCheckBox** class,[4] I found it kind of interesting to see that it was, in fact, based on the **JToggleButton** class that you just read about. This makes sense because toggle buttons and check boxes both have a simple on/off state and react when clicked. Using this knowledge, you can easily create an application based on the **ToggleButton** code that has some check boxes. Figure 8-2 shows the some sample output of this application.

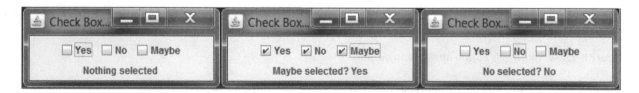

Figure 8-2. Sample output for check boxes

Listing 8-2 shows one way that this can be done.[5] A point of interest is how the event handler uses the **getText()** method (line 31) to retrieve the text of the check box that caused the state change method to be called. As mentioned earlier, this allows the check boxes to share the same event handler.

---

[4] See http://docs.oracle.com/javase/8/docs/api/javax/swing/JCheckBox.html.
[5] Initially, I had the code to create and add each **JCheckBox** to the frame on a single line. Width limitations for these listings, however, meant that it would be best, at least for this example, to create and use the **addCB()** method in lines 9-15 instead.

Listing 8-2. CheckBoxes Class

```
 8|class CheckBoxes( java.lang.Runnable ) :
 9|    def addCB( self, pane, text ) :
10|        pane.add(
11|            JCheckBox(
12|                text,
13|                itemStateChanged = self.toggle
14|            )
15|        )
16|    def run( self ) :
17|        frame = JFrame(
18|            'Check Boxes',
19|            layout = FlowLayout(),
20|            size   = ( 250, 100 ),
21|            defaultCloseOperation = JFrame.EXIT_ON_CLOSE
22|        )
23|        cp = frame.getContentPane()
24|        self.addCB( cp, 'Yes' )
25|        self.addCB( cp, 'No'  )
26|        self.addCB( cp, 'Maybe' )
27|        self.label = frame.add( JLabel( 'Nothing selected' ) )
28|        frame.setVisible( 1 )
29|    def toggle( self, event ) :
30|        cb    = event.getItem()
31|        text  = cb.getText()
32|        state = [ 'No', 'Yes' ][ cb.isSelected() ]
33|        self.label.setText( '%s selected? %s' % ( text, state ) )
```

■ **Note** This example doesn't use the **selected** parameter of the **JCheckBox** constructor, so each of the check boxes starts with the state as deselected.

Radio Buttons

One of the differences between check boxes and radio buttons is that radio buttons are most useful when they are grouped. This allows one, and only one, radio button in the group to be selected at a time. Take a look at the previous example again; this time, however, it uses radio buttons instead of check boxes.

Figure 8-3 shows sample output of this simple application, which is now using radio buttons instead of check boxes.

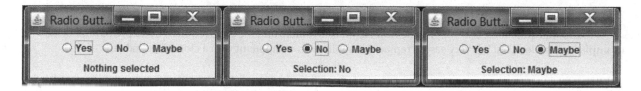

Figure 8-3. Sample output for radio buttons

Listing 8-3 shows the **RadioButtons** class that generates the output shown in Figure 8-3. What, if anything, do you notice about this class? Take a few moments to compare it to the **CheckBoxes** class in Listing 8-2. You should find very few differences between these two classes.

Listing 8-3. RadioButtons Class

```
 9|class RadioButtons( java.lang.Runnable ) :
10|    def addRB( self, pane, bg, text ) :
11|        bg.add(
12|            pane.add(
13|                JRadioButton(
14|                    text,
15|                    itemStateChanged = self.toggle
16|                )
17|            )
18|        )
19|    def run( self ) :
20|        frame = JFrame(
21|            'Radio Buttons',
22|            layout = FlowLayout(),
23|            size   = ( 250, 100 ),
24|            defaultCloseOperation = JFrame.EXIT_ON_CLOSE
25|        )
26|        cp = frame.getContentPane()
27|        bg = ButtonGroup()
28|        self.addRB( cp, bg, 'Yes' )
29|        self.addRB( cp, bg, 'No'  )
30|        self.addRB( cp, bg, 'Maybe' )
31|        self.label = frame.add( JLabel( 'Nothing selected' ) )
32|        frame.setVisible( 1 )
33|    def toggle( self, event ) :
34|        text = event.getItem().getText()
35|        self.label.setText( 'Selection: ' + text )
```

As mentioned earlier, you also need a **ButtonGroup**[6] to indicate the collection to which the new **JRadioButton**[7] object should be added. This **ButtonGroup** is created on line 27 and passed to the **addRB()** method on lines 28-30. So that shouldn't be too much of a surprise. Were you surprised that with one statement—in lines 11-18—you can:

- Create a radio button (line 13)

- Specify the associated text (line 14)

- Specify the **ActionListener** (i.e., **itemStateChanged**) event handler (line 15)

- Add the **ActionListener** to the specified pane (line 12)

- Add the **ActionListener** to the specified button group (line 11)

I found this quite nice, and I appreciate how easy it is to understand the code required to do this. Granted, the example isn't perfect, but it is very easy to replace an application component with a closely related one.

---

[6]See http://docs.oracle.com/javase/8/docs/api/javax/swing/ButtonGroup.html.
[7]See http://docs.oracle.com/javase/8/docs/api/javax/swing/JRadioButton.html.

Toggle Buttons in a Button Group

In the first part of this chapter I mentioned how the radio buttons of my parents' car were similar to toggle buttons. Thinking of this made me wonder how difficult it would be to simulate this feature in a script. All you need to do is place a bunch of toggle buttons in a button group, right? Well, that's pretty much the case. There are a few extra things that you need to do (initialize one of the buttons as selected and display the correct message), but that's pretty much it. Figure 8-4 shows the sample output for this application.

Figure 8-4. *A group of toggle buttons*

What does it take to do this? Not much. In fact I think that you'll agree that Listing 8-4 looks very similar to Listing 8-3, where you used a button group to identify a group of radio buttons.

Listing 8-4. ButtonGroupDemo

```
class ButtonGroupDemo( java.lang.Runnable ) :
    def addRB( self, pane, bg, text ) :
        bg.add(
            pane.add(
                JToggleButton(
                    text,
                    selected = ( text == '1' ),
                    itemStateChanged = self.toggle
                )
            )
        )
    def run( self ) :
        frame = JFrame(
            'ToggleButton Group',
            layout = FlowLayout(),
            size   = ( 265, 100 ),
            defaultCloseOperation = JFrame.EXIT_ON_CLOSE
        )
        cp = frame.getContentPane()
        bg = ButtonGroup()
        for i in range( 1, 6 ) :
            self.addRB( cp, bg, `i` )
        self.label = frame.add( JLabel( 'Selection: 1' ) )
        frame.setVisible( 1 )
    def toggle( self, event ) :
        text = event.getItem().getText()
        self.label.setText( 'Selection: ' + text )
```

Here's a question for you. Do toggle buttons in a button group act any differently than those that aren't in a button group? The answer is yes they do. Once a toggle button within a button group is selected, it can't be deselected. In fact, this is the same behavior shown when radio buttons are used. Initially, you can have all of the radio buttons (or toggle buttons) in a button group deselected, but once one has been selected, one will always be selected.[8]

Summary

This chapter, even though it is fairly short, discusses and describes selectable input components. One of the interesting things that I found while investigating these components was the fact that all the selectable classes are based on the **JToggleButton** class. This is what led me to investigate using multiple toggle buttons within a button group. I hope that you find these an interesting addition to your collection of user interface components.

---

[8]Unless, of course, you have something like an event handler deselect everything in the group.

CHAPTER 9

■ ■ ■

Providing Choices, Making Lists

You are likely to encounter situations where it would be nice to provide your users with a list of choices. For example, you've probably selected the name of the city where you live from a list. Maybe you want to build an application to keep track of the books or movies that you own. Fortunately, Swing provides the JList[1] component, which allows programmers to build and display lists of this sort. In this chapter, you learn how to build and display a list of items. You will also learn how to manipulate a list in the event handler method associated with another component, such as a button.

Making a List and Checking It Twice

How hard is it to make a list? Not very. Listing 9-1 shows how little code is required to create a list using a group of words from a string. Another version of this script, called List1a.py, is provided that shows you how to build a JList using a java.util.Vector.

Listing 9-1. The List1 Class

```
class List1( java.lang.Runnable ) :
    def run( self ) :
        frame = JFrame(
            'List1',
            size = ( 250, 200 ),
            defaultCloseOperation = JFrame.EXIT_ON_CLOSE
        )
        data = 'Now is the time for all good spam'.split( ' ' )
        frame.add( JList( data ) )
        frame.setVisible( 1 )
```

What can you do with a default JList? Figure 9-1 shows that you can select one or more items on this list with no additional code; you simply need to press the Ctrl key while additional items are selected.

---

[1]See http://docs.oracle.com/javase/8/docs/api/javax/swing/JList.html.

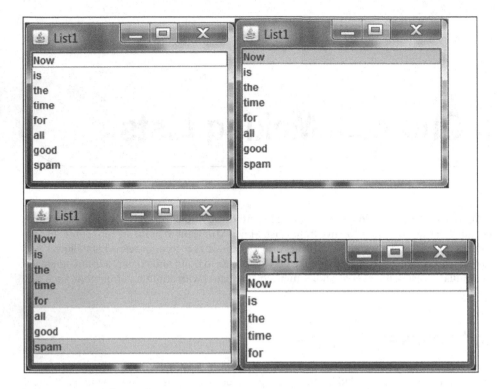

Figure 9-1. *List1's sample output*

Wow, that was easy, right? You're all done and can move on to the next topic, right? Not quite. There are lots of things that you need to consider when your applications deal with lists. For example, the last image shows one problem that occurs when the size of the frame isn't large enough to show all of the entries in the list. There is no indication that additional items exist. Even worse, if you use the cursor down arrow to move the selection down the list, you can select items that are not visible to the user. What can you do about that?

Optional Scroll Bars

If your list has a limited (small) number of items (such as the days of the week), you might want to use something like a JComboBox[2] instead of a JList. Frequently, however, the number of items on the list won't easily fit in the application window. When this happens, you only need to wrap the JList instance within a JScrollPane.[3] This is so easy to do that it is hard to imagine why you wouldn't want to always put your JList instance in a scroll pane. Listing 9-2 shows just how easy this can be. Compare line 15 to line 14 in Listing 9-1.

Listing 9-2. Wrapping a JList in a Scroll Pane

```
 7|class List2( java.lang.Runnable ) :
 8|    def run( self ) :
 9|        frame = JFrame(
10|            'List2',
```

---

[2]As discussed in section 7.2.
[3]See http://docs.oracle.com/javase/8/docs/api/javax/swing/JScrollPane.html.

```
11|            size = ( 250, 100 ),
12|            defaultCloseOperation = JFrame.EXIT_ON_CLOSE
13|        )
14|        data = 'Now is the time for all good spam'.split( ' ' )
15|        frame.add( JScrollPane( JList( data ) ) )
16|        frame.setVisible( 1 )
```

What does this do to the application? Well, if the list contains more items than can be displayed in the available area, vertical and/or horizontal scroll bars will be added, as needed, to allow the users to determine which parts of the available information they want to view. Figure 9-2 shows the output of the List2 application. It has space for fewer lines and therefore requires a vertical scrollbar.[4] Once the size of the frame is large enough to display the complete list, the vertical scrollbar automatically disappears.

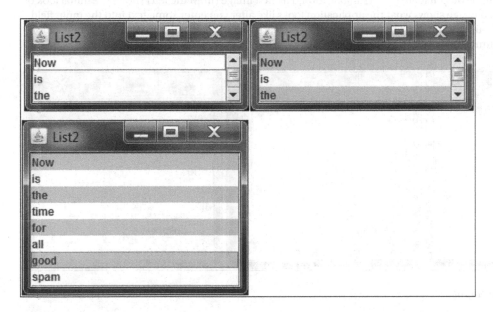

Figure 9-2. *List2's sample output*

The ScrollPane Viewport

The JScrollPane Javadoc includes a diagram that shows the relationship between the ScrollPane instance and the child component contained in it. One of the important concepts to note is that a JViewport[5] is created to determine the portion of the child component to be displayed.

■ **Tip**   If you are interested in learning more about scroll panes, viewports, and scroll bars, I encourage you to take a look at the "How to Use Scroll Panes"[6] portion of the Java Swing Tutorials. This book doesn't delve into more detail about viewports, but they do show up in Chapter 12, where tables are discussed in detail.

---

[4]In case you are wondering, I simply held the Ctrl key and selected the odd list entries to produce these images.
[5]See http://docs.oracle.com/javase/8/docs/api/javax/swing/JViewport.html.
[6]See http://docs.oracle.com/javase/tutorial/uiswing/components/scrollpane.html.

Manipulating the List

You will frequently need your applications to manipulate a list in some way. For example, you may want to add, remove, or replace items on a list. To do this, you need to use the interface provided by the list model. What's a list model? It is the component that actually contains the list contents and provides methods that allow your applications to manipulate the list. If one is not passed to the JList constructor, a DefaultListModel[7] will be created to for you.[8] You previously saw this separation of the component and its data in Chapter 7, which discussed the SpinnerModel class.

Counting List Items

Let's take a quick look at how a list model can be used to count the number of times a specific value occurs on the list. Figure 9-3 shows some sample output for the List3 application. The first image (from the left) shows the initial look of the application. The second image shows what the application looks like after you enter some text into the input field (i.e., "the") and click the Count button. Note how the input field is cleared and the message portion of the application is updated to reflect the number of occurrences of the specified word.

Figure 9-3. *List3's sample output*

Listings 9-3 and 9-4 show the List3 class produces the output shown in Figure 9-3. Lines 21-25 show how the list of words is created, again using a simple array of strings. Lines 26-32 show how the list is wrapped in a scroll pane and added to the top of the application window using the BorderLayout.NORTH position constant.

Listing 9-3. List3's run( ) Method

```
13|class List3( java.lang.Runnable ) :
14|    def run( self ) :
15|        frame = JFrame(
16|            'List3',
17|            size = ( 200, 200 ),
18|            layout = BorderLayout(),
19|            defaultCloseOperation = JFrame.EXIT_ON_CLOSE
20|        )
```

---

[7]See http://docs.oracle.com/javase/8/docs/api/javax/swing/DefaultListModel.html.
[8]This book discusses the use of the DefaultListModel, not the AbstractListModel, the ListModel, or the more interesting SortedListModel class discussed at http://java.sun.com/developer/technicalArticles/J2SE/Desktop/sorted_jlist/

```
21|          data = (
22|              'Now is the time for all good spam ' +
23|              'to come to the aid of their eggs'
24|          ).split( ' ' )
25|          self.info = JList( data )
26|          frame.add(
27|              JScrollPane(
28|                  self.info,
29|                  preferredSize = ( 200, 110 )
30|              ),
31|              BorderLayout.NORTH
32|          )
33|          panel = JPanel( layout = GridLayout( 0, 2 ) )
34|          panel.add(
35|              JButton(
36|                  'Count',
37|                  actionPerformed = self.count
38|              )
39|          )
40|          self.text = panel.add( JTextField( 10 ) )
41|          frame.add( panel, BorderLayout.CENTER )
42|          self.msg  = JLabel( 'Occurance count' )
43|          frame.add( self.msg, BorderLayout.SOUTH )
44|          frame.setVisible( 1 )
```

The middle portion of the application, containing the Count button and text input fields, is created and positioned on the application window in lines 33-41. Finally, the status message (a label field) is created and placed on the bottom of the application window in lines 42 and 43.

Listing 9-4 shows the count() method, which is identified as the button's actionListener event handler, on line 37 in Listing 9-3, when the button is created. It is here that you need to use the list model to count the number of times a specified value occurs in the associated list.[9]

Listing 9-4. List3's count() Method

```
45|    def count( self, event ) :
46|        word = self.text.getText()
47|        model = self.info.getModel()
48|        occurs = 0
49|        for index in range( model.getSize() ) :
50|            if model.getElementAt( index ) == word :
51|                occurs += 1
52|        self.msg.setText(
53|            '"%s" occurs %d time(s)' %
54|            ( word, occurs )
55|        )
56|        self.text.setText( '' )
```

---

[9]You wouldn't want to use this technique on an unbounded list. And, if your list was large, you would want the list model processing to be performed on a separate thread (i.e., by a SwingWorker class instance).

Limiting the Selectable Items

Other list-manipulation actions include adding and removing items to and from the list. Before you take a look at what these operations require, think about it for a moment. When you want to add an item to the list, where do you want to add it? Should it be added to the beginning of the list, at the end, or somewhere in the middle? You also might need to consider if multiple occurrences of a value should be allowed on the list.

Do you want to allow multiple items to be selected? This might make sense if you want to allow the users to remove multiple items with a single button click, but this might not always make sense. For example, if you want to allow the users to select an item on the list, and then allow a new item to be added, either before or after the selected item, then it doesn't make sense to allow multiple items to be selected at one time.

Earlier, you saw that the default list properties allow you to select multiple list items. How do you disable this? The JList class includes a selection mode attribute that can define the number of list items that can be selected. Table 9-1 describes the list selection mode values.

Table 9-1. *List Selection Mode Examples*

Selection Mode	Description
SINGLE_SELECTION	Either zero or one item may be selected.
SINGLE_INTERVAL_SELECTION	Only one contiguous group of items may be selected.
MULTIPLE_INTERVAL_SELECTION	The default mode allows multiple groups of items to be selected.

In Java applications, you would normally use the JList setSelectionMode() method to identify the mode to be used. In Jython, you can use this method call or you can use the selectionMode keyword argument when you create the JList object. Listing 9-5 shows an example of how easily this can be done using the constructor keyword argument

Listing 9-5. Using the List Selection Mode Keyword Argument

```
|26|        self.info = JList(                                         |
|27|            data,                                                  |
|28|            selectionMode = ListSelectionModel.SINGLE_SELECTION    |
|29|        )                                                          |
```

Reacting to List-Selection Events

Can you think of a reason that your application needs to know when an item on a list has been selected? What kinds of things might you want to do with the selected item? You might want to remove it, modify it, or insert a new item before or after the selected item. You might also want to initiate some more complex operation based on the user selection. It's all up to you.

If no item is selected, what kinds of things might you want to be able to do? What about adding items to the list? Where might you be able to add an item if you have to reference it (a selected item)? What about adding a new item first or last on the list? Those options make sense, don't they?

The reason I'm asking these questions is to help you think about things that you might want to consider as you are creating your own applications.

Do list selection events exist to be monitored? Sure. The challenge is trying to figure out what you want to do when a list selection event occurs. What do you want to happen when the users select a list item? It depends on what your application looks like and what it does.

What if you partition the application output to have the scrollable list and a text input field on top and some buttons below? Figure 9-4 shows one way to do this.

Figure 9-4. List4's sample output

Listing 9-6 shows how easily this can be done using Jython. To partition the application window, the frame uses a BorderLayout, with the scrollable pane containing the list instance positioned using the BorderLayout.NORTH constant (line 35), and another pane that uses a GridLayout to position the text field and buttons within it (lines 37-43). Then, this pane is positioned on the application frame using the BorderLayout.SOUTH constant (line 44).

Listing 9-6. List4's Class

```
14|class List4( java.lang.Runnable ) :
15|    def run( self ) :
16|        frame = JFrame(
17|            'List4',
18|            size = ( 200, 222 ),
19|            layout = BorderLayout(),
20|            defaultCloseOperation = JFrame.EXIT_ON_CLOSE
21|        )
22|        data = (
23|            'Now is the time for all good spam ' +
24|            'to come to the aid of their eggs'
25|        ).split( ' ' )
26|        self.info = JList(
27|            data,
28|            selectionMode = ListSelectionModel.SINGLE_SELECTION
29|        )
30|        frame.add(
31|            JScrollPane(
32|                self.info,
33|                preferredSize = ( 200, 100 )
34|            ),
35|            BorderLayout.NORTH
36|        )
37|        panel = JPanel( layout = GridLayout( 0, 2 ) )
38|        self.text = panel.add( JTextField( 10 ) )
39|        panel.add( self.button( 'First'  ) )
40|        panel.add( self.button( 'Last'   ) )
41|        panel.add( self.button( 'Before' ) )
42|        panel.add( self.button( 'After'  ) )
43|        panel.add( self.button( 'Remove' ) )
44|        frame.add( panel, BorderLayout.SOUTH )
45|        frame.setVisible( 1 )
46|    def button( self, text ) :
47|        return JButton( text, actionPerformed = self.insert )
48|    def insert( self, event ) :
49|        todo = event.getActionCommand()
50|        word = self.text.getText()
51|        print '%s: "%s"' % ( todo, word )
```

Now that you have an idea how the application will look, you might be able to figure out what you want to happen when a list item is selected. You can also think about changing the appearance of the application if you don't like the way it looks. What if you had the buttons and text field on the left and the list of items on the right? What would that look like? It takes very little time and effort to figure this out. Figure 9-5 shows the result of making these changes.

Figure 9-5. *List5's sample output*

Looking at Listing 9-7, you can see how few changes were needed to produce this output. Additionally, you now have an event handler that is called when a list selection operation has occurred (lines 35 and 51-54).

This method currently only produces output on the console, but it provides you with information about when a selection event occurs, as well as informs you that you can use the available information to determine whether a list item has been selected. You can do this by looking at the Javadoc for the ListSelectionListener class[10] and verifying that you only need to identify the valueChanged() method (see line 35).

Listing 9-7. List5's Class Reacting to List Selection Events

```
13|class List5( java.lang.Runnable ) :
14|    def run( self ) :
15|        frame = JFrame(
16|            'List5',
17|            size = ( 200, 220 ),
18|            layout = GridLayout( 1, 2 ),
19|            defaultCloseOperation = JFrame.EXIT_ON_CLOSE
20|        )
21|        panel = JPanel( layout = GridLayout( 0, 1 ) )
22|        panel.add( self.button( 'Remove' ) )
23|        panel.add( self.button( 'First'  ) )
24|        panel.add( self.button( 'Last'   ) )
25|        panel.add( self.button( 'Before' ) )
26|        panel.add( self.button( 'After'  ) )
27|        self.text = panel.add( JTextField( 10 ) )
28|        frame.add( panel )
29|        data = (
30|            'Now is the time for all good spam ' +
31|            'to come to the aid of their eggs'
32|        ).split( ' ' )
33|        self.info = JList(
34|            data,
```

---

[10]See http://docs.oracle.com/javase/8/docs/api/javax/swing/event/ListSelectionListener.html.

```
35|            valueChanged = self.selection,
36|            selectionMode = ListSelectionModel.SINGLE_SELECTION
37|        )
38|        frame.add(
39|            JScrollPane(
40|                self.info,
41|                preferredSize = ( 200, 100 )
42|            )
43|        )
44|        frame.setVisible( 1 )
45|    def button( self, text ) :
46|        return JButton( text, actionPerformed = self.insert )
47|    def insert( self, event ) :
48|        todo = event.getActionCommand()
49|        word = self.text.getText()
50|        print '%s: "%s"' % ( todo, word )
51|    def selection( self, e ) :
52|        index = e.getSource().getSelectedIndex()
53|        if not e.getValueIsAdjusting() :
54|            print 'selected %d' % index
```

Reacting to User (Text) Input

All right, you've given some thought as to how you want the application to look and decided that you want to do something when a list item is selected. What do you want to happen next? Wouldn't it be neat to have the application's buttons be enabled or disabled based on the user input? For example, it makes sense to enable the Remove button when a list item is selected. What about the other buttons? When do you want them to be enabled? What if you only enable the buttons related to list insertion when the user specifies some text in the text input field?

The InputMethodListener class[11] looks easy to use, right? But will it solve the problem at hand? Unfortunately, it is not going to work in this scenario. The List6.py script contains an attempt to add an InputMethodListener event handler.[12] Unfortunately, when you try to execute this script you get an AttributeError exception. Why? Because the addInputMethodListener() method is provided by the javax.swing.text.JTextComponent class, not the Runnable or InputMethodListener classes.

Listing 9-8. List6.py Script Interesting Lines

```
15|from   java.awt.event     import InputMethodListener
16|class List6( java.lang.Runnable, InputMethodListener ) :
  |    ...
29|        self.addInputMethodListener( self )
  |    ...
69|    def caretPositionChanged( self, e ) :
70|        print 'caretPositionChanged() :', e
71|    def inputMethodTextChanged( self, e ) :
72|        print 'inputMethodTextChanged() :', e
```

---

[11]See http://docs.oracle.com/javase/8/docs/api/java/awt/event/InputMethodListener.html.

[12]Please note that the line in List6.py that corresponds to line 29 in Listing 9-8 is commented out. To see the exception you need to remove the "#" in column one of that statement before executing the script.

Listing 9-8 shows how easy it is to make these kinds of changes. Why do I encourage you to look at failures? Well, there are a few very important reasons to do so:

- To try new things
- To learn how to fail gracefully
- To learn from your mistakes

It only takes a few moments to search for AWT and Swing methods related to events that might be called when the users enter text. It only required you to insert or modify seven lines of code. Was this a huge investment of time and effort? No, and what you learned was priceless.

Is there another way to use an InputMethodListener? Certainly, you can create a class to implement the InputMethodListener interface and see if that works. The List6a.py script contains this attempt. Listing 9-9 shows the modified lines from List6.py to demonstrate this iteration.

Listing 9-9. List6a.py Script, Unique Lines Only

```
15|from    java.awt.event     import InputMethodListener
16|class IML( InputMethodListener ) :
17|    def caretPositionChanged( self, e ) :
18|        print 'caretPositionChanged() :', e
19|    def inputMethodTextChanged( self, e ) :
20|        print 'inputMethodTextChanged() :', e
21|class List6a( java.lang.Runnable ) :
  |    ...
33|        self.text = panel.add( JTextField( 10 ) )
34|        self.text.addInputMethodListener( IML() )
```

Unfortunately, if you test this script, you will see that modifying the input field does not generate any output. Additional research shows that another approach might be more viable. For this iteration, you see what you need to use a DocumentListener instead of an InputMethodListener. This example is found in List6b.py; the modified lines are shown in Listing 9-10.

Listing 9-10. List6b.py Script, Unique Lines Only

```
15|from    javax.swing.event import DocumentListener
16|class DL( DocumentListener ) :
17|    def changedUpdate( self, e ) :
18|        print 'changedUpdate() :', e
19|    def insertUpdate( self, e ) :
20|        print 'insertUpdate() :', e
21|    def removeUpdate( self, e ) :
22|        print 'removeUpdate() :', e
23|class List6b( java.lang.Runnable ) :
  |    ...
35|        self.text = panel.add( JTextField( 10 ) )
36|        self.text.getDocument().addDocumentListener( DL() )
```

It is interesting to note that in order to have a DocumentListener for the input field, you can use the getDocument() method of the JTextField class to identify the actual Document object that is associated with this input field. If you test this iteration, as shown in Figure 9-6, you can see that events are being generated and the corresponding DocumentListener methods are being called. The particular events were the result of typing a character and then using the Backspace key to delete it from the input field.

This approach might not be the best way to monitor changes to an input field, especially with something simple like the JTextField, which is used in these examples. Fortunately, there is another approach that you can investigate.

```
insertUpdate() : [javax.swing.text.GapContent$InsertUndo@...]
removeUpdate() : [javax.swing.text.GapContent$RemoveUndo@...]
```

Figure 9-6. *List6b's DocumentListener sample output*

For this example, you are going to look at what happens when you add a listener to the input field for KeyListener events.[13]

```
text: "b"
text: "ba"
text: "bac"
text: "baco"
text: "bacon"
```

Figure 9-7 shows that you can monitor the text input field using a KeyListener keyReleased() method call. Listings 9-11 and 9-12 show the List7 class used to produce this output.

```
text: "b"
text: "ba"
text: "bac"
text: "baco"
text: "bacon"
```

Figure 9-7. *List7's sample output*

Listing 9-11. List7's run() Method

```
16|class List7( java.lang.Runnable, KeyListener ) :
17|    def run( self ) :
18|        frame = JFrame(
19|            'List7',
20|            size = ( 200, 220 ),
21|            layout = GridLayout( 1, 2 ),
22|            defaultCloseOperation = JFrame.EXIT_ON_CLOSE
23|        )
```

---

[13]See http://docs.oracle.com/javase/8/docs/api/java/awt/event/KeyListener.html.

```
24|          panel = JPanel( layout = GridLayout( 0, 1 ) )
25|          self.buttons = {}
26|          for name in 'First,Last,Before,After,Remove'.split( ',' ) :
27|              self.buttons[ name ] = panel.add( self.button( name ) )
28|          self.text = panel.add(
29|              JTextField(
30|                  10,
31|                  keyReleased = self.typed
32|              )
33|          )
34|          frame.add( panel )
35|          data = (
36|              'Now is the time for all good spam ' +
37|              'to come to the aid of their eggs'
38|          ).split( ' ' )
39|          model = DefaultListModel()
40|          for word in data :
41|              model.addElement( word )
42|          self.info = JList(
43|              model,
44|              valueChanged = self.selection,
45|              selectionMode = ListSelectionModel.SINGLE_SELECTION
46|          )
47|          frame.add(
48|              JScrollPane(
49|                  self.info,
50|                  preferredSize = ( 200, 100 )
51|              )
52|          )
53|          frame.setVisible( 1 )
```

Listing 9-11 shows the run() method and Listing 9-12 shows the rest of the methods from this class.

Listing 9-12. The Remaining List7 Class Methods

```
54|      def button( self, text ) :
55|          return JButton(
56|              text,
57|              enabled = 0,
58|              actionPerformed = self.doit
59|          )
60|      def doit( self, event ) :
61|          todo = event.getActionCommand()
62|          word = self.text.getText().strip()
63|          List = self.info
64|          pos  = List.getSelectedIndex()
65|          print '%s: "%s"  pos: %d' % ( todo, word, pos )
66|          if todo == 'Remove' :
67|              List.getModel().remove( pos )
68|              self.buttons[ todo ].setEnabled( 0 )
69|      def selection( self, e ) :
70|          if e.getValueIsAdjusting() :
```

```
71|              si = e.getSource().getSelectedIndex()
72|              self.buttons[ 'Remove' ].setEnabled( si > -1 )
73|    def typed( self, e ) :
74|        print 'text: "%s"' % self.text.getText().strip()
```

Figure 9-8 shows the progress in the application output using the next iteration of the script. This one is found in the List8.py script file. You can see which buttons are enabled before any text is entered, after some text is entered, after a single item is selected, and finally after a button is used to insert the new word on the list.

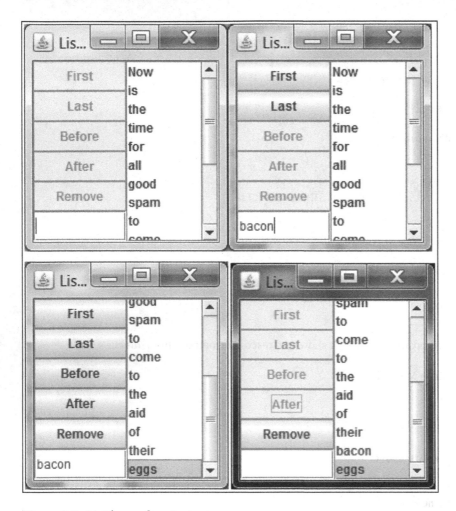

Figure 9-8. *List8's sample output*

You can look at the iterations of the application and see how small changes have been made with each. Finally, you get to the final iteration, which is found in the List10.py script file. This version includes the small improvement of putting the removed item text in the text input field. This allows you to do:

1. Select a the first item.

2. Click the Remove button (thus putting the item value into text field).

3. Click the Last button to move the first item to the end of the list.

Listing 9-13 contains the List10 class methods that allow your application to do these things. The run() method is not included because it's almost identical to the run() method found in Listing 9-11. The List10 class does, however, include some interesting properties. You might not agree that these are advantages. Specifically, List10 takes advantage of the named keyword arguments to use the textCheck() method as:

- A KeyListener keyReleased() method

- A ListSelectionListener valueChanged() method

- A simple textCheck() class

Java purists may take offense at this flexibility. However, I think that most Jython programmers can see the value provided by the use of keyword argument lists in this type of application.

Listing 9-13. Remaining List10 Methods

```
57|   def doit( self, event ) :
58|       todo  = event.getActionCommand()
59|       word  = self.text.getText().strip()
60|       List  = self.List
61|       pos   = List.getSelectedIndex()
62|       model = List.getModel()
63|       if todo == 'Remove' :
64|           self.text.setText( List.getSelectedValue() )
65|           model.remove( pos )
66|       else :
67|           if todo == 'First' :
68|               model.insertElementAt( word, 0 )
69|           elif todo == 'Last' :
70|               model.insertElementAt( word, model.getSize() )
71|           elif todo == 'Before' :
72|               model.insertElementAt( word, pos )
73|           else :
74|               model.insertElementAt( word, pos + 1 )
75|           self.text.setText( '' )
76|       self.textCheck()
77|   def textCheck( self, e = None ) :
78|       word  = self.text.getText().strip()
79|       index = self.List.getSelectedIndex()
80|       for name in 'First,Last'.split( ',' ) :
81|           self.buttons[ name ].setEnabled( len( word ) > 0 )
82|       for name in 'Before,After'.split( ',' ) :
83|           self.buttons[ name ].setEnabled(
84|               len( word ) > 0 and index > -1
85|           )
86|       self.buttons[ 'Remove' ].setEnabled( index > -1 )
```

One of the most impressive things about this example is that it demonstrates how easy it is to quickly produce applications. Being able to produce a rapid prototype is enormously valuable to programmers because they can then easily manipulate and interact with the application and decide what they like and dislike about the way it looks, as well as the way it responds to user input.

Summary

This chapter covered how to display and manipulate lists of items with an emphasis on iterating the application to test various representations of components on the frame as well as using a variety of listeners to improve your understanding of how each might or might not enhance the usability of the application. You saw just how quickly and easily a script can be modified to test a new approach so that you can discard those that don't fit your specific needs.

Note: One point that this chapter didn't cover was the fact that once modifications have been made to the list of values, the application should retrieve the current list's contents using the `ListModel` methods.

CHAPTER 10

Menus and MenuItems

Menus are one of the most common input mechanisms that applications use. When was the last time that you worked with a graphical application that didn't include some sort of menu structure and hierarchy?

The main reason for creating and using menus in your applications is that it conveys to the users some of the actions that they can perform with the application. So this is all about setting expectations and communicating at least some of the things that the applications can do.

This chapter shows how easily you can add a menu to your applications and how to make your applications react when the user selects a menu item.

The JMenu Class Hierarchy

You may not realize it, but menus are a kind of button. This makes a lot of sense when you think about what happens when you click a button and when you click on a menu item. Each causes some kind of event that needs an event handler to perform the desired action. There are differences, though. If there weren't, you wouldn't need another class. Take a moment to think about it. How would you describe a menu? I think that you'll agree that they are almost always a collection of individual words that convey information to the users. Each word or menu entry can be selected and then displays a related sub-menu or performs some kind of response. A button, on the other hand, is almost always used to initiate some kind of action or elicit a specific response.

You can see how menus and buttons are similar by looking at the JMenu class[1] Javadoc or by using the classInfo routine first mentioned in Chapter 4. The classInfo hierarchy for the JMenu class is shown in Listing 10-1.

Listing 10-1. JMenu Class Hierarchy

```
wsadmin>classInfo( JMenu )
javax.swing.JMenu
| javax.swing.JMenuItem
| | javax.swing.AbstractButton
| | | javax.swing.JComponent
| | | | java.awt.Container
| | | | | java.awt.Component
| | | | | | java.lang.Object
| | | | | | java.awt.image.ImageObserver
| | | | | | java.awt.MenuContainer
| | | | | | java.io.Serializable
| | | | java.io.Serializable
| | | java.awt.ItemSelectable
```

---

[1]See http://docs.oracle.com/javase/8/docs/api/javax/swing/JMenu.html.

```
| | | javax.swing.SwingConstants
| | javax.accessibility.Accessible
| | javax.swing.MenuElement
| javax.accessibility.Accessible
| javax.swing.MenuElement
wsadmin>
```

Unlike regular buttons, or even toggle buttons, the result of activating a menu is to cause the associated list of items to be displayed. So how do you add a JMenu to the application? Since you are using a JFrame for almost all of your applications, let's take another quick look at the JFrame hierarchy, with a focus on the methods that contain the text "menubar".

Listing 10-2 shows this hierarchy. One important point to note is that the javax.swing.JFrame class has JMenuBar getters and setters, and the java.awt.Frame class has MenuBar getters and setters.[2]

Listing 10-2. JFrame MenuBar Methods

```
wsadmin>classInfo( JFrame, meth = 'menubar' )
javax.swing.JFrame
  getJMenuBar, setJMenuBar
| java.awt.Frame
>    getMenuBar, setMenuBar
| | java.awt.Window
| | | java.awt.Container
| | | | java.awt.Component
| | | | | java.lang.Object
| | | | | java.awt.image.ImageObserver
| | | | | java.awt.MenuContainer
| | | | | java.io.Serializable
| | | javax.accessibility.Accessible
| | java.awt.MenuContainer
| javax.swing.WindowConstants
| javax.accessibility.Accessible
| javax.swing.RootPaneContainer
wsadmin>
```

What does this mean? For one, it means you need to be careful. Listing 10-3 shows what I'm talking about. Since there are getters and setters for JMenuBars as well as MenuBars, you need to be certain that you remember to include the *J*, or you'll get an exception like the one shown in lines 12 and 13.

Listing 10-3. Adding a MenuBar to the JFrame

```
1|wsadmin>from javax.swing import JFrame, JMenuBar, JMenu
2|wsadmin>
3|wsadmin>f = JFrame( 'Frame Title' )
4|wsadmin>b = JMenuBar()
5|wsadmin>m = b.add( JMenu( 'Help' ) )
6|wsadmin>f.setMenuBar( m )
7|WASX7015E: Exception running command: "f.setMenuBar( m )";
8| exception information:
```

---

[2]The Swing JMenuBar methods are used exclusively in this book.

```
 9| com.ibm.bsf.BSFException: exception from Jython:
10|Traceback (innermost last):
11|  File "<input>", line 1, in ?
12|TypeError: setMenuBar(): 1st arg can't be coerced to
13|  java.awt.MenuBar
14|wsadmin>
```

Let's take a quick look at how you can create an empty, yet colorful, menu bar so that you can more easily identify where it's placed. Figure 10-1 shows where the blue JMenuBar is positioned on the JFrame content pane. By selecting a colorful background, you don't have to add any items to the menu to see where it.

Figure 10-1. Menu1 sample output with a blue JMenuBar

Listing 10-4 shows how easily you can do this.

■ **Note**   You have to identify the preferred JMenuBar size (line 17), since it contains no JMenu entries. Otherwise no space would be allocated for the menu and it wouldn't be visible.[3]

Listing 10-4. The Menu1 Class Using Color to Show an Empty JMenuBar

```
 7|class Menu1( java.lang.Runnable ) :
 8|    def run( self ) :
 9|        frame = JFrame(
10|            'Menu1',
11|            size = ( 200, 125 ),
12|            defaultCloseOperation = JFrame.EXIT_ON_CLOSE
13|        )
14|        frame.setJMenuBar(
15|            JMenuBar(
16|                background = Color.blue,
17|                preferredSize = ( 200, 25 )
18|            )
19|        )
20|        frame.setVisible( 1 )
```

How will the application look with a couple of menu entries? Let's see…. Since the JMenuBar has a blue background color, let's make the menu entries use a color that contrasts well. Figure 10-2 shows a first attempt at doing this.

---

[3]I encourage you to comment out line 17 and test this statement yourself. Don't forget, however, to comment out the trailing comma on the previous line as well.

Figure 10-2. Menu2 sample output with a JMenuBar and entries

That's not quite what I expected. What happened to the white foreground color? Listing 10-5 shows the Menu2 class.

Listing 10-5. The Menu2 Class Specifying Foreground and Background Colors

```
 9|class Menu2( java.lang.Runnable ) :
10|    def run( self ) :
11|        frame = JFrame(
12|            'Menu2',
13|            size = ( 200, 125 ),
14|            defaultCloseOperation = JFrame.EXIT_ON_CLOSE
15|        )
16|        menuBar = JMenuBar(
17|            background = Color.blue,
18|            foreground = Color.white
19|        )
20|        fileMenu = JMenu( 'File' )
21|        fileMenu.add( JMenuItem( 'Exit' ) )
22|        menuBar.add( fileMenu )
23|        helpMenu = JMenu( 'Help' )
24|        helpMenu.add( JMenuItem( 'About' ) )
25|        menuBar.add( helpMenu )
26|        frame.setJMenuBar( menuBar )
27|        frame.setVisible( 1 )
```

The reason the menu items don't show up well is that you specified the foreground color for the JMenuBar, *not* for the menu entries. If you specify the color of the menu items, you can see the expected contrast in colors. Figure 10-3 demonstrates this expected contrast.

Figure 10-3. Menu3 sample output with colorful JMenuBar entries

Listing 10-6 shows the Menu3 class being used to generate this output. It also shows you that building a hierarchy of menu entries can make your code a bit more challenging to read.

Listing 10-6. Menu3 Class with Contrasting Menu Entries

```
 9|class Menu3( java.lang.Runnable ) :
10|    def run( self ) :
11|        frame = JFrame(
12|            'Menu3',
13|            size = ( 200, 125 ),
14|            defaultCloseOperation = JFrame.EXIT_ON_CLOSE
15|        )
16|        menuBar = JMenuBar( background = Color.blue )
17|        fileMenu = JMenu( 'File', foreground = Color.white )
18|        fileMenu.add( JMenuItem( 'Exit' ) )
19|        menuBar.add( fileMenu )
20|        helpMenu = JMenu( 'Help', foreground = Color.white )
21|        helpMenu.add( JMenuItem( 'About' ) )
22|        menuBar.add( helpMenu )
23|        frame.setJMenuBar( menuBar )
24|        frame.setVisible( 1 )
```

Looking closely at Listing 10-6, you can find three different kinds of menu-related objects:

- JMenuBar: Created on line 16[4]

- JMenu: Created on lines 17 and 20

- JMenuItem: Created on lines 18 and 21[5]

Looking again at Figure 10-3, you can see most of these distinct entries and you can use this to better understand these different menu classes. You can also see how the color scheme of the selected entries differs from the ones specified. The good news is that you don't have to describe this new scheme because it's already provided by the Java Swing classes. This is another example of the Swing library making your life as a GUI developer that much easier.

Unfortunately, not everything is this easy. Here is where you might get into a little bit of potential confusion based on names and terminology. If you ask non-programmers what the row of words across the top of an application is called, they are likely to call it a "menu," which makes sense.

For Swing developers, however, the row of words corresponds with the Java, or Jython, JMenuBar class instance and the words themselves are instances of the JMenu objects. In order to minimize confusion, this book consistently uses the Java Swing terminology. I'll call the group of words or terms the JMenuBar, whereas the individual objects are called JMenu entries.

As you can see, creating the JMenuBar and the JMenu entries, as well as the corresponding JMenuItems, requires a fair amount code. It's common practice to have a method that is responsible for the creating menu bars and their entries and items. This method makes your application constructor (or run() method) simpler, and therefore easier to read, understand, and maintain.

---

[4]See http://docs.oracle.com/javase/8/docs/api/javax/swing/JMenuBar.html.
[5]See http://docs.oracle.com/javase/8/docs/api/javax/swing/JMenuItem.html.

Reacting to Menu-Related Events

One of the nice things about menu items being a kind of abstract button is that you already know how to tell the "button" what to do when it is pressed. You can use the verbose Java addActionListen() method call or the actionPerformed keyword argument to identify the method to be called.

Consider this: It's common practice for Java Swing developers to have the application class descend from the ActionListener class. This is frequently done using the syntax shown in Listing 10-7.

Listing 10-7. Java Class Implementing ActionListener

```
public myClass implements ActionListener {
    ...
    JMenuItem menuItem = new JMenuItem( "Spam" );
    menuItem.addActionListener( this );
    ...
    publick void actionPerformed( ActionEvent e ) {
        ...
    }
    ...
}
```

Using this technique can make the actionPerformed() method more complex than it really needs to be. If every button and menu item uses the same actionPerformed() method, this event handler needs to figure out which kind of event was used to initiate the call to the actionPerformed() method. Listing 10-8, on the other hand, shows how easy it can be, using Jython, to have a simple routine for each menu item action listener event handler.

Not only does this approach simplify each event handler, it also allows each method to have a name that is more appropriate for the event being handled.

Listing 10-8. Using the actionPerformed Keyword Argument

```
 8|class Menu4( java.lang.Runnable ) :
 9|    def run( self ) :
10|        frame = JFrame(
11|            'Menu4',
12|            size = ( 200, 125 ),
13|            defaultCloseOperation = JFrame.EXIT_ON_CLOSE
14|        )
15|        menuBar = JMenuBar()
16|        fileMenu = JMenu( 'File' )
17|        exitItem = fileMenu.add(
18|            JMenuItem(
19|                'Exit',
20|                actionPerformed = self.exit
21|            )
22|        )
23|        menuBar.add( fileMenu )
24|        helpMenu = JMenu( 'Help' )
25|        aboutItem = helpMenu.add(
26|            JMenuItem(
27|                'About',
28|                actionPerformed = self.about
29|            )
30|        )
```

```
31|          menuBar.add( helpMenu )
32|          frame.setJMenuBar( menuBar )
33|          frame.setVisible( 1 )
34|    def about( self, event ) :
35|          print 'Menu4.about()'
36|    def exit( self, event ) :
37|          print 'Menu4.exit()'
38|          sys.exit()
```

Granted, in Java you don't need the ActionListener actionPerformed() method to determine which event caused the routine to be called. You could make each JMenuItem use an anonymous ActionListener class implementation. Unfortunately, this approach is much more challenging to read, use, and maintain than the Jython technique used in the Menu4 class in Listing 10-8.

Using Radio Buttons on a Menu

Up to this point, the menu items have only included text. There are times, however, when it makes sense to use radio buttons on a menu to identify only selection. I didn't have to look far to find an example of this. I often use the Notepad++ text editor, which has an Encoding menu item. The sub-menu on this entry includes five radio button menu items that identify the encoding. There is a special class for this in the Swing hierarchy, called JRadioButtonMenuItem.[6]

As you saw with radio buttons in Chapter 8, you need to be able to group all of the JRadioButtonMenuItem instances together so that the Swing framework can enforce one selected item limitation. Fortunately, you can use the same ButtonGroup class for the menu items that you used for radio buttons.

Figure 10-4. Menu5 sample output with radio button menu items

Figure 10-4 shows the sample output of the Menu5 class, which demonstrates the use of JRadioButtonMenuItem on the menu. In Listing 10-9, you can see most of the code needed to make this happen. The only routine that isn't shown is the one that creates and returns JMenuBar.

---

[6]See http://docs.oracle.com/javase/8/docs/api/javax/swing/JRadioButtonMenuItem.html.

Listing 10-9. Menu5 Class that Uses Radio Button Menu Items

```
10|class Menu5( java.lang.Runnable ) :
11|    def createMenuBar( self ) :
  |        ...
44|    def run( self ) :
45|        frame = JFrame(
46|            'Menu5',
47|            size = ( 200, 125 ),
48|            defaultCloseOperation = JFrame.EXIT_ON_CLOSE
49|        )
50|        frame.setJMenuBar( self.createMenuBar() )
51|        frame.setVisible( 1 )
52|    def spam( self, event ) : print 'Menu5.spam()'
53|    def eggs( self, event ) : print 'Menu5.eggs()'
54|    def bacon( self, event ) : print 'Menu5.bacon()'
55|    def about( self, event ) : print 'Menu5.about()'
56|    def exit( self, event ) :
57|        print 'Menu5.exit()'
58|        sys.exit()
```

I think that having the menu-creation process in a method all to itself makes the remainder of the code more understandable. Listing 10-10 shows the createMenuBar() method from this same class.

Listing 10-10 Menu5 createMenuBar() Method

```
11|    def createMenuBar( self ) :
12|        menuBar = JMenuBar()
13|        fileMenu = JMenu( 'File' )
14|        data = [
15|            [ 'Spam' , self.spam  ],
16|            [ 'Eggs' , self.eggs  ],
17|            [ 'Bacon', self.bacon ]
18|        ]
19|        bGroup = ButtonGroup()
20|        for name, handler in data :
21|            rb = JRadioButtonMenuItem(
22|                name,
23|                actionPerformed = handler,
24|                selected = ( name == 'Spam' )
25|            )
26|            bGroup.add( rb )
27|            fileMenu.add( rb )
28|        exitItem = fileMenu.add(
29|            JMenuItem(
30|                'Exit',
31|                actionPerformed = self.exit
32|            )
33|        )
34|        menuBar.add( fileMenu )
35|        helpMenu = JMenu( 'Help' )
36|        aboutItem = helpMenu.add(
```

```
37|            JMenuItem(
38|                'About',
39|                actionPerformed = self.about
40|            )
41|        )
42|        menuBar.add( helpMenu )
43|        return menuBar
```

Notice that this code (see line 24) ensures that one of the radio buttons in the group is selected. It isn't often that your event handlers (lines 52-58 in Listing 10-9) can actually be performed on a single line. But doing so shortens the listing somewhat.

Using Check Boxes on a Menu

As I'm sure you've already guessed, in addition to radio button menu items, you can also create check box menu items using the JCheckBoxMenuItem class.[7] Figure 10-5 shows some images of the same application using check box menu items.

Figure 10-5. *Menu6 sample output with check box menu items*

Now you can see another advantage of using a separate method to create the menu bar. Listing 10-11 shows only the createMenuBar() method from the Menu6 class because, other than this routine, Menu6.py and Menu5.py are the same.[8]

Listing 10-11. Menu6's createMenuBar() Class

```
10|    def createMenuBar( self ) :
11|        menuBar = JMenuBar()
12|        fileMenu = JMenu( 'File' )
13|        data = [
14|            [ 'Spam' , self.spam  ],
15|            [ 'Eggs' , self.eggs  ],
16|            [ 'Bacon', self.bacon ]
17|        ]
```

---

[7]See http://docs.oracle.com/javase/8/docs/api/javax/swing/JCheckBoxMenuItem.html.
[8]Except, of course, for the literal constants that contain the name of the script.

```
18|          for name, handler in data :
19|              fileMenu.add(
20|                  JCheckBoxMenuItem(
21|                      name,
22|                      actionPerformed = handler
23|                  )
24|              )
25|          exitItem = fileMenu.add(
26|              JMenuItem(
27|                  'Exit',
28|                  actionPerformed = self.exit
29|              )
30|          )
31|          menuBar.add( fileMenu )
32|          helpMenu = JMenu( 'Help' )
33|          aboutItem = helpMenu.add(
34|              JMenuItem(
35|                  'About',
36|                  actionPerformed = self.about
37|              )
38|          )
39|          menuBar.add( helpMenu )
40|          return menuBar
```

Separating Menu Items

Occasionally, it is convenient to use a horizontal line on a menu to separate groups of items. For example, Figure 10-6 shows how some check box menu items can be separated from one another. I think that you'll agree that the line makes them stand out significantly.

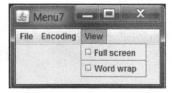

Figure 10-6. *Menu7 sample output showing menu item separation*

Interestingly enough, there are multiple ways that you can add such lines. Listing 10-12 shows three lines from the createMenuBar() method from the Menu7.py file. In it, you see these techniques and how they are used. In the first line, the familiar JMenu.add() method adds an anonymous JSeparator object.[9] This is such a simple and common operation that the JMenu class includes a method to do just this. In the second comment line, you see how the addSeparator() method adds a separator to the end of the specified JMenu. The third line shows that the JMenu has an insertSeparator() method that you can use to insert a separator line at a specified position of an existing menu.

---

[9]See http://docs.oracle.com/javase/8/docs/api/javax/swing/JSeparator.html.

Listing 10-12. Menu7 JSeparator() and addSeparator()

```
        viewMenu.add( JSeparator() )      # Using JMenu.add()
#       viewMenu.addSeparator()           # Using addSeparator()
#       viewMenu.insertSeparator( 1 )     # Using insertSeparator()
```

Menu Mnemonics and Accelerators

If you look closely at the JMenuItem constructors, you may notice that one includes something called a keyboard *mnemonic*.[10] What is this all about? Well, it lets you specify a key that can be used to select the associated menu item when the menu is visible. To better understand this idea, you'll add a mnemonic to the same menu that you saw earlier. Figure 10-7 shows the Exit menu with an underscore under the letter "x." This indicates that the user can select this entry by pressing the "x" key.

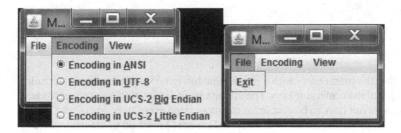

Figure 10-7. *Menu8 menu items with a mnemonic on the Exit menu item*

Figure 10-7 shows what happens to the menu items for which mnemonic values are specified. In each instance, the first instance of the specified letter in the menu item is underlined.[11] In this case, the "x" in Exit and the "A" in ANSI have menu shortcuts.

The mnemonic keystrokes are active only when the menu is being displayed. So, if you wanted to be able to use the "x" mnemonic to exit the application using the keyboard, you would need to press the F10 key to activate the first menu entry, and then press the "x" key to use the mnemonic to select this menu item.[12]

How do you define a mnemonic for a JRadioButtonMenuItem? Unlike the JMenuItem constructor, no parameter exists for a keyboard mnemonic. This is yet another example where Jython makes life so much easier for you. Instead of creating a JRadioButtonMenuItem and then using the setMnemonic() method inherited from the AbstractButton class, you can simply add a keyword argument to the constructor. Listing 10-13 shows how this is done in Menu8.py.

---

[10]See http://docs.oracle.com/javase/8/docs/api/javax/swing/JMenuItem.html#JMenuItem%28java.lang.String,%20int%29.
[11]In situations where you want to underline a different letter in the text string, use the setDisplayedMnemonicIndex() method inherited from the AbstractButton class, i.e., http://docs.oracle.com/javase/8/docs/api/javax/swing/AbstractButton.html#setDisplayedMnemonicIndex%28int%29.
[12]Of course, you could select the File menu entry using the mouse and then press the "x" key on the keyboard, but it's just as easy to use the mouse to select Exit after using it to open the File menu.

Listing 10-13. Using the Mnemonic Keyword Argument on the JRadioButtonMenuItem Constructor

```
25|          codeMenu = JMenu( 'Encoding' )
26|          data = [
27|              [ 'ANSI'                  , KeyEvent.VK_A ],
28|              [ 'UTF-8'                 , KeyEvent.VK_U ],
29|              [ 'UCS-2 Big Endian'      , KeyEvent.VK_B ],
30|              [ 'UCS-2 Little Endian'   , KeyEvent.VK_L ]
31|          ]
32|          bGroup = ButtonGroup()
33|          for suffix, mnemonic in data :
34|              name = 'Encoding in ' + suffix
35|              rb = JRadioButtonMenuItem(
36|                  name,
37|                  mnemonic = mnemonic,
38|                  selected = ( suffix == 'ANSI' )
39|              )
40|              bGroup.add( rb )
41|              codeMenu.add( rb )
```

One of the limitations of mnemonics is that the menu entry with a mnemonic has to be visible for the mnemonic key to be recognized. This brings us to the topic of to accelerator keys. The advantage of associating an accelerator key with a menu entry (or item) is that the menu does not have to be visible for the associated event to be initiated. One disadvantage of accelerator keys is that you need to use the menu item setAccelerator() method to associate an accelerator key with a menu item. Unless, of course, you're using a wonderful language like Jython that allows you to use keyword arguments on your constructor calls.

Another possible disadvantage of accelerators is that, unlike mnemonics, there is no obvious indication that an accelerator key is in effect. Listing 10-14 shows a snippet from Menu9.py, which uses a bad practice of associating an unmodified "x" accelerator key with the Exit menu item. This means that when the user presses the "x" key, the program immediately exits. This is unlikely to be an event or action that will be anticipated, or appreciated, by your users.

Listing 10-14. Example of an Unmodified Accelerator

```
18|          exitItem = fileMenu.add(
19|              JMenuItem(
20|                  'Exit',
21|                  KeyEvent.VK_X,
22|                  actionPerformed = self.exit,
23|                  accelerator = KeyStroke.getKeyStroke( 'x' )
24|              )
25|          )
```

What can and should be done about this? One possibility is to use the modified keys (Alt-X instead of simply X) .Menu10.py tries to do exactly this. Instead of "x" as shown in line 46 of Listing 10-14, Listing 10-15 defines the accelerator as Alt-X (see lines 23-27). Listing 10-15 is from Menu10a.py, which defines Alt-X as the accelerator key for the Exit menu item.

Listing 10-15. Using Alt-X as an Accelerator

```
42|          exitItem = fileMenu.add(
43|              JMenuItem(
44|                  'Exit',
45|                  KeyEvent.VK_X,
46|                  actionPerformed = self.exit,
47|                  accelerator = KeyStroke.getKeyStroke(
48|                      'x',
49|                      InputEvent.ALT_DOWN_MASK
50|                  )
51|              )
```

What does the menu item look like when you add this kind of accelerator key? Figure 10-8 shows how Swing displays this kind of information. I don't know about you, but I'm pretty impressed by Swing when I see that it automatically adds Alt-X to the menu item to clearly convey the presence of the accelerator key.

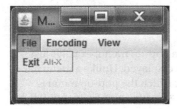

Figure 10-8. *Menu10 menu showing Alt-X accelerator key*

Unfortunately, this doesn't work for some reason. When you press Alt-X, nothing happens. Why not? Let's figure out what is wrong. What are the differences between the unmodified KeyStroke in Listing 10-14 (line 23) and the modified KeyStroke in Listing 10-15 (lines 47-50)? Listing 10-14 uses a KeyEvent constant instead a simple character string. Does it matter? Unfortunately, it does. Listing 10-16[13] shows what is returned by the KeyStroke.getKeyStroke() method using four different techniques.

Listing 10-16. Generating Modified KeyStroke Instances

```
wsadmin>from javax.swing      import KeyStroke as KS
wsadmin>from java.awt.event import ActionEvent
wsadmin>from java.awt.event import InputEvent
wsadmin>from java.awt.event import KeyEvent
wsadmin>
wsadmin>KS.getKeyStroke( 'x' )
typed x
wsadmin>KS.getKeyStroke( KeyEvent.VK_X, ActionEvent.ALT_MASK )
alt pressed X
```

---

[13]Listing 10-16 uses the KS alias for KeyStroke so the lines aren't too long.

```
wsadmin>KS.getKeyStroke( KeyEvent.VK_X, InputEvent.ALT_MASK )
alt pressed X
wsadmin>KS.getKeyStroke( 'x', ActionEvent.ALT_MASK )
alt typed x
wsadmin>
wsadmin>a = KS.getKeyStroke( KeyEvent.VK_X, ActionEvent.ALT_MASK )
wsadmin>i = KS.getKeyStroke( KeyEvent.VK_X, InputEvent.ALT_MASK )
wsadmin>a == i
1
wsadmin>
```

What does this mean for your applications? Well, it means that if you try to use the technique from Listing 10-15, line 48, your accelerator keys won't work. It isn't obvious from the user interface that there is a difference, but it's a subtle and important one at that. The last part of Listing 10-16 shows that you can use ActionEvent or InputEvent to identify the modification type—it doesn't matter. The result of the comparison is 1 (true), which means that the values are the same.

Pop-Up Menus

In addition to the menu bars, Swing applications can also use pop-up menus. What is a pop-up menu, exactly? Just as with a menu on the menu bar, when a pop-up menu is activated, its menu items are displayed. Unlike a menu bar menu, a pop-up menu is normally activated using a right-click on the component with which the pop-up menu is associated. Interestingly enough, this approach enables you to define multiple context-sensitive pop-up menus if that makes sense for your application.

Let's take a quick look at a trivial pop-up menu for a very simple application. Figure 10-9 shows the application output with two labels and two text input fields. If you right-click on either of the input fields, a small pop-up menu is displayed. Should you decide to select one of the values on the menu, that value is placed into the text field over which the right-click occurred.

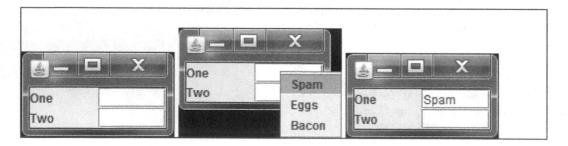

Figure 10-9. *Popup1 sample output*

Listing 10-17 shows some of the Popup1 class methods used to produce the output shown in Figure 10-9.

Listing 10-17. Popup1 actionPerformed() and run() Methods

```
11|class Popup1( java.lang.Runnable ) :
12|    def actionPerformed( self, event ) :
13|        self.target.setText( event.getActionCommand() )
14|    def run( self ) :
15|        frame = JFrame(
16|            'Popup1',
17|            layout = GridLayout( 0, 2 ),
18|            defaultCloseOperation = JFrame.EXIT_ON_CLOSE
19|        )
20|        frame.add( JLabel( 'One' ) )
21|        frame.add(
22|            JTextField(
23|                5,
24|                mousePressed  = self.PUcheck,
25|                mouseReleased = self.PUcheck
26|            )
27|        )
28|        self.PU = self.PUmenu()
29|        frame.add( JLabel( 'Two' ) )
30|        frame.add(
31|            JTextField(
32|                5,
33|                mousePressed  = self.PUcheck,
34|                mouseReleased = self.PUcheck
35|            )
36|        )
37|        frame.pack()
38|        frame.setVisible( 1 )
```

Listing 10-18 shows the remainder of the Popup1 class methods found in the Popup1.py script.

Listing 10-18. Popup1 PUmenu() and PUcheck() Methods

```
39|    def PUmenu( self ) :
40|        def MenuItem( text ) :
41|            return JMenuItem(
42|                text,
43|                actionPerformed = self.actionPerformed
44|            )
45|        popup  = JPopupMenu()
46|        popup.add( MenuItem( 'Spam' ) )
47|        popup.add( MenuItem( 'Eggs' ) )
```

```
48|         popup.add( MenuItem( 'Bacon' ) )
49|         return popup
50|    def PUcheck( self, event ) :
51|        if event.isPopupTrigger() :
52|            self.target = event.getSource()
53|            self.PU.show(
54|                event.getComponent(),
55|                event.getX(),
56|                event.getY()
57|            )
```

One of the reasons for including multiple input fields was to demonstrate that the event used to display the pop-up can also be used to determine which component to associate with the event (see line 52 in Listing 10-18). In order for the pop-up menu to have access to this information, it needs to be saved somewhere in the application. Jython makes this really easy, by allowing you to dynamically create object attributes as they are needed. You can see that the only other occurrence of the self.target object attribute is found on line 13 of Listing 10-17 in the ActionListener actionPerformed() method. Table 10-1 describes the various parts of the Popup1 class.

Table 10-1. Popup1 Class, Explained

Lines	Description
12-13	The actionPerformed() method is invoked when a pop-up menu item is selected (line 43).
14-38	Popup1 run() method, which: • Creates the application frame (lines 15-19). • Creates the labels and text fields (lines 20-36). Note the use of the mousePressed and mouseReleased keyword assignments. • Creates the pop-up menu (line 28). • Resizes and shows the frame (lines 37-38).
39-49	PUmenu() method that's used to create the JPopupMenu and MenuItems.
50-57	PUcheck() method that's invoked by mouse-listener routines to verify that a pop-up trigger occurred. If a trigger did occur, it saves the associated input field and then shows the pop-up menu based on the cursor's location.

Summary

This chapter is all about menus and menu items—more specifically, it's about JMenus and JMenuItems. It is important to remember the difference. The former are AWT classes and the latter are Swing classes. You saw how easy it is to create menu bars, pop-up menus, and the event handlers that are associated with these menu items. In the next chapter, you take a look at really useful structure—JTree—which is great for displaying hierarchical relationships between information.

CHAPTER 11

■ ■ ■

Using JTree to Show the Forest: Hierarchical Relationships of Components

This chapter is all about building and using trees to display a hierarchical relationship between elements. Trees allow you to convey a specific relationship between different pieces of information. For example, this kind of structure is great for showing something like an organizational chart. By the time you're through with this chapter, you should not only be able to use trees in your own applications, but you will also more aware of the capabilities and limitations of this useful structure.

Displaying the Servers in a WebSphere Application Server Cell

One of the really useful Swing structures is JTree,[1] which lets you show a hierarchical relationship of components. A simple WebSphere Application Server cell will have a number of nodes, with each node having a number of servers. This hierarchy is well suited for a tree structure. Figure 11-1 shows a sequence of images created by the Tree1.py script. Here's a description of each image, from top-left to bottom-right:

- This image only shows the cell name and the associated node names within the cell. The horizontal scroll bar shows that the tree is within a scroll bar, and that the available horizontal space isn't sufficient to display the widest node name.

- This image shows what the tree looks like with the first node expanded. The highlighting is an indication that a tree node is selected.

- This image shows what happens when the second node is expanded.

- The final image shows the application after it has been resized and has multiple nodes selected.

---

[1]See http://docs.oracle.com/javase/8/docs/api/javax/swing/JTree.html.

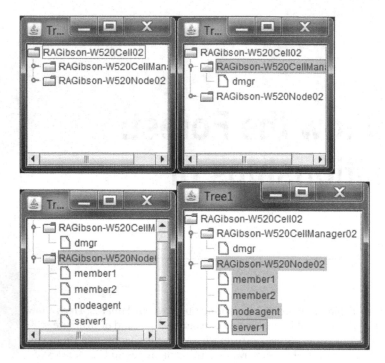

Figure 11-1. *Tree1 sample output*

The resized window is large enough to display the complete tree, so no scroll bars are necessary.

Trees display information vertically, with each line or row displaying a single piece of information, or data. Each of these data items is called a *node*, and the node at the top of the tree is called the *root node*.[2] A node may or may not have additional nodes beneath it. If it does, it is called a *branch node*, if it doesn't, it's called a *leaf node*. A branch node is also called the parent of the nodes beneath it, and they are referred to as children, or child nodes. You may have noticed that there is a bit of a terminology collision[3] here.

Figure 11-1 shows the name of the WebSphere cell as the root node, and the names of the WebSphere nodes as children of the root node of the tree. Subsequent images in this figure show how individual nodes can be selected, collapsed, or expanded using the mouse or keyboard.[4]

The second image in the figure shows an expanded branch node. In this case, the first child node beneath the root identifies the WebSphere deployment manager node that has one child (leaf) node, identified as dmgr. In this application, each leaf node represents an application server and shows the name of each server. It's important to remember that server names must be unique within the same node, but can occur multiple times within the cell.

This hierarchical representation of the names of the WebSphere cell, nodes, and servers should match your conceptual understanding of the relationship between these WebSphere configuration objects.

As Figure 11-1 illustrates, it is very likely that the JTree instance will be in a JScrollPane to allow scroll bars to displayed as needed.

---

[2]To minimize the chance of confusion, I'm going to try to be consistent and refer to Swing tree nodes as nodes, and WebSphere Application Server nodes as WebSphere nodes.

[3]This topic also came up in Chapter 10.

[4]Tree nodes can be expanded or collapsed by positioning the entry using a mouse or cursor keys and pressing Enter.

Listing 11-1 shows the Tree1 class from the Tree1.py script used to generate the output shown in Figure 11-1.[5]

Listing 11-1. Tree1 Class Using the JTree Class

```
 8|class Tree1( java.lang.Runnable ) :
 9|   def cellTree( self ) :
10|       cell = AdminConfig.list( 'Cell' )
11|       root = DefaultMutableTreeNode( self.getName( cell ) )
12|       for node in AdminConfig.list( 'Node' ).splitlines() :
13|           here = DefaultMutableTreeNode(
14|               self.getName( node )
15|           )
16|           servers = AdminConfig.list( 'Server', node )
17|           for server in servers.splitlines() :
18|               leaf = DefaultMutableTreeNode(
19|                   self.getName( server )
20|               )
21|               here.add( leaf )
22|           root.add( here )
23|       return JTree( root )
24|   def getName( self, configId ) :
25|       return AdminConfig.showAttribute( configId, 'name' )
26|   def run( self ) :
27|       frame = JFrame(
28|           'Tree1',
29|           size = ( 200, 200 ),
30|           defaultCloseOperation = JFrame.EXIT_ON_CLOSE
31|       )
32|       frame.add( JScrollPane( self.cellTree() ) )
33|       frame.setVisible( 1 )
```

Table 11-1 provides a short description of the code used to build and display the hierarchical tree structure. From the code in Listing 11-1, the description in Table 11-1, and the output in Figure 11-1, it should be clear that the JTree class is easy to use and quite powerful. With no additional code, you can select one or more items as well as expand or collapse individual nodes.[6]

Table 11-1. *Tree1 Listing Explained*

Lines	Description
9–23	cellTree() method that creates, populates, and returns a JTree instance representing the names of the WebSphere cell, nodes, and application servers. Each node in the tree is an instance of DefaultMutableTreeNode and may have zero or more child nodes (aka children).
24–25	getName() method that uses the AdminConfig.showAttribute() scripting object method call to obtain and return the name of the specified configuration object.
26–33	Tree1 run() method that creates the application frame, populates it, and displays it on the Swing event dispatch thread.

---

[5]Remember that AdminConfig is a wsadmin scripting object, and therefore is only available when wsadmin is used to execute the Jython script.
[6]See http://docs.oracle.com/javase/8/docs/api/javax/swing/tree/DefaultMutableTreeNode.html.

JTree Attributes and Methods

You can see, by looking at the cellTree() method in Listing 11-1, that it is really easy to create a JTree. You can also see, from Figure 11-1, that the default settings or attributes might not match your expectations. For example, you might not want to allow the users to select multiple entries. How do you limit the users to selecting zero or one item at a time? You'll see how to do this shortly. Before you do that, though, it is important to see how the tree structure is separated from the data being represented.

The TreeSelectionModel Class

One scenario that occurs frequently in the Swing class hierarchy is having one class to display a structure, and having a related but separate class that holds the data. This is also the case for trees. The class used by a tree to hold its data is an implementation of the TreeModel interface.[7] The only implementation of this class used by this book is the DefaultTreeModel class.[8]

In addition to the data model, the JTree class also has a TreeSelectionModel associated with it. Unless, of course, you don't want to let the users select any of the tree nodes. If this is the case, it should be set to None (or null in Java terms).

What, exactly, does this mean? Does it mean that you can't expand or collapse the tree nodes? No, it doesn't. It just means that no node can be selected. Figure 11-2 shows images similar to those Figure 11-1, but this time none of the nodes can be selected.

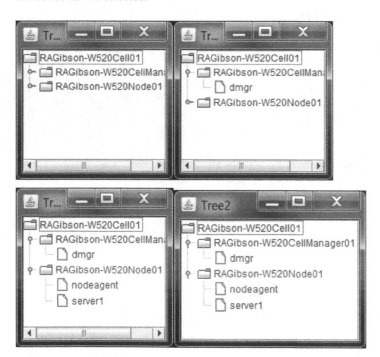

Figure 11-2. *Tree2 sample output*

---

[7]See http://docs.oracle.com/javase/8/docs/api/javax/swing/tree/TreeModel.html.
[8]See http://docs.oracle.com/javase/8/docs/api/javax/swing/tree/DefaultTreeModel.html.

What do you need to do to set this kind of limitation? Well, it's really quite simple. Listing 11-2 contains the run() method from Tree2.py, which shows that you only need to change lines 32-34, which correspond to line 32 in Listing 11-1.

Listing 11-2. Tree2 run() Method

```
26|    def run( self ) :
27|        frame = JFrame(
28|            'Tree2',
29|            size = ( 200, 200 ),
30|            defaultCloseOperation = JFrame.EXIT_ON_CLOSE
31|        )
32|        tree = self.cellTree()
33|        tree.setSelectionModel( None )
34|        frame.add( JScrollPane( tree ) )
35|        frame.setVisible( 1 )
```

Let's get back to the question raised earlier. How do you limit the selection to zero or one tree node? The answer is that you need to change the default selection mode using the setSelectionMode() method. What kinds of values does this method allow? The value must correspond to the TreeSelectionModel constants shown in Table 11-2.[9]

Table 11-2. TreeSelectionModel Constants

SINGLE_TREE_SELECTION	Allows a maximum of one tree node to be selected.
CONTIGUOUS_TREE_SELECTION	Allows a maximum of one continuous adjacent group of nodes to be selected.
DISCONTIGUOUS_TREE_SELECTION	Allows an unlimited number of nodes to be selected, with no restriction that they be adjacent.

This table may make you think about lists and how you can limit the selection of list items.[10] In fact, there is a direct correlation between the selection settings allowed by JList instances and JTree instances. In the example scripts in Chapter 9, you used the JList selectionMode keyword argument to limit the JList instances to a single item.

You might wonder if you can do a similar thing with JTree instances. Listing 11-3 shows how you can use the classInfo function, which you learned about in Chapter 4, to display the JTree class hierarchy. It also shows all of the attributes that contain the string "selectionmode". Unlike the corresponding JList class hierarchy, the JTree class does not have a selectionMode attribute. So the answer to the question is no, you can't do it quite that easily.

[9]See http://docs.oracle.com/javase/8/docs/api/javax/swing/tree/TreeSelectionModel.html.
[10]See the section in Chapter 9 entitled "Limiting the Selectable Items."

Listing 11-3 JTree class hierarchy showing selectmode attributes

```
wsadmin>from javax.swing import JTree
wsadmin>
wsadmin>classInfo( JTree, attr = 'selectionmode' )
javax.swing.JTree
  selectionModel
| javax.swing.JComponent
| | java.awt.Container
| | | java.awt.Component
| | | | java.lang.Object
| | | | java.awt.image.ImageObserver
| | | | java.awt.MenuContainer
| | | | java.io.Serializable
| | java.io.Serializable
| javax.swing.Scrollable
| javax.accessibility.Accessible
wsadmin>
```

So, how can you do it? Well, Listing 11-4 contains the run() method from Tree3.py. The statement used to limit the tree selection to a single node is performed in lines 34-36, which correspond to line 33 in Listing 11-2. From this you can see that in order to change the selection mode you need to obtain the selection model used by this tree (via a call to the getSelectionModel() method as shown in line 34). You then call the setSelectionMode() method of this model to make the change.

Listing 11-4. Tree3 run() Method, Limiting Node Selection

```
27|    def run( self ) :
28|        frame = JFrame(
29|            'Tree3',
30|            size = ( 200, 200 ),
31|            defaultCloseOperation = JFrame.EXIT_ON_CLOSE
32|        )
33|        tree = self.cellTree()
34|        tree.getSelectionModel().setSelectionMode(
35|            TreeSelectionModel.SINGLE_TREE_SELECTION
36|        )
37|        frame.add( JScrollPane( tree ) )
38|        frame.setVisible( 1 )
```

■ **Note**   It is possible to use the Jython-provided attributes to minimize the explicit calls to the specified methods, but that is likely to cause confusion. Code to do this would look something like:

```
tree.selectionModel.selectionMode = TreeSelectionModel.SINGLE_TREE_SELECTION
```

You will have to decide if using the attribute names like this instead of the getter and setter methods is worth the potential confusion that it might cause.

TreeSelectionListener

There are times when your applications will need to know when the user makes a tree node selection. For example, when the user selects a tree node it is likely that they want information about this node displayed immediately. You will need the application to display information about the selected WebSphere node as soon as the user selects the corresponding tree node.

To do this, you need to use the TreeSelectionListener interface.[11] Just like the ListSelectionListener,[12] which is described in Chapter 9, this interface has a single valueChanged() method. Can you use the valueChanged keyword argument on the JTree constructor call to identify a TreeSelectionListener method for the JTree instance? The simple quick answer to this question is yes. Figure 11-3 shows one possible use for this kind of listener.

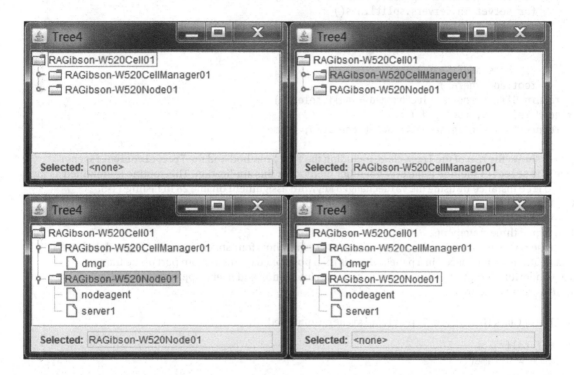

Figure 11-3. *Tree4 sample output*

In Figure 11-3, you can see how the text field is updated by the tree selection listener event handler to reflect the data from the selected node; it also shows "<none>" if no node has been selected. This will prove to be very useful, as you'll see when you build on this application. Listings 11-5 and 11-6 show the Tree4 class that this application uses.

---

[11]See http://docs.oracle.com/javase/8/docs/api/javax/swing/event/TreeSelectionListener.html.
[12]See http://docs.oracle.com/javase/8/docs/api/javax/swing/event/ListSelectionListener.html.

Listing 11-5. Tree4 Class Using a `TreeSelectionListener`

```
13|class Tree4( java.lang.Runnable ) :
14|    def cellTree( self ) :
15|        cell = AdminConfig.list( 'Cell' )
16|        root = DefaultMutableTreeNode( self.getName( cell ) )
17|        for node in AdminConfig.list( 'Node' ).splitlines() :
18|            here = DefaultMutableTreeNode(
19|                self.getName( node )
20|            )
21|            servers = AdminConfig.list( 'Server', node )
22|            for server in servers.splitlines() :
23|                leaf = DefaultMutableTreeNode(
24|                    self.getName( server )
25|                )
26|                here.add( leaf )
27|            root.add( here )
28|        return JTree( root, valueChanged = self.select )
29|    def getName( self, configId ) :
30|        return AdminConfig.showAttribute( configId, 'name' )
```

Listing 11-6 shows the rest of the Tree4 class, including the `run()` method and the `TreeSelectionListener` event handler. The `select()` method is the event handler method for this application. This routine is identified as the listener for the JTree instance by using the `valueChanged` keyword assignment on line 28 in Listing 11-5.

The `run()` method creates and populates the application frame. Lines 38-42 of Listing 11-6 show how easy it is to create the tree, limit the number of items that can be selected, and position it all on the application frame. This is accomplished in just three statements.

Setting up the rest of the frame is also as easy. Lines 43-52 show how four statements can create a label and a read-only text field. These are placed in a panel, which is then positioned on the bottom part of the frame.

This is a wonderful example of how easy it is to create an interesting and useful application using Swing components in a creative manner.

Listing 11-6. Tree4 Class Using a `TreeSelectionListener`, Continued

```
31|    def run( self ) :
32|        frame = JFrame(
33|            'Tree4',
34|            size = ( 320, 200 ),
35|            layout = BorderLayout(),
36|            defaultCloseOperation = JFrame.EXIT_ON_CLOSE
37|        )
38|        tree = self.cellTree()
39|        tree.getSelectionModel().setSelectionMode(
40|            TreeSelectionModel.SINGLE_TREE_SELECTION
41|        )
42|        frame.add( JScrollPane( tree ), BorderLayout.CENTER )
43|        panel = JPanel()
44|        panel.add( JLabel( 'Selected:' ) )
```

```
45|          self.msg = panel.add(
46|              JTextField(
47|                  '<none>',            # Initial value
48|                  20,                  # Field width (columns)
49|                  editable = 0         # Disable editing
50|              )
51|          )
52|          frame.add( panel, BorderLayout.SOUTH )
53|          frame.setVisible( 1 )
54|      def select( self, event ) :
55|          tree = event.getSource()
56|          if tree.getSelectionCount() :
57|              node = str( tree.getLastSelectedPathComponent() )
58|          else :
59|              node = '<none>'
60|          self.msg.setText( node )
```

Table 11-3 describes the important changes from the previous tree examples and the Tree4 class shown in Listings 11-4 and 11-5. I think it's impressive how easily you can use the Swing classes to build this neat little application.[13]

Table 11-3. *Tree4 Listing Explained*

Lines	Description
28	The only real difference is where you specify the valueChanged keyword on the JTree constructor to specify the TreeSelectionListener event handler routine to be called.
35	To make the presentation more aesthetically appealing, the frame uses the Border Layout Manager.
42	You position the JScrollPane instance containing the JTree in the center of the application frame.
43–52	You create a Panel container to hold the label and the disabled text field on the bottom of the application frame.
54–60	The select() method is the TreeSelectionListener valueChanged event handler. This method uses the event.getSource() method to obtain a reference to the associated tree, and if a node has been selected, it uses the getLastSelectedPathComponent() method call to identify that node.

JTree Manipulation

Some applications provide a way for the users to make changes to the tree being displayed. For example, you might want your application to provide a way for the user to change the tree node to reflect new information. This can be as simple as allowing the displayed values to be modified, or it may be appropriate to add and remove specific nodes.

---

[13]The dataType of the value returned by the getLastSelectedPathComponent() method call is an object, so it needs to be converted to a string before this value can be used to update the JTextField value.

.Let's break this example into pieces, and not just because the listing, even without comments and blank lines, is too big. To start, let's see what the application looks like when the DynamicTree.py script is executed. Figure 11-4 shows three images of this application before any changes are made.[14]

Figure 11-4. DynamicTree sample output

The first part of the DynamicTree class, shown in Listing 11-7, provides enough information to understand the layout of the application shown in Figure 11-4. The top part of the application window has a scroll pane containing the initial tree. Beneath this, there is a row of buttons. The run() method, shown in lines 59-77, creates and populates the frame, as you have seen before. For now, don't worry about the constructor (the __init__() method) or the getSuffix() method. You'll see how they are used shortly.

---

[14]This example is based on the DynamicTreeDemo from the Java Swing Tutorial, which can be found at http://docs.oracle.com/javase/tutorial/uiswing/components/tree.html#dynamic.

Listing 11-7. DynamicTree Class (Part 1 of 5)

```
53|class DynamicTree( java.lang.Runnable ) :
54|    def __init__( self ) :
55|        self.nodeSuffix = 0
56|    def getSuffix( self ) :
57|        self.nodeSuffix += 1
58|        return self.nodeSuffix
59|    def run( self ) :
60|        frame = JFrame(
61|            'DynamicTree',
62|            layout = BorderLayout(),
63|            locationRelativeTo = None,
64|            defaultCloseOperation = JFrame.EXIT_ON_CLOSE
65|        )
66|        self.tree  = self.makeTree()        # Keep references handy
67|        self.model = self.tree.getModel()
68|        frame.add(
69|            JScrollPane(
70|                self.tree,
71|                preferredSize = Dimension( 300, 150 )
72|            ),
73|            BorderLayout.CENTER
74|        )
75|        frame.add( self.buttonRow(), BorderLayout.SOUTH )
76|        frame.pack()
77|        frame.setVisible( 1 )
```

The only new thing in this run() method is line 63, which you might not have seen. What does this keyword argument do? It corresponds with the setLocationRelativeTo() method from the JFrame class that is inherited from the java.awt.Window class.[15] By initializing this value to None, which corresponds to the Java null, the application window is positioned in the center of the screen.[16] Pretty neat, eh?

The buttonRow() method, called in line 75 of Listing 11-7, can be seen on lines 78-94 in Listing 11-8. There really shouldn't be anything too surprising in this routine, which uses a GridLayout instance to position the buttons being created in one horizontal row and assigns the actionPerformed event handler for each button using a keyword argument (line 90).

Listing 11-8. DynamicTree Class (Part 2 of 5, buttonRow() Method)

```
78|    def buttonRow( self ) :
79|        buttonPanel = JPanel( GridLayout( 0, 3 ) )
80|        data = [
81|            [ 'Add'   , self.addEvent ],
82|            [ 'Remove', self.delEvent ],
83|            [ 'Clear' , self.clsEvent ]
84|        ]
```

---

[15]See http://docs.oracle.com/javase/8/docs/api/java/awt/Window.html#setLocationRelativeTo%28java.awt.Component%29.
[16]Actually, the top-left corner of the application is positioned on the center of the screen. This should be "close enough" for now.

```
85|            self.buttons = {}
86|            for name, handler in data :
87|                self.buttons[ name ] = buttonPanel.add (
88|                    JButton(
89|                        name,
90|                        actionPerformed = handler,
91|                        enabled = name != 'Remove'
92|                    )
93|                )
94|            return buttonPanel
```

Listing 11-9 shows the code for the three button event handlers that are referenced by the data array in lines 80-84 of Listing 11-8. For now, I'll just say that an event handler method is called when the button is pressed. I'll defer a discussion of these specific event handlers until a little later. For now, it makes sense to provide them here because of their references in the previous listing.

Listing 11-9. DynamicTree Class (Part 3 of 5, Button Event Handlers)

```
 95|    def addEvent( self, event ) :
 96|        sPath = self.tree.getSelectionModel().getSelectionPath()
 97|        if sPath :                         # Use selected node
 98|            parent = sPath.getLastPathComponent()
 99|        else :                             # Nothing selected, use root
100|            parent = self.model.getRoot()
101|        kids = parent.getChildCount()
102|        child = DefaultMutableTreeNode(
103|            'New node %d' % self.getSuffix()
104|        )
105|        self.model.insertNodeInto( child, parent, kids )
106|        self.tree.scrollPathToVisible(
107|            TreePath( child.getPath() )
108|        )
109|    def delEvent( self, event ) :
110|        currentSelection = self.tree.getSelectionPath()
111|        if currentSelection :
112|            currentNode = currentSelection.getLastPathComponent()
113|            if currentNode.getParent() :
114|                self.model.removeNodeFromParent( currentNode )
115|                return
116|    def clsEvent( self, event ) :
117|        self.model.getRoot().removeAllChildren()
118|        self.model.reload()
```

The DefaultTreeModel Class

Listing 11-10 shows the makeTree() method called in line 66 of Listing 11-7. It uses instances of the DefaultMutableTreeNode class, which you saw previously. What's new in this method is how the root node of the tree is passed as an argument to the DefaultTreeModel class constructor (line 126).

Listing 11-10. DynamicTree Class (Part 4 of 5, the makeTree() Method)

```
119|    def makeTree( self ) :
120|        root = DefaultMutableTreeNode( 'Root Node' )
121|        for name in 'Parent 1,Parent 2'.split( ',' ) :
122|            here = DefaultMutableTreeNode( name )
123|            for child in 'Child 1,Child 2'.split( ',' ) :
124|                here.add( DefaultMutableTreeNode( child ) )
125|            root.add( here )
126|        model = DefaultTreeModel(
127|            root,
128|            treeModelListener = myTreeModelListener()
129|        )
130|        tree = JTree(
131|            model,
132|            editable = 1,
133|            showsRootHandles = 1,
134|            valueChanged = self.select
135|        )
136|        tree.getSelectionModel().setSelectionMode(
137|            TreeSelectionModel.SINGLE_TREE_SELECTION
138|        )
139|        return tree
```

Don't forget that the JTree instance doesn't actually contain the data being displayed. It only provides a view of the data, which like most non-trivial Swing components, is provided by a component data model. In the case of the JTree class, it's almost always an instance of the DefaultTreeModel class.[17]

What does the tree model provide? Well, a lot of methods are provided by this class. Unfortunately, I don't have the time or space to investigate and describe how and when they are used. At this point, I will only take a look at a few of them, specifically the ones related to adding and removing TreeModelListeners. In fact, that's exactly what is done in line 128. The DefaultTreeModel instance is then passed to the JTree constructor in line 131. At the same time, other keyword arguments make the tree modifiable (line 132) and make the root node handle visible (line 133). Note that the valueChanged keyword assignment argument (line 134) is used to identify the TreeSelectionListener event handler for this tree instance.

Listing 11-11 shows the TreeSelectionListener event handler method for this DynamicTree class application. It is only a little different from the one you saw earlier in this chapter. This example determines if a removable node has been selected. Only non-root nodes can be selected, so you want the Remove button to be enabled only if the user has selected a non-root node. To do this, the code determines if a node has been selected, and if so, how far down the tree this selected node is. If no node has been selected, the count will be zero. The root node, by definition, has a depth of 1. This information is used in line 148 to determine if the Remove button should be enabled.

[17]See http://docs.oracle.com/javase/8/docs/api/javax/swing/tree/DefaultTreeModel.html.

Listing 11-11. DynamicTree Class (Part 5 of 5, the select() Method)

```
140|    def select( self, event ) :
141|        tree  = event.getSource()        # Get access to tree
142|        count = tree.getSelectionCount()
143|        sPath = tree.getSelectionModel().getSelectionPath()
144|        if sPath :                        # How deep is the pick?
145|            depth = sPath.getPathCount()
146|        else :                            # Nothing selected
147|            depth = 0
148|        self.buttons[ 'Remove' ].setEnabled( count and depth > 1 )
```

The TreeModelListener Interface

Now you finally get to the topic mentioned in Listing 11-10 on line 128—the TreeModelListener interface.[18] As you have seen, listeners are used when certain events occur. In this case, the methods in this listener are called when tree nodes are added, changed, or removed. In addition, another method is called when the tree structure changes. It is important to note the difference between this listener and the TreeSelectionListener discussed earlier.

By creating a class based on this listener interface, you can monitor changes that occur in the tree. The question, though, is how? Well, the TreeModelListener class is set up as a main class and isn't nested inside the application class. This demonstrates how you can use the TreeModelEvent[19] provided with each of the TreeModelListener methods in order to detect any changes that have occurred.

Listing 11-12 shows the myTreeModelListener class, which includes some common, shared methods that locate specific parts of the tree model. They identify the parent or the specific node of interest.

Listing 11-12. The myTreeModelListener Class

```
19|class myTreeModelListener( TreeModelListener ) :
20|    def getNode( self, event ) :
21|        try :
22|            parent = self.getParent( event )
23|            node = parent.getChildAt(
24|                event.getChildIndices()[ 0 ]
25|            )
26|        except :
27|            node = event.getSource().getRoot()
28|        return node
29|    def getParent( self, event ) :
30|        try :
31|            path = event.getTreePath().getPath()
32|            parent = path[ 0 ]          # Start with root node
```

---

[18]See http://docs.oracle.com/javase/8/docs/api/javax/swing/event/TreeModelListener.html.
[19]See http://docs.oracle.com/javase/8/docs/api/javax/swing/event/TreeModelEvent.html.

```
33|                for node in path[ 1: ] :   # Get parent of changed node
34|                    parent = parent.getChildAt(
35|                        parent.getIndex( node )
36|                    )
37|        except :
38|            parent = None
39|        return parent
40|    def treeNodesChanged( self, event ) :
41|        node = self.getNode( event )
42|        print ' treeNodesChanged():', node.getUserObject()
43|    def treeNodesInserted( self, event ) :
44|        node = self.getNode( event )
45|        print 'treeNodesInserted():', node.getUserObject()
46|    def treeNodesRemoved( self, event ) :
47|        print ' treeNodesRemoved(): child %d under "%s"' % (
48|            event.getChildIndices()[ 0 ],
49|            self.getParent( event )
50|        )
51|    def treeStructureChanged( self, event ) :
52|        print 'treeStructureChanged():'
```

One question that people sometimes ask is, "How do I edit a node?" The sequence of images in Figure 11-5 demonstrates this process. You begin with the tree expanded and the root node selected. The users indicate that they want to edit the node by triple-clicking the node (three left clicks in a short time interval).[20] The node text is temporarily replaced with a text field containing the selected node text. This allows users to easily replace the text when they start typing. Should they want to cancel the edit operation, they can simply press Escape. To complete the edit, thereby replacing the original node value with the new one, users simply need to press Enter. This is the point at which the TreeModelListener treeNodesChanged() method is invoked.

---

[20]It's interesting to note that the specified node is expanded or collapsed as part of the normal double-click process. That's why the tree is collapsed as part of this edit process.

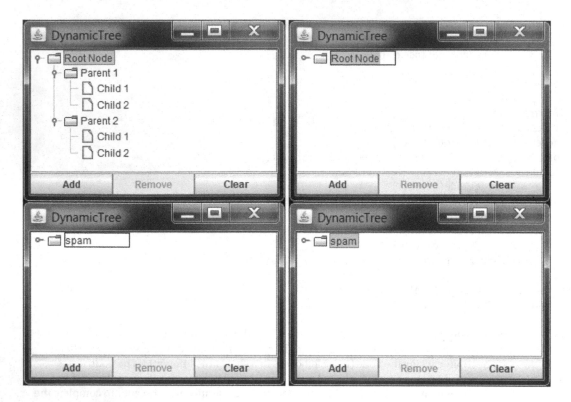

Figure 11-5. *Editing tree nodes*

How in the world would someone know this? Where is this documented? Well, if you think about it, there has to be some editor associated with the tree in order for you to modify node values. A DefaultTreeCellEditor[21] is one of the many things provided by the JTree class. This editor determines how the change is triggered, as well as the kind of edit input field to be displayed.

In addition to a default tree cell editor, the JTree constructor will also provide DefaultTreeCellRenderer[22] to determine how the tree nodes will be displayed. The fact that these support classes are part of the Swing hierarchy makes the lives of Swing application developers significantly easier.

Creating your own replacements for either of these classes is well beyond the scope of this book. However, the topic of cell renderers and editors is discussed in Chapter 12, which covers tables.

Summary

This chapter was all about creating, displaying, and manipulating trees. One of the most important points to remember about the JTree class is that it does not actually contain the data; it simply displays the hierarchical data in a form similar to an outline. The next chapter discusses the JTable class used to display data in a tabular format.

---

[21]See http://docs.oracle.com/javase/8/docs/api/javax/swing/tree/DefaultTreeCellEditor.html.
[22]See http://docs.oracle.com/javase/8/docs/api/javax/swing/tree/DefaultTreeCellRenderer.html.

■ ■ ■

CHAPTER 12

Motion to Take from the Table: Building Tables

One of the most useful structures in graphical applications is the table format, when information is displayed in an organized arrangement of rows and columns. In fact, you have seen lots of examples of tables throughout this book.

As a side note, it is interesting how often words have multiple meanings and uses. This is especially true in the technology industry. It can also be the case with natural languages such as English. If you look for the definition of the word "table," you'll find that it is often used as a noun and occasionally as a transitive verb (i.e., to place on or take off of an agenda). It is this second form that was the source for the title of this chapter,[1] just to be different.

A table is such a common idea that most people would be hard pressed to remember when the concept was first described to them. This chapter is all about how to build, display, control, manage, and manipulate information in tables.

Tables Can Be Really Easy

We use tables of information all the time. In fact, it was while I was working with a simple wsadmin Jython script that listed port numbers and EndPoint names for my WebSphere Application Server environment that I started thinking about displaying the information in a table. The name of the application was ListPorts.py and Chapter 22 is all about the iterative development of a Swing application that does this.

Over time, I've written many different versions of that ListPorts.py script file. So many that it's hard to keep track of them all. I wrote a script to locate the various instances of this script on my system and then created a table of the file date, size, and locations. Using this information, I produced a script that displays this information in table form, as shown in Figure 12-1.

---

[1] See *Robert's Rules of Order,* Article VI, Section 35.

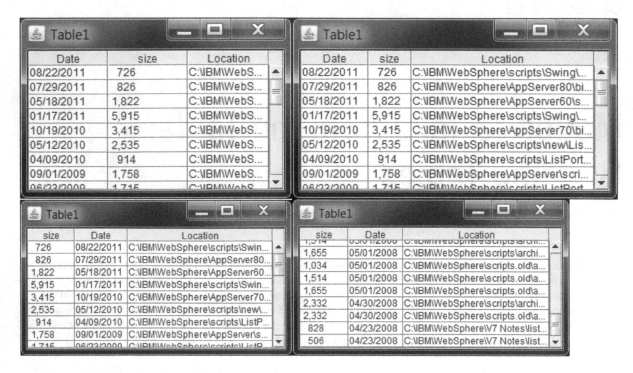

Figure 12-1. *Table1.py output images*

There are multiple images in this figure to show that the table columns can be resized and moved around easily. To resize a column, you simply drag the vertical bar between two column headings one way or the other. To reorder the columns, you drag a column heading (such as "Date") to the desired position. The other columns are reordered accordingly. All of these capabilities are provided by the JTable class.

It's also interesting to note how the right-most column, which isn't wide enough to display the complete directory path, uses an ellipse (. . .) to indicate that the data has been truncated. Just as in Listing 12-1, which shows that lines 10-39 have been left out.[2] The last image shows that the column headings stay in place, even when the data scrolls down to display other rows in the table.

Listing 12-1. Excerpts from Table1.py

```
 7|class Table1( java.lang.Runnable ) :
 8|    def __init__( self ) :
 9|        info = r'''
  |...
40|04/23/2008|    506|C:\IBM\WebSphere\V7 Notes\listports.py
41|'''
42|        self.data = [                  # list comprehension
43|            line.split( '|' )          # each row is an array
44|            for line in info.splitlines() # each line is a row
45|            if line                    # ignore blank lines
46|        ]
```

---

[2]Of course, the Java Swing table does this automatically for you, whereas I had to do this manually in Listing 12-1.

```
47|    def run( self ) :
48|        frame = JFrame(
49|            'Table1',
50|            size = ( 300, 200 ),
51|            locationRelativeTo = None,
52|            defaultCloseOperation = JFrame.EXIT_ON_CLOSE
53|        )
54|        headings = 'Date,size,Location'.split( ',' )
55|        frame.add(
56|            JScrollPane(
57|                JTable( self.data, headings )
58|            )
59|        )
60|        frame.setVisible( 1 )
```

How much code is required to provide all of this functionality? Almost none, as you can see by looking at the Table1 class in Listing 12-1. Line 57 contains the JTable[3] constructor.[4] In fact, no additional code was required to provide all of the functionality just described. It is all provided by the Java Swing class library.

Defaults Can Be Harmful to your . . . Mental Health

There's a great deal that can be said for simplicity. In other words, defaults can sometimes drive you crazy. Just remember though—you get what you pay for. By that, I mean it is extremely unlikely that you will be able to have a really useful application that uses all of the Swing class defaults.

Let's take another look at the simple table created by the Table1.py script. Did you notice that all of the columns in the first image are the same width? Unfortunately, the data found in each column isn't all the same width. But the default settings allocate each column the same amount of column space and each column is expected to contain the same type of data (i.e., a string).

You'll investigate column manipulation a little later in this chapter (in the section entitled "Column Manipulation"). For now, don't worry about it. First, I describe other aspects of tables.

Picky, Picky, Picky. . . Selecting Parts of a Table

What parts of the table can be selected? As you can see in Figure 12-2, multiple groups of rows can be selected. This figure also shows that cell values can be edited. When a cell is edited,[5] the cell highlighting is distinctly different and the cell has a more pronounced border. One of the challenges with the defaults is that every cell within the table is considered a string, so (almost) any kind of character data can be entered. For example, while editing the selected cell in Figure 12-2, you could easily enter any text you want. The caveat is that some characters will cause the edit mode to terminate (such as the Tab and Enter keys).

---

[3]See http://docs.oracle.com/javase/8/docs/api/javax/swing/JTable.html.

[4]As you have seen before, it is a really good idea to place a potentially large component, such as a JTable instance, in a JScrollPane, as shown in lines 56-58.

[5]Either by double-clicking on the cell or positioning the focus on a cell using cursor control keys and pressing the spacebar.

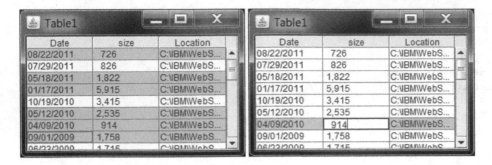

Figure 12-2. `Table1` *output: row selection and editing*

This provides you with a quick overview about some of the aspects related to Swing tables. The rest of the chapter discusses tailoring them to act in ways that make sense.

Row, Row, Row Your . . . Table? Working with Rows

If you play with the `Table1.py` application, you'll see that when you click on any cell in the table, the whole row is selected. In Figure 12-2, you can see that multiple groups of rows can, by default, be selected.[6] How can you change the row selection behavior? That's easy; the `JTable` class has a row `selectionMode` property that uses the same constants used when you were working with lists and trees. Table 12-1 describes the possible selection values.

Table 12-1. *Selection Mode Constants*

Selection Mode Constant	Description
SINGLE_SELECTION	Zero or one row can be selected.
SINGLE_INTERVAL_SELECTION	One contiguous group of rows can be selected.
MULTIPLE_INTERVAL_SELECTION	The default mode allows multiple groups of rows to be selected.

You can see, by looking at the `JTable` class Java documentation, that there is a setter but not a getter for the `selectionMode` property.[7] Don't be confused by the fact that there is a getter and setter for the `selectionModel` property; this is not what we're talking about. The fact that the class provides only a setter method means that you can use the setter (`table.setSelectionMode()`) method or you can specify the `selectionMode` keyword argument when the table is constructed, as shown in Listing 12-2, which is from `Table2.py`.

[6]Press and hold the Ctrl key as you use the mouse to select or deselect an individual row. If you hold the Shift key while making a selection, you can select multiple contiguous rows.
[7]I looked all over, but have yet to find any explanation for the lack of getter for this table property.

Listing 12-2. Specifying the selectionMode Using a Keyword Argument

```
 6|from    javax.swing import ListSelectionModel as LSM
  | ...
56|        frame.add(
57|            JScrollPane(
58|                JTable(
59|                    self.data,
60|                    headings,
61|                    selectionMode = LSM.SINGLE_SELECTION
62|                )
63|            )
64|        )
```

Does the presence of the selectionMode attribute in the JTable class mean that you can access its value
(the operation normally performed by a getter method)? No, it doesn't. If you try to do that, you'll get an exception like
the one shown in Listing 12-3.

Listing 12-3. Write-Only Attributes

```
wsadmin>from javax.swing import JTable
wsadmin>
wsadmin>data = [ [ '1.1', '1.2' ], [ '2.1', '2.2' ] ]
wsadmin>head = [ 'Uno', 'Dos' ]
wsadmin>
wsadmin>table = JTable( data, head )
wsadmin>
wsadmin>table.selectionMode
WASX7015E: Exception running command: "table.selectionMode";
 exception information:
 com.ibm.bsf.BSFException: exception from Jython:
Traceback (innermost last):
  File "<input>", line 1, in ?
AttributeError: write-only attr: selectionMode

wsadmin>
```

What does that mean for your applications? Basically, it means that if your application needs to display and
modify this attribute, it needs to provide some way to maintain the property value as well as monitor any changes
made to it.

Selecting Columns

The JTable class has columnSelectionAllowed and rowSelectionAllowed attributes. Interestingly enough, the former doesn't appear on the Javadoc page of the JTable class, but it does exist, as you can see in Listing 12-4.

Listing 12-4. JTable selectionAllowed Attributes

```
wsadmin>from javax.swing import JTable
wsadmin>
wsadmin>classInfo( JTable, attr = 'SelectionAllowed' )
javax.swing.JTable
  columnSelectionAllowed, rowSelectionAllowed
| javax.swing.JComponent
| | java.awt.Container
| | | java.awt.Component
| | | | java.lang.Object
| | | | java.awt.image.ImageObserver
| | | | java.awt.MenuContainer
| | | | java.io.Serializable
| | java.io.Serializable
| javax.swing.event.TableModelListener
| | java.util.EventListener
| javax.swing.Scrollable
| javax.swing.event.TableColumnModelListener
| | java.util.EventListener
| javax.swing.event.ListSelectionListener
| | java.util.EventListener
| javax.swing.event.CellEditorListener
| | java.util.EventListener
| javax.accessibility.Accessible
| javax.swing.event.RowSorterListener
| | java.util.EventListener
wsadmin>
```

Selecting Individual Cells

If you look at the JTable documentation, you should be able to find the cellSelectionEnabled attribute. Notice that it has been obsolete since version 1.3. How do you allow your table cells to be selected? Well, a cell can be selectable only when both rowSelectionAllowed and columnSelectionAllowed are true.

Interestingly enough, both a getter and a setter are provided for the cellSelectionEnabled attribute. The setter is used to assign the specified (Boolean) value to the rowSelectionAllowed and columnSelectionAllowed attributes, and the getter returns true only if both attributes are true. Table 12-2 shows the values returned by the rowSelectionAllowed, columnSelectionAllowed, and cellSelectionEnabled getter methods after the statement or method call listed in column 1 of the table has been executed.

Table 12-2. *Row, Column, and Cell Selection Values*

Statement Executed	Row	Col	Cell
JTable()	1	0	0
setColumnSelectionAllowed(1)	1	1	1
setRowSelectionAllowed(0)	0	1	0
setRowSelectionAllowed(1)	1	1	1
setCellSelectionEnabled(0)	0	0	0
setCellSelectionEnabled(1)	1	1	1

One question that might come to mind, especially if you have seen the TableSelectionDemo application[8] from the Java Swing Tutorial website, is "Aren't the Row, Column, and Cell selection attributes affected by the selection mode?" The answer is no, they aren't. The developer of that application has added this association, but this is not something that the JTable class does. So, the values in Table 12-2 are the same, regardless of the table selectionMode setting. However, this does point out how developers can choose to enhance classes to provide functionality for their applications.

I Am the Very Model of a Modern Major General: Table Models[9]

One of the many things that you haven't read about yet about JTable instances is the fact that the displayed information isn't stored in the JTable. The table actually provides a view to the data. The JTable class isn't the first complex Swing class that you've seen that does this. In Chapter 11, you learned how the JTree class used a data model to hold the information and the class used to display it.

What are the advantages to separating it like this? For one, it allows the view (the JTable class) to do things like determine the column order to be displayed and to rearrange it, if necessary. In case you are interested, you can disable the movement of columns. Listing 12-5 shows how you can use the JTable getTableHeader() method to access the JTableHeader[10] instance for this table. You then call the setReorderingAllowed() method with a value of 0 (false) to indicate that column reordering is not allowed.

Listing 12-5. Disabling Column Reordering

```
table.getTableHeader().setReorderingAllowed( 0 )
```

Types of Table Models

What kinds of table models exist in the Swing class hierarchy for your applications to use? There is an AbstractTableModel[11] class as well as a DefaultTableModel.[12] I'll let you guess which class is used as the default should one not be provided for your JTable constructor call.

---

[8]See http://docs.oracle.com/javase/tutorial/uiswing/examples/components/TableSelectionDemoProject/src/components/TableSelectionDemo.java.
[9]With thanks and homage to Gilbert and Sullivan for their marvelous works
[10]See http://docs.oracle.com/javase/8/docs/api/javax/swing/table/JTableHeader.html.
[11]See http://docs.oracle.com/javase/8/docs/api/javax/swing/table/AbstractTableModel.html.
[12]See http://docs.oracle.com/javase/8/docs/api/javax/swing/table/DefaultTableModel.html.

Looking at the DefaultTableModel class documentation, you'll find more than two dozen methods, as well as another dozen inherited from the AbstractTableModel base class. What do these methods allow you to do with your table data? Well, from the user interface perspective, you can do things like add, move, and remove rows of data. One of the most important methods, however, is the isCellEditable() method, which is used by the JTable class to determine whether users are allowed to modify data in the specified cell. Listing 12-6 shows just how easily this can be used.

Listing 12-6. Creating a Read-Only TableModel Class

```
 9|class roTM( DefaultTableModel ) :
10|    def __init__( self, data, headings ) :
11|        DefaultTableModel.__init__( self, data, headings )
12|    def isCellEditable( self, row, col ) :
13|        return 0
14|class Table3( java.lang.Runnable ) :
  |...
62|            frame.add(
63|                JScrollPane(
64|                    JTable(
65|                        roTM( self.data, headings ),
66|                        selectionMode = LSM.SINGLE_SELECTION
67|                    )
68|                )
69|            )              .
```

The interesting point about the table model is how it is used, automatically, by the JTable class to determine what information is to be displayed and how. How does the JTable class determine how the data is displayed? It calls the tableModel getColumnClass(...) method, inherited from the base AbstractTableModel class, which you can and should override.

Wait a minute, what does this mean? Previously, you learned that the default data type for each cell is a string. Really, it's an *object* that's represented as a string by default. You can and should provide your own table model getColumnClass(...) instance to identify the appropriate data type for each column. Why a column? One simplifying implementation choice made by the Swing designers was to guarantee that all data in a JTable column would be of a single type. This shouldn't be too much of a restriction though since you can choose to identify the data type of the column as an object and figure out how to display and manipulate the actual data.

Listing 12-7 shows a relatively simple table model descendent class that only allows the values in column one (the second column)[13] to be modified (every other column is read-only). It also includes the getColumnClass(...) method, which identifies the appropriate data type for each column.

Listing 12-7. My Table Model Class

```
13|class myTM( DefaultTableModel ) :
14|    def __init__( self, data, headings ) :
15|        info = []
16|        df   = DateFormat.getDateInstance( DateFormat.SHORT )
```

---

[13]Remember that Jython and Java both use zero origin array indexing.

```
17|        for date, size, path in data :
18|            info.append(
19|                [
20|                    df.parse( date ),
21|                    Integer( size.strip().replace( ',', '' ) ),
22|                    String( path )
23|                ]
24|            )
25|        DefaultTableModel.__init__( self, info, headings )
26|    def getColumnClass( self, col ) :
27|        return [ Date, Integer, String ][ col ]
28|    def isCellEditable( self, row, col ) :
29|        return col == 1
```

Figure 12-3, shows the resulting output of this application (the source for which is in Table4.py). Is the way the information is displayed in the table what you expected? Perhaps, perhaps not. Did you notice how the middle column is now right-aligned, whereas all of the others are left-aligned? Why do you think that is?

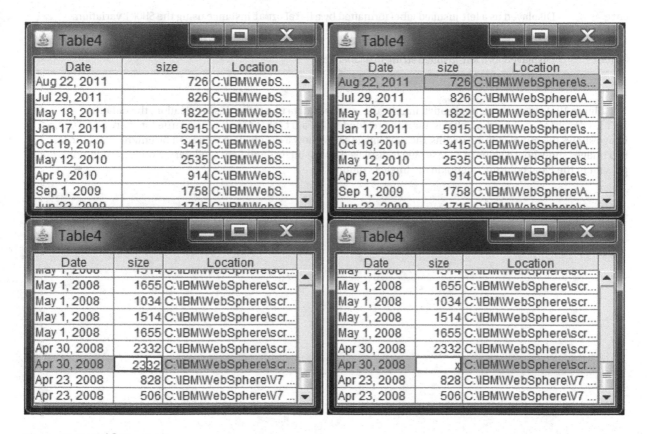

Figure 12-3. Table4 output

Cell Renderers

Another important aspect of the complex JTable class is the fact that each data type has a renderer instance that determines how the information should be presented to the user. Unless you provide one, an instance of the DefaultTableCellRenderer[14] class will be used. It is this renderer instance that displays the Integer values in the middle column using right justification. What kind of cell renderers are provided by Swing? Table 12-3 provides this information.

Table 12-3. *Data Type-Specific Cell Renderers*

Data Type	Renderer Description
Boolean	Displayed as a check box.
Number	Displayed as a right-justified label.
Double	Like Number, but the value is provided by a NumberFormat instance, which is locale-specific.
Float	Same as Double.
Date	Displayed as a left-justified label formatted by a DateFormat instance using the SHORT variation.
Icon	Displayed as a centered label.
Object	Displayed as a left-justified string in a label field.

Figure 12-4 shows some application images using various data types. For this application, the default isCellEditable(...) method, that is, the one provided by DefaultTableModel, returns true for every cell. The first image shows the initial column widths, the next image shows how a simple date value can be entered, and the last two images show how a value of 1234567890 is displayed by the integer and float renderers. Notice how commas are present in the Float column, but not in the Integer column.

---

[14]See http://docs.oracle.com/javase/8/docs/api/javax/swing/table/DefaultTableCellRenderer.html.

Figure 12-4. Table5 *output: data type rendering*

Custom Cell Renderers

I have a question for you to consider: what do you think about representing a Boolean value as a check box? This might make sense, at least as long as the data is editable. It is also very likely that Boolean values will be editable.

While working on this chapter, I wondered if the selection model had any impact on the row, column, and cell selection values. So I wrote a little Swing application to answer this question. The results of this test are displayed in Table 12-2.

Three versions of the application can be found in the TableSelection#.py script files, where # is 1, 2, or 3. The first version uses the simple expedient of not providing a TableModel, so all of the table cells default to being an object, the default representation of which is a left-justified string value.

A reasonable improvement or iteration is to provide a simple table model that identifies each cell as being of type Boolean, which results in the values being displayed using a check box centered in the cell. That's exactly what the other versions of the application do. This is the point at which I wondered what it would take to provide my own renderer, one that displays the Boolean value as a 0 or a 1. That's what the third version of the application does. Since a simple table model class already exists to identify each cell as a Boolean, and since a default renderer for type Boolean already exists (see Table 12-3), you have to figure out how to replace this default Boolean renderer with one of your own, specifically one that displays each value as a digit, centered in the cell. Figure 12-5 shows images from all three verisons of this application.

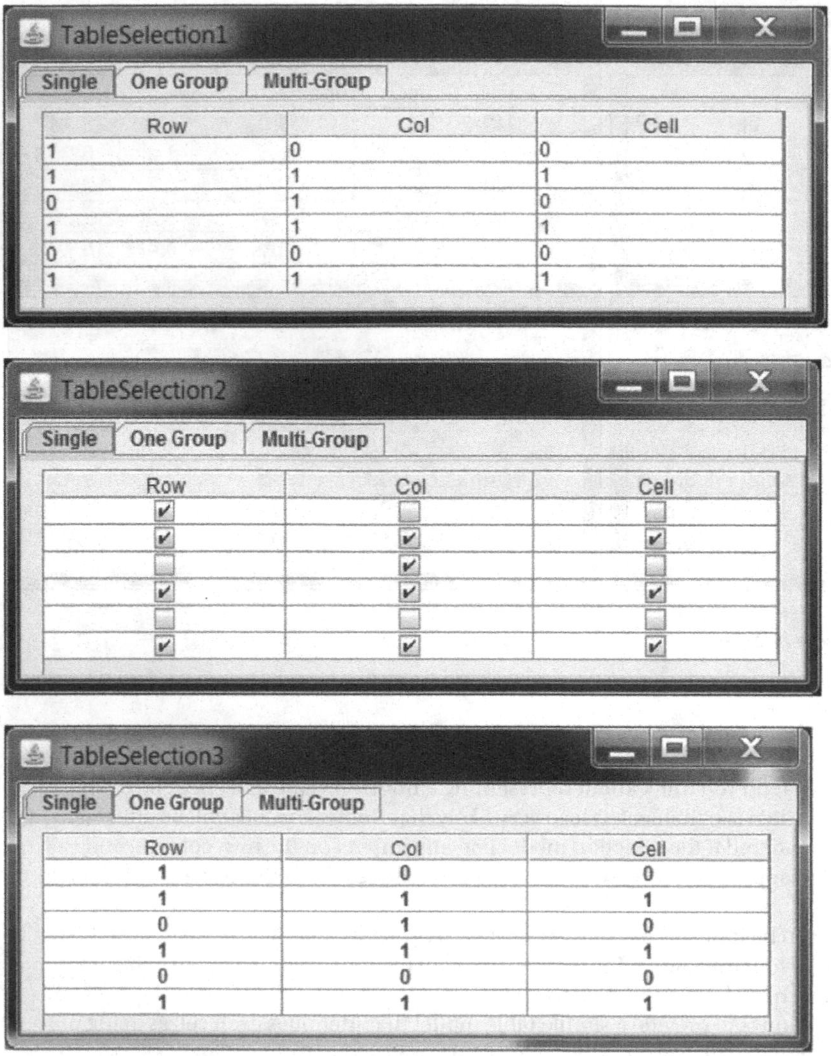

TableSelection1

Row	Col	Cell
1	0	0
1	1	1
0	1	0
1	1	1
0	0	0
1	1	1

TableSelection2

Row	Col	Cell
✔	☐	☐
✔	✔	✔
☐	✔	☐
✔	✔	✔
☐	☐	☐
✔	✔	✔

TableSelection3

Row	Col	Cell
1	0	0
1	1	1
0	1	0
1	1	1
0	0	0
1	1	1

Figure 12-5. TableSelection output with default and custom renderer

The first application, TableSelection1.py, simply creates each JTable instance using the defaults. The second image, generated by TableSelection2.py, uses a table model that identifies each cell as being of type Boolean. The last image, generated by TableSelection3.py, replaces the default renderer of Boolean values with the one shown in Listing 12-8 (line 81).

Listing 12-8: Custom Renderer for Boolean Values

```
| 17|class boolRenderer( DefaultTableCellRenderer ) :                    |
| 18|    def __init__( self ) :                                          |
| 19|        self.result = JLabel(                                       |
| 20|            horizontalAlignment = SwingConstants.CENTER             |
| 21|        )                                                           |
| 22|    def getTableCellRendererComponent(                              |
| 23|        self,                                                       |
| 24|        table,                  # JTable  - table containing value  |
| 25|        value,                  # Object  - value being rendered    |
| 26|        isSelected,             # boolean - Is value selected?      |
| 27|        hasFocus,               # boolean - Does this cell have focus?|
| 28|        rowIndex,               # int     - Row # (0..N)            |
| 29|        vColIndex,              # int     - Col # (0..N)            |
| 30|    ) :                                                             |
| 31|        self.result.setText( value.toString() )                    |
| 32|        return self.result                                         |
|...|  ...                                                               |
| 81|        bTable.setDefaultRenderer( Boolean, boolRenderer() )        |
|...|  ...                                                               |
```

A Few Cautions. . .

As you can see in Listing 12-8 as well as in the Javadoc for the DefaultTableCellRenderer class and the TableCellRenderer interface[15] on which it is based, only one method class exists. When providing a custom TableCellRenderer, it is important that you realize the potential performance impacts that can occur because of how the getTableCellRendererComponent(...) method is used. So, take a few moments to read the "Implementation Note" on the DefaultTableCellRenderer documentation page.

One of the important things that a custom TableCellRenderer should do is reuse a component instance, instead of instantiating a new one on each call to the getTableCellRendererComponent(...) method. Listing 12-8 shows how this class creates a common JLabel component instance in the constructor and reuses it on each use (lines 31 and 32).

It's interesting to note that if, for some reason, you don't like the column-centric technique for choosing the cell renderer, it is possible to create a table class based on JTable, which provides a getCellRenderer(...) method that uses a different technique. However, as you might imagine, the difficulties associated with a drastic approach such as this is not something to be underestimated. Although possible, it should rarely be considered a viable option.

---

[15]See http://docs.oracle.com/javase/8/docs/api/javax/swing/table/TableCellRenderer.html.

Which Cell Renderer to Use?

For tables that contain a variety of data types, it is quite possible that multiple cell renderer instances exist. When this occurs, it might not be clear how the table determines which one to use. How is this determined? Well, if a renderer has been defined for the specified table column, it takes precedence. If not, the renderer for the data type for that column will be used. So, if you want to use a custom renderer, you have to decide if you want all cells of the same type to be rendered in the same fashion or if you only want the data in a specific column to use this custom renderer. This should help you decide which technique to use to specify the custom renderer.

What would be a good example of this kind of decision? Consider a situation whereby your table contains a number of columns containing floating-point values. You might want some of these rendered using one format (such as a percentage, with a specific number of decimal places) and another column as a completely different format (such as in currency).

You just saw how to set up a cell renderer for a specific data type. How do you set up a column-specific one? First, you need to access the TableColumn[16] instance for the specific table column in question. Fortunately, this is easily done by using the getColumn(...) method of the TableColumnModel[17] instance that is used to hold the column information for the specific table instance. This TableColumn class includes a setCellRenderer(...) method, which allows you to specify the renderer instance for this particular table column. Listing 12-9 shows how easy this is. Please note how the col variable identifies the column number for which this renderer instance is being specified.

Listing 12-9. Defining a Column-Specific Cell Renderer

```
t = JTable( ... )
t.getColumnModel().getColumn( col ).setCellRenderer( myRenderer() )
```

Don't JLabel Me

The custom renderer used in Listing 12-8 used an instance of the JLabel class. Can some other component class be used? Certainly! In fact, it appears to be quite reasonable to use something like the JFormattedTextField class that you first saw in Chapter 7.

Figure 12-6 shows some sample images of the first attempt to use a JFormattedTextField as the component returned for the custom renderer of the last column of the table. This column, which contains values of type Double, has exactly two digits after the decimal point. Notice how the editor displays the cell data.

---

[16]See http://docs.oracle.com/javase/8/docs/api/javax/swing/table/TableColumn.html.
[17]See http://docs.oracle.com/javase/8/docs/api/javax/swing/table/TableColumnModel.html.

Figure 12-6. *Table6a output with a custom renderer*

Unfortunately, it isn't quite right, is it? For example, when the first row is selected, the last cell isn't highlighted the same way that the rest of the row is. Additionally, the numeric values, although they are displayed with exactly two decimal places, are left aligned in the cell. Nor does the cell have a border when it is selected, as the other cells in the row do. Listing 12-10 shows the first attempt at a renderer, which uses a JFormattedTextField instance to display the values.

Listing 12-10. Table6a.py: First Attempt at Custom Renderer

```
18|class myRenderer( DefaultTableCellRenderer ) :
19|    def __init__( self ) :
20|        nf = NumberFormat.getInstance()
21|        nf.setMinimumFractionDigits( 2 )
22|        nf.setMaximumFractionDigits( 2 )
23|        self.result = JFormattedTextField( nf )
24|    def getTableCellRendererComponent(
25|        self,
26|        table,              # JTable  - table containing value
27|        value,              # Object  - value being rendered
28|        isSelected,         # boolean - Is value selected?
29|        hasFocus,           # boolean - Does this cell have focus?
30|        rowIndex,           # int     - Row # (0..N)
31|        vColIndex           # int     - Col # (0..N)
32|    ) :
33|        self.result.setValue( value )
```

```
34|          return self.result
  |...
74|          model = myTM( self.data, headings )
75|          table = JTable(
76|              model,
77|              selectionMode = ListSelectionModel.SINGLE_SELECTION
78|          )
79|          table.getColumnModel().getColumn(
80|              model.getColumnCount() - 1 # i.e., last column
81|          ).setCellRenderer(
82|              myRenderer()
83|          )
```

Let's start by fixing the alignment problem. A little investigation into the JFormattedTextField Javadoc[18] shows that it inherits the horizontal alignment property from the JTextField class.[19] This allows you to add a horizontalAlignment keyword argument to the JFormattedTextField constructor call. Listing 12-11 shows this minor modification.

Listing 12-11. Table6b.py with Horizontal Alignment

```
19|class myRenderer( DefaultTableCellRenderer ) :
20|    def __init__( self ) :
21|        nf = NumberFormat.getInstance()
22|        nf.setMinimumFractionDigits( 2 )
23|        nf.setMaximumFractionDigits( 2 )
24|        self.result = JFormattedTextField(
25|            nf,
26|            horizontalAlignment = JTextField.RIGHT
27|        )
```

What does this do to the application's output? Figure 12-7 shows how this change affects the cells' appearance. This does improve things a little bit, but additional challenges remain.

---

[18]See http://docs.oracle.com/javase/8/docs/api/javax/swing/JFormattedTextField.html.
[19]See http://docs.oracle.com/javase/8/docs/api/javax/swing/JTextField.html.

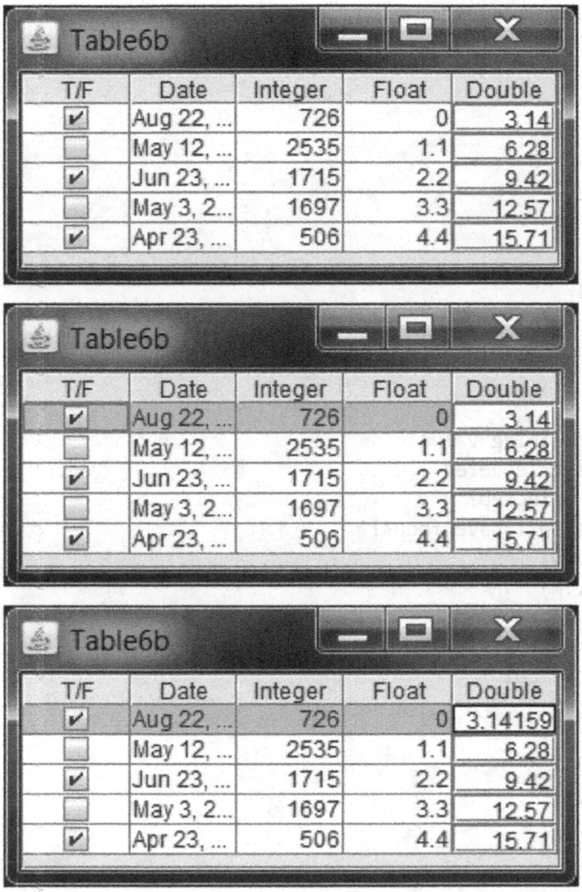

Figure 12-7. *FormattedTextField with horizontal alignment fix*

You can use the fact that the DefaultTableCellRenderer already does a lot of the work for you to resolve another issue. With a little bit of code, you should be able to take advantage of this fact. Listing 12-12 shows one way to use the DefaultTableCellRenderer class to solve some of the custom rendering issues.

Listing 12-12. Table6c.py: One Solution to the Custom Rendering Issues

```
19|class myRenderer( DefaultTableCellRenderer ) :
20|    def __init__( self ) :
21|        nf = NumberFormat.getInstance()
22|        nf.setMinimumFractionDigits( 2 )
23|        nf.setMaximumFractionDigits( 2 )
24|        self.result = JFormattedTextField(
25|            nf,
26|            border = None,
27|            horizontalAlignment = JTextField.RIGHT
28|        )
29|        self.DTCR = DefaultTableCellRenderer()
30|    def getTableCellRendererComponent(
31|        self,
32|        table,                 # JTable  - table containing value
33|        value,                 # Object  - value being rendered
34|        isSelected,            # boolean - Is value selected?
35|        hasFocus,              # boolean - Does this cell have focus?
36|        row,                   # int     - Row # (0..N)
37|        col                    # int     - Col # (0..N)
38|    ) :
39|        comp = self.DTCR.getTableCellRendererComponent(
40|            table, value, isSelected, hasFocus, row, col
41|        )
42|        result = self.result
43|        result.setForeground( comp.getForeground() )
44|        result.setBackground( comp.getBackground() )
45|        result.setBorder( comp.getBorder() )
46|        result.setValue( value )
47|        return result
```

What does this mean as far as this output is concerned? Well, as you can see in Figure 12-8 when a row is selected, all of the cells in the row have the same color scheme. The second image shows that when a cell in the last column is selected, a slightly darker border is visible. And finally, the last image shows that when an invalid value is specified, this fact is highlighted in a very obvious fashion. So it appears that using the default cell renderer is a viable solution for some of these display issues.

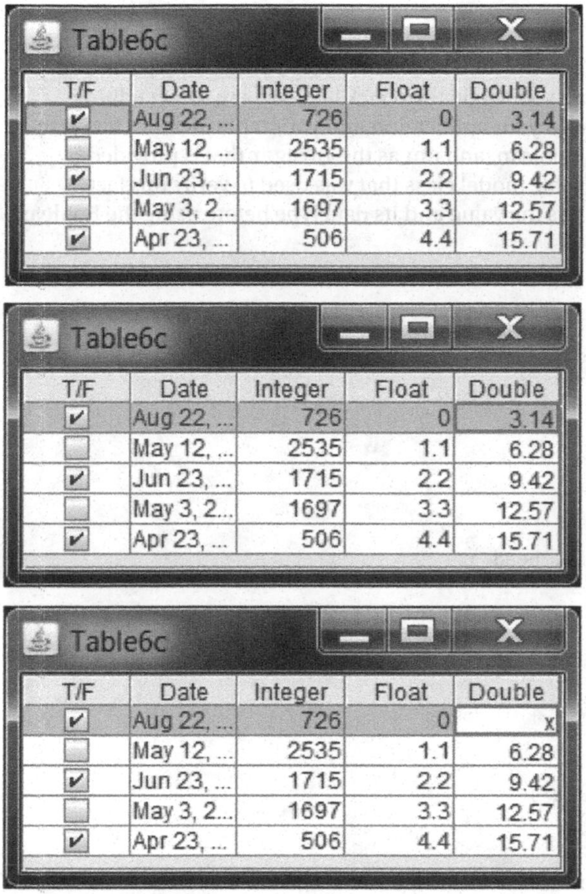

Figure 12-8. Table6c *output showing expected results*

Using Cell Editors

Another important part of displaying information in a tabular form is the fact that you'll often want to allow the user to modify the information. This is where a cell editor comes into play. For this purpose, the Swing hierarchy includes a CellEditor,[20] a TableCellEditor[21] interface, and a DefaultCellEditor[22] class. Which of these are important for providing your own cell editor? Well, the base CellEditor interface provides a group of methods that are rarely replaced or overridden. So, it is best if you just leave them alone.

On the other hand, the TableCellEditor interface provides a method called getTableCellEditorComponent(...) that enables developers to provide or specify an editor component with a table.

---

[20]See http://docs.oracle.com/javase/8/docs/api/javax/swing/CellEditor.html.
[21]See http://docs.oracle.com/javase/8/docs/api/javax/swing/table/TableCellEditor.html.
[22]See http://docs.oracle.com/javase/8/docs/api/javax/swing/DefaultCellEditor.html.

Boolean Cell Editors

You've already seen some of the simple, default, cell editors. Consider for a moment what you are doing when you have a table display Boolean values with a check box. Every time you toggle the check box, you are in fact editing the value in that cell. That's why, if you have a table model class in your application and your table includes Boolean values, the setValueAt(...) method must save the value as a Boolean, and not as the Integer that is provided by the setValueAt(...) method. Listing 12-13 shows the simple table model class that was used to verify this fact. Notice how the setValueAt(...) method, in lines 27-29, displays the value and its data type before using the Boolean constructor to save the appropriate kind of value.

Listing 12-13. BoolEdit.py Table Model Class

```
13|class tm( DefaultTableModel ) :
14|    def __init__( self ) :
15|        head = 'Name,Value'.split( ',' )
16|        self.data = [
17|            [ 'False', Boolean( 0 ) ],
18|            [ 'True' , Boolean( 1 ) ]
19|        ]
20|        DefaultTableModel.__init__( self, self.data, head )
21|    def getColumnClass( self, col ) :
22|        return [ String, Boolean ][ col ]
23|    def isCellEditable( self, row, col ) :
24|        return col == 1
25|    def getValueAt( self, row, col ) :
26|        return self.data[ row ][ col ]
27|    def setValueAt( self, value, row, col ) :
28|        print 'tm.setValueAt():', value, type( value )
29|        self.data[ row ][ col ] = Boolean( value )
```

Figure 12-9 shows a couple of images of the application, as well as the output that is generated by the setValueAt(...) method. Note how the value that is provided to the method is a Python integer. This is why you need to convert it to a Boolean before saving it in the data array instance.

```
Press <Enter> to terminate the application:
tm.setValueAt(): 1 org.python.core.PyInteger
tm.setValueAt(): 0 org.python.core.PyInteger
tm.setValueAt(): 1 org.python.core.PyInteger
```

Figure 12-9. BoolEdit sample output

Did you notice that you didn't even have to provide a custom or specialized editor for this example? In Table 12-3, you can see how Swing provides a renderer for Boolean types. Since the possible values are very limited, you don't need to worry about an editor for Boolean types.

Numeric Cell Editors

What about the numeric types? What do the default renderers and editors for these types provide? Figure 12-10 shows some images from the sample NumbEdit.py application that show the minimum values for each type in the top rows and the maximum values for each type in the bottom rows.

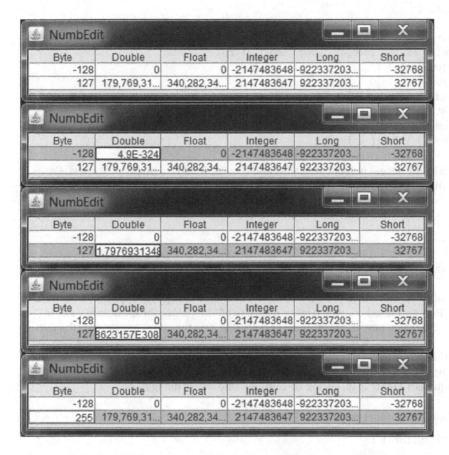

Figure 12-10. NumbEdit.py *output: default numeric renderers and editors*

At first glance, it may seem that the minimum Double and Float values should be something other than zero. The fact that they are non-zero, just very small, as is evident when the default editor for either value is used. The second image shows that the minimum Double value is 4.9E-324, which is very close to 0. So close, in fact, that the default renderer displays a value of zero instead. The third and fourth images show that the largest Double value has too many significant digits to be displayed in the available space (it has a value of 1.7976931348623157E308). so elipses are used to indicate that the values have been truncated.

The last image shows what happens when a user attempts to enter a value that is outside of the range of valid values. The default editor highlights the cell using a red border, and the user is unable to move the focus away from the cell.

One question that frequently comes to mind relates to the setValueAt(...) method that is called to save user-specified values of various types. Java examples frequently use a switch statement or nested if-then-else statements to deal with this type of thing. Jython, on the other hand, can make this kind of thing trivial, as shown in Listing 12-14.[23]

Listing 12-14. NumbEdit.py getValueAt(...) and setValueAt.(...) Methods

```
11|class tm( DefaultTableModel ) :
  |    ...
29|    def getColumnClass( self, col ) :
30|        return [ Byte, Double, Float, Integer, Long, Short ][ col ]
31|    def getValueAt( self, row, col ) :
32|        return self.data[ row ][ col ]
33|    def setValueAt( self, value, row, col ) :
34|        print 'tm.setValueAt():', value, type( value )
35|        Type = self.getColumnClass( col )
36|        self.data[ row ][ col ] = Type( value )
```

All of this capability is provided by the default numeric renderers and editors, which is actually pretty neat. Can you think of a situation where you might need to provide your own numeric editor? What about the situation where you want to allow a specific range of values? You might be able to use a numeric JSpinner as was discussed in Chapter 7, but let's start with something a little simpler. What does it take to provide a custom numeric editor that verifies the user input before it is accepted?

Custom Numeric Cell Editors

First, you need to decide the range of value with which you want to work. For example, say your application wants to work with a simple concept like TCP/IP port numbers, which range from 0 to 65535.[24] Since the maximum value is larger than Short.MAX_VALUE (i.e., 32767), you have to use an Integer type field, and the editor has to verify the user input before accepting it.

How, exactly, is the custom editor class supposed to check the user input? Well, first, you have to realize that the editor has to provide some sort of input field. If you base the custom editor on DefaultCellEditor,[22] you can use the fact that one of the constructors requires a JTextField. Listing 12-15 shows one way of doing this.

Listing 12-15. portEditor Class and Table Model from PortEdit.py

```
14|class portEditor( DefaultCellEditor ) :
15|    def __init__( self ) :
16|        self.textfield = JTextField(
17|            horizontalAlignment = JTextField.RIGHT
18|        )
19|        DefaultCellEditor.__init__( self, self.textfield )
20|    def stopCellEditing( self ) :
```

---

[23]Again, this script uses a temporary variable, Type, so the line isn't too long.
[24]Ignore the fact that a port number is in fact an *unsigned* short integer, which Java doesn't support.

```
21|        try :
22|            val = Integer.valueOf( self.textfield.getText() )
23|            if not ( -1 < val < 65536 ) :
24|                raise NumberFormatException()
25|            result = DefaultCellEditor.stopCellEditing( self )
26|        except :
27|            self.textfield.setBorder( LineBorder( Color.red ) )
28|            result = 0                # false
29|        return result
30|class tm( DefaultTableModel ) :
31|    def __init__( self ) :
32|        head = 'Name,Value'.split( ',' )
33|        self.data = [
34|            [ 'Min Port', Integer(   0   ) ],
35|            [ 'Max Port', Integer( 65535 ) ]
36|        ]
37|        DefaultTableModel.__init__( self, self.data, head )
38|    def isCellEditable( self, row, col ) :
39|        return col == 1
40|    def getColumnClass( self, col ) :
41|        return [ String, Integer ][ col ]
42|    def getValueAt( self, row, col ) :
43|        return self.data[ row ][ col ]
44|    def setValueAt( self, value, row, col ) :
45|        print 'tm.setValueAt():', value, type( value )
46|        self.data[ row ][ col ] = Integer( value )
  |...
55|        table = JTable( tm() )
56|        table.setDefaultEditor( Integer, portEditor() )
```

This example shows how easy it is (line 27) to duplicate the technique used by DefaultCellEditors (that is, highlight the cell with a red border). It's also good to note that since the custom cell editor is based on a JTextField, the value provided to the setValueAt(...) table model method (lines 44-47) is a string, not an integer as you might expect.

How hard do you think it would be to change the code so it would display the port number using a different format (for example, in hexadecimal, octal, or even using a comma for values larger than 999)? Think about this for a moment. One significant decision you need to make is how, exactly, you want to represent port values. If you want to display (render) them using hexadecimal characters, should they be maintained, verified, and edited as character strings, or do you need to work with integer values elsewhere in the application?

These are the kinds of things that you need to consider as an application developer. How should the values be displayed (rendered) for the users? How do you expect the users to provided new values (editor)? What do you need to do to verify user input? Just think of the fun you have ahead of you.

JComboBox Cell Editors

If you look at the constructors for the DefaultCellEditor class,[22] you see one that accepts a JCheckBox argument (which is likely to be the one used by the default Boolean cell editor), one that accepts a JTextField argument, like the one you just saw, and one that accepts a JComboBox argument. What does that look like? Figure 12-11 shows some sample application images for the cbEdit1.py script that use a combo box editor for the values in column 1.

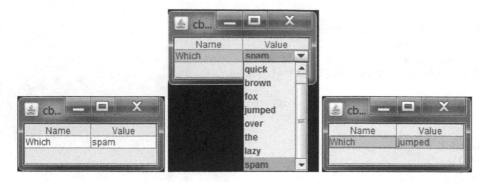

Figure 12-11. cbEdit1.py *output using a JComboBox editor*

It's interesting to note that you can't tell, from the initial display, that a combo box or drop-down list will be displayed, until you invoke the editor on the value displayed in column 1. Is there a way to show this? Certainly! All you have to do is set the cell renderer and the editor. Figure 12-12 shows some images from the cbEdit2.py application, which does this.

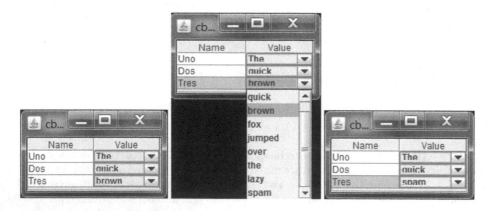

Figure 12-12. cbEdit2.py *output using a JComboBox editor and renderer*

A Slight Detour: Table Row Height

Figure 12-12 shows that the default might not always be optimal. So, how do you change the height of the table rows? When one of these kinds of questions arises, the first place that you should look is at the documentation for the class in question. In this case, the JTable[3] class. Search for "rowheight" and you'll find a (protected) rowHeight attribute, as well as some getter and setter methods.

The fact that the class includes multiple getter and setters, as shown in Table 12-4 illustrates that this class provides an opportunity to control the row height used by the rows in the table. In addition, each row can have a different height.

Table 12-4. `JTable rowHeight` *Getter and Setter Methods*

Getter/Setter Name	Description
`getRowHeight()`	Returns the `JTable rowHeight` (in pixels).
`getRowHeight( int row )`	Returns the `rowHeight` of the specified `JTable` row.
`setRowHeight( int rowHeight )`	Specifies the `rowHeight` to be used by all table rows, in pixels, and initiates a table revalidation and repainting.
`setRowHeight( int row,` `int rowHeight )`	Specifies the `rowHeight` to be used by the specified row and initiates a table revalidation and repaint.

The results of using the `rowHeight` keyword attribute on the `JTable` constructor call is shown in Figure 12-13. Remember that since the frame containing the `JTable` instance is contained in a scroll pane, simply changing the height of the rows isn't sufficient. You also need to increase the height of the frame if you don't want the scroll bar to be displayed.

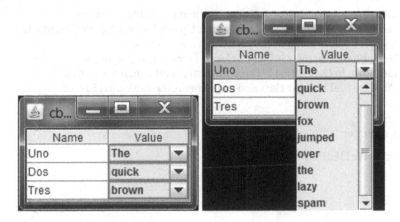

Figure 12-13. `cbEdit3.py` *output with slightly larger rows*

Interestingly enough, the second image shows that the height of the drop-down list (the `ComboBox`) isn't affected by the `JTable` row height. This shouldn't be too much of a surprise when you think about it. The row height that you changed was in the table, not in the `ComboBox`.

Listing 12-16 shows the slight modifications required to make the application easier to use. The only changes are found in lines 54, where the height of the frame is slightly larger (from 112 to 125 pixels). The other change can be seen in line 58, where you specify the `rowHeight` keyword argument used to assign the value of 20 (pixels) for each row.

Listing 12-16. The cbEdit3 Class's run Method

```
51|class cbEdit3( java.lang.Runnable ) :
52|    def run( self ) :
53|        frame = JFrame(
54|            'cbEdit3',
55|            size = ( 200, 125 ),
56|            locationRelativeTo = None,
57|            defaultCloseOperation = JFrame.EXIT_ON_CLOSE
58|        )
59|        table = JTable( tm(), rowHeight = 20 )
60|        table.setDefaultRenderer( JComboBox, cbRenderer() )
61|        table.setDefaultEditor( JComboBox, cbEditor() )
62|        frame.add( JScrollPane( table ) )
63|        frame.setVisible( 1 )
```

Warning: Ugliness Ahead

Up to this point, I have been completely avoiding the fact that the version of Jython that is provided with the WebSphere Application Server product is, in a word, ancient. I'm sorry, but it's true. Up until now, it hasn't caused any problems, at least nothing significant. Now, however, you're going to see where it makes a difference.

When I tried to implement a simple cell editor based on the JSpinner[25] class, I converted a simple Java application, an abbreviated version of which is shown in Listing 12-17. The point that I want to make with this example is the fact that the class extends the AbstractCellEditor class and implements the TableCellEditor interface, as you can see in lines 12 and 13.

Listing 12-17. SpinEditor.java JSpinner Cell Editor

```
12|public class SpinEditor extends AbstractCellEditor
13|    implements TableCellEditor
14|{
15|    JSpinner spinner;
16|    public SpinEditor()
17|    {
18|        String values[] = { "Spam", "Eggs", "Bacon" };
19|        spinner = new JSpinner( new SpinnerListModel( values ) );
20|        spinner.setEditor( new JSpinner.ListEditor( spinner ) );
21|    }
22|    public Component getTableCellEditorComponent(
23|        JTable table,
24|        Object value,
25|        boolean isSelected,
26|        int row,
27|        int column
28|    )
```

---

[25]SpinEditor.java is incompletely shown here; only enough is shown for discussion purposes.

```
29|    {
30|        spinner.setValue( value );
31|        return spinner;
32|    }
33|    public Object getCellEditorValue()
34|    {
35|        return spinner.getValue();
36|    }
37|    public static void main(String[] args)
38|    {
  |        ...
63|    }
64|}
```

Why use this approach? The main reason for doing so relates to the fact that the previous examples used the DefaultCellEditor constructors, as shown in Table 12-5. The Java example, shown in Listing 12-17, illustrates how you might go about creating a different kind of table cell editor, using a totally different component type.

Table 12-5. *DefaultCellEditor Constructor Signatures*

```
DefaultCellEditor( JCheckBox checkBox )

DefaultCellEditor( JComboBox comboBox )

DefaultCellEditor( JTextField textField )
```

What does this look like when you convert it to Jython? You are likely to get an editor class similar to Listing 12-18. Notice how easy the conversion from Java to Jython is. This might be of assistance to you in the future, should you want to convert a Java Swing application to Jython.

Listing 12-18. SpinEdit1.py Editor Class

```
14|class editor( AbstractCellEditor, TableCellEditor ) :
15|    def __init__( self ) :
16|        values = 'Bacon,Eggs,Spam'.split( ',' )
17|        self.spinner = JSpinner( SpinnerListModel( values ) )
18|        self.spinner.setEditor(
19|            JSpinner.ListEditor( self.spinner )
20|        )
21|    def getCellEditorValue( self ) :
22|        return self.spinner.getValue()
23|    def getTableCellEditorComponent(
24|        self,                       # object reference
25|        table,                      # JTable
26|        value,                      # Object
27|        isSelected,                 # boolean
28|        row,                        # int
29|        column                      # int
30|    ) :
31|        self.spinner.setValue( value );
32|        return self.spinner;
```

179

Unfortunately, if you were to execute this script using the wsadmin utility from a WebSphere Application Server installation and click one of the values in the right-most column, you would see an exception like the one shown in Figure 12-14.

```
Press <Enter> to terminate the application:Exception in thread
  "AWT-EventQueue-0" Traceback (innermost last):
  (no code object) at line 0
AttributeError: abstract method "isCellEditable" not implemented
```

Figure 12-14. *The* wsadmin *exception about the* isCellEditable *method*

The really strange thing is that when I tried to use this same script with the latest stable build of Jython (Jython 2.5.3), it worked just fine. But how do you get it to work with the version of Jython provided by the WebSphere product?

Instead of inheriting from AbstractCellEditor and TableCellEditor, as shown in Listing 12-17, you can base the editor class on the DefaultCellEditor class, as shown in Listing 12-19.

Listing 12-19. SpinEdit2.py Editor Class Based on DefaultCellEditor

```
13|class editor( DefaultCellEditor ) :
14|    def __init__( self ) :
15|        DefaultCellEditor.__init__( self, JTextField() )
16|        values = 'Bacon,Eggs,Spam'.split( ',' )
17|        self.spinner = JSpinner( SpinnerListModel( values ) )
18|        self.spinner.setEditor(
19|            JSpinner.ListEditor( self.spinner )
20|        )
21|    def getCellEditorValue( self ) :
22|        return self.spinner.getValue()
23|    def getTableCellEditorComponent(
24|        self,                      # object reference
25|        table,                     # JTable
26|        value,                     # Object
27|        isSelected,                # boolean
28|        row,                       # int
29|        column                     # int
30|    ) :
31|        self.spinner.setValue( value );
32|        return self.spinner;
```

This script works using the wsadmin utility and Jython 2.5.3. Since this book is primarily intended for WebSphere script writers, subsequent scripts will be based on the DefaultCellEditor class, and not on the AbstractCellEditor class and the TableCellEditor interface. Nonetheless, it was worth noting, so you don't waste the same kind of time that I did when I first encountered this issue.

Figure 12-15 shows some images from this application. The first two use an application frame height of 106 pixels, with each table row using 20 pixels. The next two images show what happens when each row uses 25 pixels and the frame height is set to 116 pixels.

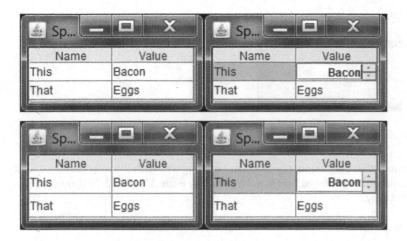

Figure 12-15. *SpinEdit2.py output images*

The interesting note about these images is that when you use a uniform row height for each table row to better display the cell editor representation, the table representation might look quite right. This is due to the fact that you chose to display the cell values using a text, or string renderer, instead of a spinner renderer. If you use a custom renderer instead, you'll see that each cell in this column uses the spinner icons, as shown in Figure 12-16.

Figure 12-16. *SpinEdit3.py output images using a JSpinner renderer*

Did you notice how the cell being edited in the second image shows the text of the spinner selection in bold? It's little things like this that make your application more user friendly. That's one of the best reasons for using a robust and well-designed framework like Swing to build your applications.

Are there other improvements that you should make? Take another look at the application. In fact, let's make this more obvious by comparing the outputs of SpinEdit2 and SpinEdit3, side by side, when the first row in the table is selected. See Figure 12-17.

Figure 12-17. SpinEdit2 and SpinEdit3 renderer differences

Seeing them like this makes it more obvious that the custom renderer isn't dealing well with the cell colors. This shouldn't be too difficult to fix, right? Listing 12-12 showed how to solve a similar issue. Listing 12-20 shows the revision of the sRenderer class from SpinEdit4.py.

Listing 12-20. SpinEdit4.py sRenderer Class

```
34|class sRenderer( DefaultTableCellRenderer ) :
35|    def __init__( self ) :
36|        self.DTCR    = DefaultTableCellRenderer()
37|        self.spinner = JSpinner( SpinnerListModel( choices ) )
38|    def getTableCellRendererComponent(
39|        self,
40|        table,              # table containing cell being rendered
41|        value,              # Object  - value being rendered
42|        isSelected,         # boolean - Is value selected?
43|        hasFocus,           # boolean - Does this cell have focus?
44|        row,                # int     - Row # (0..N)
45|        col                 # int     - Col # (0..N)
46|    ) :
47|        comp = self.DTCR.getTableCellRendererComponent(
48|            table, value, isSelected, hasFocus, row, col
49|        )
50|        result = self.spinner
51|        result.setForeground( comp.getForeground() )
52|        result.setBackground( comp.getBackground() )
53|        result.setValue( value )
54|        return result
```

Unfortunately, this doesn't resolve the problem because the JSpinner class has its own model-specific editor. In order to "fix" this—that is, to have the spinner renderer reflect the appropriate colors—you need to change the text editor field that the spinner is using.

Listing 12-21 shows the revised spinner renderer class from the SpinEdit5.py sample application. Figure 12-18 shows what this does to the application's output.

Listing 12-21. SpinEdit5.py with Fixed sRenderer Class

```
34|class sRenderer( DefaultTableCellRenderer ) :
35|    def __init__( self ) :
36|        self.DTCR    = DefaultTableCellRenderer()
37|        self.spinner = JSpinner( SpinnerListModel( choices ) )
38|    def getTableCellRendererComponent(
39|        self,
```

```
40|        table,              # table containing cell being rendered
41|        value,              # Object  - value being rendered
42|        isSelected,         # boolean - Is value selected?
43|        hasFocus,           # boolean - Does this cell have focus?
44|        row,                # int     - Row # (0..N)
45|        col                 # int     - Col # (0..N)
46|    ) :
47|        comp = self.DTCR.getTableCellRendererComponent(
48|            table, value, isSelected, hasFocus, row, col
49|        )
50|        tf = self.spinner.getEditor().getTextField()
51|        tf.setForeground( comp.getForeground() )
52|        tf.setBackground( comp.getBackground() )
53|        self.spinner.setValue( value )
54|        return self.spinner
```

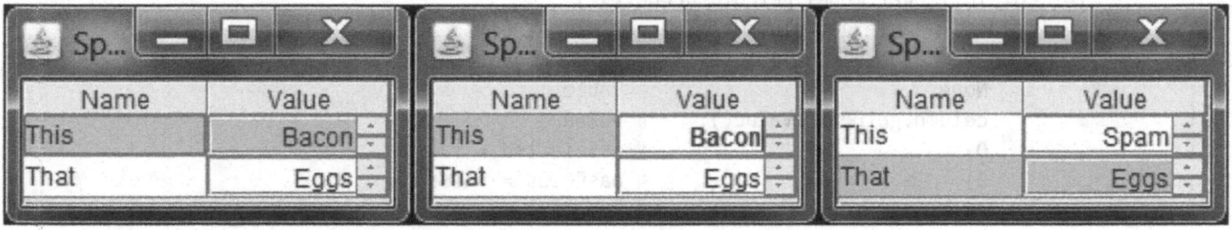

Figure 12-18. SpinEdit5 output

Column Manipulation

Up to this point, you haven't learned much about column adjustments and manipulations. Back in Figure 12-1, you saw how the default table settings allow users to reorder the columns. Listing 12-3 shows how this feature can be disabled. Now, you're going to take a look at ways that you can manipulate your table columns.

Column Widths

In the section entitled, "Defaults Can Be Harmful to Your . . . Mental Health," you learned that, by default, the available horizontal space will be shared equally among each of the columns. If that is not the best appearance for your application, you need to take control of the way the column space is allocated. The first thing to realize is that your table might not have column headings. If it does, the information in these headings might not affect the way that column space is, or should be, allocated. For example, if the information in your column headings is always wider than the table data, this can greatly simplify the way that column space should be allocated. On the other hand, if the data is sometimes wider than your column headings, you need to take this into account when your application determines how wide each column should be.

Column Heading Width

In order to determine the amount of space (the width) that should be used to comfortably display your headings, the program needs to make use of the renderer used by the table header. The fact that the table header has its own renderer shouldn't be too much of a surprise to you. Remember that the header will almost always contain strings, whereas the table data will have various types of data in each column. Besides, you previously learned about the JTableHeader class,[10] when you learned how to disable the reordering of columns.

Now, you're going to use this class to obtain the renderer used to display the table header. Let's revisit the application, last seen in Table6c.py, and revise it to adjust the width of the columns using the width of the column headings.

Listing 12-22 shows the code used to do this. You may be surprised by the row number of -1, in line 105. The Javadoc for the TableCellRenderer interface[15] includes a comment in the section on the getTableCellRendererComponent(...) method that states, "When drawing the header, the value of row is -1."

Listing 12-22. Table7.py: Specifying the Column Width Using Header Information Only

```
 97|        hRenderer = table.getTableHeader().getDefaultRenderer()
 98|        for col in range( model.getColumnCount() ) :
 99|            column = table.getColumnModel().getColumn( col )
100|            comp = hRenderer.getTableCellRendererComponent(
101|                None,                       # Table
102|                column.getHeaderValue(),    # value
103|                0,                          # isSelected = false
104|                0,                          # hasFocus = false
105|                -1,                         # row #
106|                col                         # col #
107|            )
108|            width = comp.getPreferredSize().width
109|            column.setPreferredWidth( width )
```

This attempt fails because the preferred size is only a suggestion, not an absolute and firm limitation or restriction.[26] If you want to do this, you have to set the minimum and maximum column widths. Be careful though. In some classes the method and attribute names have minimum and maximum spelled out entirely. The TableColumn class,[16] on the other hand, has setMinWidth(...), and setMaxWidth(...) methods instead. So, by replacing line 109 in Listing 12-20 with two statements, one to set the minimum column width and one to set the maximum column width, you get the output in Figure 12-19, which was generated using the Table8.py script.

---

[26]And thirdly, the code is more what you'd call "guidelines" than actual rules.

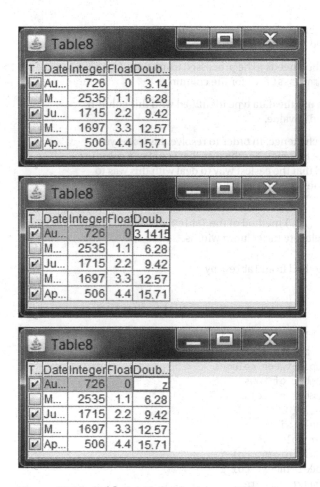

Figure 12-19. *Table8 with fixed column widths*

Determining Column Width

Well, that's a big failure. You certainly don't want to fix the column widths solely on the widths of the column headers, at least not for this kind of column headings that this application is using. Instead, you can process the data in the table, one column at a time, and compute the maximum preferred width for each value in the column. Then, you set the preferred width for the column using the maximum of the preferred header width and the maximum preferred width of all of the values in this column.

That doesn't sound too terribly bad. Are there any problems with this? Yes, unfortunately, there are. While working on a general function for this purpose, I encountered the following issues:

- The data returned by the getValueAt(...) method needs to be processed using the appropriate data type (the result of the getColumnClass(...) for the column).

  This wasn't too difficult to resolve since you can use the data type identified with this column to provide the renderer with the appropriate kind of value.

- Dealing with Date values can be somewhat of a challenge. In order to resolve this issue, you have to use the appropriate DateFormat instance that matches the way that your Date columns are displayed in the table. In this case, it seemed that the easiest way to deal with this was to use a DefaultRenderer and have it determine the preferred width of the string representation of the formatted date strings.

Listing 12-23 shows excerpts from the setColumnWidths(...) method of the Table9.py sample application. You might want to use something like this to determine how to allocate the column widths.

Listing 12-23. Excerpts from the setColumnWidths(...) Method from Table9.py

```
21|def setColumnWidths( table ) :
22|    header = table.getTableHeader()
  |    ...
27|    tcm    = table.getColumnModel()          # Table Column Model
28|    data   = table.getModel()                # To access table data
29|    margin = tcm.getColumnMargin()           # gap between columns
30|    rows = data.getRowCount()                # Number of rows
31|    cols = tcm.getColumnCount()              # Number of cols
32|    df     = DateFormat.getDateInstance( DateFormat.MEDIUM )
33|    tWidth = 0                               # Table width
34|    for i in range( cols ) :                 # For col 0..N
35|        col = tcm.getColumn( i )             # TableColumn: col i
36|        idx = col.getModelIndex()            # model index: col i
37|        render = col.getHeaderRenderer()     # header renderer,
38|        if not render :                      #
39|            render = hRenderer               #   or a default
40|        if render :
41|            comp = render.getTableCellRendererComponent(
  |                ...
48|            )
49|            cWidth = comp.getPreferredSize().width
50|        else :
51|            cWidth = -1
52|        Type = data.getColumnClass( i )          # dataType: col i
53|        for row in range( rows ) :
54|            v = data.getValueAt( row, idx )      # value
55|            if Type == Date :
56|                val = df.format( v )             # formatted date
57|                r = table.getDefaultRenderer( String )
```

```
58|            else :
59|                val = Type( v )
60|                r = table.getCellRenderer( row, i )
61|            comp = r.getTableCellRendererComponent(
  |                ...
68|            )
69|            cWidth = max( cWidth, comp.getPreferredSize().width )
70|        if cWidth > 0 :
71|            col.setPreferredWidth( cWidth + margin )
72|        tWidth += col.getPreferredWidth()
73|    table.setPreferredScrollableViewportSize(
  |        ...
78|    )
```

I think that you'll agree that the column widths shown in Figure 12-20 are a great improvement over the ones in Figure 12-19.

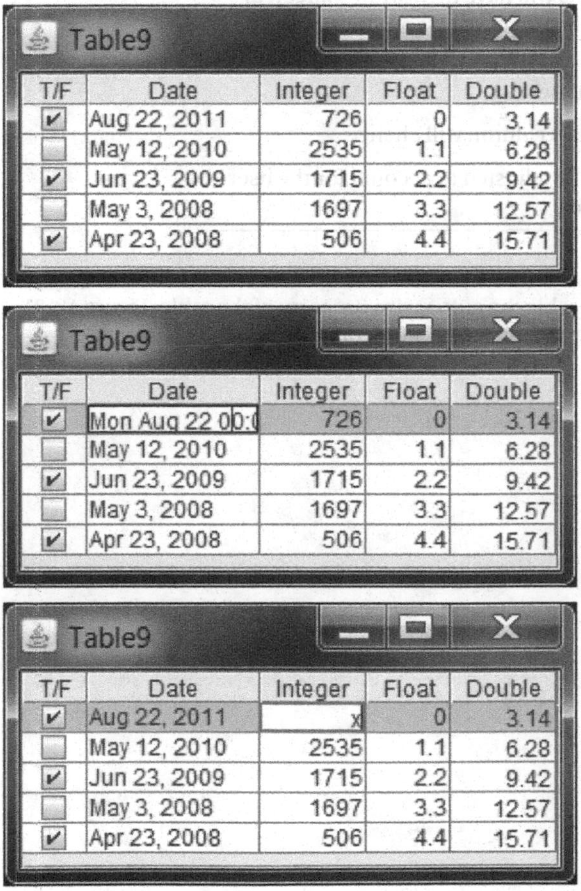

Figure 12-20. `Table9` *with compute column widths*

Column Adjustments

If you have played with any of the table samples, you may have wondered why the columns react in the way that they do when you change the column widths. (Drag the vertical bar separating two column headers to the left or to the right to change the widths.)

Did you notice how all of the subsequent columns are adjusted to maintain the table width? Why is this? Well, the JTable class includes a property called AutoResizeMode that the table uses to determine changes to the other columns' widths. Table 12-6 shows the constants used to modify this JTable property.

Table 12-6. JTable *Auto Resize Constants*

JTable Auto Resize Constant	Description
AUTO_RESIZE_OFF	Columns will not be adjusted automatically.
AUTO_RESIZE_NEXT_COLUMN	Only the next column width will be affected by column width changes.
AUTO_RESIZE_SUBSEQUENT_COLUMNS	All subsequent columns will have their widths affected, in order to distribute the effects across any subsequent columns.
	Note: This is the default setting.
AUTO_RESIZE_LAST_COLUMN	Only the width of the last column will change.
AUTO_RESIZE_ALL_COLUMNS	All table columns will be adjusted to account for the user-specified width changes.

Let's see what this means in a real application. To start, disable the auto resize property of the table. Figure 12-21 shows the application when the AUTO_RESIZE_OFF and setColumnWidths(...) functions are used, as shown in Listing 12-21.

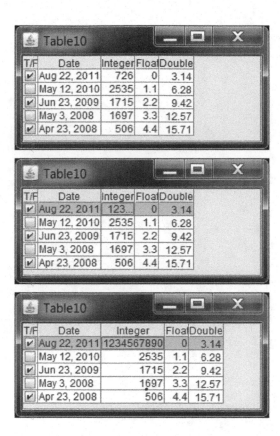

Figure 12-21. `Table10.py`: *computing column widths with auto resize off*

What would it take to have a simple table application that allowed you to dynamically change the auto resize mode, and then see how each setting affects the application? Figure 12-22 shows the results.

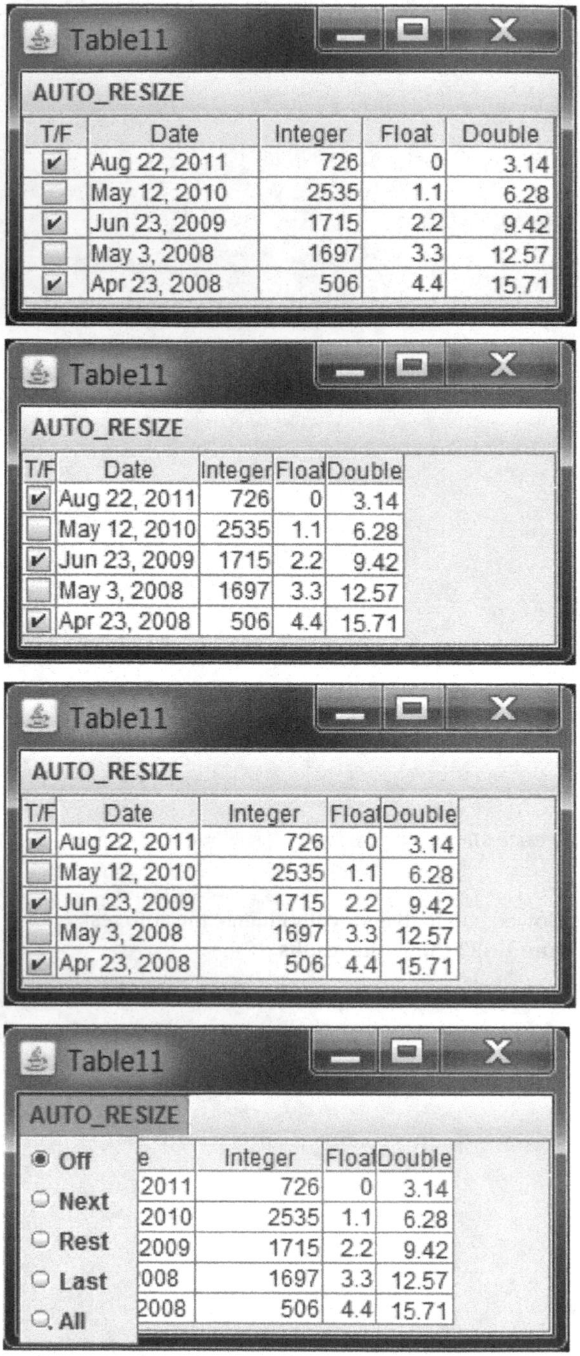

Figure 12-22. `Table11.py`: *dynamically selecting auto resize mode*

You can see that the application has a menu that allows you to select a different auto resize setting. Listing 12-24 shows parts of the Table11.py script that were used to produce the output in Figure 12-22. All of the radio button menu items identify the handler method as the action listener event handler. All this routine has to do is match the text of the user selection to the corresponding JTable auto resize constant and use this to change the auto resize mode on the table.

Listing 12-24. Selected Parts of Table11.py

```
130|class Table11( java.lang.Runnable ) :
   |     ...
144|        self.info = [
145|            [ 'Off' , JTable.AUTO_RESIZE_OFF                ],
146|            [ 'Next', JTable.AUTO_RESIZE_NEXT_COLUMN        ],
147|            [ 'Rest', JTable.AUTO_RESIZE_SUBSEQUENT_COLUMNS ],
148|            [ 'Last', JTable.AUTO_RESIZE_LAST_COLUMN        ],
149|            [ 'All' , JTable.AUTO_RESIZE_ALL_COLUMNS        ]
150|        ]
   |     ...
185|    def handler( self, event ) :
186|        cmd = event.getActionCommand()
187|        for name, value in self.info :
188|            if cmd == name :
189|                self.table.setAutoResizeMode( value )
190|                self.table.repaint()
```

This kind of script is easy to produce, and it provides you with a simple test environment to better understand the implications of a table's property. In this case, you're looking at the auto resize property.

Summary

This chapter has illustrated some of the power and flexibility of the JTable class. It is important to remember that with great power there must also come great responsibility. This is just a reminder that you can quickly create a table in your application. However, if you do so, it is quite likely that the default settings are going to need some testing, manipulation, and tweaking in order to fit your exact needs. As this chapter has shown, iterating your script with various enhancements isn't that difficult. You are encouraged to use this technique to help improve your knowledge of tables and their characteristics.

CHAPTER 13

Keystrokes, Actions, and Bindings, Oh My!

There are a number of ways that graphical applications obtain user input. This chapter focuses on how applications deal with user input from the keyboard. This is all about what happens when the user presses a key, and how applications perceive and react to this kind of event.

Getting in a Bind: Looking at Bindings

In the section entitled "Menu Mnemonics and Accelerators" in Chapter 10, you learned how convenient it is to associate a particular keystroke[1] with an `ActionListener`[2] for menu items. This association is called a *binding*. Doing this allowed you to simplify the process of causing some menu-related action to occur. Thus, you were able to initiate the associated menu action using the specified keystroke.

In this chapter, you learn how other parts of your applications can be set up to react to specific keystrokes. You will also learn how to enhance the friendliness of your applications with these kinds of bindings.

What Is Meant by Binding?

Menu entries aren't the only place in Swing where you can build an association between a keystroke and an action. In fact, creating this kind of association is called *binding*. A keystroke is bound to an action. One point you have to realize is that key bindings relate to a specific context. This has the potential of causing the users some confusion. For example, say you use a keystroke in a particular way for one context and in a different way in a different context. This might confuse or frustrate your users, so consider the consequences of such bindings carefully.

InputMaps and ActionMaps

How are bindings created? To begin, it is important to realize that the abstract `JComponent` class[3] includes `actionMap` and `inputMap` attributes, as you can see in Listing 13-1.[4]

---

[1] See http://docs.oracle.com/javase/8/docs/api/javax/swing/KeyStroke.html.
[2] See http://docs.oracle.com/javase/8/docs/api/java/awt/event/ActionListener.html.
[3] See http://docs.oracle.com/javase/8/docs/api/javax/swing/JComponent.html.
[4] The `classInfo` function can be found in `code\Chap_04\classInfo.py`.

Listing 13-1. JComponent Map Attributes

```
wsadmin>from javax.swing import JComponent
wsadmin>
wsadmin>classInfo( JComponent, attr = 'map' )
javax.swing.JComponent
  actionMap, inputMap
| java.awt.Container
| | java.awt.Component
| | | java.lang.Object
| | | java.awt.image.ImageObserver
| | | java.awt.MenuContainer
| | | java.io.Serializable
| java.io.Serializable
wsadmin>
```

Let's take a look at a specific class that descends from JComponent; for example, the JTable class.[5] If you use the classInfo function to display the methods that have the word "map" somewhere in their names, you get the output in Listing 13-2. This makes sense, since it shows that you have getter and setter methods for the inputMap and actionMap attributes. It is important to note, however, that the output of this function can be incomplete.

Listing 13-2. JTable Map Methods

```
wsadmin>from javax.swing import JTable
wsadmin>
wsadmin>classInfo( JTable, meth = 'map' )
javax.swing.JTable
| javax.swing.JComponent
>   getActionMap, getInputMap, setActionMap, setInputMap
| | java.awt.Container
| | | java.awt.Component
| | | | java.lang.Object
| | | | java.awt.image.ImageObserver
| | | | java.awt.MenuContainer
| | | | java.io.Serializable
| | java.io.Serializable
| javax.swing.event.TableModelListener
| | java.util.EventListener
| javax.swing.Scrollable
| javax.swing.event.TableColumnModelListener
| | java.util.EventListener
| javax.swing.event.ListSelectionListener
| | java.util.EventListener
| javax.swing.event.CellEditorListener
| | java.util.EventListener
| javax.accessibility.Accessible
| javax.swing.event.RowSorterListener
| | java.util.EventListener
wsadmin>
```

---

[5]See http://docs.oracle.com/javase/8/docs/api/javax/swing/JTable.html.

If you look at the JTable Javadoc,[5] you'll find the inputMap and actionMap getters and setters listed in Table 13-1. The interesting point is that there are two inputMap getters, one without an argument and the other with. What's that all about?

Table 13-1. JTable inputMap *and* actionMap *Getters and Setters*

Method return type and signature	Description
InputMap getInputMap()	Returns the inputMap that is used when the component has focus.
InputMap getInputMap(int condition)	Returns the inputMap that is used during condition.
void setInputMap(int condition, InputMap map)	Sets the inputMap to use with the condition to map.
ActionMap getActionMap()	Returns the actionMap used to determine what action to fire for a particular KeyStroke binding.
void setActionMap(ActionMap am)	Sets the actionMap to am.

The condition argument used by the second getter identifies which of three possible inputMaps should be returned to the caller. The constants that should be used are found in the JComponent class and are shown in Table 13-2.

Table 13-2. JComponent *Condition (Binding-Related) Constants*

Constant Name	Binding Context
WHEN_FOCUSED	Binding applies when the component has the focus.
WHEN_ANCESTOR_OF_FOCUSED_COMPONENT	Binding applies when the receiving component is an ancestor of the focused component or is itself the focused component.
WHEN_IN_FOCUSED_WINDOW	Binding applies when the receiving component is in the window that has the focus or is itself the focused component.

So, it looks like you can use one of these JComponent constants as the condition argument to the getInputMap() method in order to retrieve the KeyStroke InputMap. But which constant is the right one to use?

You have a few options available. You could use all three and see which one results in inputMaps that contain information. Or you could take a look at the JComponent Javadoc[3] and read about the interesting and potentially useful methods that exist. Which ones, you might wonder? Well, the ones listed in Table 13-3 caught my attention (and aren't marked as obsolete).

Table 13-3. *JComponent Keystrokes and Actions Methods*

Method return type and signature	Description
KeyStroke[] getRegisteredKeyStrokes()	Returns the keystrokes that will initiate registered actions.
int getConditionForKeyStroke(KeyStroke aKeyStroke)	Returns the condition that determines whether a registered action occurs in response to the specified keystroke.
ActionListener getActionForKeyStroke(KeyStroke aKeyStroke)	Returns the object that will perform the action registered for a given keystroke.

Okay, I admit it. I didn't know to look into the JComponent class for these methods until I used the classInfo function and it showed the KeyStroke methods. Listing 13-3 shows the result of doing this.

Listing 13-3. Keystroke Methods in JTable Hierarchy

```
wsadmin>from javax.swing import JTable
wsadmin>
wsadmin>classInfo( JTable, meth = 'keystroke' )
javax.swing.JTable
  getSurrendersFocusOnKeystroke, setSurrendersFocusOnKeystroke
| javax.swing.JComponent
>   getActionForKeyStroke, getConditionForKeyStroke
>   getRegisteredKeyStrokes
| | java.awt.Container
| | | java.awt.Component
| | | | java.lang.Object
| | | | java.awt.image.ImageObserver
| | | | java.awt.MenuContainer
| | | | java.io.Serializable
| | java.io.Serializable
| javax.swing.event.TableModelListener
| | java.util.EventListener
| javax.swing.Scrollable
| javax.swing.event.TableColumnModelListener
| | java.util.EventListener
| javax.swing.event.ListSelectionListener
| | java.util.EventListener
| javax.swing.event.CellEditorListener
| | java.util.EventListener
| javax.accessibility.Accessible
| javax.swing.event.RowSorterListener
| | java.util.EventListener
wsadmin>
```

JTable Keystrokes

Let's take advantage of these methods to see how many keystroke bindings exist for the JTable class. Listing 13-4 shows a simple script that can be used to determine how many of these bindings exist, as well as determine the ones associated specifically with the spacebar.

Listing 13-4. The Keystrokes.py Script

```
 1|from javax.swing import JTable
 2|table = JTable()
 3|keys  = [
 4|             str( key )
 5|             for key in table.getRegisteredKeyStrokes()
 6|        ]
 7|print 'Number of JTable KeyStrokes:', len( keys )
 8|width = max( [ len( key ) for key in keys ] )
 9|print 'JTable "Space" Keys:'
10|print '\n'.join(
11|                [
12|                    '%*s' % ( width, key )
13|                    for key in keys if key.endswith( 'SPACE' )
14|                ]
15|            )
```

The output of this script is shown in Figure 13-1. It contains a few interesting things to consider. First, notice that there are almost six dozen keystroke bindings for JTable instances. This should explain why the rest of the output is limited to instances of bindings for the spacebar key. The other point of interest is the way that the keystroke modifiers are presented.

```
Number of JTable KeyStrokes: 71
JTable "Space" Keys:
            pressed SPACE
        ctrl pressed SPACE
       shift pressed SPACE
    shift ctrlpressed SPACE
```

Figure 13-1. Keystrokes.py output

Additional tests of the keystroke modifiers show that each of the keystrokes has the four possible modifiers seen in Figure 13-1. This made me wonder how hard it might be to get the names of the actions for these keystrokes.

Listing 13-5 shows the KeyStrokes2.py script, which was written to answer these questions.

197

Listing 13-5. KeyStrokes2.py Showing Bound Actions

```
1|from javax.swing import JTable
2|table = JTable()
3|keys  = [
4|          key
5|              for key in table.getRegisteredKeyStrokes()
6|      ]
7|print 'Number of JTable KeyStrokes:', len( keys )
8|width = max( [ len( str( key ) ) for key in keys ] )
9|print 'JTable "Space" Keys:'
10|for key in keys :
11|    if str( key ).endswith( 'SPACE' ) :
12|        cond = table.getConditionForKeyStroke( key )
13|        act  = table.getInputMap( cond ).get( key )
14|        print '%*s : %s' % ( width, str( key ), act )
```

The resulting output is shown in Figure 13-2. I don't know about you, but I find this really fascinating.

```
Number of JTable KeyStrokes: 71
JTable "Space" Keys:
            pressed SPACE : addToSelection
       ctrl pressed SPACE : toggleAndAnchor
      shift pressed SPACE : extendTo
 shift ctrl pressed SPACE : moveSelectionTo
```

Figure 13-2. Keystrokes2.py output

Putting It All Together

What would it take to create a simple application that displays a table of information showing the keystroke bindings for the JTable class? You can use a number of things that you've learned up to this point to do just that.

locationRelativeTo = None

While creating this application, you can also get a better understanding of something that you have been taking for granted up to now. Back in Chapter 11, you started seeing some examples that used the locationRelativeTo keyword argument to position the JFrame instance "in the middle of the screen." So what exactly does that mean, and why am I bringing it up here?

Until this application, you didn't really have much of a reason to dig into it. This application changed that because it became more obvious what setting the locationRelativeTo attribute to None actually does. Essentially, using this setting causes the top-left corner of your application to be placed in the center of the screen. When your application isn't too big for the screen, this is a very easy and convenient way to position the application window near the center of the screen.

Centering the Application

If you want to center the application's window in the middle of the screen, the application must be able to determine or compute the following:

- The size of the screen

- The size of the application (frame)

Then you have compute the best location for the top-left corner for the application using some simple math; so far, so good. The question is, what's the best way to determine the size of the screen? There's a simple answer to that question because that's something that GUI application developers have needed to know for a long time. Figure 13-3 shows just how easily this can be done.

```
wsadmin>from java.awt import Toolkit
wsadmin>
wsadmin>Toolkit.getDefaultToolkit().getScreenSize()
java.awt.Dimension[width=1920,height=1080]
wsadmin>
```

Figure 13-3. *Determining screen size*

Unfortunately, you might not actually need to use this technique. Consider for a moment what using the locationRelativeTo keyword argument does. It places the application in the center of the screen. To correctly position the application, you only need to reposition it using the size of the application (which you can obtain using the JFrame getSize() method) and the center of the screen (which you can obtain using the JFrame getLocation() method). Listing 13-6 is an excerpt from the KeyBindings.py script; it shows one way that this can be done.

Listing 13-6. Centering an Application

```
134|        size = frame.getSize()
135|        loc  = frame.getLocation()
136|        frame.setLocation(
137|            Point(
138|                loc.x - ( size.width  >> 1 ),
139|                loc.y - ( size.height >> 1 )
140|            )
141|        )
```

The code expects that the JFrame instance is in the variable named frame, and that it has been properly populated and sized before the statement in line 134 is executed. It is important to realize what kinds of values are returned by the method calls in lines 134 and 135. The size value is an instance of the java.awt.Dimension class[6] (just like you saw in Figure 13-3). This makes perfect sense since the application has a width and height. On the other hand, the call to the getLocation() method returns an instance of the java.awt.Point class,[7] because only the X and Y coordinates are needed to identify a point on the screen.

The call to the setLocation(...) method should be fairly clear, once you realize that the positioning adjustment requires that you move the X coordinate by half the width of the application and move the Y coordinate by half the height of the application. This is exactly what the expressions on lines 138 and 139 are doing.

[6]See http://docs.oracle.com/javase/8/docs/api/java/awt/Dimension.html.
[7]See http://docs.oracle.com/javase/8/docs/api/java/awt/Point.html.

Defining the Table Properties

With a little thought, you'll likely realize that this table will be composed of strings and you need to prevent the users from being able to modify the table's contents. You can define a trivial table model containing only the getColumnClass(...) and isCellEditable(...) methods. Listing 13-7 shows just how simple this class can be.

Listing 13-7. Trivial Custom Table Model Class

```
75|class myTM( DefaultTableModel ) :
76|    def getColumnClass( self, col ) :
77|        return String
78|    def isCellEditable( self, row, col ) :
79|        return 0
```

Computing the Table Data

Most of the work needed to create this application has already been completed. The biggest challenge is using the stuff that you learned about earlier—using KeyStrokes.py and KeyStrokes2.py to build the two-dimensional array of strings. The first column should hold the keystroke name and then each of the columns can hold the action name for the corresponding keystroke-modifier column. Listing 13-8 shows the data(...) method, which builds and returns this table for the application.

Listing 13-8. KeyBindings.py Method to Build Table Data

```
80|class KeyBindings( java.lang.Runnable ) :
81|    def data( self ) :
82|        table = JTable()      # use an empty (default) table
83|        iMap  = table.getInputMap(
84|            JComponent.WHEN_ANCESTOR_OF_FOCUSED_COMPONENT
85|        )
86|        keystrokes = [
87|            ( key, iMap.get( key ) )
88|            for key in table.getRegisteredKeyStrokes()
89|        ]
90|        keys = {}       # Dict, index = key name  -> modifiers
91|        acts = {}       # Dict, index = keyStroke -> actionName
92|        for key, act in keystrokes :
93|            val = str( key )       # e.g., shift ctrl pressed TAB
94|            acts[ val ] = act      # e.g., selectNextColumnCell
95|            pos = val.rfind( ' ' )
96|            prefix, name = val[ :pos ], val[ pos + 1: ]
97|            if keys.has_key( name ) :
98|                keys[ name ].append( prefix )
99|            else :
100|                keys[ name ] = [ prefix ]
101|        names = keys.keys()
102|        names.sort()
103|        prefixes = [
104|            'pressed',           # unmodified keystroke
105|            'ctrl pressed',      # Ctrl-<keystroke>
```

```
106|              'shift pressed',      # Shift-<keystroke>
107|              'shift ctrl pressed'  # Shift-Ctrl-<keystroke>
108|          ]
109|          result = []               # The 2D table of strings
110|          for name in names :       # For each key name (e.g., TAB)
111|              here = [ name ]       # Current table row
112|              for prefix in prefixes :
113|                  kName = ' '.join( [ prefix, name ] )
114|                  here.append( acts.get( kName, '' ) )
115|              result.append( here )
116|          return result
```

Table 13-4 explains how this method produces the desired result. It may help you to realize that the cells for which no bindings exist will contain empty strings.

Table 13-4. KeyBindings.py data() Method, Explained

Lines	Description
82	Instantiates a JTable to simplify access to its methods.
83-85	Obtains an inputMap of the context used for all key bindings.
86-89	List-comprehension statement that builds a list of tuples for all the keystroke bindings and their associated action names.
90-100	Builds a dictionary, named keys, indexed by the key name (e.g., TAB) and identifying the modifier bindings. Also builds a dictionary, named acts, indexed by the keystroke (e.g., pressed TAB) containing the bound action.
101-102	Builds a sorted list of the bound (unmodified) keystroke names (e.g., SPACE and TAB).
103-108	Builds a list of the keystroke modifiers in column order.
109-116	Builds the table to be returned by the data() method (i.e., the two-dimensional array of strings).

The Fruits of Your Labor

Figure 13-4 shows the results of executing the KeyBindings.py application, before any row selection has been made.

KeyStroke	Unmodified	Ctrl	Shift	Shift-Ctrl
A		selectAll		
BACK_SLASH		clearSelection		
C		copy		
COPY	copy			
CUT	cut			
DELETE			cut	
DOWN	selectNextRow	selectNextRowChangeLead	selectNextRowExtendSelection	selectNextRowExtendSelection
END	selectLastColumn	selectLastRow	selectLastColumnExtendSelection	selectLastRowExtendSelection
ENTER	selectNextRowCell		selectPreviousRowCell	
ESCAPE	cancel			
F2	startEditing			
F8	focusHeader			
HOME	selectFirstColumn	selectFirstRow	selectFirstColumnExtendSelection	selectFirstRowExtendSelection
INSERT		copy	paste	
KP_DOWN	selectNextRow	selectNextRowChangeLead	selectNextRowExtendSelection	selectNextRowExtendSelection
KP_LEFT	selectPreviousColumn	selectPreviousColumnChangeLead	selectPreviousColumnExtendSelection	selectPreviousColumnExtendSelection
KP_RIGHT	selectNextColumn	selectNextColumnChangeLead	selectNextColumnExtendSelection	selectNextColumnExtendSelection
KP_UP	selectPreviousRow	selectPreviousRowChangeLead	selectPreviousRowExtendSelection	selectPreviousRowExtendSelection
LEFT	selectPreviousColumn	selectPreviousColumnChangeLead	selectPreviousColumnExtendSelection	selectPreviousColumnExtendSelection
PAGE_DOWN	scrollDownChangeSelection	scrollRightChangeSelection	scrollDownExtendSelection	scrollRightExtendSelection
PAGE_UP	scrollUpChangeSelection	scrollLeftChangeSelection	scrollUpExtendSelection	scrollLeftExtendSelection
PASTE	paste			
RIGHT	selectNextColumn	selectNextColumnChangeLead	selectNextColumnExtendSelection	selectNextColumnExtendSelection
SLASH		selectAll		
SPACE	addToSelection	toggleAndAnchor	extendTo	moveSelectionTo
TAB	selectNextColumnCell		selectPreviousColumnCell	
UP	selectPreviousRow	selectPreviousRowChangeLead	selectPreviousRowExtendSelection	selectPreviousRowExtendSelection
V		paste		
X		cut		

Figure 13-4. *KeyBindings.py's output, with no row selected*

One of the really neat things about this application is that you can use what you see to understand the results of using these bindings. For example, take a look at the TAB row and the Unmodified column. The action that is seen here is selectNextColumnCell and the one in you can see that when you press either the Tab or the Shift-Tab key, the table selection moves in the expected fashion.

Take a look at the actions associated with the Ctrl-A and Ctrl-BACK_SLASH keys. Try pressing these keys and see if the results meet your expectations. You should realize that not all of the actions will be allowed. Why not? Well, some of them require that the current cell be editable (e.g., cut or paste). Others depend on the current values of the columnSelectionAllowed and rowSelectionAllowed table attributes. In spite of that, I find the output of this application quite useful. I hope that you do as well.

Binding Reuse

You might be wondering what you can do with this information. I'll get to that, but first I want to explain how I came to investigate keystroke bindings.

I was working with an application that used some JTable instances. One of the challenges that I encountered was that my tables had some read-only and read-write columns. I expected that the users of the application might want to skip from one read-write cell to another using the Tab and Shift-Tab keys. In order to do this, I first had to figure out how the current keystroke bindings worked.

Looking again at Figure 13-4, you can see that the Tab and Shift-Tab keys correspond to `selectNextColumnCell` and `selectPreviousColumnCell`, respectively. What can be done with this information? Well, what you want to do is have the Tab and Shift-Tab keys be bound to actions something like `selectNextEditableColumnCell` and `selectPreviousEditableColumnCell`.

I don't know about you, but I would much prefer to use existing code instead of figuring out how to rewrite these two `ActionListeners`. That should make sense. How should you go about doing that? You have a number of options from which to choose. Let's start with something simple and decide if and when you can improve things.

Where to Begin: Finding the Appropriate Action Class

With what kind of class do you need to start? Let's see if you can get by with something easy, like the `AbstractAction` class.[8] According to the Javadoc for that class, "The developer need only subclass this abstract class and define the `actionPerformed` method." This sounds ideal for this situation.

The next question you need to ask is, "What will our class instance need to access in order to perform its role?" Well, since you are specifically concerned with `JTable` actions, it would seem likely that the action will need to know with which table instance the action should be working. Additionally, it will need to know the action it will be using to perform its role. In the case of `selectNextEditableColumnCell`, it needs to know that it will need to use `selectNextColumnCell`. Or will it? Do you really need to create a completely new action and replace the keystroke binding of the Tab key from `selectNextColumnCell` to a completely new action? What if your new action simply identifies itself as the original action and uses the original action to perform its role? That seems like a reasonable and fairly simple approach. It also simplifies the code that you need to write to perform the desired action.

What Do You Need to Worry About? Boundary Conditions

Whenever you create something like this, you need to be concerned with *boundary conditions*. What are those in this case? Well, consider a situation in which you have a read-only table. What should happen when the `selectNextEditableColumnCell` action is invoked? If you're not careful, you might create an infinite loop situation, which would be a bad thing. You need to be certain that your action deals well with a read-only table.

What's the next worst-case scenario? In my mind, it would be a table with only one editable cell. In that case, how many cells would your action need to check in order to find the next editable cell? Well, that would depend on the size of the table. Can you figure that out? Given access to the table, you can use the `table.getRowCount()` and `table.getColumnCount()` methods to determine how many cells exist.

Listing 13-9 shows a simple implementation of this approach. It includes a call to the default toolkit `beep()` method if no editable cells are found in the table. You can test this application, which can be found in the `code\Chap_13\WoT.py` script. You may want to modify the `isCellEditable(...)` method to return a `0` (`false`) in order to test the read-only table scenario.

---

[8]See `http://docs.oracle.com/javase/8/docs/api/javax/swing/AbstractAction.html`.

Listing 13-9. findEditableCell Class from WoT.py

```
39|class findEditableCell( AbstractAction ) :
40|    def __init__( self, table, action ) :
41|        self.table    = table
42|        self.original = table.getActionMap().get( action )
43|        self.table.getActionMap().put( action, self )
44|        self.beep     = Toolkit.getDefaultToolkit().beep
45|    def actionPerformed( self, actionEvent ) :
46|        table = self.table
47|        numCells = table.getRowCount() * table.getColumnCount()
48|        for cell in range( numCells ) :
49|            self.original.actionPerformed( actionEvent )
50|            if table.isCellEditable(
51|                table.getSelectedRow(),
52|                table.getSelectedColumn()
53|            ) :
54|                return
55|        self.beep()
  |...
70|        findEditableCell( table, 'selectNextColumnCell' )
71|        findEditableCell( table, 'selectPreviousColumnCell' )
```

Summary

This chapter explained how Java Swing applications deal with keystrokes. Rather than have the application monitor the user input, the environment determines the action to be performed for the keystroke event based on the current context. It is important to know how this works so your applications can take advantage of the existing infrastructure.

The next chapter discusses events and event handlers.

CHAPTER 14

■ ■ ■

It's the Event of the Year: Events in Swing Applications

I have been referencing events, of all sorts, in many of the preceding chapters. It seems like a good time to take a better look at how events are handled in Swing applications.

This chapter is all about events, such as mouse clicks, and preparing an application to handle these kinds of events when they occur. You'll also see how easy it is in Jython to associate a method with an event. It is important to note that methods that are called when specific events occur are called *listeners*. The association of a listener method with a specific kind of event is a kind of registration. Let's begin this chapter by taking a look at the number of classes that have something to do with events and listeners.

If an Event Occurs and No One Hears It . . .

If you look at the "complete list of Java classes,[1] " you'll find over 4,000 items. Of these, almost 12 dozen have "event" somewhere in their name and another seven dozen have "listener" in their name. What are all these things?

You've seen a number of them already. For example, when you were working with the JButton class,[2] you learned that in order to be able to react to user input, you needed an ActionListener[3] or some descendant class instance containing an actionPerformed(...) method. Until you did this association, no method would be called when the event occurred and the events were lost.

What type of argument is supplied to the actionPerformed(...) method? An ActionEvent,[4] that's what. An ActionEvent is an object instance that is used to indicate that some kind of component action has occurred. It can be used by an event handler to do things like identify the component that generated the event. Since ActionEvents are passed to registered listening methods, this chapter focuses more on listeners than on the details about ActionEvents.

Many of the Java Swing examples that you'll investigate are almost certain to include a listener of some type, as well as the method it defines or requires. The interesting thing about many of the Jython script examples that you've seen is that they don't have to explicitly identify, include, and use the particular listener class that is needed for the kind of event to be handled. You simply use the appropriate keyword argument to identify the method to be called when the event occurs.

---

[1]See http://docs.oracle.com/javase/8/docs/api/allclasses-noframe.html.
[2]See http://docs.oracle.com/javase/8/docs/api/javax/swing/JButton.html.
[3]See http://docs.oracle.com/javase/8/docs/api/java/awt/event/ActionListener.html.
[4]See http://docs.oracle.com/javase/8/docs/api/java/awt/event/ActionEvent.html.

Is this always a good thing? Maybe, maybe not. Consider for a moment the perspective of an experienced Java Swing developer. Their experience may have trained them to look at Swing applications in a specific way to locate event handlers. Their first instinct may be to search for calls to the add*Listener(...) method. Are they going to locate them in Jython scripts that use the appropriate keyword argument? I don't think so, do you?

Personally, I find the use of the keyword argument to be a better approach for a number of reasons, including (but not limited to) these:

- It forces the developer to identify the event handler during component instantiation.

- It allows the event handler routine to be named something other than the generic actionPerformed(...) method name. For example, I prefer to see a method named buttonPressed(...) rather than the ubiquitous actionPerformed(...) variation, don't you?

- It allows multiple event handlers to be defined as part of the same application class. In this way, each button instance can have its own unique event handler, instead of having to share a single actionPerformed(...) method that must determine how it was invoked. This allows each event handler method to be simpler and uncluttered by code that needs to determine or identify the exact source of the associated event that caused the routine to be called.

- It allows the developer to avoid using multiple inheritance in their application class (for example, to include the ActionListener as one of its base classes).

Are there times when it might be a bad idea to use the keyword argument to identify the event handler to be invoked? Think about it for a moment. What does a method name like add*Listener(...) imply? It tells you that there are situations where multiple listeners may be appropriate. If this is the case then you are likely to be better served by using add*Listener(...) to identify all of the event handlers to be registered as event listeners. Otherwise, using the keyword argument approach may very well be the best. I'll talk more about this later in this chapter.

Using Listener Methods

Most of the examples that you've seen have focused on a small number of listeners.[5] For example, in all of the JButton examples, you have only seen the ActionListener and its actionPerformed(...) method. Is that the only listener available for the JButton class? If you think so, you are sadly mistaken and in for a big surprise. Listing 14-1 shows the various listener methods and class hierarchy where each is defined.

Listing 14-1. JButton Listeners

```
wsadmin>from javax.swing import JButton
wsadmin>
wsadmin>classInfo( JButton, meth = 'listener' )
javax.swing.JButton
| javax.swing.AbstractButton
>    addActionListener, addChangeListener, getActionListeners
>    getChangeListeners, getItemListeners, removeActionListener
>    removeChangeListener
| | javax.swing.JComponent
> >    addAncestorListener, addVetoableChangeListener
> >    getAncestorListeners, getVetoableChangeListeners
> >    removeAncestorListener, removeVetoableChangeListener
```

---

[5]The primary exception was shown in Table 6-2, where there were more than a dozen listeners for the JTextArea class.

```
| | | java.awt.Container
> > >   addContainerListener, addPropertyChangeListener
> > >   getContainerListeners, removeContainerListener
| | | | java.awt.Component
> > > >   addComponentListener, addFocusListener
> > > >   addHierarchyBoundsListener, addHierarchyListener
> > > >   addInputMethodListener, addKeyListener
> > > >   addMouseListener, addMouseMotionListener
> > > >   addMouseWheelListener, addPropertyChangeListener
> > > >   getComponentListeners, getFocusListeners
> > > >   getHierarchyBoundsListeners, getHierarchyListeners
> > > >   getInputMethodListeners, getKeyListeners, getListeners
> > > >   getMouseListeners, getMouseMotionListeners
> > > >   getMouseWheelListeners, getPropertyChangeListeners
> > > >   removeComponentListener, removeFocusListener
> > > >   removeHierarchyBoundsListener, removeHierarchyListener
> > > >   removeInputMethodListener, removeKeyListener
> > > >   removeMouseListener, removeMouseMotionListener
> > > >   removeMouseWheelListener, removePropertyChangeListener
| | | | | java.lang.Object
| | | | | java.awt.image.ImageObserver
| | | | | java.awt.MenuContainer
| | | | | java.io.Serializable
| | | java.io.Serializable
| | java.awt.ItemSelectable
> >   addItemListener, removeItemListener
| | javax.swing.SwingConstants
| javax.accessibility.Accessible
wsadmin>
```

Is it likely that your applications will be using all of these listeners? No, but there are quite a few that are worth investigating. The information in Listing 14-1 shows a large number of listener methods that are part of the java.awt.Component class. The variety and type of listeners in the hierarchy should encourage you, as a developer, and give you confidence that your application will be able to monitor any type of event you need.

Put Your Listener Where Your Component Is

In this section, you learn what it takes to create a MouseListener[6] for a component.[7] Before you begin, though, it is important to realize that if your application is interested in mouse movement, this requires a different kind of listener (MouseMotionListener).[8] For the moment, however, this section focuses on what it takes to create a MouseListener.

Table 14-1 shows the events defined by the MouseListener class. Each of these methods has a MouseEvent parameter that is passed to the event handler method.

---

[6]See http://docs.oracle.com/javase/8/docs/api/java/awt/event/MouseListener.html.
[7]It's interesting to note that, at least at the time of this writing, the version 7 java.awt.event.MouseListener Javadoc page has a bad link. The "Tutorial: Writing a Mouse Listener" link should actually point to http://docs.oracle.com/javase/tutorial/uiswing/events/mouselistener.html. This bad link has been corrected on the version 8 page.
[8]See http://docs.oracle.com/javase/8/docs/api/java/awt/event/MouseMotionListener.html.

Table 14-1. MouseListener *Methods*

Method Name	Invoked When the Mouse ...
mouseEntered(...)	Enters a component.
mousePressed(...)	Button has been pressed on a component.
mouseReleased(...)	Button has been released on a component.
mouseClicked(...)	Button has been pressed and released on a component.
mouseExited(...)	Exits a component.

Listing 14-2 shows just how easily you can add a MouseListener to a component like a button. Note how the listener class, in lines 10-24, needs to be provided with access to the specific application component, in this case, a JTextArea. This is because it's external to the Listen1 application class.

Listing 14-2. Adding a MouseListener to a Button

```
10|class listener( MouseListener ) :
11|    def __init__( self, textArea ) :
12|        self.textArea = textArea
13|    def mouseClicked( self, me ) :
14|        self.logEvent( me )
15|    def mouseEntered( self, me ) :
16|        self.logEvent( me )
17|    def mouseExited( self, me ) :
18|        self.logEvent( me )
19|    def mousePressed( self, me ) :
20|        self.logEvent( me )
21|    def mouseReleased( self, me ) :
22|        self.logEvent( me )
23|    def logEvent( self, me ) :
24|        self.textArea.append( me.toString() + '\n' )
25|class Listen1( java.lang.Runnable ) :
26|    def run( self ) :
27|        frame = JFrame(
28|            'Listen1',
29|            layout = FlowLayout(),
30|            locationRelativeTo = None,
31|            size = ( 512, 256 ),
32|            defaultCloseOperation = JFrame.EXIT_ON_CLOSE
33|        )
34|        self.button   = frame.add( JButton( 'Button' ) )
35|        self.textarea = JTextArea( rows = 10, columns = 40 )
36|        self.button.addMouseListener( listener( self.textarea ) )
37|        frame.add( JScrollPane( self.textarea ) )
38|        frame.setVisible( 1 )
```

Figure 14-1 shows an image from the Listen1.py application. In this case, I moved the mouse over the button, clicked the button, and then moved the mouse elsewhere. Figure 14-1 shows every event that occurred, in the order that they are shown in Table 14-1.

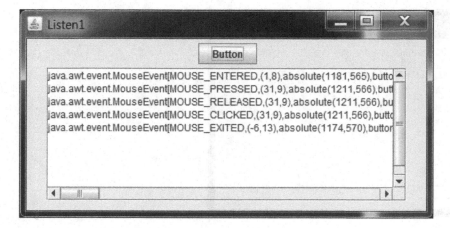

Figure 14-1. Listen1.py *sample output*

What if you aren't interested in monitoring all of the possible events that class provides? Well, one trivial technique is to have the uninteresting methods do nothing (they can contain a simple, pass or return statement). This can be a possible source of confusion and error. I've had at least one instance where I didn't realize that I duplicated a listener method name, where the second instance inadvertently replaced the first. It took me a while to realize and resolve my mistake. What can you do about this kind of situation?

Adapt or Die: Using Adapter Classes

The Swing designers have been very kind to its developers. The hierarchy includes about two dozen "adapter" classes that contain most, if not all, of the methods you'll need, all with empty placeholder statements. Using these as a base class is a great place to start.

One way to find the class you need is by looking at the Javadoc and paying particular interest to the "See Also" sections. For example, the MouseListener Javadoc[6] has, as its first reference in this section, the MouseAdapter class.[9] Using that as a base class for your listener allows you to simplify the listener class from the Listen1 application. Listing 14-2 contains the original listener class in lines 10-24. Listing 14-3 shows a simplified class that assumes you are interested in one only of the available methods.

Listing 14-3. Listen2.py Using MouseAdapter

```
10|class listener( MouseAdapter ) :
11|    def __init__( self, textArea ) :
12|        self.textArea = textArea
13|    def mouseClicked( self, me ) :
14|        self.textArea.append( me.toString() + '\n' )
```

Figure 14-2 shows sample output from this iteration of the Listen#.py script. Note that Listen2.py is only interested in mouseClicked events, so you only see references to those events in the text area. You no longer see the other events shown in Figure 14-1.

---

[9]See http://docs.oracle.com/javase/8/docs/api/java/awt/event/MouseAdapter.html.

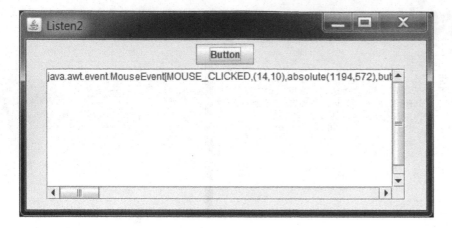

Figure 14-2. Listen2.py *sample output*

Listening for Keyboard Events

What if you wanted your application to monitor keystrokes as they are entered, so that the application can be dynamically updated to reflect various information about the user input? If your application has more than one kind of information to be displayed, based on this input, this could make things a little interesting for the developers. One approach would be to have one KeyListener for the user input field that updates multiple fields based on the user's input. One problem with this, though, is that as you continue to add fields to the application, this listener becomes more complex.

Another approach is to have a more generic listener class that is used to monitor one simple property, and then update a single application field based on this property. What would this kind of listener class need in order to perform this role? It would need to have the following parts of the application specified during its instantiation or construction:

- The input field being monitored

- The output field to be updated

- The function used to determine the result displayed in the output field

Say you had a single input field that you wanted to monitor. When the user enters a value, it needs to be checked to see if the value is an even number (integer). That's not too difficult. What if you also wanted the field to indicate when the value was an odd integer value? It might also be interesting to have a field display whether the value is a prime number.

In order to create this kind of application, you need to understand the kinds of events that are generated for KeyListener objects.[10] How does this class work? Table 14-2 shows the three methods that are part of the KeyListener interface. Each event handler method has a KeyEvent argument that will be passed to the method.

---

[10]See http://docs.oracle.com/javase/8/docs/api/java/awt/event/KeyListener.html.

Table 14-2. *KeyListener Methods*

Method Name	Description
keyPressed(...)	Invoked when a key is pressed.
keyReleased(...)	Invoked when a key is released.
keyTyped(...)	Invoked when a key is typed.

Unfortunately, the description for each method is kind of lacking. What does each mean, and what's the difference between them? When might you be concerned with using one method versus another?

The best way to answer questions like this is to write a program that tries them out. You can then learn more about the methods by seeing the output they produce. Using Listen1.py as a starting point, you can replace MouseListener with KeyListener, replacing each MouseListener method with the appropriate KeyListener method. The result is shown in Listing 14-4.

Listing 14-4. KeyListener Descendant Class from Listen3.py

```
13|class listener( KeyListener ) :
14|    def __init__( self, textArea ) :
15|        self.textArea = textArea
16|    def keyPressed( self, ke ) :
17|        self.logEvent( ke )
18|    def keyReleased( self, ke ) :
19|        self.logEvent( ke )
20|    def keyTyped( self, ke ) :
21|        self.logEvent( ke )
22|    def logEvent( self, ke ) :
23|        self.textArea.append( ke.toString() + '\n' )
```

Sample output from the Listen3.py application is shown in Figure 14-3. The first image shows what happens when you press and hold (and finally release) the Right-Shift key. Notice how multiple KEY_PRESSED events, only one KEY_RELEASED event, and no KEY_TYPED events were generated. The second image shows the key events that were generated when you quickly press and release the 0 key. And the third image shows the keystroke events that can occur when a normal key, in this case the 0 key, is pressed and held just long enough to generate two repeated 0's in the input field.

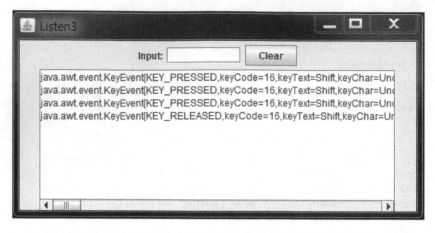

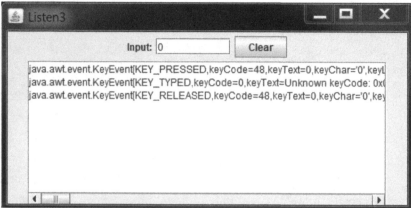

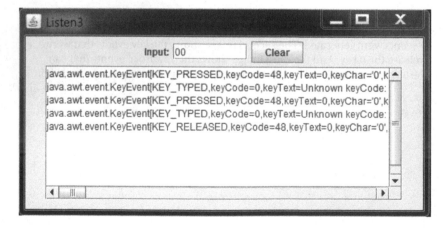

Figure 14-3. `Listen3.py` *sample output*

From these images, you can see that:

- For repeated keystrokes of characters that don't produce input (such as the Shift key), only KEY_PRESSED events occur.

- For repeated keystrokes of characters that produce input (such as any of the letters and the numeric keys), the KEY_PRESSED and KEY_TYPED events occur in an alternating pattern.

- The KEY_RELEASED event only occurs once for each key.

You are encouraged to use the Listen3.py script and see the events that are generated when you press and release combinations of keys (such as Ctrl-Shift-Spacebar). Are you surprised, or do you observe what you expected? This exercise should help you better understand the keystroke events that are generated.

Listing 14-5 shows almost all of the Listen3 class that was used to produce the output shown in Figure 14-3. At this point, you shouldn't be too surprised by how easy it is to create this kind of application.

Listing 14-5. Listen3 Class from Listen3.py

```
24|class Listen3( java.lang.Runnable ) :
25|    def run( self ) :
26|        frame = JFrame(
27|            'Listen3',
28|            layout = FlowLayout(),
29|            locationRelativeTo = None,
30|            size = ( 512, 256 ),
31|            defaultCloseOperation = JFrame.EXIT_ON_CLOSE
32|        )
33|        frame.add(
34|            JLabel(
35|                'Input:',
36|                horizontalAlignment = SwingConstants.RIGHT
37|            )
38|        )
39|        self.text = frame.add( JTextField( 8 ) )
40|        frame.add(
41|            JButton(
42|                'Clear',
43|                actionPerformed = self.clear
44|            )
45|        )
46|        self.textArea = JTextArea( rows = 10, columns = 40 )
47|        frame.add( JScrollPane( self.textArea ) )
48|        self.text.addKeyListener( listener( self.textArea ) )
49|        frame.setVisible( 1 )
```

Listing 14-6, on the other hand, may contain a surprise or two. Initially, I intended that the button should only be used to clear the application TextArea. However, after playing with the application for a very short time, I soon realized that it would also be useful to clear the input text field. The potential surprise, however, is related to the last method call in this routine.

What, exactly, does the requestFocusInWindow() method do, and how did I know to use it? Before including this method call, I was forced to use the mouse to click on the input field to give it focus after the button was pressed. The alternative would be to use the Tab key to move the focus from the button to the input field. The problem with this approach is that it generates input that's written to TextArea.

So, I looked for methods in JTextField that had "focus" in their name. The first one that I found was JComponent.requestFocus(),[11] which looked promising, at least until I read that the use of this routine is discouraged. The good news is that the documentation for this method also provided the name of the recommended routine to be used, instead. So, the purpose of the call to the requestFocusInWindow() method is to restore focus to the input field after the button is pressed.

Listing 14-6. The ActionListener Method Used by the Button

```
50|    def clear( self, event ) :
51|        self.text.setText( '' )
52|        self.textArea.setText( '' )
53|        self.text.requestFocusInWindow()
```

All in all, this is a useful application, especially when you are interested in learning about keystroke events that can be generated and the sequence in which they occur.

Most Objects Never Really Listen

At the beginning of this chapter, you read that there are times when it makes sense for multiple listeners to monitor a particular component for the same kind of event. Fortunately, this is something that can easily be accomplished. Before you looked at the kind of keystroke events that can be generated, you saw an application that had multiple listeners monitoring an input field, each one updating a component based on the value contained in the input field.

Before you look at an example, take a moment to think about situations in which it would make sense to do this. Listing 14-7 provides one example. The class constructor for this listener requires that three things be provided:

- The input field being monitored

- The output field to be updated (in this example, a JLabel)

- The function to be used to determine the message value to be specified

Listing 14-7. Listener Class from Listen4.py

```
10|class listener( KeyAdapter ) :
11|    def __init__( self, input, msg, fun ) :
12|        self.input = input
13|        self.msg   = msg
14|        self.fun   = fun
15|    def keyReleased( self, ke ) :
16|        text = self.input.text
17|        if text :
18|            try :
19|                value = int( self.input.text )
20|                msg = [ 'No', 'Yes' ][ self.fun( value ) ]
21|            except :
22|                msg = 'invalid integer'
23|        else :
24|            msg = ''
25|        self.msg.setText( msg )
```

---

[11]See http://docs.oracle.com/javase/8/docs/api/javax/swing/JComponent.html#requestFocus%28%29.

This listener class, as you can see, descends from the KeyAdapter class,[12] not from the abstract KeyListener class.[10] This allows you to simplify the class because you can choose to implement only the keyReleased(...) method.[13]

Maybe you are confused by the syntax shown on line 20. Here, we take advantage of some of the power of Jython.

The first part of the expression—"['No', 'Yes']"—identifies a list containing two values. The second part of the expression—"[self.fun(value)]"—identifies the index used to select the desired value from the list. In order to determine the value to be used, which should be zero or one, you call the user-specified function (provided when the class was instantiated; see lines 11-14) and pass the value of the user-specified input field (after converting it from a string to an integer).

■ **Note** In case you are wondering, the try/except statement is necessary in case the user specifies an invalid input and the conversion fails.

Listing 14-8. Listen4 Class from Listen4.py

```
26|class Listen4( java.lang.Runnable ) :
27|    def run( self ) :
28|        def isEven( num ) :
29|            return not ( num & 1 )
30|        def isOdd( num ) :
31|            return num & 1
32|        def isPrime( num ):
33|            result = 0                        # Default = False
34|            if num == abs( int( num ) ) :    # Only integers allowed
35|                if num == 1 :                # Special case
36|                    pass                     #   use default (false)
37|                elif num == 2 :              # Special case
38|                    result = 1               #
39|                elif num & 1 :               # Only odd numbers...
40|                    for f in xrange( 3, int( num**0.5 ) + 1, 2 ) :
41|                        if not num % f :
42|                            break            # f is a factor...
43|                    else :
44|                        result = 1           # we found a prime
45|            return result
46|        def label( text ) :
47|            return JLabel(
48|                text + ' ',
49|                horizontalAlignment = SwingConstants.RIGHT
50|                )
```

---

[12]See http://docs.oracle.com/javase/8/docs/api/java/awt/event/KeyAdapter.html.
[13]Initially, I mistakenly used the keyTyped(...) method, thinking that it would be the one invoked after the keystroke had been processed. But I was wrong. Fortunately, it was a trivial thing to change the name of the routine from keyTyped(...) to keyReleased(...).

```
51|          frame = JFrame(
52|              'Listen4',
53|              layout = GridLayout( 0, 2 ),
54|              locationRelativeTo = None,
55|              size = ( 200, 128 ),
56|              defaultCloseOperation = JFrame.EXIT_ON_CLOSE
57|          )
58|          frame.add( label( 'Integer:' ) )
59|          text  = frame.add( JTextField( 10 ) )
60|          frame.add( label( 'Even?' ) )
61|          even  = frame.add( JLabel( '' ) )
62|          text.addKeyListener( listener( text, even, isEven ) )
63|          frame.add( label( 'Odd?' ) )
64|          odd   = frame.add( JLabel( '' ) )
65|          text.addKeyListener( listener( text, odd, isOdd ) )
66|          frame.add( label( 'Prime?' ) )
67|          prime = frame.add( JLabel( '' ) )
68|          text.addKeyListener( listener( text, prime, isPrime ) )
69|          frame.setVisible( 1 )
```

Lines 62, 65, and 68 of Listing 14-8 show how the application has three KeyListener methods for the same input field (the JTextField), as well as specifying different output (JLabel) fields and functions to be called to determine the message to be displayed in each.

Figure 14-4 shows some sample output from the Listen4.py application, which has multiple listeners for a single input field.

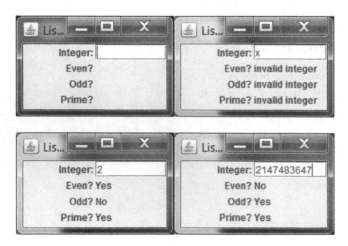

Figure 14-4. Listen4.py output

Looking for a Listener in a Haystack

Up to this point, things have sort of been handed to you on a platter, so to speak. Unfortunately, that approach is only useful up to a point. Let's take a look at how a developers can determine the best way to do something.

One of the many challenges with designing and developing an application is trying to figure out what size it should be. Along those lines, I wondered how much time and effort would be required to have the application monitor any resize requests that might occur.

Why would I want to do this? Consider, for a moment, that I have no idea how large or small for that matter, to make my application. I could simply let Swing determine the size for me by using the JFrame pack()(inherited) method.

Unfortunately, I haven't always been happy with the default size. So, I did a quick look at the listeners and the Java Swing Tutorial[14] to see if I could find something useful. It didn't take me long to realize that my photographic memory was out of film, and I would have to use a different technique.

Using one of the various Internet search engines, you can search for "java swing resize listener," which will quickly point you to the "How to Write a Component Listener" swing tutorial page.[15] Looking at the sample application on that page, called ComponentEventDemo.java,[16] I was able to find some things worth investigating.

- This application, like most from the Java Swing Tutorial pages, has the main(...) method use an anonymous Runnable class within its call to the SwingUtilities invokeLater(...) method.

- Invariably, the run(...) method in this class simply calls the createAndShowGUI(...) method within the application class.

- This application class (ComponentEventDemo) extends JPanel, so the createAndShowGUI(...) method creates JFrame instances and uses the JPanel that is created by the application class as a replacement for the JFrame ContentPane. I haven't used this technique, but it appears to be a common one used by many of the sample applications in the Swing Tutorial pages.

- The sample applications that extend a base class like JPanel almost always use the Java technique of calling the super(...) method to invoke the base class constructor. Unfortunately, this isn't available to Jython developers, so instead, you'll have to invoke the base class constructor—that is, call the JPanel.__init__(self) method.

- The only expression that can't be used "as-is" occurs in the component event handler methods, and looks like this: e.getComponent().getClass().getName(). If you try to use expressions like these in your Jython scripts, you'll get an exception something like this:

  ```
  TypeError: getName(): expected 1 args; got 0
  ```

---

[14]See https://docs.oracle.com/javase/tutorial/uiswing/.
[15]See http://docs.oracle.com/javase/tutorial/uiswing/events/componentlistener.html.
[16]See http://docs.oracle.com/javase/tutorial/uiswing/examples/events/ComponentEventDemoProject/src/events/ComponentEventDemo.java.

The reason that this happens is because Jython has two ways for calling a method instance[17]:

- `theInstance.theMethod( args )`

- `TheClass.theMethod( theInstance, args )`

Unfortunately, you are trying to use the first technique, but Jython prefers the second. How can you fix this? You have a couple of different options available. You can use the syntax preferred by Jython, which is an expression like this one:

```
java.lang.Class.getName( e.getComponent().getClass() )
```

Unfortunately, this results in a string something like "`javax.swing.JButton`", instead of the preferred "`JButton`". A somewhat simpler approach is to use the fact that you can use `str( e.getComponent().getClass() )` to get this same string value, then split the string with "`.`" as a delimiter. Finally, you use the negative list indexing technique to access the final part of the list of strings:

```
name = str( e.getComponent().getClass() ).split( '.' )[ -1 ]
```

Before you take a look at Jython script that I produced, try to convert the original Java application to Jython yourself. This exercise should provide you with some practice at reading an original Java Swing application and trying to produce a script using the same kind of components and organization.

Using the original Java version—or the one you created, or even the one that can be found in code\Chap_14\ ComponentEventDemo.py—take a look at the events generated when you do something simple like make the application window a tiny bit taller. Figure 14-5 shows multiple images produced by using the Jython script at various times. The most interesting one, at least to me, is the last image, which shows just how many "Moved" events are generated when you make the window a little bit larger.[18] Also interesting is the fact that only one "Resized" event is generated. The really interesting part is that the event identifies the component that was resized, in this case, the JFrame object.

---

[17]Thanks to Jeff Emanuel for providing this explanation on the jython-users mailing list.
[18]This is why my version of the script includes a counter showing the number of events that have been encountered.

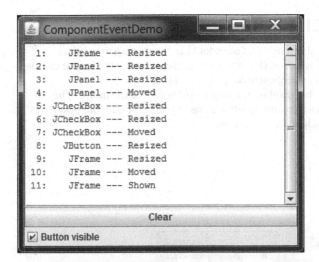

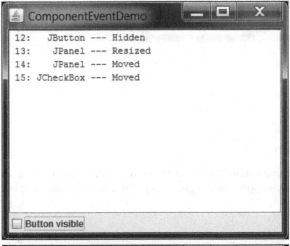

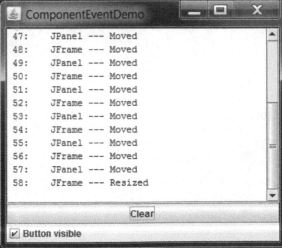

Figure 14-5. ComponentEventDemo sample output

Using a ComponentAdapter to Monitor Changes

Using this ComponentEventDemo application made me think about using a ComponentListener[15] to gain a better understanding about the size and position of an application window. Of course, if you aren't interested in monitoring all of the Component events, you might want to consider using a ComponentAdapter[19] instead.

What do you think it would take to have an application that displays the width and height of the frame? The images in Figure 14-6 show one possible representation. Take a few moments and see if you can figure out how to do this before looking at the source, which is available in code\Chap_14\Frame1.py.

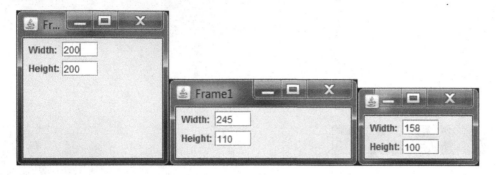

Figure 14-6. Frame1 sample output

Issues you might want to consider:

- Which Layout Manager do you want to use?

- For which events does the application need to listen?

Listing 14-9 shows the Frame1 class from the script of the same name. Notice how the Layout Manager attribute of the frame constructor is initialized to None. That means that this application is going to position each component by specifying its size and location.

Listing 14-9. Frame1 Class from Frame1.py

```
16|class Frame1( java.lang.Runnable ) :
17|    def run( self ) :
18|        self.frame = frame = JFrame(
19|            'Frame1',
20|            size = ( 200, 200 ),
21|            layout = None,
22|            locationRelativeTo = None,
23|            defaultCloseOperation = JFrame.EXIT_ON_CLOSE
24|        )
25|        frame.addComponentListener( listener( self ) )
26|        insets = frame.getInsets()
27|        self.width  = JTextField( 4 )
28|        self.height = JTextField( 4 )
```

---

[19]See http://docs.oracle.com/javase/8/docs/api/java/awt/event/ComponentAdapter.html.

```
29|         items = [
30|             [ JLabel( 'Width:'  ),  7,  7 ],
31|             [ self.width         , 50,  5 ],
32|             [ JLabel( 'Height:' ),  7, 31 ],
33|             [ self.height        , 50, 30 ]
34|         ]
35|         for item in items :
36|             thing = frame.add( item[ 0 ] )
37|             size  = thing.getPreferredSize()
38|             thing.setBounds(
39|                 insets.left + item[ 1 ],
40|                 insets.top  + item[ 2 ],
41|                 size.width,
42|                 size.height
43|             )
44|         frame.setVisible( 1 )
```

Listing 14-10 shows the simple listener class that is a descendant of the abstract `ComponentAdapter` class. This allows you to simplify your class and only specify methods of interest, which in this case is the `componentResized()` method.[20]

Listing 14-10. Listener Class from `Frame1.py`

```
 8|class listener( ComponentAdapter ) :
 9|    def __init__( self, app ) :
10|        self.app = app
11|    def componentResized( self, ce ) :
12|        app   = self.app
13|        size  = app.frame.getSize()
14|        app.width.setText( `size.width` )
15|        app.height.setText( `size.height` )
```

What would it take to have an application that shows the position or location on the screen, in addition to the size? It would be a good exercise for you to try to expand `Frame1.py` to add this kind of functionality. Why don't you take some time to do this before you take a look at the one found in `code\Chap_14\Frame2.py`?

Listing 14-11 shows the revised listener class that was used to generate the output shown in Figure 14-7. Note how additional `ComponentListener` methods have been included. This allows the application to update the position, that is the X and Y fields, as the application frame is moved. In order to do this, the `frame.getBounds()` method is called to acquire the current size and position of the frame. In Listing 14-8, you were only using the size of the application, so the `frame.getSize()` method was used instead.

---

[20]If you are unfamiliar with the backtic operator, it converts the expression within as a printable string. See the Jython `repr()` built-in function.

Listing 14-11. Listener Class from Frame2.py

```
 8|class listener( ComponentAdapter ) :
 9|    def __init__( self, app ) :
10|        self.app = app
11|    def updateInfo( self ) :
12|        app    = self.app
13|        bounds = app.frame.getBounds()
14|        app.width.setText( `bounds.width` )
15|        app.height.setText( `bounds.height` )
16|        app.x.setText( `bounds.x` )
17|        app.y.setText( `bounds.y` )
18|    def componentMoved( self, ce ) :
19|        self.updateInfo()
20|    def componentResized( self, ce ) :
21|        self.updateInfo()
22|    def componentShown( self, ce ) :
23|        self.updateInfo()
```

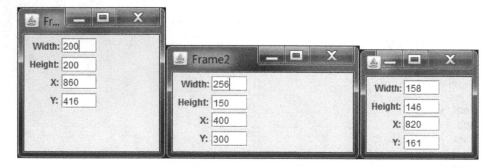

Figure 14-7. Frame2 sample output

Listing 14-12 shows just how little needed to be modified in order to have the application monitor the location as well as the size. It also shows how tedious it can be to determine the components' positions so that they can be identified without using a Layout Manager.

Why did I choose to use the absolute layout technique? The primary reason was because I didn't want the components to move around on the application as it moved and was resized.

Listing 14-12. Modified Statements from the Frame2 Class

```
24|class Frame2( java.lang.Runnable ) :
  |    ...
34|        self.width  = JTextField( 4 )
35|        self.height = JTextField( 4 )
36|        self.x      = JTextField( 4 )
37|        self.y      = JTextField( 4 )
38|        items = [
39|            [ JLabel( 'Width:' ) , 11,  7 ],
40|            [ self.width         , 50,  5 ],
41|            [ JLabel( 'Height:' ),  7, 31 ],
```

```
42|            [ self.height      , 50, 30 ],
43|            [ JLabel( 'X:' )    , 35, 55 ],
44|            [ self.x            , 50, 53 ],
45|            [ JLabel( 'Y:' )    , 35, 79 ],
46|            [ self.y            , 50, 78 ]
47|        ]
  |    ...
```

Monitoring the Input Fields

Using the mouse to move and resize the application window can be a frustrating experience, especially if you are trying to precisely adjust a specific value (such as the height). Wouldn't it be useful to also allow users to enter a value in any of these input fields as well? If you do allow user input, you'll need to verify that input before it is used. For example, it doesn't make any sense to allow users to specify a negative width or height. On the other hand, it may make sense for the location values to be negative. On my system, I have a second display, and when I put the application frame in the middle of it, the value of X is -775.

So how do you go about monitoring the input fields? One way is to have an ActionListener for each field. In fact, you could have a different one for each field so that you don't have to figure out which value was modified. Listing 14-13, which can be found in Frame3.py, shows one way that this can be done.

Listing 14-13. Unique ActionListener for Each Input Field

```
24|class Frame3( java.lang.Runnable ) :
25|    def changeWidth( self, event ) :
26|        value = event.getActionCommand()
27|        try :
28|            width = int( value )
29|            size  = self.frame.getSize()
30|            self.frame.setSize( width, size.height )
31|        except :
32|            print 'Invalid Width: "%s"' % value
  |    ...
57|    def run( self ) :
  |        ...
66|        self.width  = JTextField(
67|            4, actionPerformed = self.changeWidth
68|        )
69|        self.height = JTextField(
70|            4, actionPerformed = self.changeHeight
71|        )
72|        self.x      = JTextField(
73|            4, actionPerformed = self.changeX
74|        )
75|        self.y      = JTextField(
76|            4, actionPerformed = self.changeY
77|        )
  |        ...
```

Unfortunately, this isn't a great approach for a number of reasons, including these:

- Using `ActionListeners` means that the values aren't verified until the user presses Enter, which isn't very user friendly. It would probably be better if verification occurred when the user does one of the following:

- Presses the Enter key

- Tries to change focus (using the Tab key, Shift-Tab, or even a mouse event)

- Enters the text

- Each `ActionListener` is very similar. You might be able to refactor, but the technique used to indicate that an invalid value was specified isn't very good or user friendly. Nor does it use the Swing interface, which is a bad thing.

Back in Chapter 7, you read a little about the `JFormattedTextField` class,[21] including how it is used to restrict user input. Let's revisit that class and see if it can help you improve the user experience of this application. What part of a `JFormattedTextField` will help you with this application? Well, there are some things in the Javadoc that you should be aware of. Specifically, it contains information about using one of the following:

- A `PropertyChangeListener`[22] for monitoring editing changes

- An `InputVerifier`[23] to keep focus from being lost when an invalid value is specified

Using a PropertyChangeListener

One of the interesting things about the `JFormattedTextField` class is that, in addition to the text attribute that it inherits from `JTextField`, it also defines a value attribute.[24] Why does it have both a text and a value attribute? More importantly, what does that mean for your applications?

Consider the following scenario: a formatted text field has some kind of value, for example, some kind of currency. When this field has focus, it may be an indication that the user wants to modify the value, which is great. Users start typing and as they do so, the text that they enter might not be valid. As user input is being provided, the text attribute reflects what the user has entered. When entry is complete, the contents of the text attribute can be used to determine if the information is valid or appropriate for the field.

So, the value attribute maintains a valid value, formatted using the appropriate pattern. The text attribute, on the other hand, reflects the current, unverified, and unformatted user input. It's when the user entry process is complete that the verification and formatting can occur, but only if the user-specified value is acceptable. At least that way it is supposed to work, if your applications use the available capabilities.

Let's start by looking at the `PropertyChangeListener` to see how it fits into this strategy. To begin, consider an application that has a couple of formatted text fields with a property change listener event handler routine to tell you about the `PropertyChangeEvents` that occur. This routine can update a text area with information about the events, including the `PropertyName`, the `OldValue`, and the `NewValue` attributes identified by `PropertyChangeEvent`.[25]

Listing 14-14 shows the `PropertyChangeListener` and `ActionListener` event handler routines from the `PropertyListener.py` sample application.

---

[21]See `http://docs.oracle.com/javase/8/docs/api/javax/swing/JFormattedTextField.html`.

[22]See `http://docs.oracle.com/javase/8/docs/api/java/beans/PropertyChangeListener.html`.

[23]See `http://docs.oracle.com/javase/8/docs/api/javax/swing/InputVerifier.html`.

[24]In spite of the fact that the Javadoc for this class doesn't identify this fact, at least not explicitly in the "Field Summary" section.

[25]See `http://docs.oracle.com/javase/8/docs/api/java/beans/PropertyChangeEvent.html`.

Listing 14-14. PropertyChangeListener Event Handler Routine

```
17|class PropertyListener( java.lang.Runnable ) :
18|    def changed( self, pce ) :
19|        format  = '    Name: %(name)s\n'
20|        format += 'OldValue: %(old)s\n'
21|        format += 'NewValue: %(new)s\n\n'
22|        name     = pce.getPropertyName()
23|        old      = 'pce.getOldValue()'
24|        new      = 'pce.getNewValue()'
25|        self.textArea.append( format % locals() )
26|    def clear( self, e ) :
27|        self.textArea.setText( '' )
```

Figure 14-8 shows some images from this application. I'm not sure what I was expecting, but I didn't realize the kind of PropertyChangeEvents that would be generated (which is exactly why this kind of script is so useful).

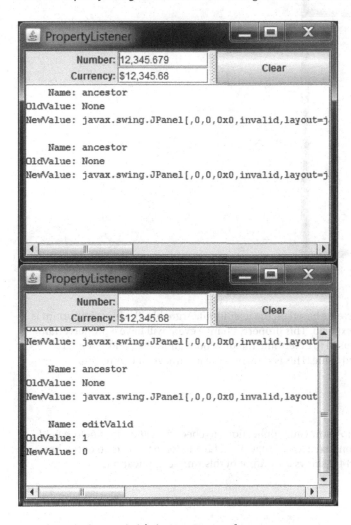

Figure 14-8. PropertyListener.py *sample output*

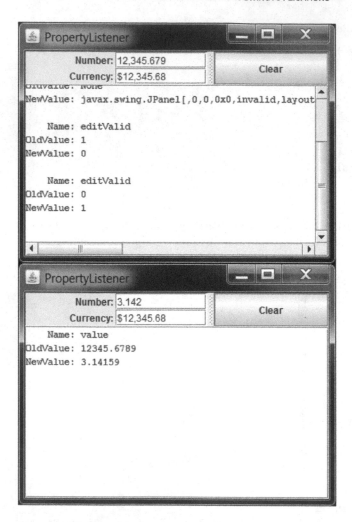

Figure 14-8. (*continued*)

The images in Figure 14-8 demonstrate various events based on the user input. Arguably, the most important is when the user enters a valid value for the formatted text field. This property change event will have a property name of value, as well as an OldValue attribute that can be used to determine the previous valid value, and a NewValue attribute that can be used to identify the newly entered value. This is shown in the last image in Figure 14-8.

Using an InputVerifier

As mentioned earlier, the InputVerifier class exists to allow your applications to check for valid input before field focus is enabled. Let's take a look at a trivial application that uses an InputVerifier to force the user to enter the value pass before the input focus can change. Figure 14-9 shows the output of this simple application.

Figure 14-9. `VerifyTest1.py` *sample output*

Listing 14-15 shows how the `InputVerifier` only needs to implement the `verify(...)` method. As long as this `verify(...)` method returns a value of `false` (0), the input focus isn't allowed to change.

Listing 14-15. Trivial Input Verification from `VerifyTest1.py`

```
 9|class inputChecker( InputVerifier ) :
10|    def verify( self, input ) :
11|        return input.getText() == "pass"
12|class VerifierTest1( java.lang.Runnable ) :
13|    def run( self ) :
14|        frame = JFrame(
15|            'VerifierTest1',
16|            locationRelativeTo = None,
17|            defaultCloseOperation = JFrame.EXIT_ON_CLOSE
18|        )
19|        frame.add(
20|            JTextField(
21|                'Enter "pass"',
22|                inputVerifier = inputChecker()
23|            ),
24|            BorderLayout.NORTH
25|        )
26|        frame.add(
27|            JTextField( 'TextField 2' ),
28|            BorderLayout.SOUTH
29|        )
30|        frame.pack()
31|        frame.setVisible( 1 )
```

The problem with this trivial implementation is that the user doesn't get much feedback that the current value is unacceptable. Wouldn't it be better if you used some of the available techniques to explain to the user that something is wrong?

Figure 14-10 shows one possible approach. Notice what happens when the user simply tries to change focus by pressing the Tab key. The border color around the input field changes to RED and the field text is selected. I don't know about you, but I find this to be a pretty strong indication that something is wrong here.

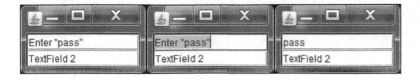

Figure 14-10. `VerifyTest2.py` *sample output*

Listing 14-16 shows this modified InputVerifier descendant class. In it, the verify(...) method does a little more than the previous version. This additional functionality requires fewer than a dozen lines of code. However, there is a world of difference between the usability of the two applications, don't you think?

Listing 14-16. A Slightly More Involved Input Verifier from VerifyTest2.py

```
11|class inputChecker( InputVerifier ) :
12|    def __init__( self ) :
13|        self.border = None    # holder for "original" border
14|    def verify( self, input ) :
15|        text = input.getText()
16|        if not self.border : # The first time, save the border
17|            self.border = input.getBorder()
18|        result = input.getText() == "pass"
19|        if result :           # valid? Restore original border
20|            input.setBorder( self.border )
21|        else :                # invalid? change border color
22|            input.setBorder( LineBorder( Color.red ) )
23|            input.selectAll()
24|        return result
```

Is there anything missing from this application? Consider what happens when an invalid value is entered. Nothing, that's what. The InputVerifier isn't invoked because it is associated with events that attempt to change the keyboard focus. Pressing the Enter key doesn't do that. This event is associated with ActionEvents, not with InputVerifier events.

Figure 14-11 shows what happens when you associate an ActionListener with the first input field that invokes the InputVerifier to validate the user input. The second image shows that, when the user presses the Enter key without changing the text, the InputVerifier indicates that the text is invalid. The final image shows what happens when the user enters valid text and presses Enter. Note that focus remains with the input field because the change of focus is not a normal result of this action.

Figure 14-11. VerifyTest3.py *sample output*

Listing 14-17 shows how simple it can be to have the ActionListener event handler routine invoke the InputVerifier shouldYieldFocus() method to initiate input verification.

Listing 14-17. Using an ActionListener Method to Verify Input from VerifyTest3.py

```
25|class VerifierTest3( java.lang.Runnable ) :
26|    def verify( self, e ) :
27|        self.verifier.shouldYieldFocus( e.getSource() )
28|    def run( self ) :
  |        ...
34|        self.verifier = inputChecker()
35|        frame.add(
36|            JTextField(
37|                'Enter "pass"',
38|                actionPerformed = self.verify,
39|                inputVerifier = self.verifier
40|            ),
41|            BorderLayout.NORTH
42|        )
  |        ...
```

Summary

This chapter covered some of events that your Swing applications will encounter. It is important to be familiar with these events so that your applications can react well to user input. Remember, though, that there are many, many events in the Swing class hierarchy. This chapter provides exposure to some of them.

In Chapter 15, you'll investigate how to use open source software libraries to enhance your applications.

CHAPTER 15

■ ■ ■

Nuts to Soup: Using Jsoup to Enhance Applications

Up to this point, the applications in this book have been pretty simple. In this chapter, you learn what it will take to create an application "as you go." By that, I mean you can start simple and iterate over its creation and development, with the intent of making it more useful based on what you learn as you go along. Additionally, you will use an existing open source software (OSS) Java class library to create a useful application built on the work of others.

Using Existing Classes: Creating an HTML Retrieval Application from Scratch

Based on the number of times that I've referred to the Java Swing documentation pages (the Javadoc for the Swing class hierarchy), along with the number of footnote references that point to various class pages, it would be useful if you had an application to help you with this kind of lookup, don't you think? So, what will such an application need to do?

Wouldn't it be great if this application were able to access and process the Javadoc pages directly? What would that take to achieve? This application needs to be able to access a remote website, request a specific page, and process the results.

Are there any classes in the Swing hierarchy that you might be able to use? Listing 15-1 shows the list of classes on the Java "All Classes" page[1] that include HTML somewhere in their class name.[2]

Listing 15-1. Java "HTML" Classes

```
BasicHTML
HTML
HTML.Attribute
HTML.Tag
HTML.UnknownTag
HTMLDocument
HTMLDocument.Iterator
HTMLEditorKit
HTMLEditorKit.HTMLFactory
```

---

[1]See http://docs.oracle.com/javase/8/docs/api/allclasses-noframe.html.
[2]This list of classes can be obtained by executing the following command. jython getLinks.py http://docs.oracle.com/javase/8/docs/api/allclasses-noframe.html | grep HTML. Then edit the result to remove the URLs that are listed with each class. The getLinks.py script is discussed later in this chapter.

```
HTMLEditorKit.HTMLTextAction
HTMLEditorKit.InsertHTMLTextAction
HTMLEditorKit.LinkController
HTMLEditorKit.Parser
HTMLEditorKit.ParserCallback
HTMLFrameHyperlinkEvent
HTMLWriter
MinimalHTMLWriter
```

This would appear to be a reasonable place to start an investigation. How could you use some of these classes in order to:

- Connect to a remote website using a uniform resource locator (URL)

- Retrieve the hypertext markup language (HTML) from that page

- Process the contents, with the purpose of locating the hyperlinks[3] and the associated text

After a bit of investigation and work, I was able to get the routine shown in Listing 15-2 working. There may be some way to refactor the code to make it slightly shorter, but I don't see any easy way to make it easier to read and understand.

Listing 15-2. The getLinks Routine

```
 8|def getLinks( page ) :
 9|    url  = URI( page ).toURL()
10|    conn = url.openConnection()
11|    isr  = InputStreamReader( conn.getInputStream() )
12|    br   = BufferedReader( isr )
13|    kit  = HTMLEditorKit()
14|    doc  = kit.createDefaultDocument()
15|    parser = ParserDelegator()
16|    callback = doc.getReader( 0 )
17|    parser.parse( br, callback, 1 )
18|    iterator = doc.getIterator( HTML.Tag.A )
19|    while iterator.isValid() :
20|        try :
21|            attr   = iterator.getAttributes()
22|            src    = attr.getAttribute( HTML.Attribute.HREF )
23|            start  = iterator.getStartOffset()
24|            fini   = iterator.getEndOffset()
25|            length = fini - start
26|            text   = doc.getText( start, length )
27|            print '%40s -> %s' % ( text, src )
28|        except :
29|            pass
30|        iterator.next()
```

---

[3]See http://en.wikipedia.org/wiki/Hyperlink.

What does the output of the script containing this routine look like? Well, Listing 15-3 shows the (slightly massaged) output of the script, which allows the output to fit in the available space. This figure shows the hyperlinks found on the IBM website (http://www.ibm.com).[4]

Listing 15-3. Absolute Links from http://www.ibm.com

```
United States -> http://www.ibm.com/planetwide/select/selector.html
        IBM?? -> http://www.ibm.com/us/en/
     Site map -> http://www.ibm.com/sitemap/us/en/
```

Figure 15-1 shows output from the Merriam Webster page. It contains a number of relative hyperlinks instead of the absolute links shown in Listing 15-3.

```
                  -> /
     "Cartouche" -> /dictionary/cartouche
    "Praemunire" -> /dictionary/praemunire
    "Positivity" -> /dictionary/positivity
Quizzes & Games -> /game/index.htm
Word of the Day -> /word-of-the-day/
          Video -> /video/index.php
      New Words -> http://nws.merriam-webster.com/opendictionary/
    My Favorites -> /my-saved-words/manage-list.htm
```

Figure 15-1. *Relative links from http://www.merriam-webster.com/*

Dealing with relative versus absolute hyperlinks is just the kind of thing that your application should take into consideration. Additionally, dealing with HTML includes the risk that it may not be well formed (i.e., syntactically correct).

Based on the hope that others are likely to have encountered and already solved these kinds of problems, I decided to search the Internet for possible solutions.

An initial search for "Jython HTML parsing" results in some interesting possibilities. Unfortunately, subsequent investigation identifies some prohibiting factors, including the fact that some Python modules (such as urllib2, HTMLParser, BeautifulSoup, and lxml) don't work well or at all with Jython environments or the possible solutions have significant performance issues.

Wouldn't It Be Nice: Using Java Libraries

If the Jython or Python modules can't help , what's left? Don't forget that one of the most significant advantages to Jython is that it is running on a Java Virtual Machine. So, you can investigate the possibility of using one or more Java libraries to help.

---

[4]This output is the result of executing wsadmin -f %SwJCode%\Chap_15\getLinks.py -conntype none with the SwJCode environment variable containing the path to the code folder that contains the book's scripts.

233

When I asked on the Jython user's mailing list[5] for suggestions, the *Jsoup*[6] *library* was quickly recommended. Jsoup is a Java library for working with "real-world" HTML (such as pages with syntax issues). The Jsoup page includes the following quote:

■ **Note**   Jsoup is a Java library for working with real-world HTML. It provides a very convenient API for extracting and manipulating data, using the best of DOM, CSS, and jQuery-like methods.

Jsoup implements the WHATWG HTML5[7] specification and parses HTML to the same DOM as modern browsers do.

This sounds exactly like the kind of thing you need in this case, don't you think?

Working with the Jsoup Library

Follow these steps to use a new library with wsadmin and Jython:

1. First, you need to download the Jsoup archive library:

   • Point your favorite browser to http://jsoup.org/.

   • Select the Download link.

   • Right-click on the core library file[8] and save it in a convenient directory.

2. For wsadmin, you need to add this Java archive to the classpath. Fortunately, a wsadmin command-line option exists to do exactly this. If the Jsoup JAR file is in the C:\temp directory, this can be as simple as:[9]

   ```
   wsadmin -wsadmin_classpath c:\temp\jsoup-1.8.1.jar -f scriptName.py
   ```

   For Jython, you only need to have this library (JAR file) as part of the JYTHONPATH environment variable. For example:

   ```
   Set JYTHONPATH=C:\Programs\jsoup\jsoup-1.8.1.jar;%JYTHONPATH%
   jython scriptName.py
   ```

---

[5]See jython-users@lists.sourceforge.net.
[6]See http://jsoup.org/.
[7]See http://whatwg.org/html.
[8]At the time of this writing, it was jsoup-1.8.1.jar.
[9]The first time that Jython is told about this Java archive, you will see a message something like this to indicate that Jython is aware of the archive and has processed it to store information about the JAR file for later use by Jython scripts.

```
*sys-package-mgr*: processing new jar, 'C:\temp\jsoup-1.8.1.jar'.
```

Listing 15-4 shows a simple, interactive `wsadmin` session that demonstrates how easy it is for scripts to use the Jsoup library.

Listing 15-4. Simple Jsoup Demonstration

```
 1|wsadmin>from org.jsoup import Jsoup
 2|wsadmin>
 3|wsadmin>doc = Jsoup.connect( 'http://www.ibm.com' ).get()
 4|wsadmin>doc.title()
 5|'IBM - United States'
 6|wsadmin>for link in doc.getElementsByTag( 'a' ) :
 7|wsadmin>    print link.attr( 'abs:href' )
 8|wsadmin>
 9|http://www.ibm.com/planetwide/select/selector.html
10|http://www.ibm.com/us/en/
11|http://www.ibm.com/sitemap/us/en/
12|http://www.ibm.com/software/marketing-solutions/benchmark-hub/...
13|http://www.ibm.com/systems/infrastructure/us/en/it-infrastruct...
14|http://www-935.ibm.com/services/us/en/it-services/business-con...
15|http://www.ibm.com/common/twitter/ibm.xml
16|http://www.ibm.com/news/us/en
17|...
```

Table 15-1 contains a description of each line of the simple interactive session.

Table 15-1. *Simple Jsoup Demonstration, Explained*

Lines	Description
1	Import statement used to add the Jsoup library to the current namespace.
2	An empty line to make the session input easier to read.
3	A statement used to retrieve the contents of the `www.ibm.com` web page. **Note:** It is possible for an exception to be raised.
4	Demonstration of using the `title()` method[10] to display the title of the retrieved web page.
6-8	For loop used to retrieve the HTML links and display the absolute URLs[11] to which they refer.
9...	The remainder of the session shows the first few lines that are output by the previous loop.

Isn't this easier to read, understand, and use than the ones from the Swing hierarchy? I think so, and I'm pretty sure that you'll agree.

---

[10]See `http://jsoup.org/apidocs/org/jsoup/nodes/Document.html#title()`.
[11]See `http://jsoup.org/cookbook/extracting-data/working-with-urls`.

Jsoup Call May Appear to Hang

So now you're all set, right? No, not quite. Remember that the Swing applications need to be able to deal with events. More importantly, you don't want the application to wait or appear to be "hung," while waiting for things (such as like the retrieval of web pages) to complete. As mentioned before, you're going to start simple and make decisions based on how things look.

First you need a descendant of the SwingWorker class to perform the Jsoup retrieval and to process requests on a separate thread. Listing 15-5 shows the soupTask class from this simple application.

Listing 15-5. soupTask Class from javadocInfo_01.py

```
23|class soupTask( SwingWorker ) :
24|    def __init__( self, comboBox, label, url ) :
25|        self.cb  = comboBox      # Save provided references
26|        self.msg = label
27|        self.url = url           # URL to be used
28|        self.doc = None
29|        SwingWorker.__init__( self )
30|    def doInBackground( self ) :
31|        try :
32|            self.msg.setText( 'working...' )
33|            self.doc = Jsoup.connect( self.url ).get()
34|            self.msg.setText( 'ready' )
35|        except :
36|            Type, value = sys.exc_info()[ :2 ]
37|            print 'Error:', str( Type )
38|            print 'value:', str( value )
39|            self.msg.setText( str( value ) )
40|        if self.doc :
41|            self.cb.removeAllItems()
42|            for link in self.doc.getElementsByTag( 'a' ) :
43|                self.cb.addItem( str( link.text() ) )
44|    def done( self ) :
45|        pass
```

Figure 15-2 shows some sample images from the first Swing application using the Jsoup library.

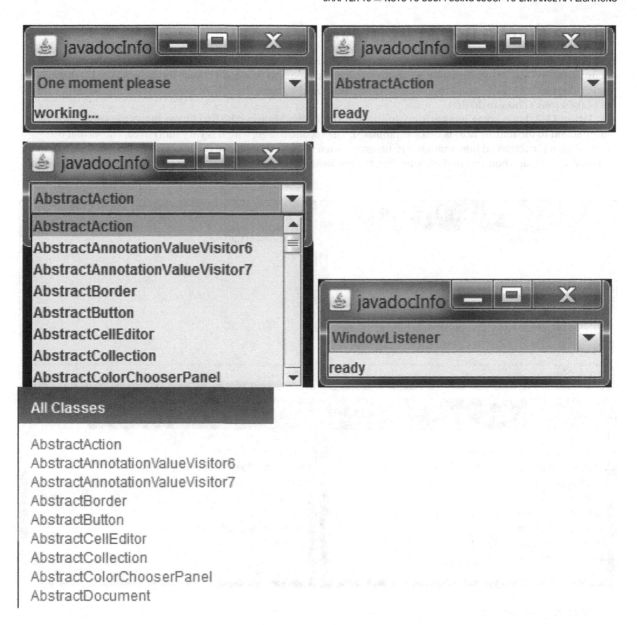

Figure 15-2. javadocInfo_01.py sample output

The last image in Figure 15-2 shows that a browser appears when the same URL is used. It certainly looks like the Jsoup application is working as expected.

From a Combo Box to a List Box

That application is quite simple and demonstrates the feasibility of using the Jsoup library to process the current Java documentation URL.[12] Unfortunately, a combo box doesn't appear to be a good choice for showing the list of available entries, does it? What else is missing? Well, I would like to be able to see the URL of the selected entry, wouldn't you? Let's take a look at how to do that.

Figure 15-3 shows some images from this iteration of the application. The first image shows the application as a connection to the remote host is being established. The second image, which is very short lived, shows that the processing of the retrieved information is in progress. Then you see an image of the list of items from the page, and finally, you see that when you make a selection, the text field is updated to reflect the associated URL for the selection.

Figure 15-3. javadocInfo_02.py sample output

To make this happen, you have to change the JComboBox into a JList, which allows you to display more entries. This means that you need to change the soupTask class to deal with these changes. Additionally, a new argument is added to this constructor, so that the task can return a dictionary of the links found on the page, indexed by the text associated with each link. Listing 15-6 shows the most significant changes that were made to the application.

---

[12]See http://docs.oracle.com/javase/8/docs/api/allclasses-noframe.html.

Listing 15-6. soupTask, Iteration 2, from javadocInfo_02.py

```
26|class soupTask( SwingWorker ) :
27|    def __init__( self, List, label, url, result ) :
28|        self.List = List                 # Save provided references
29|        self.msg  = label
30|        self.url  = url                   # URL to be used
31|        self.doc  = None
32|        self.docLinks = result            # lookup result
33|        SwingWorker.__init__( self )
34|    def doInBackground( self ) :
35|        try :
36|            self.msg.setText( 'connecting...' )
37|            self.doc = Jsoup.connect( self.url ).get()
38|            self.msg.setText( 'processing...' )
39|            model = DefaultListModel()
40|            for link in self.doc.getElementsByTag( 'a' ) :
41|                name = link.text()
42|                href = link.attr( 'abs:href' )
43|                self.docLinks[ name ] = href
44|                model.addElement( name )
45|            self.List.setModel( model )
46|            self.msg.setText( 'Make a selection' )
47|        except :
48|            Type, value = sys.exc_info()[ :2 ]
49|            Type, value = str( Type ), str( value )
50|            print 'Error:', Type
51|            print 'value:', value
52|            self.msg.setText( value )
53|    def done( self ) :
54|        pass
```

That's pretty good, but it's still not a great application. What else can you do to make it more useful and usable?

Listing 15-7 shows the main application class of the second iteration of the Javadoc lookup application. Overall, it's amazing how much this little application can do with fewer than 100 lines of Jython code.

Listing 15-7. javadocInfo_02 Application Class

```
55|class javadocInfo_02( java.lang.Runnable ) :
56|    def run( self ) :
57|        frame = JFrame(
58|            'javadocInfo_02',
59|            locationRelativeTo = None,
60|            size = ( 350, 225 ),
61|            defaultCloseOperation = JFrame.EXIT_ON_CLOSE
62|        )
63|        model = DefaultListModel()
64|        model.addElement( 'One moment please...' )
65|        self.List = JList(
66|            model,
67|            valueChanged = self.pick,
68|            selectionMode = ListSelectionModel.SINGLE_SELECTION
69|        )
```

239

```
70|          frame.add(
71|              JScrollPane( self.List ),
72|              BorderLayout.CENTER
73|          )
74|          self.msg = JTextField()
75|          frame.add( self.msg, BorderLayout.SOUTH )
76|          self.Links = {}
77|          soupTask(
78|              self.List,          # The visible JList instance
79|              self.msg,           # The message area (JTextField)
80|              JAVADOC_URL,        # Remote web page URL to be processed
81|              self.Links          # Dictionary of links found
82|          ).execute()
83|          frame.setVisible( 1 )
```

Listing 15-8 shows the ListSelectionListener[13] event handler that's invoked when the user makes a selection. It takes a bit of work (code) to figure out when this handler actually has some work to do. Why is that? One reason is that it is invoked when a ListSelectionEvent[14] occurs. So, the first thing it does is determine if the event that occurred is related to a selection adjustment, which is ignored. Then it checks the number of entries on the list. If only one element is present, which only occurs when the list is created with the "One moment please. . ." message, this event is ignored.

Finally, it checks to see if an element is selected, in which case the URL associated with this item is displayed in the message text field. Otherwise, the "Make a selection" message is displayed.

Listing 15-8. javadocInfo_02.py ListSelectionListener Event Handler

```
84|    def pick( self, e ) :
85|        if not e.getValueIsAdjusting() :
86|            List  = self.List
87|            model = List.getModel()
88|            if model.getSize() > 1 :
89|                index = List.getSelectedIndex()
90|                if index > -1 :
91|                    choice = model.elementAt( index )
92|                    self.msg.setText( self.Links[ choice ] )
93|                else :
94|                    self.msg.setText( 'Make a selection' )
```

Adding a TextArea to Show the HTML

From here, it's easy to imagine how useful it would be to retrieve the contents of the page that is selected by the user. You really don't need to create another web browser.[15] It is potentially useful if the application can retrieve, process, and analyze a user-selectable page. Let's begin by displaying the page's contents (the HTML), and then decide how best to proceed. Listing 15-9 contains the modified textTask class, which is where the most interesting changes occur.

---

[13]See http://docs.oracle.com/javase/8/docs/api/javax/swing/event/ListSelectionListener.html.
[14]See http://docs.oracle.com/javase/8/docs/api/javax/swing/event/ListSelectionEvent.html.
[15]In fact, if you try to display a complete HTML page using one of the HTML-aware components, you are likely to encounter a large number of Java exceptions.

240

Listing 15-9. textTask Class from javadocInfo_03.py

```
60|class textTask( SwingWorker ) :
61|    def __init__( self, area, url ) :
62|        self.area = area              # Save area to be updated
63|        self.url  = url               # URL to be retrieved
64|        SwingWorker.__init__( self )
65|    def doInBackground( self ) :
66|        try :
67|            self.area.setText( 'connecting...' )
68|            doc = Jsoup.connect( self.url ).get()
69|            self.area.setText( str( doc.normalise() ) )
70|        except :
71|            Type, value = sys.exc_info()[ :2 ]
72|            Type, value = str( Type ), str( value )
73|            self.area.setText(
74|                '\nError: %s\nValue: %s' % ( Type, value )
75|            )
76|    def done( self ) :
77|        pass
```

Figure 15-4 shows some sample output from the javadocInfo_03.py script. The first image shows the HTML text from the JFrame Javadoc web page. It should be no surprise that the TextArea containing the HTML needs to be in a scroll pane. The second image shows the portion of the HTML that describes the Field Summary portion of the page. The last image shows how this HTML is displayed in a browser.

Figure 15-4. javadocInfo_03 sample output

241

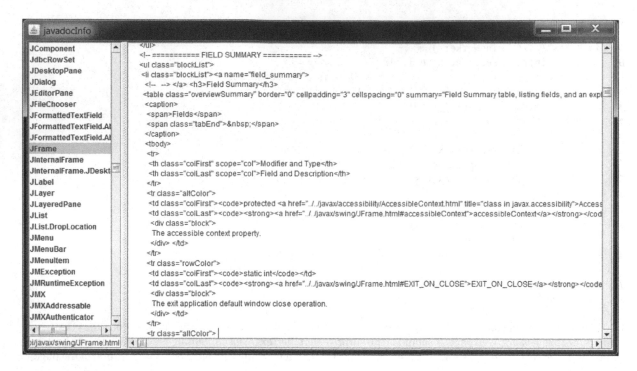

Field Summary

Fields		
Modifier and Type	**Field and Description**	
protected AccessibleContext	accessibleContext	
	The accessible context property.	
static int	EXIT_ON_CLOSE	
	The exit application default window close operation.	
protected JRootPane	rootPane	
	The JRootPane instance that manages the contentPane and optional menuBar for this frame, as well as the glassPane.	
protected boolean	rootPaneCheckingEnabled	
	If true then calls to add and setLayout will be forwarded to the contentPane.	

Figure 15-4. (*continued*)

Rendering HTML

It certainly would be nice if you could actually use HTML tags to tell how the Swing component should display information. Well, you can, at least to a limited extent. Some, but not all, Swing components are capable of using HTML tags to determine how information should be displayed. You saw from the most recent application output in Figure 15-4 that the JTextArea component doesn't do this.

Don't get your hopes up too quickly. You won't be able to create a fully capable web browser in your applications simply by selecting the "right" Swing components.

Another caveat you need to be aware of is the fact that the HTML specification implemented in the Swing component hierarchy is 3.2, so it's not as feature-rich as the latest HTML specification (version 5), which is starting to show up on the Internet.

What does it take to have one of the HTML capable components display text as the HTML tags indicate? Well, it's as simple as having the text attribute string begin with <html>.

Listing 15-10 contains the trivial script that demonstrates just how easy it is to use HTML to do this. Please be careful though—just because you can do something, doesn't mean that you should.

Listing 15-10. HTMLtext_01.py Script Showing an HTML Label

```
 1|from javax.swing import JFrame
 2|from javax.swing import JLabel
 3|frame = JFrame(
 4|            'HTMLtext_01',
 5|            size = ( 200, 200 ),
 6|            locationRelativeTo = None,
 7|            defaultCloseOperation = JFrame.EXIT_ON_CLOSE
 8|        )
 9|text  = '<html>'
10|text += '<sup>My</sup> '
11|text += '<sub><i>Label</i></sub> '
12|text += '<font color="#FF0000">is</font> '
13|text += '<font color="#00FF00"><b>far</b></font> '
14|text += '<font color="#0000FF">too busy,</font> '
15|text += "<u>isn't it?</u>"
16|label = frame.add( JLabel( text ) )
17|frame.setVisible( 1 )
18|raw_input()
```

Figure 15-5 demonstrates this axiom quite vividly. Keep in mind that you should be interested in making your application more appealing, not less.

Figure 15-5. HTMLtext_01.py sample output

If you are familiar with HTML, you know that you can do all sorts of interesting things with it. For example, as you can see in Figure 15-6, you can create a simple unordered list tag (starts on line 10 and ends on line 14 of Listing 15-?) to display a bulleted list with each item in a different color.

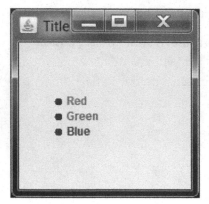

Figure 15-6. *HTMLtext_02.py sample output*

Listing 15-11 shows the trivial script used to produce the output in Figure 15-6. As you can see, it's up to the developer how to build the string. In this case, using multiple concatenation steps to build the HTML string makes for a better and more complete understanding of the various parts of the HTML.

Listing 15-11. HTMLtext_02.py Source

```
 1|from javax.swing import JFrame
 2|from javax.swing import JLabel
 3|frame = JFrame(
 4|            'HTMLtext_02',
 5|            size = ( 200, 200 ),
 6|            locationRelativeTo = None,
 7|            defaultCloseOperation = JFrame.EXIT_ON_CLOSE
 8|        )
 9|text = '<html>'
10|text += '<ul compact>'
11|text += '<li><font color="red">Red</font></li>'
12|text += '<li><font color="green">Green</font></li>'
13|text += '<li><font color="blue">Blue</font></li>'
14|text += '</ul>'
15|label = frame.add( JLabel( text ) )
16|frame.setVisible( 1 )
17|raw_input()
```

Modifying the HTML Text

In addition to static components, your applications might have some dynamic components that might be improved by the users of the HTML. Do you remember the JToggleButton component discussed in Chapter 8? Figure 15-7 shows one way to use HTML to make the button state more obvious to the users.

Figure 15-7. *HTMLtext_03.py sample output*

Listing 15-12 shows part of the HTMLtext_03.py script that was used to produce this output. If you're uncomfortable with the statement in lines 24-29, don't worry. It uses Jython's flexibility to determine which color and text values should be used by indexing an array using the result of calling the button.isSelected() method.

Listing 15-12. Using HTML in a JToggleButton from HTMLtext_03.py

```
 6|class HTMLtext_03( java.lang.Runnable ) :
 7|    def run( self ) :
 8|        frame = JFrame(
 9|            'HTMLtext_03',
10|            size = ( 100, 100 ),
11|            locationRelativeTo = None,
12|            defaultCloseOperation = JFrame.EXIT_ON_CLOSE
13|        )
14|        text  = '<html><font color="red">Off</font>'
15|        label = frame.add(
16|            JToggleButton(
17|                text,
18|                itemStateChanged = self.toggle
19|            )
20|        )
21|        frame.setVisible( 1 )
22|    def toggle( self, event ) :
23|        button = event.getItem()
24|        button.setText(
25|            '<html><font color="%s">%s</font>' % [
26|                ( 'red'  , 'Off' ),
27|                ( 'green', 'On'  )
28|            ][ button.isSelected() ]
29|        )
```

Listing 15-13 shows some additional ways that this might be done.[16] I'm quite certain that you can come up with some other alternatives yourself.

Listing 15-13. Alternative Ways of Setting the JToggleButton Text

```
 if button.isSelected() :
     text = '<html><font color="red">Off</font>'
 else :
     text = '<html><font color="green">On</font>'
 button.setText( text )

   ... or even ...

 if button.isSelected() :
     color, value = 'red', 'Off'
 else :
     color, value = 'green', 'On'
 text = '<html><font color="%s">%s</font>' % ( color, value )
 button.setText( text )
```

Identifying the Sections

Now that you've learned about the components that you can use to display text that's been marked up in HTML, it's time to return to Jsoup to see what you can do to improve your Javadoc application.

Note in Figure 15-4 that the HTML for a Swing class can be quite extensive. The application that I'm considering, at least for this chapter, can display a subset of the information that's available on the user selected entry, not the complete details.

Let's work on this in steps, so that you can learn as you go along. To begin, let's see what it takes to build a tiny application that will display the header text for a specific Javadoc page. The getHeaders class that is used in all three of the getHeader scripts is shown in Listing 15-14. As you can see, it is a simple application that uses a SwingWorker descendent class to populate a scrollable text area with the HTML heading tags from the JFrame Javadoc URL.

Listing 15-14. The getHeaders Class[17]

```
62|class getHeaders1( java.lang.Runnable ) :
63|    def run( self ) :
64|        frame = JFrame(
65|            'JFrame headers',
66|            size = ( 500, 250 ),
67|            locationRelativeTo = None,
68|            defaultCloseOperation = JFrame.EXIT_ON_CLOSE
69|        )
```

---

[16]This is a kind of a tip of the hat to Perl's "Tim Toady" (TMTOWTDI) motto at http://en.wikipedia.org/wiki/There%27s_more_than_one_way_to_do_it and the "Zen of Python," which can be seen at http://www.python.org/dev/peps/pep-0020/.
[17]The complete URL of the JFrame Javadoc is http://docs.oracle.com/javase/8/docs/api/javax/swing/JFrame.html.

```
70|          textArea = JTextArea()
71|          frame.add( JScrollPane( textArea ) )
72|          url = '.../docs/api/javax/swing/JFrame.html'
73|          headerTask( url, textArea ).execute()
74|          frame.setVisible( 1 )
```

Listing 15-15 shows the headerTask that uses the Jsoup library to retrieve the specified HTML, process it, and display the result in the user-specified area. If you watch closely while executing any of these getHeader scripts, you might be able to see the connecting... and processing... messages that this class produces.

It is important to note that this class uses the Jsoup items to process the retrieved HTML. The ones new to this application are found in the getPlainText(...) method, as shown on lines 38-42.

Listing 15-15. The headerTask Class from the getHeader1.py Script Files

```
38|class headerTask( SwingWorker ) :
39|    def __init__( self, url, result ) :
40|        self.url    = url                # URL to be retrieved
41|        self.result = result
42|        SwingWorker.__init__( self )
43|    def getPlainText( self, element ) :
44|        visitor = FormattingVisitor( self.url )
45|        walker  = NodeTraversor( visitor )
46|        walker.traverse( element )
47|        return visitor.toString()
48|    def doInBackground( self ) :
49|        try :
50|            self.result.setText( 'connecting...' )
51|            doc = Jsoup.connect( self.url ).get()
52|            self.result.setText( 'processing...' )
53|            self.text = self.getPlainText( doc )
54|        except :
55|            Type, value = sys.exc_info()[ :2 ]
56|            Type, value = str( Type ), str( value )
57|            print '\nError:', Type
58|            print 'value:', value
59|            self.result.setText( 'Exception: %s' % value )
60|    def done( self ) :
61|        self.result.setText( self.text )
```

The FormattingVisitor(...) method is a descendant of the Jsoup NodeVisitor class, and its implementation is shown in Listing 15-16. This is the only class in the three getHeader#.py scripts that changes. In this class, the application appends the text of any HTML header tags that it finds to be displayed in the application text area.

Listing 15-16. The FormattingVisitor() Method from getHeader1.py

```
23|class FormattingVisitor( NodeVisitor ) :
24|    def __init__( self, url ) :
25|        self.result = StringBuilder()
26|    def append( self, text ) :
27|        newline = [ '', '\n' ][ self.result.length() > 0 ]
28|        self.result.append( newline + text )
29|    def head( self, node, depth ) :
30|        name = node.nodeName()
31|        if name in [ 'h1', 'h2', 'h3', 'h4', 'h5', 'h6' ] :
32|            if node.hasText() :
33|                self.append( '%s: %s' % ( name, node.text() ) )
34|    def tail( self, node, depth ) :
35|        name = node.nodeName()
36|    def toString( self ) :
37|        return str( self.result )
```

The only method that changes in the three getHeader scripts is head(...). The one from getHeader2.py is shown in Listing 15-17. Note how this iteration is only interested in the H3 (Header 3) tags.

Listing 15-17. The head(...) Method from getHeader2.py

```
29|    def head( self, node, depth ) :
30|        name = node.nodeName()
31|        if name == 'h3' :
32|            if node.hasText() :
33|                self.append( '%s: %s' % ( name, node.text() ) )
```

Listing 15-18 shows the last version of the head(...) method. This version is only interested in H3 tags whose text doesn't contain the word "inherited."

Listing 15-18. The head(...) Method from getHeader3.py

```
29|    def head( self, node, depth ) :
30|        name = node.nodeName()
31|        if name == 'h3' and node.hasText() :
32|            text = node.text()
33|            if text.find( 'inherited' ) < 0 :
34|                self.append( '%s: %s' % ( name, text ) )
```

Figure 15-8 shows the output of these three getHeader scripts. From this output, it shouldn't be too much of a leap to figure out how to change the Javadoc script to display the most useful H3 text. Before you do that, though, take a moment to figure out where you want to go next.

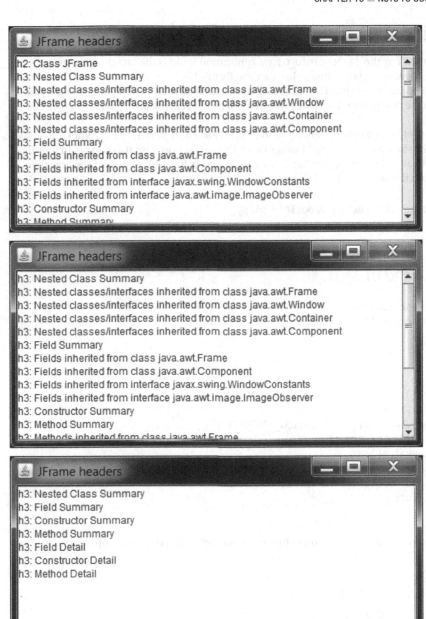

Figure 15-8. Sample output from the getHeader scripts

Fixing the Great Divide

One of the problems that I have with the way the javadocInfo_03.py application looks is the fact that the divider doesn't provide enough space to see the longer class names. How can you fix this?

To begin with, it's a good idea to adjust the position to something more convenient. If you do that, though, you need to have the application tell you the new position, so that you can use it as the starting position for the revised application.

You need to add a PropertyChangeListener event handler to the JSplitPane and watch for the right kind of changes. This is all very easy to say, but how easy is it to do? Listing 15-19 shows just how easy this can be. In line 109, you see how to specify the PropertyChangeListener event handler method, and in lines 137-146, you see how the event handler determines and displays the divider-related changes.

Listing 15-19. PropertyChangeListener Changes in javadocInfo_04.py

```
      |    ...
104|        frame.add(
105|            JSplitPane(
106|                JSplitPane.HORIZONTAL_SPLIT,
107|                pane,
108|                JScrollPane( self.area ),
109|                propertyChange = self.propChange
110|            )
111|        )
      |    ...
137|    def propChange( self, pce ) :
138|        src  = pce.getSource()          # Should be our JSplitPane
139|        prop = pce.getPropertyName()
140|        if prop == JSplitPane.LAST_DIVIDER_LOCATION_PROPERTY :
141|            curr = src.getDividerLocation()
142|            last = pce.getNewValue()
143|            prev = pce.getOldValue()
144|            print '\nlast: %4d  prev: %4d  curr: %4d' % (
145|                last, prev, curr
146|            ),
```

Figure 15-9 shows the sample output from an execution of the script that determined a more appropriate divider value.

```
last:    -1  prev:     0  curr:   129
last:   129  prev:    -1  curr:   129
last:    -1  prev:   129  curr:   129
last:   129  prev:    -1  curr:   271
last:   271  prev:   129  curr:   271
last:   129  prev:   271  curr:   271
```

Figure 15-9. SplitPane PropertyChangeListener output

So what can you do with this newfound knowledge? Well, my initial attempt consisted of adding a dividerLocation keyword argument to the JSplitPane[18] constructor call. Unfortunately, this caused an exception indicating that this is a read-only value.

Looking at the Javadoc, you can see that there are multiple setDividerLocation(...) methods, which is likely to be the source of the problem. So you need to call one of these setter methods after JSplitPane has been instantiated. Listing 15-20 shows how this is done in the javadocInfo_05.py script.

Listing 15-20. Using a DividerLocation Setter Method Call

```
106|        sPane = JSplitPane(
107|                    JSplitPane.HORIZONTAL_SPLIT,
108|                    pane,
109|                    JScrollPane( self.area ),
110|                    propertyChange = self.propChange
111|                )
112|        sPane.setDividerLocation( 234 )
```

Filtering the List

One of the problems with the complete list of classes that's initially displayed by the javadocInfo script is that it's too long. If you drag the scroll bar down, you'll quickly see that there are something like 4,000 classes listed. This makes it harder for the users to deal with.

Wouldn't it be nice to use the JTextField as an input field filter that allowed users to enter text to be matched? That's what you'll do next. The changes that need to be made include the following:

- Locate the places in the script where the setText(...) method is used to show the URL associated with the user selection.

- Add a listener to JTextField that allows you to monitor user input and locate class names containing the user-specified text. For this, I chose to use a CaretListener and check for changes in the user-specified text.

The javadocInfo_06.py script contains these changes and Figure 15-10 shows some sample screens.

---

[18]See http://docs.oracle.com/javase/8/docs/api/javax/swing/JSplitPane.html.

Figure 15-10. javadocInfo_06.py sample output with list filtering

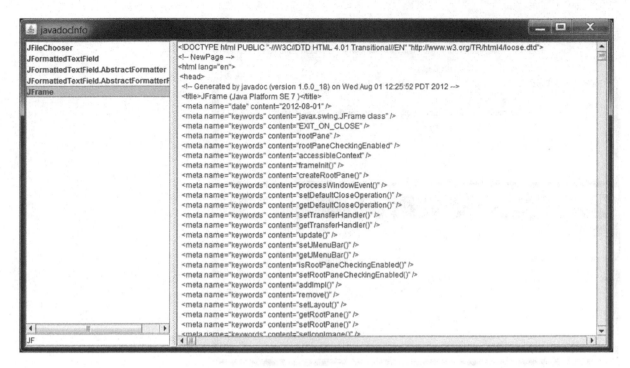

Figure 15-10. (*continued*)

Using Jsoup to Pick Up the Tab: Adding a JTabbedPane

I wonder how difficult it would be for the Jsoup library to process the Javadoc HTML and find the tables that are frequently found in the heading 3 (h3) sections of the documentation? While I was thinking about this, it came to me that I might be able to use a JTabbedPane, with the tab name being the heading 3 text and the contents being the HTML table.

You could even use a suitable pane to render the table properly. This is sounding interesting. To simplify things during my testing (and learning) phases, I chose to start with the getHeaders script.

Figure 15-11 shows the sample output of the getHeaders5.py script, which retrieves and processes the Javadoc for the JFrame class.

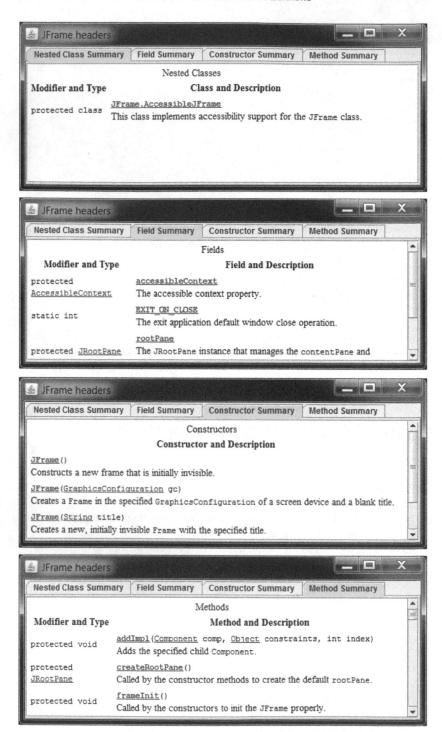

Figure 15-11. getHeaders5.py output with JFrame h3 tables on JTabbedPane

The most significant changes are shown in Listing 15-21, which contains the FormattingVisitor class from the getHeaders5.py script.

Listing 15-21. FormattingVisitor Class Used to Build the JTabbedPane

```
25|class FormattingVisitor( NodeVisitor ) :
26|    def __init__( self, url ) :
27|        self.Tabs   = JTabbedPane()
28|        self.header = re.compile( '[hH][1-6]$' )
29|        self.h3Text = ''
30|    def head( self, node, depth ) :
31|        name = node.nodeName()
32|        if re.match( self.header, name ) :
33|            self.h3Text = [ '', node.text() ] [ name[ 1 ] == '3' ]
34|    def tail( self, node, depth ) :
35|        name = node.nodeName()
36|        if self.h3Text and name == 'table' :
37|            ePane = JEditorPane(
38|                'text/html',                # mime type
39|                '<html>' + str( node ),     # content
40|                editable = 0
41|            )
42|            self.Tabs.addTab( self.h3Text, JScrollPane( ePane ) )
43|    def toString( self ) :
44|        tp = self.Tabs
45|        return '\n'.join(
46|            [
47|                tp.getTitleAt( i )
48|                for i in range( tp.getTabCount() )
49|            ]
50|        )
```

Table 15-2 explains how this class works, in detail.

Table 15-2. FormattingVisitor Class, Explained

Lines	Description
26-29	Class constructor used to instantiate the JTabbedPane, as well as define a regular expression (RegExp) to identify heading tags, specifically h3 tags.
30-33	The head(...) method is called by the NodeTraversor() method as the HTML is processed. It is invoked when any open tag is encountered (such as <h2> or <table...>). The value of the h3Text variable is set to an empty string (when any other head level is encountered) or to the text associated with the heading tag when an h3 tag is found.
34-42	The tail(...) method is called as the HTML is processed, specifically when an end tag (such as </h3> or </table>) is found. When a table "end" tag is found after an <h3> tag, a read-only JEditorPane is created containing the whole <table> HTML. This JEditorPane instance is placed in a JScrollPane and added as a tab to the JTabbedPane.
43-50	The toString(...) method is provided and returns a string with all of the JTabbedPane tab names, separated by newline \n characters.

The only other significant difference in this script relates to how the SwingWorker descendent class (headerTask) updates the application in a way that allows the updates to be shown to the users. Listing 15-22 shows the headerTask class from getHeader5.py.

Listing 15-22. The headerTask Class from the getHeaders5.py Script

```
51|class headerTask( SwingWorker ) :
52|    def __init__( self, url, frame ) :
53|        self.url   = url              # URL to be retrieved
54|        self.frame = frame
55|        SwingWorker.__init__( self )
56|    def doInBackground( self ) :
57|        try :
58|            print 'connecting...'
59|            doc = Jsoup.connect( self.url ).get()
60|            print 'processing...'
61|            visitor = FormattingVisitor( self.url )
62|            walker  = NodeTraversor( visitor )
63|            walker.traverse( doc )
64|            self.frame.add( visitor.Tabs )
65|            self.frame.validate()
66|        except :
67|            Type, value = sys.exc_info()[ :2 ]
68|            Type, value = str( Type ), str( value )
69|            print '\nError:', Type
70|            print 'value:', value
71|    def done( self ) :
72|        print 'done'
```

Table 15-3 describes the headerTask class in detail. The most important part of this is how this class informs the Swing framework that it needs to validate the application (frame) updates. If this isn't done, the user won't see any of the changes.

Table 15-3. *The headerTask Class, Explained*

Lines	Description
52-55	Class constructor used to save the specified URL, as well as a reference to the application frame to be modified. This method also has to invoke the SwingWorker constructor in order to properly initialize the class as a SwingWorker instance.
56-70	The doInBackground() method is where the actual (generally long-running) processing occurs.
59	This is where the HTML from the specified URL is retrieved.
61-63	A NodeVisitor call uses the FormattingVisitor instance to process the Javadoc from the specified URL.
64	The result of the processing is a JTabbedPane instance, which is added to the application's JFrame instance. Unfortunately, this call to the frame.add(...) method is not likely to happen in a way that lets the Swing framework know that a change has occurred.
65	The call to frame.validate() forces the framework to recognize that it needs to process the changes and update the user display.
	Note: Lines 58, 60, and 72 write messages to the console to let you know that things are progressing. They certainly aren't required and may be commented out.
	If you comment out line 72, you also need to add a pass statement to satisfy language syntax requirements.

The Jsoup library is quite powerful. Even a tiny bit of testing shows some neat capabilities. For example, I find the output shown in Figure 15-11 a bit hard to read. When I looked at the HTML found in the Javadoc pages, I saw that all of the tables have a border="0" attribute that keeps the grid lines between columns and rows from being shown. Do you know how difficult it is to use the Jsoup library to change the table border attributes to "1"?

Take a look at Listing 15-22, specifically at line 54 where the HTML document is retrieved from the remote website. All you need to do is add the statement in Listing 15-23 after the HTML has been retrieved, and before it is processed by the rest of the code.

Listing 15-23. Changing the border Attribute of All the Tables

```
doc.select( 'table' ).attr( 'border', '1' )
```

It's as simple as that. The result of adding this statement can be seen in Figure 15-12.

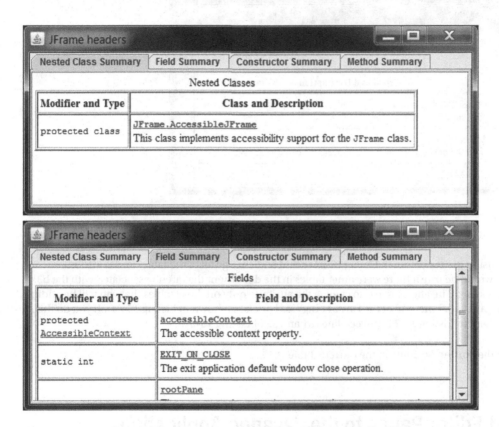

Figure 15-12. *getHeaders6.py output with JFrame h3 tables on JTabbedPane*

Figure 15-12. (*continued*)

If you think about it, using the statement in Listing 15-23 to find and change all of the table border attributes might be extra work. This would be true if there were other tables in the document that aren't associated with the h3 sections that you want to display. The alternative is to change the attribute only on those tables that you will be adding to the JEditorPane in the tail(...) method of the FormattingVisitor class (shown in Listing 15-21). If you do this, you need to add the statement in Listing 15-24 between lines 31 and 32 of Listing 15-21.

Listing 15-24. Changing the border Attribute of the Current Table

```
node.attr( 'border', '1' )
```

Adding Tabbed Editor Panes to the Javadoc Application

What do you need to do in order to add the functionality of the getHeader6.py script to the latest javadocInfo_06.py script?

- The right pane needs to be changed. It isn't a simple JTextArea instance any longer. You have to decide what you want to display when nothing is selected, and you have to figure out how to display the JTabbedPane after a class' HTML has been processed.

- What do you want the application to do as the data is being retrieved and processed? Currently, you can display a status message in the JTextArea. It would seem that you need to dynamically change the right panel of SplitPane, based on what needs to be displayed.

In order for the application to display different kinds of panes in the frame, you need to use a JSplitPane method that wasn't covered in Chapter 5. Since the SplitPane has left and right parts, you need to use the setRightComponent(...) method to dynamically replace that part of the application.

In order for the application to display tabbed JEditorPanes, you'll also need to replace the textTask class (as seen in Listing 15-9) with a modified version of the headerTask class shown in Listing 15-22. This class needs to have the right information so that it can display a status message or the final JTabbedPane result in the application's SplitPane.

What's the result of making these changes? Figure 15-13 shows some sample images from the modified script (javadocInfo_07.py).

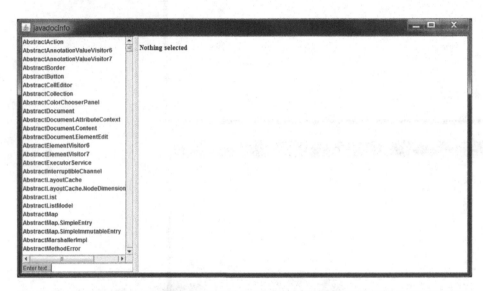

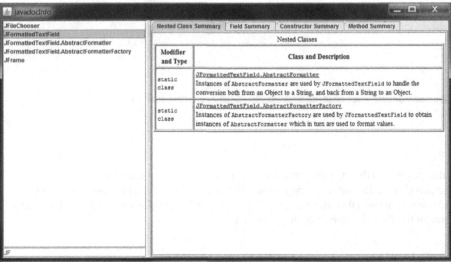

Figure 15-13. *javadocInfo_07.py sample output*

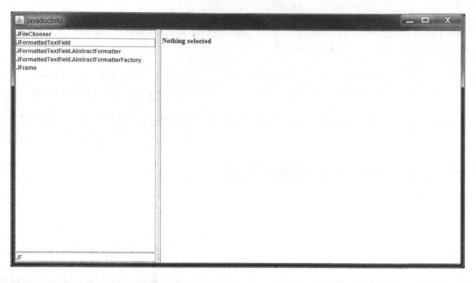

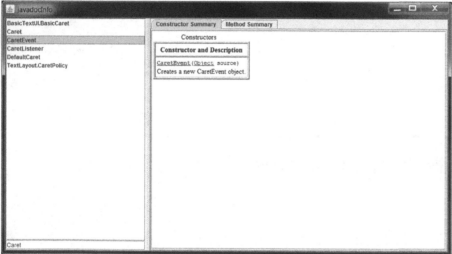

Figure 15-13. (*continued*)

Were there any surprises that happened during this combination process? A few, but not nearly as many as I feared. The biggest surprise was that the first attempt showed that when the JTabbedPane replaced the right component of the SplitPane, the width of the left component used to display the list of classes narrowed drastically. So, I had to set the minimum size of the JScrollPane containing this list.

What Improvements/Enhancements Remain?

As is frequently the case when using any program, possible enhancements come to mind. You might want to consider adding some menu items. This would make sense if you wanted to allow the users to specify the URL of the page from which it should load the list of Java classes. Another possible menu entry might be used to allow the user to filter class entries (such as AWT and Swing).

You might also want to add a tab to the tabbed pane that shows the class hierarchy produced by the `classInfo` function mentioned in Chapter 4.

If you are really ambitious, you could add functionality to the Editor Panes so that the links in the displayed HTML open the specified website in a browser.

I haven't delved too deeply into the subject of Editor Panes. There is a decent page in the Java Swing Tutorials entitled "How to Use Editor Panes and Text Panes"[19] that you might want to take a look at.

Summary

One of the useful things about this chapter is that it demonstrates how easy it is to use existing Java classes and libraries. There is an enormous number of class libraries on the Internet. Hopefully, this chapter gives you the courage to use them in your Jython scripts.

The next chapter discusses dialog boxes and how they can be used to interact with users to obtain input for scripts.

---

[19]See `http://docs.oracle.com/javase/tutorial/uiswing/components/editorpane.html`.

■ ■ ■

Conversing with a User with Dialog Boxes

According to several dictionaries, a "dialogue" is an exchange of information between two entities, at least one of whom is a person. Maybe that's why a window for providing input to an application is called a "dialog box."

Way back in Chapter 1, you read all about the top-level containers. The examples throughout the book have used the JFrame class as the top-level container of choice. Now you're going take some time to learn about the JDialog[1] container class and dialog boxes in general. This chapter also touches on a few related issues. In Chapter 17, you'll continue by learning about some specialized dialog boxes that you can use to make your life as an application developer much easier.

This chapter is all about using dialog boxes to get information from the user into an application. It starts by discussing where dialog boxes fit in the Swing class hierarchy. Then is discusses how you position them, especially when multiple displays exist. Additionally, you'll see how various dialog boxes can be created using JOptionPane methods.

What Are Dialog Boxes?

Dialog boxes are separate windows that are used to convey information to, and from, the application user. They can also be used to interact with the user to obtain input that is returned to the application. You are likely very familiar with the kind of message windows that display informational, warning, and error messages. It is also likely that you've used a dialog box to provide information to applications. Now you'll see what you need to do to use these dialog boxes in your applications.

What's a JDialog?

Listing 16-1 shows the class hierarchy for the JDialog class. It's interesting to note how similar this hierarchy is to the JFrame class,[2] shown in Listing 16-2.

---

[1]See http://docs.oracle.com/javase/8/docs/api/javax/swing/JDialog.html.
[2]See http://docs.oracle.com/javase/8/docs/api/javax/swing/JFrame.html.

Listing 16-1. JDialog Class Hierarchy

```
wsadmin>from javax.swing import JDialog
wsadmin>
wsadmin>classInfo( JDialog )
javax.swing.JDialog
| java.awt.Dialog
| | java.awt.Window
| | | java.awt.Container
| | | | java.awt.Component
| | | | | java.lang.Object
| | | | | java.awt.image.ImageObserver
| | | | | java.awt.MenuContainer
| | | | | java.io.Serializable
| | | javax.accessibility.Accessible
| javax.swing.WindowConstants
| javax.accessibility.Accessible
| javax.swing.RootPaneContainer
wsadmin>
```

This similarity should help you understand that JDialog instances should be able to contain the same kind of Swing components that JFrame instances do.

Listing 16-2. JFrame Class Hierarchy

```
wsadmin>from javax.swing import JFrame
wsadmin>
wsadmin>classInfo( JFrame )
javax.swing.JFrame
| java.awt.Frame
| | java.awt.Window
| | | java.awt.Container
| | | | java.awt.Component
| | | | | java.lang.Object
| | | | | java.awt.image.ImageObserver
| | | | | java.awt.MenuContainer
| | | | | java.io.Serializable
| | | javax.accessibility.Accessible
| | java.awt.MenuContainer
| javax.swing.WindowConstants
| javax.accessibility.Accessible
| javax.swing.RootPaneContainer
wsadmin>
```

These similarities made me wonder just how similar the two top-level containers might be as well. Using the final version of the javadocInfo.py script file discussed in Chapter 15,[3] take a quick look at the JDialog methods shown in Figure 16-1.

---

[3]Which is ...\Code\Chap_15\javadocInfo_07.py.

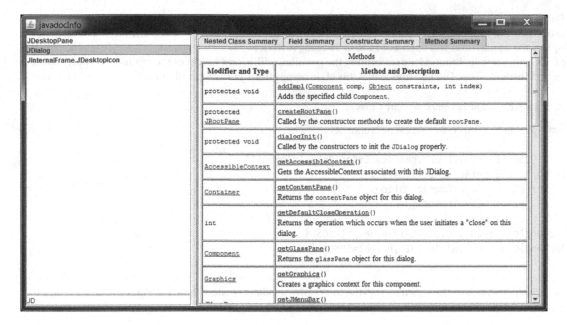

Figure 16-1. *JDialog methods*

It also makes me feel good about the effort that was invested in creating that script/application. After starting it, you only need to type two letters and use two mouse clicks to display the information about the class methods:

1. Type JD to filter the list of classes.

2. Select the JDialog entry on the short list of classes.

3. Select the Method Summary tab. You're done!

A quick glance at these methods shows that the JFrame and JDialog classes both have RootPanes, ContentPanes, GlassPanes, MenuBars, and many other things in common. There are a number of differences as well. If you start by looking at the class constructors for each class, it should quickly become obvious that there are a lot more JDialog constructors than there are JFrame constructors. It seems that this is the result of the presence in the JDialog constructors of two additional parameters:

- The owner argument (dialog, frame, or window)

- The modality argument (a Boolean flag or a Dialog.ModalityType)

What's the GraphicsConfiguration Component Do?

One issue that pops up time and time again in the Javadocs for various Swing-related classes is that they contain so much information that it is often difficult to comprehend. This is a long way of saying that the first few (perhaps dozen) times that I looked at the JFrame and JDialog Javadoc pages, I didn't take the time or effort to see the GraphicsConfiguration[4] parameter in some of the constructors.

---

[4]See http://docs.oracle.com/javase/8/docs/api/java/awt/GraphicsConfiguration.html.

When I finally did see it, it took me a while to realize how useful this particular parameter can be. However, this is only the case when the users can have multiple displays. You can use this parameter to identify on which of the available displays the application will open a JFrame or JDialog instance.

Listing 16-3 shows one technique for determining the position, width, and height of the available displays using the GraphicsEnvironment class. Did you notice that this class comes from java.awt and not the javax.swing library?

Listing 16-3. Using the GraphicsEnvironment Class

```
wsadmin>from java.awt import GraphicsEnvironment
wsadmin>
wsadmin>LGE = GraphicsEnvironment.getLocalGraphicsEnvironment()
wsadmin>for SD in LGE.getScreenDevices() :
wsadmin>    for GC in SD.getConfigurations() :
wsadmin>        print GC.getBounds()
wsadmin>
java.awt.Rectangle[x=1920,y=0,width=1920,height=1080]
java.awt.Rectangle[x=0,y=0,width=1920,height=1080]
wsadmin>
```

Table 16-1 describes each of the statements in the interactive wsadmin session shown in Figure 16-1.

Table 16-1. Using the GraphicsEnvironment Session

Lines	Description
1	Add the GraphicsEnvironment class from the java.awt library to the local namespace.
3	Use the getLocalGraphicsEnvironment() method to obtain information about the local graphics environment.
4	Loop over the ScreenDevice objects in the environment.
5	Loop over the GraphicConfiguration objects in each ScreenDevice object.
6	Display the bound instance values for the current GraphicConfiguration object.
8 - 9	Results generated by the print statement in line 6.

The output shown in Listing 16-3 is specific to my environment and shows that it has two displays, logically configured to be side by side, with the primary display on the right. How do you tell this? Well, the primary display ("Screen 0") is considered to be at location [x=0, y=0]. The next display ("Screen 1") has a positive x value, which indicates that it is logically to the right of the primary display. If a third display were present that was logically considered to be on the left of the primary display, it would have a negative value of x. Adding the values of x and width from the second display (1920 + 1920 = 3840) results in the logical width of the combined display.

Using a GraphicsConfiguration Object

Listing 16-4 shows how to obtain a GraphicsConfiguration object from a ScreenDevice object. Once you have it, how can it be used? The JDialog and JFrame classes both have constructors that include GraphicsConfiguration objects. So, once you have a configuration object that identifies a display, this can be provided on the JDialog or JFrame constructor call to identify the display with which the application should be associated. Listing 16-4 shows an example class that uses a GraphicsConfiguration object to identify the user display on which the JFrame instance should be displayed.

Listing 16-4. Using a GraphicsConfiguration Object

```
 8|class ScreenLoc( java.lang.Runnable ) :
 9|   def run( self ) :
10|       d   = 0
11|       LGE = GraphicsEnvironment.getLocalGraphicsEnvironment()
12|       for GD in LGE.getScreenDevices() :
13|           CO = GD.getDefaultConfiguration()
14|           for GC in GD.getConfigurations() :
15|               b = GC.getBounds()
16|               frame = JFrame(
17|                   'Screen: %d' % d,
18|                   CO,
19|                   size = (
20|                       int( b.getWidth()  ) >> 1,
21|                       int( b.getHeight() ) >> 3
22|                   ),
23|                   defaultCloseOperation = JFrame.EXIT_ON_CLOSE
24|               )
25|               d += 1
26|               frame.add( JLabel('CO' ) )
27|               frame.setVisible( 1 )
```

Table 16-2 explains the ScreenLoc class shown in Listing 16-4 in detail. One way to figure out what the code is doing is to keep an eye out while viewing the Javadoc pages of the code snippets. In this case, some of this is explained on the GraphicsConfiguration and GraphicsDevice pages, which help explain how they can be used. The ScreenLoc class in Figure 16-1 is based on these code snippets.

Table 16-2. ScreenLoc Class Explained

Lines	Description
8-9	Define the class as a descendent of the java.lang.Runnable class; its run() method will be called by the Swing Dispatch thread.
10	d is a simple integer identifying the device number 0..N-1.
11	Call the static getLocalGraphicsEnvironment() method from the GraphicsEnvironment[5] class to obtain information about the local graphics environment (LGE).
12-26	Process each GraphicsDevice[6] (GD) in the local graphics environment.
13	Get the default GraphicsConfiguration object (CO) associated with the current device.
14-24	Process all of the GraphicsConfiguration (GC) objects for the current GraphicsDevice.
15	Get the bounds (java.awt.Rectangle[7]) describing the device coordinates.
16-23	Create a JFrame instance on the current GraphicsDevice using the configuration object. **Note:** Since only the size is provided, the JFrame instance will be positioned in the top-left corner of the display.
19-22	The size of the frame is defined to be half the display width and an eighth of the display height.
24	Increment the display counter (d).
25	Add a JLabel instance to the current frame containing the information about the configuration object.
26	Make the frame instance visible.

Is a GraphicsConfiguration Object Really Necessary?

If you want to create a frame or a dialog window using a configuration object, you can. But it would be just as easy to use the device bounds rectangle to position the window, especially in Jython. Listing 16-5 shows the ScreenPos class, from the script of the same name, which shows how easily this can be done.

Listing 16-5. Using Device Bounds to Position Items

```
 8|class ScreenPos( java.lang.Runnable ) :
 9|    def run( self ) :
10|        d    = 0
11|        LGE = GraphicsEnvironment.getLocalGraphicsEnvironment()
12|        for GD in LGE.getScreenDevices() :
13|            for GC in GD.getConfigurations() :
14|                b = GC.getBounds()
15|                w = int( b.getWidth()  ) >> 1
16|                h = int( b.getHeight() ) >> 3
17|                x = int(
18|                    ( int( b.getWidth()  - w ) >> 1 ) + b.getX()
19|                )
```

[5]See http://docs.oracle.com/javase/8/docs/api/java/awt/GraphicsEnvironment.html.
[6]See http://docs.oracle.com/javase/8/docs/api/java/awt/GraphicsDevice.html.
[7]See http://docs.oracle.com/javase/8/docs/api/java/awt/Rectangle.html.

```
20|                    y = int(
21|                        ( int( b.getHeight() - h ) >> 1 ) + b.getY()
22|                    )
23|                    frame = JFrame(
24|                        'Screen: %d' % d,
25|                        bounds = ( x, y, w, h ),
26|                        defaultCloseOperation = JFrame.EXIT_ON_CLOSE
27|                    )
28|                    d += 1
29|                    frame.add( JLabel('GC' ) )
30|                    frame.setVisible( 1 )
```

Table 16-3 explains the statements shown in Listing 16-5 in detail. Remember that these listings sometimes have more lines than might normally be used only because of the narrow width required for these pages.

Table 16-3. *ScreenPos Example, Explained*

Lines	Description
8-9	Define the class as a descendent of the java.lang.Runnable class; its run() method will be called by the Swing Dispatch thread.
10	d is a simple integer identifying the device number 0..N-1.
11	Call the static getLocalGraphicsEnvironment() method from the GraphicsEnvironment class to obtain information about the local graphics environment (LGE).
12-29	Process each GraphicsDevice (GD) in the local graphic environment.
13-29	Process all of the GraphicsConfiguration (GC) objects for the current GraphicsDevice.
14	Get the bounds (b) Rectangle defining the GraphicsDevice.
15	The width (w) of the window to be instantiated should be half the width of the graphic device on which it will be seen.
16	The height (h) of the window should be an eighth the height of the display screen.
17-19	The window's upper-left corner (the X coordinate) is half the screen width minus the width of the window. Adding the screen's X coordinate positions it properly.
20-22	The window's upper-left corner (the Y coordinate) is half the screen height minus the height of the window. Adding the screen's Y coordinate positions it properly.
23-26	Instantiate the JFrame using the given title and the previously computed coordinates.
27	Increment the display counter (d).
28	Add a JLabel instance to the current frame containing the information about the GraphicsConfiguration object.
29	Make the frame instance visible.

The result of all of this simply shows that using a GraphicsConfiguration object isn't required. It is generally easier to use the Rectangle object available with the GraphicsDevice to determine where to position the window, based on the window and screen sizes.

What About an Owner?

In the section entitled, "What's a JDialog?," I mentioned that there are two parameters that exist in most of the JDialog constructors that don't exist in the JFrame constructors. These are the owner and modality parameters, and they are closely associated. When a JDialog instance is configured to be modal and the window is visible, all user input is blocked to all of the other application windows. This forces the user to interact with the modal dialog window first.

■ **Note** If the owner parameter is specified as None, then a shared, hidden frame will be identified as the owner.

Figure 16-2 shows some sample output generated by the SimpleDialog.py script. It shows how you can create multiple non-modal dialog windows, but only one modal one.

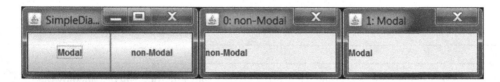

Figure 16-2. *SimpleDialog sample output*

Listing 16-6 shows the SimpleDialog class from this application. It only needs an ActionListener event handler to respond to when one of the application buttons is clicked. Note how the JDialog constructor specifies the owner using a value of None (line 36). This forces the Swing library to use a (shared) hidden frame, which forces the modal dialog box to be handled first.

Listing 16-6. The SimpleDialog Class from SimpleDialog.py

```
 9|class SimpleDialog( java.lang.Runnable ) :
10|    def run( self ) :
11|        self.frame = frame = JFrame(
12|            'SimpleDialog',
13|            size = ( 250, 100 ),
14|            layout = GridLayout( 0, 2 ),
15|            locationRelativeTo = None,
16|            defaultCloseOperation = JFrame.EXIT_ON_CLOSE
17|        )
18|        frame.add(
19|            JButton(
20|                'Modal',
21|                actionPerformed = self.makeDialog
22|            )
23|        )
24|        frame.add(
25|            JButton(
26|                'non-Modal',
27|                actionPerformed = self.makeDialog
28|            )
29|        )
```

```
30|          self.boxNum = 0
31|          frame.setVisible( 1 )
32|     def makeDialog( self, event ) :
33|          cmd = event.getActionCommand()
34|          isModal = ( cmd == 'Modal' )
35|          dialog = JDialog(
36|              self.frame,                    # Try None as owner...
37|              title = '%d: %s' % ( self.boxNum, cmd ),
38|              modal = isModal,
39|              size = ( 200, 100 ),
40|              locationRelativeTo = self.frame
41|          )
42|          self.boxNum += 1
43|          dialog.add( JLabel( cmd ) )
44|          dialog.setVisible( 1 )
```

What happens if you iconify the application when non-modal dialog windows exist? Well, if they were instantiated with the owner parameters specified as None, nothing happens to them. They remain as they are. However, if the application is identified as the owner (in this case specifying an argument of self.frame), then all of the associated non-modal windows will be iconified as well. And if you deiconify the application, all of the non-modal windows will follow suit. Knowing this might help you decide if you want to specify the owner argument when you instantiate your JDialog instance.

Where's the Dialog?

At the start of this chapter, you saw that a dialog is about communication. Up to now, you haven't done anything with the JDialog instances that you've created other than make them appear and disappear. Where's the communication in that? This section explains how you enable a JDialog instance to communicate with the application or the component that created it.

Let's start with the simple case. If your application creates a modal JDialog instance, the application will be in suspended animation until the dialog is hidden or closed. Since the application created the object instance, it can now call any of its getter methods to retrieve information from the object. Figure 16-3 shows some sample output from a trivial application that uses a custom JDialog box to obtain user input.

Figure 16-3. CustomDialog1.py sample output

Listing 16-7 shows the CustomDialog class from this sample application. Since there are some points of interest, this section will describe in more detail how this application works.

Listing 16-7. CustomDialog Sample Class

```
12|class CustomDialog( java.lang.Runnable ) :
13|    def run( self ) :
14|        self.frame = frame = JFrame(
15|            'CustomDialog',
16|            size = ( 200, 100 ),
17|            locationRelativeTo = None,
18|            defaultCloseOperation = JFrame.EXIT_ON_CLOSE
19|        )
20|        self.label = frame.add( JLabel( '' ) )
21|        frame.add(
22|            JButton(
23|                'Prompt user',
24|                actionPerformed = self.popup
25|            ),
26|            BorderLayout.SOUTH
27|        )
28|        frame.setVisible( 1 )
29|    def popup( self, event ) :
30|        self.dialog = dialog = JDialog(
31|            self.frame,
32|            'Name prompt',
33|            1,
34|            layout = GridLayout( 0, 2 ),
35|            locationRelativeTo = self.frame
36|        )
37|        dialog.add( JLabel( "What's your name?" ) )
38|        self.text = dialog.add(
39|            JTextField(
40|                10,
41|                actionPerformed = self.enter
42|            )
43|        )
44|        self.result = None
45|        dialog.pack()
46|        dialog.setVisible( 1 )
47|        self.label.setText( 'Name = "%s"' % self.result )
48|    def enter( self, event ) :
49|        self.result = self.text.getText()
50|        self.dialog.setVisible( 0 )
```

Table 16-4 describes the CustomDialog class shown in Listing 16-7 in more detail. For simplicity's sake, the code that's similar to other examples is described in less detail.

Table 16-4. *CustomDialog Class, Explained*

Lines	Description
13-28	CustomDialog run() method that populates the JFrame instance and displays it for the user.
20	The popup() ActionListener method needs to access the label field, so addressability to it must be saved.
29-47	popup() ActionListener event handler, which is invoked when the button is activated.
30-36	Create a modal JDialog instance that identifies the application frame as the owner and tell the Swing library to display the JDialog instance relative to it.
37-46	Populate the JDialog and make it visible.
47	This is the point where control returns when the JDialog is no longer visible (it's either closed or hidden).
48-50	ActionListener event handler for the JDialog user input field (JTextField). **Note:** This event handler expects to be associated with a modal dialog instance. It does not include any protection from concurrency issues.

The last row of Table 16-4 includes one of the significant reasons for using modal dialog boxes. Dealing with concurrency issues can add complexity to your applications. So think carefully before using non-modal dialog boxes that can update values in the component that creates it.

Multiple Modal Dialog Boxes Are Annoying

Please be considerate of your users. Even though it's possible for your application to create multiple modal dialog boxes, don't do it. Unfortunately, I see this quite often, especially when a web application uses Adobe Flash. I tend to see something like the image shown in Figure 16-4. Unfortunately, these boxes can stack up, so I find myself clicking on the Deny ("No") button a lot. This can be frustrating. As a user, I try to avoid using this kind of application whenever possible. Keep this in mind when you create your applications. Don't create a "user-hostile" application that does something annoying like this.

Figure 16-4. *Please take "no" for an answer*

Using JOptionPane Methods

It's commonplace to come across applications that use modal dialog boxes to obtain user input, so it should be no surprise that there's an easy way to create a variety of commonly used dialog boxes.

There are four major and two minor variants of methods in the JOption class for creating modal dialog boxes to obtain user input. All of these methods have names that adhere to the following naming convention: show%1%2Dialog(), where %2 represents the major portion, which will be one of the following four types:

- Input
- Confirm
- Message
- Option

And %1 represents the minor portion, which will be empty or internal. This means that you should be able to produce the complete list of method names by using a simple nested loop, right? Listing 16-8 shows this simple list.

Listing 16-8. JOption show*Dialog Method Name Variants

```
wsadmin>num = 1
wsadmin>for minor in [ '', 'Internal' ] :
wsadmin>    for major in [ 'Input', 'Confirm', 'Message', 'Option' ] :
wsadmin>        print '%2d: show%s%sDialog()' % ( num, minor, major )
wsadmin>        num += 1
wsadmin>
 1: showInputDialog()
 2: showConfirmDialog()
 3: showMessageDialog()
 4: showOptionDialog()
 5: showInternalInputDialog()
 6: showInternalConfirmDialog()
 7: showInternalMessageDialog()
 8: showInternalOptionDialog()
wsadmin>
```

Unfortunately, it doesn't take into consideration the fact that Java allows method overloading, so each method name can have multiple signatures. What does this mean for Jython programmers? It means that you have to take this into consideration.

■ **Note**   For now, ignore the showInternal variants. You'll see them again in Chapter 19, where you learn about JInternalFrames.

The JOptionPane.showMessageDialog() Method

The simplest dialog box that can be displayed by the JOptionPane class is called a MessageDialog. It is the simplest primarily because it returns no value. The purpose of a MessageDialog is to inform users about some event. Since it doesn't provide the user with any opportunity to provide input, the showMessageDialog() method doesn't have to return any value.

Figure 16-5 shows the Java method signature and a simple image from the `MessageDialogDemo.py` application. Notice that the dialog box has a simple title of "Message," an informational icon, and an OK button.

```
| showMessageDialog(
|     Component parentComponent,
|     Object    message
| )
```

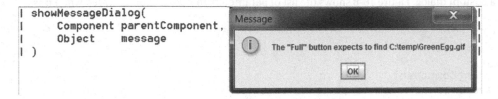

Figure 16-5. *Simple `MessageDialog` signature and sample image*

Figure 16-6 shows another `showMessageDialog()` method signature, as well as an example image from the `MessageDialogDemo.py` application. This version of the method allows you to specify the title to be displayed in the title bar. It also allows you to specify the `messageType` and an optional icon to be displayed. If an icon isn't provided, then the icon that is displayed on the `MessageDialog` is based on the `messageType` that was specified.

```
| showMessageDialog(
|     Component parentComponent,
|     Object    message,
|     String    title,
|     int       messageType,
|     Icon      icon
| )
```

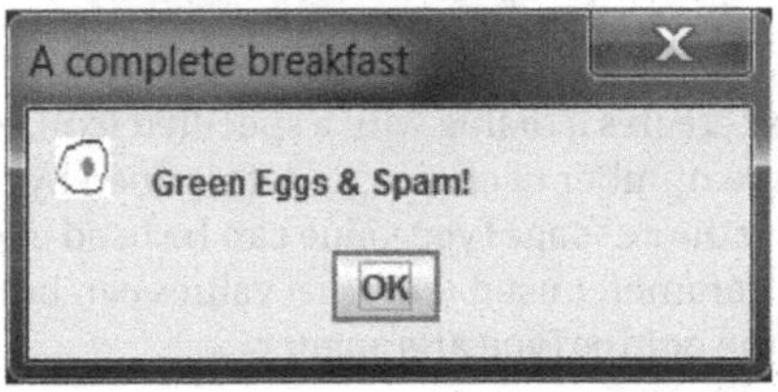

Figure 16-6. *Complete `MessageDialog` signature and sample image*

Figure 16-7 shows the list of `MessageType` constants that are defined in the `JOptionPane` class. These should be used for `messageType` arguments in the `show*Dialog()` method calls. If you don't provide an icon parameter, the icon displayed on the dialog box will be based on the `MessageType`.

```
PLAIN_MESSAGE

ERROR_MESSAGE

INFORMATION_MESSAGE

WARNING_MESSAGE

QUESTION_MESSAGE
```

Figure 16-7. *`MessageType` constants defined in the `JOptionPane` class*

The JOptionPane.showOptionDialog() Method

The next most useful show*Dialog method is showOptionDialog(). It is useful, and frequently used, because of its flexibility. It can display a custom dialog. Figure 16-8 shows the list of parameters that should be specified when this method is called.

```
showOptionDialog(
    Component parentComponent,
    Object    message,
    String    title,
    int       optionType,
    int       messageType,
    Icon      icon,
    Object[]  options,
    Object    initialValue
)
```

Figure 16-8. *Complete showOptionDialog signature*

This method creates a dialog with a specified icon, where the initial choice is determined by the initialValue parameter and the number of choices is determined by the optionType parameter.

You saw how the messageType value can be used to determine the icon to be shown if it's not specified. How is the optionType parameter used and what values can be specified? Figure 16-9 shows the JOptionPane constants that can be used for the optionType argument.

```
DEFAULT_OPTION

YES_NO_OPTION

YES_NO_CANCEL_OPTION

OK_CANCEL_OPTION
```

Figure 16-9. *OptionType constants defined in the JOptionPane class*

It would seem that you can use the optionType and messageType arguments to tell the showOptionDialog() method how many buttons to display, as well as their labels. Listing 16-9 shows the simplest form of a call to the showOptionDialog() method. Note how you can use an optionType of DEFAULT_OPTION and None for the options and initialValue arguments.

Listing 16-9. Sample showOD() Method Used to Call showOptionDialog

```
26|    def showOD( self, event ) :
27|        options = 'Bacon,Eggs,Spam'.split( ',' )
28|        result = JOptionPane.showOptionDialog(
29|            self.frame,                        # parentComponent
30|            'What goes good with spam?',        # message text
31|            'This is a test!',                  # title
```

```
32|               JOptionPane.DEFAULT_OPTION,          # optionType
33|               JOptionPane.QUESTION_MESSAGE,        # messageType
34|               None,                                # icon
35|               None,                                # options
36|               None                                 # initialValue
37|           )
38|           self.label.setText( 'result = %d' % result )
```

Figure 16-10 shows the different buttons that are displayed on the OptionDialog when you specify the various constants listed in Figure 16-9.

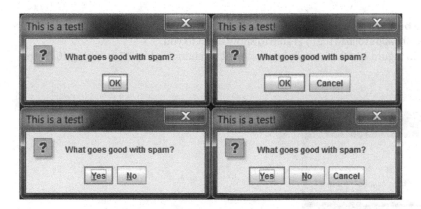

Figure 16-10. *Simple OptionDialog examples*

What if you don't like these kinds of buttons? Can you specify button labels other than Yes, No, OK, and Cancel? Sure, that's what the options and initialValue arguments are for. Listing 16-10 shows how to provide your own button labels for the OptionDialog box.

Listing 16-10. Modified showOD() Method Specifying Options

```
26|     def showOD( self, event ) :
27|         options = 'Bacon,Eggs,Spam'.split( ',' )
28|         result = JOptionPane.showOptionDialog(
29|             self.frame,                          # parentComponent
30|             'What goes good with spam?',         # message text
31|             'This is a test!',                   # title
32|             JOptionPane.DEFAULT_OPTION,          # optionType
33|             JOptionPane.QUESTION_MESSAGE,        # messageType
34|             None,                                # icon
35|             options,                             # options
36|             options[ -1 ]                        # initialValue
37|         )
38|         self.label.setText( 'result = %d' % result )
```

Figure 16-11 shows the OptionDialog that results from this showOD() method.

Figure 16-11. OptionDialog *example using non-standard button labels*

Are you limited to one, two, or three buttons? As a matter of fact, you're not. If you provide an array (list) of options with more than three values, the showOptionDialog() is able to show them to you.

The example OptionDialog shown in Figure 16-12 can easily be produced by changing line 27 in Listing 16-10 to the statement in Listing 16-11.

Figure 16-12. OptionDialog *example with eight buttons*

Listing 16-11. Specifying Many OptionDialog Button Labels

```
27|        options = 'Now is the time for all good spam'.split( ' ' )
```

Certainly this example is a bit excessive, but it does demonstrate an interesting point. It should also raise a question or two. When you display a variety of buttons on a dialog box, how can you tell which one the user pressed? If you use one of the standard OptionDialog objects, you can use the return value constants defined in the JOptionPane class and listed in Figure 16-13 to make this determination.

```
YES_OPTION

NO_OPTION

CANCEL_OPTION

OK_OPTION

CLOSED_OPTION
```

Figure 16-13. JOptionPane *constants for the* showOptionDialog *returned value*

If you specify your own list of button labels, you can use the returned value as an index into the options array to determine the label of the selected button. Be careful, though. Before using it as an index, you should check to see if a value of -1 (the JOptionPane.CLOSED_OPTION) was returned in case the user closed the dialog box.

The JOptionPane.showConfirmDialog() Method

By now, you should be very comfortable with the parameters that exist for the JOptionPane.show*Dialog() methods. This will make the explanation of the showConfirmDialog() method that much easier. The simplest form of this method is shown in Figure 16-14.

```
showConfirmDialog(
    Component parentComponent,
    Object    message
)
```

Figure 16-14. *Simple showConfirmDialog() arguments*

This method can be used to display a simple dialog box with three choices (buttons): Yes, No, and Cancel. This is identical to calling the showOptionDialog() method and specifying an optionType value of JOptionPane.YES_NO_CANCEL_OPTION. The default title is "Select an Option," and you can use the JOptionPane constants listed in Figure 16-13 to determine which selection the user chose.

The other showConfirmDialog() signatures follow this same pattern, with one allowing an optionType, the next having an optionType as well as a messageType, and the last allowing these two arguments in addition to an icon.

Again, when the optionType is provided, it determines the number of buttons and which values should be shown. The messageType identifies the icon to be shown, if the icon parameter isn't specified.

The JOptionPane.showInputDialog() Method

The last of the show*Dialog() methods discussed in this chapter is showInputDialog(). It has a number of variations. You'll take a look at these variations so you can decide which make most sense for your needs. Let's start by looking at the simplest one, which has only one parameter and work your way toward the most complex version, which has seven parameters.

Figure 16-15 shows the simplest variant, which requires only a string parameter containing the message to be displayed. In fact, there are two forms of this variant—with and without the parentComponent parameter.

```
showInputDialog(
    Object    message
)
```

```
showInputDialog(
    Component parentComponent,
    Object    message
)
```

Figure 16-15. *Simplest showInputDialog() method signatures*

Listing 16-12 shows the showID() method from the InputDialogDemo.py application, with the optional parentComponent specified.

Listing 16-12. Simplest showInputDialog() Example

```
26|    def showID( self, event ) :
27|        result = JOptionPane.showInputDialog(
28|            self.frame,                     # parentComponent
29|            'What is your favorite color?'  # message text
30|            )
31|        self.label.setText( 'result = "%s"' % result )
```

The result of executing the showInputDialog() method call shown in Listing 16-12 is illustrated in Figure 16-16. Personally, I haven't been able to figure out a difference between these two variants. Regardless of whether the optional parentComponent is specified, you see a dialog box with a title of "Input" and the specified message, as well as OK and Cancel buttons.

Figure 16-16. Sample showInputDialog() window

One interesting thing to note is that the value that is returned is not an integer, as you have seen with other show*Dialog() methods. It is either the user-specified string (the contents of the input field) or None if the dialog box is closed (which is done by using the Close icon or pressing the Cancel button).

Figure 16-17 shows the next pair of signatures for this method. In it you see that an initial value for the input field can be specified. Again, there are two variants of this showInputDialog() method, with the parentComponent being optional.

```
| showInputDialog(                            |
|     Object    message,                      |
|     Object    initialSelectionValue         |
| )                                           |
```

```
| showInputDialog(                            |
|     Component parentComponent,              |
|     Object    message,                      |
|     Object    initialSelectionValue         |
| )                                           |
```

Figure 16-17. showInputDialog() with initialSelectionValue specified

Listing 16-13 shows an example of this method call from the InputDialogDemo.py sample application. In this particular example, the optional parentComponent is specified in line 28. Feel free to try this version and then comment out that line and try it again.

Listing 16-13. showInputDialog() with an Initial Value

```
26|    def showID( self, event ) :
27|        result = JOptionPane.showInputDialog(
28|            self.frame,                      # parentComponent
29|            'What is your favorite color?',  # message text
30|            'Spam'                           # initialValue
31|        )
32|        self.label.setText( 'result = "%s"' % result )
```

When I tried this, I saw output similar to what is shown in Figure 16-18. Note how the initial value is provided and selected.

Figure 16-18. *Sample showInputDialog() window showing an initial value*

The next variation allows you to specify the title of the dialog box, as well as the messageType parameter that determines the icon to display. The signature for this version is shown in Figure 16-19.

```
| showInputDialog(                              |
|     Component parentComponent,                |
|     Object    message,                        |
|     String    title,                          |
|     int       messageType                     |
| )                                             |
```

Figure 16-19. *showInputDialog() method with messageType parameter*

Listing 16-14 shows how the title and messageType parameters are specified. The constants to be used for the messageType parameter can be found in Figure 16-7.

Listing 16-14. showInputDialog() with Title and messageType Parameters

```
26|    def showID( self, event ) :
27|        result = JOptionPane.showInputDialog(
28|            self.frame,                     # parentComponent
29|            'What is your favorite color?',  # message text
30|            'Asked by the bridge guardian',  # title
31|            JOptionPane.QUESTION_MESSAGE     # messageType
32|        )
33|        self.label.setText( 'result = "%s"' % result )
```

The output of the version of the showID() method in Listing 16-14 is shown in Figure 16-20.

Figure 16-20. *Sample output showing the title and messageType*

Finally, you get to the last of the showInputDialog() method variants. As mentioned earlier, its signature is shown in Figure 16-21. The main difference between this method and the other signatures just discussed is the presence of the icon, selectionValues, and initialSelectionValue arguments.

```
| showInputDialog(                                    |
|     Component parentComponent,                      |
|     Object    message,                              |
|     String    title,                                |
|     int       messageType,                          |
|     Icon      icon,                                 |
|     Object[]  selectionValues,                      |
|     Object    initialSelectionValue                 |
| )                                                   |
```

Figure 16-21. *Seven argument showInputDialog() method signature*

Listing 16-15 shows an example of this seven argument variant of the showInputDialog() method.[8] As mentioned, if an icon isn't provided, the icon that's displayed on the MessageDialog is based on the specified messageType value.

---

[8]As you've seen previously, the lines have been shortened to fit in the available space. This is most obvious with lines 27 and 28, which really don't require two statements.

Listing 16-15. Sample Use of Seven Argument showInputDialog() Method

```
26|    def showID( self, event ) :
27|        COLORS = 'Red,Orange,Yellow,Green,Blue,Indigo,Violet'
28|        colors = COLORS.split( ',' )
29|        result = JOptionPane.showInputDialog(
30|            self.frame,                       # parentComponent
31|            'What is your favorite color?',  # message text
32|            'Asked by the bridge guardian',  # title
33|            JOptionPane.QUESTION_MESSAGE,     # messageType
34|            None,                             # icon
35|            colors,                           # selectionValues
36|            colors[ -1 ]                      # initialSelectionValue
37|        )
38|        self.label.setText( 'result = "%s"' % result )
```

Figure 16-22 shows images from the application containing the method shown in Listing 16-15. This variant of the showInputDialog() method provides a combo box containing the values provided by the selectionValues argument. The last parameter is used to identify the initial combo box entry to be displayed.

Figure 16-22. *Sample output from seven argument showInputDialog() call*

Summary

This chapter has been all about dialog boxes and some of the ways they can be used in your applications. You've seen how simple these techniques can be. The large variety of ways that dialog boxes can be created and used should be a clue about how useful they can be. I encourage you to take a look at the sample scripts in the code\Chap_16 directory and modify them to test the various techniques described in this chapter.

Additionally, you are encouraged to take a look at the "How to Make Dialogs"[9] portion of the Java Swing Tutorial, which contains much of this same information but uses Java instead of Jython as the programming language. One thing you'll take away from reading that document is how much easier it can be to create and use dialog boxes in Jython.

In the next chapter, you investigate specialized dialog boxes, including how to create and use them in your applications.

---

[9]See http://docs.oracle.com/javase/tutorial/uiswing/components/dialog.html.

■ ■ ■

Specialized Dialog Boxes

In Chapter 16, you saw how to create a completely customized dialog box using the JDialog[1] class. You also saw how to take advantage of the JOptionPane[2] methods to quickly and easily display some simple, generalized dialog boxes. Now you are going to look at some dialog boxes that can be used to make your life as a developer significantly easier. You'll be able to use dialog boxes that have been designed, implemented, and tested for you. The chapter begins by looking at the JFileChooser[3] class, which the Swing developers were kind enough to provide for creating dialog boxes. These are great examples of the kind of user input that can be performed by dialog boxes. Keep these in mind when you encounter a situation where you want to provide your own dialog boxes.

The JFileChooser Class

One of the most common types of dialog boxes is the ones that let the users traverse the filesystem and specify a file or directory to be used by the application. It is important to remember, though, that the JFileChooser instance helps your application to interact with the users to choose a particular file or directory. It is the responsibility of the application to do something with the specified file or directory.

Let's take a look at just how difficult it is to use the JFileChooser class. Listing 17-1 shows a simple event handler that displays a File Chooser dialog box that allows the users to traverse the local filesystem and select a file to be opened.

Listing 17-1. Trivial Sample JFileChooser() Routine

```
26|    def showFC( self, event ) :
27|        fc = JFileChooser()
28|        result = fc.showOpenDialog( None )
29|        if result == JFileChooser.APPROVE_OPTION :
30|            message = 'result = "%s"' % fc.getSelectedFile()
31|        else :
32|            message = 'Request canceled by user'
33|        self.label.setText( message )
```

Figure 17-1 shows an example dialog box after the user has moved about the filesystem; it's displaying the contents of the C:\IBM\WebSphere directory.

---

[1]See http://docs.oracle.com/javase/8/docs/api/javax/swing/JDialog.html.
[2]See http://docs.oracle.com/javase/8/docs/api/javax/swing/JOptionPane.html.
[3]See http://docs.oracle.com/javase/8/docs/api/javax/swing/JFileChooser.html.

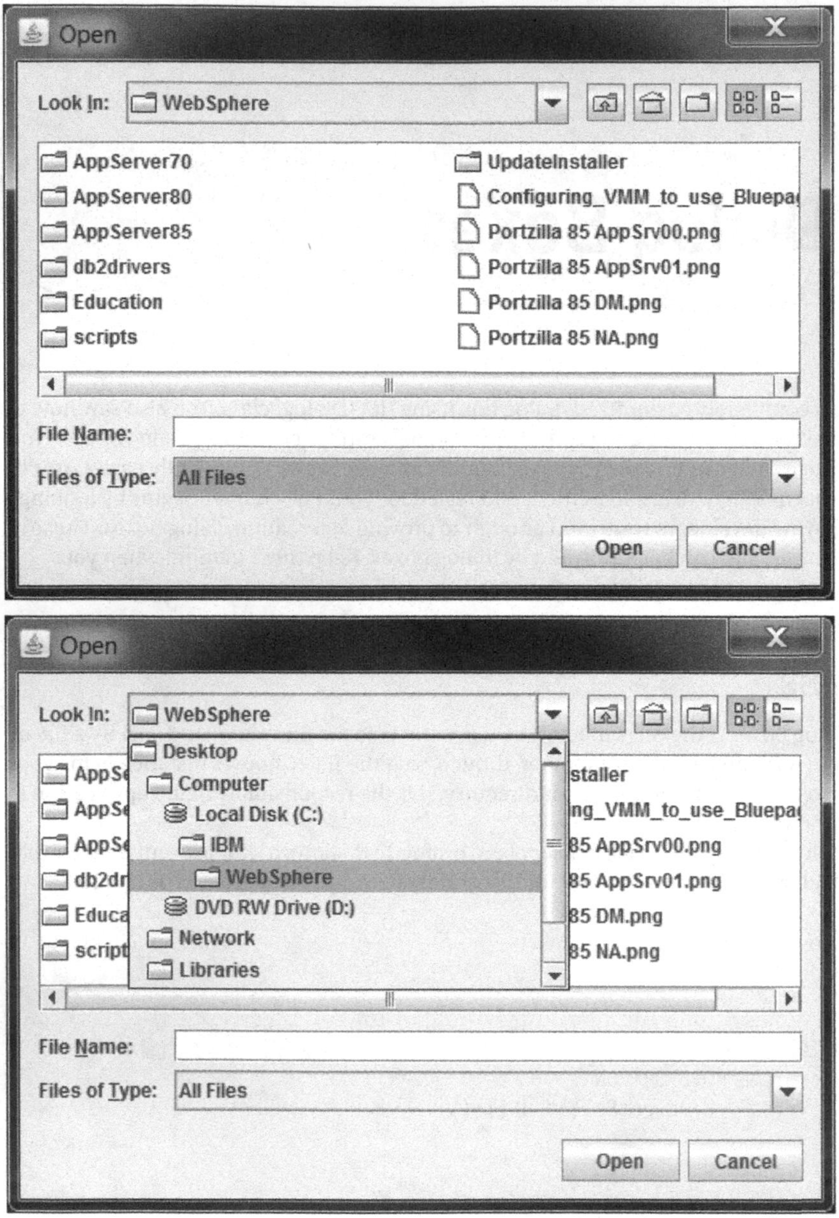

Figure 17-1. *Sample JFileChooser() Open dialog box from FileChooserDemo1.py*

It doesn't take much to realize how powerful this dialog box can be. For example, clicking on the Look In drop-down shows a combo box with indented entries for each directory level, as well as some specialized icons to indicate directories and disk drives.

Now let's take a look at which constructors are available with the JFileChooser class, so that you can have your applications create the appropriate kind of JFileChooser instance best suited for your needs.

JFileChooser Constructors

Which constructors exist for the JFileChooser class? Table 17-1 shows the Java constructor signatures and includes a short description about each constructor. The first constructor is the one that was used in Listing 17-1, in line 27. The next two signatures allow you to identify the starting view of the JFileChooser dialog box using either java.io.File or java.lang.String to identify the initial view to be shown. That makes it easy to indicate the starting directory to be displayed by the JFileChooser instance.

Table 17-1. *JFileChooser Constructors*

Signature	Description
JFileChooser()	Constructs a JFileChooser pointing to the user's default directory.
JFileChooser(File currentDirectory)	Constructs a JFileChooser using the given File as the path.
JFileChooser(String currentDirectoryPath)	Constructs a JFileChooser using the given Path.
JFileChooser(FileSystemView fsv)	Constructs a JFileChooser using the given FileSystemView.
JFileChooser(File currentDirectory, FileSystemView fsv)	Constructs a JFileChooser using the given currentDirectory and FileSystemView.
JFileChooser(String currentDirectoryPath, FileSystemView fsv)	Constructs a JFileChooser using the given currentDirectoryPath and FileSystemView.

The last three JFileChooser constructors include a FileSystemView parameter that can be used to limit the portion of the filesystem that the JFileChooser can display to the user. This way, you don't have to allow the user to see the whole filesystem, just the portion they need.

Using a FileSystemView

The default FileSystemView instance that is used by the JFileChooser allows you to access the complete filesystem. Listing 17-2 shows a verbose way to provide or identify the default FileSystemView instance. It is, in fact, identical to the default JFileChooser( ) instantiation when no parameter is specified.

Listing 17-2. JFileChooser( ) Instance with Default FileSystemView from FileChooserDemo2.py

```
27|    def showFC( self, event ) :
28|        fc = JFileChooser( FileSystemView.getFileSystemView() )
29|        result = fc.showOpenDialog( None )
30|        if result == JFileChooser.APPROVE_OPTION :
31|            message = 'result = "%s"' % fc.getSelectedFile()
32|        else :
33|            message = 'Request canceled by user'
34|        self.label.setText( message )
```

If, on the other hand, you are interested in limiting the user to a specific subset of the filesystem, you can implement a class that identifies the virtual "root" of the filesystem that you want the user to be able to traverse. Listing 17-3 shows one implementation of this kind of FileSystemView descendent class.[4]

Listing 17-3. FileSystemView Class that Limits Filesystem Access from FileChooserDemo3.py

```
11|class RestrictedFileSystemView( FileSystemView ) :
12|    def __init__( self, root ) :
13|        FileSystemView.__init__( self )
14|        self.root  = root
15|        self.Roots = [ root ]
16|    def createNewFolder( self, containingDir ) :
17|        folder = File( containingDir, 'New Folder' )
18|        folder.mkdir()
19|        return folder
20|    def getDefaultDirectory( self ) :
21|        return self.root
22|    def getHomeDirectory( self ) :
23|        return self.root
24|    def getRoots( self ) :
25|        return self.Roots
```

Listing 17-4 shows how this RestrictedFileSystemView class might be used to limit the JFileChooser to the specified directory and its subdirectories. It is unlikely, however, that you are going to want the "root" directory specified using a string like this one. It would be more reasonable to include statements to determine the root system based on the specific environment in which the script is executing.

Listing 17-4. JFileChooser() Using RestrictedFileSystemView from FileChooserDemo3.py

```
43|    def showFC( self, event ) :
44|        fc = JFileChooser(
45|            RestrictedFileSystemView(
46|                File( r'C:\IBM\WebSphere' )
47|            )
48|        )
49|        result = fc.showOpenDialog( None )
50|        if result == JFileChooser.APPROVE_OPTION :
51|            message = 'result = "%s"' % fc.getSelectedFile()
52|        else :
53|            message = 'Request canceled by user'
54|        self.label.setText( message )
```

Figure 17-2 shows some sample images from the application from Listings 17-3 and 17-4. It is interesting to see how the initial directory is WebSphere, and that the "up one level" button is disabled because WebSphere is considered the "root" directory of this restricted filesystem.

---

[4]Note: The FileSystemView roots attribute is read-only, so this class works around that limitation by using a variable named Roots instead.

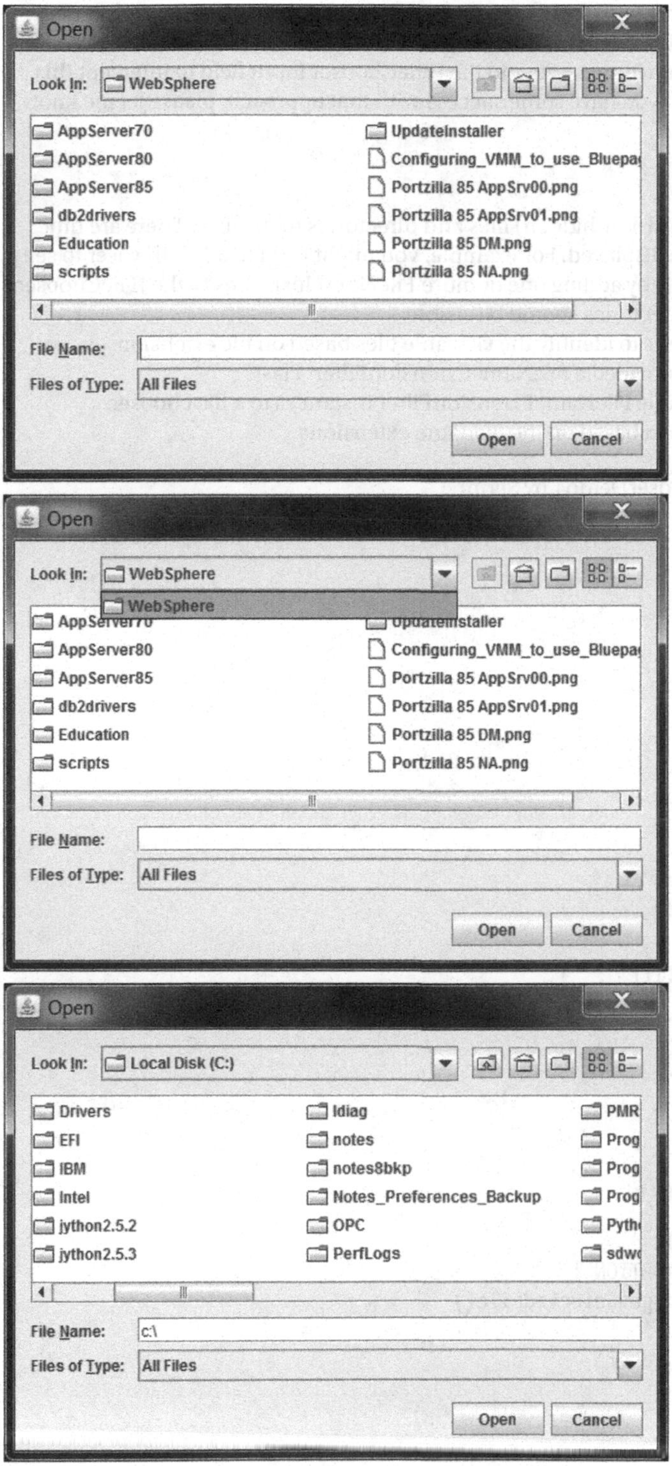

Figure 17-2. Sample RestrictedFileSystem JFileChooser() images

Does this FileSystemViewer class completely limit the users from accessing the rest of the system? No, not really. For example, if the user enters something like C:\ in the File Name input field, the view will display the contents of that directory, unfortunately. There may be a way to add an input verifier to the JFileChooser input field to intercept this kind of thing, but I haven't investigated that option. If you have some success with that approach, please let me know.

File Filtering

By default, a JFileChooser instance will show all of the (non-hidden) files and directories to the user. There are times when you might prefer to limit the kinds of files to be displayed. For example, you might want to allow the user to see only the XML, text, or image files. The way to do this is by adding one or more FileFilter[5] instances to the JFileChooser. The JFileChooser then determines which files and directories should be visible.

One of the most common FileFilter mechanisms is to identify the viewable files based on file extension. To simplify this process, the Swing developers have provided a FileNameExtensionFilter[6] class.

Listing 17-5 shows how easily you can add multiple FileNameExtensionFilter instances to a file chooser. This allows users to select the kinds of files to be shown based on the filename extensions.

Listing 17-5. The showFC Method from the FileChooserDemo4.py Script

```
44|    def showFC( self, event ) :
45|        fc = JFileChooser(
46|            RestrictedFileSystemView(
47|                File( r'C:\IBM\WebSphere' )
48|            )
49|        )
50|        fc.addChoosableFileFilter(
51|            FileNameExtensionFilter(
52|                'XML files',
53|                [ 'xml' ]
54|            )
55|        )
56|        fc.addChoosableFileFilter(
57|            FileNameExtensionFilter(
58|                'Image files',
59|                'bmp,jpg,jpeg,gif,png'.split( ',' )
60|            )
61|        )
62|        fc.addChoosableFileFilter(
63|            FileNameExtensionFilter(
64|                'Text files',
65|                [ 'txt' ]
66|            )
67|        )
68|        result = fc.showOpenDialog( None )
69|        if result == JFileChooser.APPROVE_OPTION :
70|            message = 'result = "%s"' % fc.getSelectedFile()
71|        else :
72|            message = 'Request canceled by user'
73|        self.label.setText( message )
```

---

[5]See http://docs.oracle.com/javase/8/docs/api/javax/swing/filechooser/FileFilter.html.
[6]See http://docs.oracle.com/javase/8/docs/api/javax/swing/filechooser/FileNameExtensionFilter.html.

Figure 17-3 shows an example image from the FileChooserDemo4.py script. It shows the filters available when the Files of Type combo box is selected. It is interesting to note that the initial filter to be displayed is the last one that was added. It is also interesting to note that the All Files filter is available by default. So, if you don't want this filter to be available, you need to use the removeChoosableFileFilter() method and pass it the result of calling the getAcceptAllFileFilter(). The FileChooserDemo5.py script includes these calls, in case you are interested.

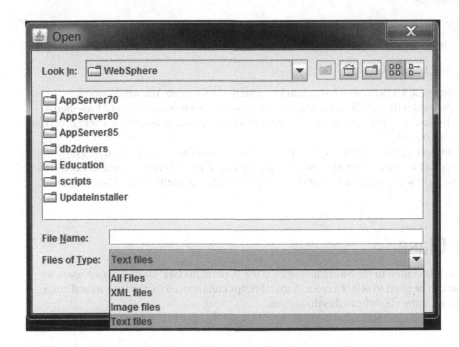

Figure 17-3. *Sample output from the FileChooserDemo4.py script*

Chooser Dialog Types

Up to now, all of the examples that you've seen have used the showOpenDialog() method to display the modal dialog box. In each of these, the primary button displayed the Open text. There are two other ways to display the dialog box. The first uses the showSaveDialog() method, which includes a Save button. This shouldn't be too much of a surprise. The second allows you to customize the text to be displayed on the primary button and uses the showDialog() method to do so. In each case, the application uses the return value to determine which choice the user made so that the appropriate action can be taken. The possible return values are:

- JFileChooser.APPROVE_OPTION
- JFileChooser.CANCEL_OPTION
- JFileChooser.ERROR_OPTION

The last of these occurs only if some kind of error is encountered or if the dialog is somehow dismissed.

Selection Types

There are times when you'll want your users to be able to choose something other than a file. For these times, you need to tell the JFileChooser instance the kinds of selections that are acceptable. To do this, you can use the setFileSelectionMode() method or the fileSelectionMode attribute keyword on the constructor call. In either case, the values that can be specified are as follows:

- JFileChooser.FILES_ONLY

- JFileChooser.DIRECTORIES_ONLY

- JFileChooser.FILES_AND_DIRECTORIES

The default value is JFileChooser.FILES_ONLY, which shouldn't be much of a surprise. You might wonder why the primary button isn't disabled when this in effect. I was a little surprised about this myself, until I selected a directory and clicked on the Open button. The JFileChooser understood this to be the same as double-clicking on the directory, so I guess it does make some sense.

You might want to use the JFileChooser.DIRECTORIES_ONLY value for a chooser that allows the user to identify a source or destination directory for some operation (such as for copying files). There are a number of other JFileChooser methods as well. You might want to take a look at the Swing Tutorial page entitled "How to Use File Choosers"[7] if you are interested.

The JColorChooser Class

Another specialized dialog box that is included in the Swing hierarchy is the JColorChooser[8] class. It allows users to display a variety of techniques that can be used to select a color. A trivial script can be used to display a modal color chooser dialog box. Figure 17-4 shows some views from this dialog box.

---

[7]See http://docs.oracle.com/javase/tutorial/uiswing/components/filechooser.html.
[8]See http://docs.oracle.com/javase/8/docs/api/javax/swing/JColorChooser.html.

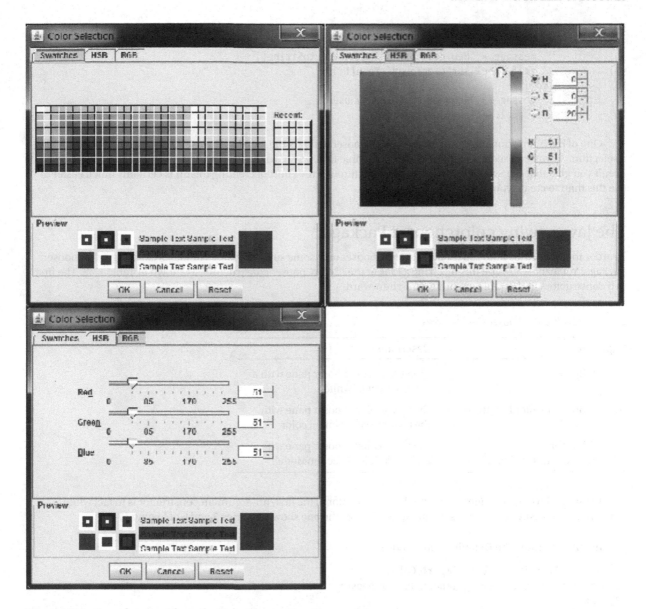

Figure 17-4. *Sample output from the ColorChooserDemo1.py script*

Listing 17-6 shows the showCC ActionListener event handler method from the ColorChooserDemo1.py script used to generate the output shown in Figure 17-4.

Listing 17-6. The showCC Method from the ColorChooserDemo1.py Script

```
27|     def showCC( self, event ) :
28|         result = JColorChooser().showDialog(
29|             None,                      # Parent component
30|             'Color Selection',         # Dialog title
31|             self.label.getForeground() # Initial color
```

```
32|        )
33|        if result :
34|            message = 'New color: "%s"' % result.toString()
35|            self.label.setForeground( result )
36|        else :
37|            message = 'Request canceled by user'
38|        self.label.setText( message )
```

One of the interesting things about this color chooser dialog is the fact that the user has multiple ways of making a selection. As you can see in Figure 17-4, there are three tabs, any of which can be used by the user to pick a color. Aren't you glad that the Swing developers have gone through the effort of creating this? It is certainly much easier to use this than to create your own.

The javax.swing.colorchooser Package

In order to provide this functionality, the JColorChooser uses some support classes in the javax.swing.colorchooser package. You can determine this by taking a look at the JColorChooser constructors, as shown in Table 17-2. The first two constructors in this table are pretty straightforward.

Table 17-2. *JColorChooser Constructors*

Signature	Description
JColorChooser( )	Creates a color chooser pane with a default color of white.
JColorChooser(Color initialColor)	Creates a color chooser pane with the user-specified initial color.
JColorChooser (ColorSelectionModel model)	Creates a color chooser pane with the given ColorSelectionModel.

Paranoid developers might wonder if the default color of the first, no-argument constructor is in fact white. In fact, you can easily verify this using an expression like the one shown on lines 5 and 6 of Listing 17-7.

Listing 17-7. Verifing the Default JColorChooser Color

```
1|wsadmin>from java.awt     import Color
2|wsadmin>from javax.swing import JColorChooser
3|wsadmin>
4|wsadmin>cc = JColorChooser()
5|wsadmin>cc.getColor() == Color.white
6|1
7|wsadmin>
8|wsadmin>csm = cc.getSelectionModel()
9|wsadmin>print csm.toString().split( '.' )[ -1 ]
10|DefaultColorSelectionModel@768b768b
11|wsadmin>
```

You might wonder about the last of the constructors shown in Table 17-2. What is a ColorSelectionModel?[9] The Javadoc says that it is an interface, and not a simple class. That same page says that the DefaultColorSelectionModel[10] class is the only implementation class that is provided by in the Swing hierarchy. In lines 8-10 of Figure 17-5, you can see that the default ColorSelectionModel that is associated with a JColorChooser instance is one of these DefaultColorSelectionModel instances.

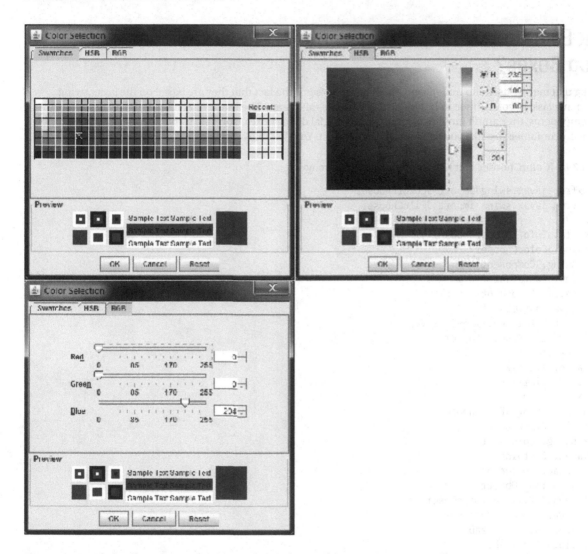

Figure 17-5. JColorChooser sample output after making a change

Looking at the Javadoc for the DefaultColorSelectionModel class, you see that it allows you to listen for changes to the color. As you have seen before, this is the standard way that can be monitored. From this experience, you should be able to make an educated "guess" as to how the JColorChooser works. Take another look at the

[9]See http://docs.oracle.com/javase/8/docs/api/javax/swing/colorchooser/ColorSelectionModel.html.
[10]See http://docs.oracle.com/javase/8/docs/api/javax/swing/colorchooser/DefaultColorSelectionModel.html.

ColorChooserDemo1.py sample script. What is the initial color that is displayed? Take a look at each of the tabs and you should see that the same color shown in the preview pane is represented on each tab in a consistent fashion. What happens when you pick another color and then select the other tabs? How do you think that this is done? Figure 17-5 shows some sample images after one color change has been made. You are encouraged to test this application yourself to see the JColorChooser in full size.

What Else Do You Need to Know About These "Special" Dialog Boxes?

One thing that may be useful to understand about these classes is the fact that they are based on the javax.swing. JComponent class, as you can see in Listing 17-8. What does this mean? The interesting thing is that since they are both JComponents, they aren't limited to being used as modal dialog boxes. You can, if you want, add an instance of either to any container, just like you can for any JComponent. You don't have to, but it's something to consider.

Listing 17-8. JColorChooser and JFileChooser Class Hierarchy

```
wsadmin>from javax.swing import JColorChooser
wsadmin>from javax.swing import JFileChooser
wsadmin>
wsadmin>classInfo( JColorChooser )
javax.swing.JColorChooser
| javax.swing.JComponent
| | java.awt.Container
| | | java.awt.Component
| | | | java.lang.Object
| | | | java.awt.image.ImageObserver
| | | | java.awt.MenuContainer
| | | | java.io.Serializable
| | java.io.Serializable
| javax.accessibility.Accessible
wsadmin>
wsadmin>classInfo( JFileChooser )
javax.swing.JFileChooser
| javax.swing.JComponent
| | java.awt.Container
| | | java.awt.Component
| | | | java.lang.Object
| | | | java.awt.image.ImageObserver
| | | | java.awt.MenuContainer
| | | | java.io.Serializable
| | java.io.Serializable
| javax.accessibility.Accessible
wsadmin>
```

Summary

This chapter covered some specialized dialog boxes that are highly functional and generally useful all at the same time. The ones you learned about here are related to user selection—selecting a color, a file, or a directory. Hopefully, you have seen just how easily they can be added to your scripts. Coming up in the next chapter, you'll learn how your applications can monitor progress and report it back to the users.

■ ■ ■

Monitoring and Indicating Progress

As you've no doubt seen, many graphical applications include a progress indicator of some sort to convey how quickly something is happening. I don't know about you, but I tend to be somewhat impatient, so I find these progress bars very helpful. I hate it when a program just sits there—is it still working, has it hung, who knows? This chapter covers some different ways to measure progress and communicate it to your users.

Changing the Cursor

Sometimes you'll need to tell the users that the program is busy and let them know that they have to wait for a (hopefully short) amount of time. The easiest way to do this is to change the Cursor[1] from its default value to one that indicates that the application is busy. The Cursor class includes a number of predefined constants that can be used for this purpose. For this particular situation, you can use WAIT_CURSOR. How do you do that? Listing 18-1 shows a basic example of how to use it.

Listing 18-1. Using the WAIT_CURSOR Method from WaitCursor1.py

```
23|    def wait( self, event ) :
24|        source = event.getSource()
25|        prev   = source.getCursor()
26|        source.setCursor(
27|            Cursor.getPredefinedCursor( Cursor.WAIT_CURSOR )
28|        )
29|        sleep( 5 )
30|        source.setCursor( prev )
```

This method is from the WaitCursor1.py script in the code\Chap_18 directory. If you execute the script and press the Wait button, the cursor will change from its default value to the WAIT_CURSOR for five seconds. Remember to change it back. Otherwise, you are likely to confuse your users into thinking that the script is still busy. Figure 18-1 shows some sample images from my system when I executed this script.

---

[1]See http://docs.oracle.com/javase/8/docs/api/java/awt/Cursor.html.

Figure 18-1. WaitCursor images from a Windows 7 environment

■ **Note**   It is important to note that the way that the cursor looks is dependent on the operating system. It's also important to remember that WAIT_CURSOR is visible only when the cursor is over the component for which the cursor was changed. Because of this, you may want to call the setCursor() method for your highest-level container (for example, your frame instance).

What if you want to enable WAIT_CURSOR in one part of your application and change it back somewhere else? You either have to save the original cursor setting somewhere, so it can be restored using this saved value, or you can simply use the Cursor.DEFAULT_CURSOR constant. Listing 18-2 demonstrates this constant using a JToggleButton. An even easier technique is to use None as an argument to the setCursor(...) method, which will force the specified component to use the cursor setting of its parent component.

Listing 18-2. Setting the Cursor Shape Based on isSelected() from WaitCursor2.py

```
22|    def wait( self, event ) :
23|        source = event.getSource()
24|        cursor = [
25|            Cursor.DEFAULT_CURSOR,     # isSelected() == 0 (false)
26|            Cursor.WAIT_CURSOR         # isSelected() == 1 (true)
27|        ][ source.isSelected() ]
28|        source.setCursor( Cursor.getPredefinedCursor( cursor ) )
```

When the ActionListener event handler is called, the cursor state will be based on the result of calling the JToggleButton isSelected() method (which returns zero for false and one for true).

Are there any problems with using the cursor to indicate that the application is busy? Think about it. When you use this technique, you are telling the user to wait. How happy do you think the users are when they are told to wait? I, for one, hate when I get a "wait" message. Since your applications are supposed to be event driven, you want them to be able to continue running even though a different part might be busy doing something. If your script needs to be interacting with the user while another part is doing something else, it needs to be doing these other operations on separate threads. Remember the SwingWorker class first mentioned in Chapter 6? That's how you're going to do it.

Showing a Progress Bar

Have you ever had an application appear to stop working and wonder what was going on? It happens to me all of the time. Even though I have a fairly capable laptop, there are times when every application appears to be hung. Sometimes the title bars show a "(Not Responding)" message, but that isn't very reassuring. Unless an operation is expected to complete in less than half a second, it is best to consider communicating to the user some kind of indication of the expected wait time. That's the purpose of a progress bar. Let's take a look at the JProgressBar[2] class and see what it takes to make use of it. It's always a good idea to begin by looking at the class constructors. Table 18-1 contains the constructors for the JProgressBar class.

Table 18-1. JProgressBar Constructors

Signature	Description
JProgressBar()	Creates a horizontal progress bar that displays a border but no progress string.
JProgressBar(BoundedRangeModel newModel)	Creates a horizontal progress bar that uses the specified model to hold the progress bar's data.
JProgressBar(int orient)	Creates a progress bar with the specified orientation, which can be SwingConstants.VERTICAL or SwingConstants.HORIZONTAL.
JProgressBar(int min, int max)	Creates a horizontal progress bar with the specified minimum and maximum.
JProgressBar(int orient, int min, int max)	Creates a progress bar using the specified orientation, minimum, and maximum.

As is often the case, at least for me, the description that is provided in the Javadoc isn't always clear. Take a look at the default JProgressBar instance. The first implementation can be found in ProgressBar0.py; sample images from this implementation are shown in Figure 18-2.

Figure 18-2. Sample images from the ProgressBar0.py output

---

[2]See http://docs.oracle.com/javase/8/docs/api/javax/swing/JProgressBar.html.

How was this done? The primary (ProgressBar) class for this script is shown in Listing 18-3. There really shouldn't be too many surprises here. The only part that you might wonder about is using the setBorder(...) method call on lines 46-48.

It's sometimes confusing that you have to use the frame.getContentPane() method to access the particular pane to which you want to add an "empty" border. Note also the call to the BorderFactory[3].createEmptyBorder(...) method to create a little space or gap around the components in the JPanel. You might want to take a look at the "How to Use Borders" section of the Java Swing Tutorials[4] to obtain a better understanding about borders and how they can be used in Swing applications.

Listing 18-3. ProgressBar Class from ProgressBar0.py

```
38|class ProgressBar0( java.lang.Runnable ) :
39|    def run( self ) :
40|        frame = JFrame(
41|            'ProgressBar0',
42|            size = ( 280, 125 ),
43|            locationRelativeTo = None,
44|            defaultCloseOperation = JFrame.EXIT_ON_CLOSE
45|        )
46|        frame.getContentPane().setBorder(
47|            BorderFactory.createEmptyBorder( 20, 20, 20, 20 )
48|        )
49|        panel = JPanel()
50|        self.button = panel.add(
51|            JButton(
52|                'Start',
53|                actionPerformed = self.start
54|            )
55|        )
56|        self.progressBar = panel.add( JProgressBar() )
57|        frame.add(
58|            panel,
59|            BorderLayout.NORTH
60|        )
61|        frame.setVisible( 1 )
62|    def start( self, event ) :
63|        progressTask(
64|            self.button,
65|            self.progressBar
66|        ).execute()
```

The ActionListener event handler routine, shown in lines 62-66 of Listing 18-3, creates the progressTask instance. Immediately after that, the thread starts executing. Details about this class are shown in Listing 18-4.

[3]See http://docs.oracle.com/javase/8/docs/api/javax/swing/BorderFactory.html.
[4]See http://docs.oracle.com/javase/tutorial/uiswing/components/border.html.

Listing 18-4. The progressTask class from ProgressBar0.py

```
14|class progressTask( SwingWorker ) :
15|    def __init__( self, button, progressBar ) :
16|        self.btn = button              # Save provided references
17|        self.PB  = progressBar
18|        SwingWorker.__init__( self )
19|    def doInBackground( self ) :
20|        self.btn.setEnabled( 0 )       # Disable the "start" button
21|        try :
22|            random   = Random()
23|            progress = 0
24|            self.PB.setValue( progress )
25|            while progress < 100 :
26|                sleep( ( random.nextInt( 1400 ) + 100 ) / 1000.0 )
27|                progress = min(
28|                    progress + random.nextInt( 10 ) + 1, 100
29|                )
30|                self.PB.setValue( progress )
31|        except :
32|            Type, value = sys.exc_info()[ :2 ]
33|            print 'Error:', str( Type )
34|            print 'value:', str( value )
35|            sys.exit()
36|    def done( self ) :
37|        self.btn.setEnabled( 1 )       # Enable the "start" button
```

Is this a great example of a SwingWorker descendent class? No, not really. For one thing, it needs to know too much about the invoking application. This should be obvious when you see that the constructor needs to have references to specific application components provided when the object is instantiated. This should be a dead giveaway. There has to be a better way, don't you think?

SwingWorker Progress

Are there any methods in the SwingWorker class related to "progress"? How can you find out? Chapter 4, introduced the classInfo utility class. Listing 18-5 shows the output of this function. It tells you that a getter method exists for a property named progress. Looking at the Javadoc for the SwingWorker[5] class shows you that a setter method exists, but it is protected, so any descendent classes that you define have to do something special to access that setter method.

Listing 18-5. SwingWorker "Progress" Methods

```
wsadmin>from javax.swing import SwingWorker
wsadmin>
wsadmin>classInfo( SwingWorker, meth = 'progress' )
javax.swing.SwingWorker
  getProgress
```

---

[5]See http://docs.oracle.com/javase/8/docs/api/javax/swing/SwingWorker.html.

```
| java.lang.Object
| java.util.concurrent.RunnableFuture
| | java.lang.Runnable
| | java.util.concurrent.Future
wsadmin>
```

How do I know this? When I tried to use a simple call to the SwingWorker setProgress(...) method, an AttributeError exception was raised and the setProgress name was the source of the error.[6]

So, what can you do? The Jython developers were kind enough to provide a way to access this kind of protected method. A Java programmer can use the @Override annotation to allow the doInBackground(...) method to use the setProgress(...) method. In Jython, you have to use the following syntax to call the setProgress(...) method. In the SwingWorker descendent class, use this:

```
self.super__setProgress( value )[7]
```

Listing 18-6 shows the modified progressTask class from the working ProgressBar2.py script. Note the simplifications, which include the fact that this class now has no references to the application components. That means it's completely contained, meaning that all references to the class attributes exist only in the class.

Listing 18-6. The progressTask Class from ProgressBar2.py

```
15|class progressTask( SwingWorker ) :
16|    def __init__( self ) :
17|        SwingWorker.__init__( self )
18|    def doInBackground( self ) :
19|        try :
20|            random   = Random()
21|            progress = 0
22|            self.super__setProgress( progress )
23|            while progress < 100 :
24|                sleep( ( random.nextInt( 1400 ) + 100 ) / 1000.0 )
25|                progress = min(
26|                    progress + random.nextInt( 10 ) + 1, 100
27|                )
28|                self.super__setProgress( progress )
29|        except :
30|            Type, value = sys.exc_info()[ :2 ]
31|            print 'Error:', str( Type )
32|            print 'value:', str( value )
33|            sys.exit()
34|    def done( self ) :
35|        pass
```

Listing 18-7 shows the modified ProgressBar class from this same script. Since the SwingWorker descendent class knows nothing about the class components defined here, you have to make this class a descendent of the PropertyChangeListener class, as shown on lines 36 and 65-70.

---

[6]The script containing the "first attempt" is the ProgressBar1.py file found in the code\Chap_18 directory.
[7]Yes, there really are two underscores between super and setProgress.

Listing 18-7. The ProgressBar Class from ProgressBar2.py

```
36|class ProgressBar2( java.lang.Runnable, PropertyChangeListener ) :
37|    def run( self ) :
38|        frame = JFrame(
39|            'ProgressBar2',
40|            size = ( 280, 125 ),
41|            locationRelativeTo = None,
42|            defaultCloseOperation = JFrame.EXIT_ON_CLOSE
43|        )
44|        frame.getContentPane().setBorder(
45|            BorderFactory.createEmptyBorder( 20, 20, 20, 20 )
46|        )
47|        panel = JPanel()
48|        self.button = panel.add(
49|            JButton(
50|                'Start',
51|                actionPerformed = self.start
52|            )
53|        )
54|        self.progressBar = panel.add( JProgressBar() )
55|        frame.add(
56|            panel,
57|            BorderLayout.NORTH
58|        )
59|        frame.setVisible( 1 )
60|    def start( self, event ) :
61|        self.button.setEnabled( 0 )
62|        task = progressTask()
63|        task.addPropertyChangeListener( self )
64|        task.execute()
65|    def propertyChange( self, event ) :
66|        if event.getPropertyName() == 'progress' :
67|            progress = event.getNewValue()
68|            self.progressBar.setValue( progress )
69|            if progress == 100 :
70|                self.button.setEnabled( 1 )
```

Showing Progress Details

So far, this is a pretty good way to display progress, albeit a bit vague. Wouldn't it be nice if you were able to display the percentage complete on the progress bar? The developers of the Swing classes thought about this, and have made it really easy for you to do. All you have to do is enable the stringPainted property of the JProgressBar instance. In Jython, this is as simple as adding the stringPainted keyword to the JProgressBar constructor call. Listing 18-8 shows this process.

Listing 18-8. ProgressBar Constructor Call with the stringPainted Keyword

```
56|        self.progressBar = panel.add(
57|            JProgressBar( stringPainted = 1 )
58|        )
```

After making this change, you can see that the progress bar includes a string representation of the completion as a percentage value. Figure 18-3 shows some sample images from `ProgressBar4.py`, which incorporates this change.

Figure 18-3. Sample images with stringPainted enabled from ProgressBar4.py

Specifying a Progress Bar Range

Some of the JProgressBar constructors shown in Table 18-1 allow you to define the minimum and maximum values for your progress bar. What does this do, and what does this mean as far as the SwingWorker progress?

If you specify minimum and maximum values for a progress bar, you become responsible for tracking its updates. The separation of the progressTask (SwingWorker) instance from the ProgressBar class means that only the progress bar is aware of the new minimum and maximum values. In the progressTask instance, it is measuring a percentage of the progress, as shown in Figure 18-3.

So, if your application needs to use non-default minimum and maximum values in a progress bar instance, it needs to take this into account. Listing 18-9 shows one approach that you might want to consider using. Regardless of the minimum and maximum values you choose for the JProgressBar instance, it uses the progress value of the progressTask instance as a percentage complete value to determine the value that's assigned to the JProgressBar instance (as shown on line 74).

Listing 18-9. propertyUpdate() Method from ProgressBar5.py

```
68|    def propertyUpdate( self, event ) :
69|        if event.getPropertyName() == 'progress' :
70|            progress = event.getNewValue()  # integer % complete
71|            lo    = self.progressBar.getMinimum()
72|            hi    = self.progressBar.getMaximum()
73|            here  = int( ( hi - lo ) * 0.01 * progress ) + lo
74|            self.progressBar.setValue( here )
75|            if progress == 100 :
76|                self.button.setEnabled( 1 )
```

Indeterminate ProgressBar Range

Sometimes, you won't know how long an action will take. For example, if your application needs to communicate with a remote host to transfer data from there to here, there is likely to be some delay while communication is being established. Once that has occurred, the amount of data can be provided before the copying initiates. While this is happening, it is considered good practice to tell the users that something is happening.

For this purpose, the JProgressBar class includes an indeterminate attribute. When this attribute[8] is enabled, the progress bar will show movement, but no change in progress completion percentage. The ProgressBar6. py sample script shows one way that this attribute can be used. It includes a random delay in the progressTask doInBackground(...) method to simulate some kind of initialization delay before progress changes occur. Figure 18-4 shows some images of the progress bar when the indeterminate attribute is true.

Figure 18-4. *Sample images of indeterminate progress*

Listing 18-10 shows the lines in ProgressBar6.py that relate to using the indeterminate attribute in your application progress bar instance. In the ActionListener event handler invoked when the Start button is selected, you see how the indeterminate attribute is enabled. Then, in the PropertyChangeListener event handler in line 74, you can see how the state of the indeterminate attribute is disabled and the actual progress is determined.

Listing 18-10. Indeterminate Related Code from ProgressBar6.py

```
65|    def start( self, event ) :
66|        self.button.setEnabled( 0 )
67|        self.progressBar.setIndeterminate( 1 )
68|        task = progressTask( self.propertyUpdate )
69|        task.execute()
70|    def propertyUpdate( self, event ) :
71|        if event.getPropertyName() == 'progress' :
72|            progress = event.getNewValue()  # integer % complete
73|            PB = self.progressBar
74|            PB.setIndeterminate( 0 )
75|            lo = PB.getMinimum()
76|            hi = PB.getMaximum()
77|            here  = int( ( hi - lo ) * 0.01 * progress ) + lo
78|            PB.setValue( here )
79|            if progress == 100 :
80|                self.button.setEnabled( 1 )
```

---

[8]Interestingly enough, the JProgressBar Javadoc doesn't explicitly identify indeterminate as an actual attribute or field. But if you use the classInfo function from Chapter 4, you can see that it does exist and your Jython scripts can access it directly, even though this practice is discouraged.

ProgressMonitor Objects

In many ways, instances of the ProgressMonitor[9] class appear to be similar to the dialog boxes described in Chapters 16 and 17. This is a bit misleading, though. Listing 18-11 shows that the ProgressMonitor class is a descendent of the java.lang.Object class. JDialog descends from the java.awt.Dialog class, and JColorChooser and JFileChooser both descend from the javax.swing.JComponent class, as you learned in Chapter 17.

Listing 18-11. ProgressMonitor Class Hierarchy

```
wsadmin>from javax.swing import ProgressMonitor
wsadmin>
wsadmin>classInfo( ProgressMonitor )
javax.swing.ProgressMonitor
| java.lang.Object
| javax.accessibility.Accessible
wsadmin>
```

What does this mean for your applications? For one, ProgressMonitor instances are going to act very different from descendants of the JComponent class. Additionally, you can't add a ProgressMonitor instance to a Swing container. This provides additional information as to why this dialogue-like box is being discussed here, instead of in Chapter 17. How do you use a ProgressMonitor object? Let's begin with the constructor and then discuss how the instance can and should be used. Take a look at the ProgressMonitor constructors shown in Table 18-2.

Table 18-2. *ProgressMonitor Constructor*

Signature	Description
ProgressMonitor(Component parentComponent, Object message, String note, int min, int max)	Instantiates an object for the purpose of showing progress.

It's kind of interesting to see that this class has only one constructor. Most of the previous Swing classes you've learned about had many more. The constructor parameters shouldn't be too much of a surprise. The kinds of questions that I had when I first encountered this constructor were mostly concerned with the message and note arguments. Mostly, I wondered about how they differ and how they should be used.

Listing 18-12 shows how simple it can be to demonstrate a progress monitor. If you want to enter this example in your own interactive session, remember that the last (i.e., empty) line is significant. It tells the Jython interpreter that the while statement is complete, and that the contents of the loop should be executed.

---

[9]See http://docs.oracle.com/javase/8/docs/api/javax/swing/ProgressMonitor.html.

Listing 18-12. Interactive `wsadmin` Session Showing `ProgressMonitor`

```
wsadmin>from javax.swing import ProgressMonitor
wsadmin>from java.util   import Random
wsadmin>from time        import sleep
wsadmin>
wsadmin>random = Random()
wsadmin>progress = 0
wsadmin>
wsadmin>pm = ProgressMonitor( None, 'Message text', None, 0, 100 )
wsadmin>while progress < 100 :
wsadmin>    sleep( ( random.nextInt( 1400 ) + 100 ) / 1000.0 )
wsadmin>    progress = min( 100, progress + random.nextInt( 10 ) )
wsadmin>    pm.setProgress( progress )
wsadmin>
```

Figure 18-5 shows some images of a `ProgressMonitor` instance.

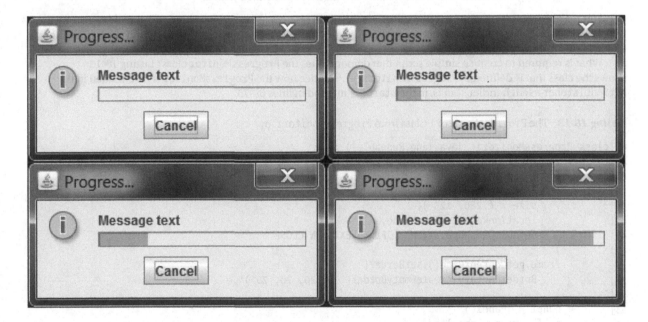

Figure 18-5. Images from the interactive session ProgressMonitor instance in Listing 18-12

■ **Note**   A `ProgressMonitor` instance shouldn't be reused. A new instance should be instantiated instead.

From these, you can see the following about the dialog box:

- A title of Progress...

- A Close icon in the upper-right corner

- An Information icon

- The user-supplied message text

- A progress bar

- A Cancel (or local equivalent) button

Based on this first attempt and on the previous investigation into JDialog instances, you may be surprised to learn that you have no control over:

- The title of the ProgressMonitor dialog box.

- The icon that is displayed

- The buttons that are displayed

- The text that is shown on the button

Some other big differences between ProgressMonitor instances and the other dialog boxes that you've seen are:

- ProgressMonitor dialog box instances are not modal.

- The ProgressMonitor class doesn't have any listeners associated with it.

You may be wondering why I used an interactive wsadmin session, as shown in Listing 18-12, to demonstrate the ProgressMonitor class. One big reason was to show that once the progress reaches the maximum value (100%), the dialog is automatically hidden.

What is required to create a simple script that demonstrates the ProgressMonitor class? Listing 18-13 shows the class that is defined in ProgressMonitor1.py.[10] Notice how the ProgressMonitor is instantiated in the ActionListener event handler, that is, in the start(.) method in lines 65-75.

Listing 18-13. The ProgressMonitor1 Class from ProgressMonitor1.py

```
42|class ProgressMonitor1( java.lang.Runnable ) :
43|    def run( self ) :
44|        frame = JFrame(
45|            'ProgressMonitor',
46|            size = ( 280, 125 ),
47|            locationRelativeTo = None,
48|            defaultCloseOperation = JFrame.EXIT_ON_CLOSE
49|        )
50|        frame.getContentPane().setBorder(
51|            BorderFactory.createEmptyBorder( 20, 20, 20, 20 )
52|        )
53|        panel = JPanel()
54|        self.button = panel.add(
55|            JButton(
56|                'Start',
57|                actionPerformed = self.start
58|            )
59|        )
60|        frame.add(
61|            panel,
62|            BorderLayout.NORTH
63|        )
```

---

[10]Note that the class name can't be the same as the Java Swing class you are trying to use.

```
64|        frame.setVisible( 1 )
65|    def start( self, event ) :
66|        self.button.setEnabled( 0 )
67|        self.PM = ProgressMonitor(
68|            None,              # parentComponent
69|            'Message text',    # message
70|            None,              # note
71|            0,                 # minimum value
72|            100                # maximum value
73|        )
74|        task = progressTask( self.propertyUpdate )
75|        task.execute()
```

Listing 18-14 shows the PropertyChangeListener event handler that is defined in the propertyUpdate() method. Note its similarity to the PropertyChangeListener event handler in the progress bar scripts.

Listing 18-14. PropertyChangeListener from ProgressMonitor1.py

```
76|    def propertyUpdate( self, event ) :
77|        if event.getPropertyName() == 'progress' :
78|            progress = event.getNewValue()  # integer % complete
79|            PM = self.PM
80|            lo = PM.getMinimum()
81|            hi = PM.getMaximum()
82|            here  = int( ( hi - lo ) * 0.01 * progress ) + lo
83|            PM.setProgress( here )
84|            if progress == 100 :
85|                self.button.setEnabled( 1 )
```

ProgressMonitor Cancellation

Using ProgressMonitor1.py, you can easily demonstrate the cancellation process. Start the application and press the Start button. Watch what happens when the ProgressMonitor dialog appears. You shouldn't be too surprised that the dialog box goes away. You might wonder why the Start button is still disabled ... at least for a short time.

What is happening? Consider that, when the ProgressMonitor was canceled, the progressTask continued to execute on the separate thread. Until this task completes, PropertyChangeEvents will continue to be generated, which will result in the PropertyChangeListener method being called. Once the progress reaches 100, the Start button will be enabled. Is this the right way to handle the cancellation event? I don't think so.

In order to properly react to the cancellation of a ProgressMonitor, you need to be able to determine that it has occurred. Fortunately, the Swing designers have provided an isCanceled() method as part of the ProgressMonitor API. You can use it to detect the situation. What should you do when it occurs? Well, one of the important things that you should do is terminate the progressTask that was created to perform the job being monitored. Again, the Swing designers come to the rescue. The SwingWorker API includes a cancel() method that allows developers to terminate the thread.

Is that all you need to worry about? No, you also have to include code in the progressTask class and the PropertyChangeListener event handler to deal with the possible cancellation of these different objects.

Listing 18-15 shows the modifications found in the second script—ProgressMonitor2.py—to deal with the cancellation of a ProgressMonitor object.

Listing 18-15. Differences Found in ProgressMonitor2.py

```
14|class progressTask( SwingWorker ) :
  |    ...
23|    def doInBackground( self ) :
24|        try :
25|            random   = Random()
26|            progress = 0
27|            self.super__setProgress( progress )
28|            sleep( ( random.nextInt( 1400 ) + 100 ) / 1000.0 )
29|            while progress < 100 :
30|                sleep( ( random.nextInt( 1400 ) + 100 ) / 1000.0 )
31|                progress = min(
32|                    progress + random.nextInt( 10 ) + 1, 100
33|                )
34|                self.super__setProgress( progress )
35|        except KeyboardInterrupt, ki :
36|            pass
37|        except :
38|            Type, value = sys.exc_info()[ :2 ]
39|            print 'Error:', str( Type )
40|            print 'value:', str( value )
41|            sys.exit()
  |    ...
44|class ProgressMonitor2( java.lang.Runnable ) :
  |    ...
67|    def start( self, event ) :
68|        self.button.setEnabled( 0 )
69|        self.PM = ProgressMonitor(
70|            None,              # parentComponent
71|            'Message text',   # message
72|            None,              # note
73|            0,                 # minimum value
74|            100                # maximum value
75|        )
76|        self.task = progressTask( self.propertyUpdate )
77|        self.task.execute()
78|    def propertyUpdate( self, event ) :
79|        if event.getPropertyName() == 'progress' :
80|            progress = event.getNewValue()  # integer % complete
81|            PM, task = self.PM, self.task
82|            lo, hi   = PM.getMinimum(), PM.getMaximum()
83|            here     = int( ( hi - lo ) * 0.01 * progress ) + lo
84|            PM.setProgress( here )
85|            done = task.isDone()
86|            if PM.isCanceled() or done :
87|                if not done :
88|                    task.cancel( 1 )
89|                self.button.setEnabled( 1 )
```

Table 18-3 identifies the changes that you nee to make in order to deal with the cancellation of ProgressMonitor or progressTask more appropriately. It is interesting to see how little code is needed in order to adequately handle these cancellation events.[11]

Table 18-3. *Explanation of Changes in* ProgressMonitor2.py

Lines	Description
35-36	The except clause in the progressTask doInBackground() method now silently ignores KeyboardInterrupt exceptions. All others will continue to display information about the exception before the application is terminated.
76	A reference is saved in the object instance to the task object. The PropertyChangeListener event handler needs this reference.
86-88	If the ProgressMonitor was canceled, you might need to cancel the progressTask instance.
89	If the ProgressMonitor was canceled or if the progressTask instance is completed, the Start button will be enabled.

The ProgressMonitor Message

Take another look at the ProgressMonitor constructor in Table 18-2. What data type is the message parameter? It's an object. What does that mean and why isn't it a String? According to the Javadoc, the message argument is an object so that it can be used in different ways, as described in the JOptionPane.message[12] documentation. Additionally, it is important to note that the message portion of the ProgressMonitor object will not change during the life of the ProgressMonitor. Let's see what you can do with the message.

The ProgressMonitor3.py script uses the same technique as shown in Chapter 16 to specify the message as an ImageIcon. I tried this approach first because I wanted to see if I could use this technique to display a different icon on the ProgressMonitor. Unfortunately, as you can see in Figure 18-6, the ImageIcon is displayed in addition to the Information icon.

Figure 18-6. ProgressMonitor *with an* ImageIcon *message*

Can you use HTML in the message? According to the JOptionPane.message documentation, you would expect strings to be displayed in a JLabel. Since the JLabel class allows HTML text, you might be able to do some interesting things.

Figure 18-7 shows what happens when you try using an HTML message, as well as an ordered and unordered list.[13] Unfortunately, it appears that an excessively "long" HTML message can cause some problems. From the little testing that I did, it appears to be related to the horizontal space that is allowed for the message. I guess you need to determine just how much information, and in what form, should be displayed in this message field.

---

[11]A Java application would need to catch a java.lang.InterruptedException instead.

[12]See http://docs.oracle.com/javase/8/docs/api/javax/swing/JOptionPane.html#message.

[13]All of these output images were generated by ProgressMonitor4.py. You will have to edit the source script and uncomment the desired assignment statement in the start() method to duplicate these different outputs.

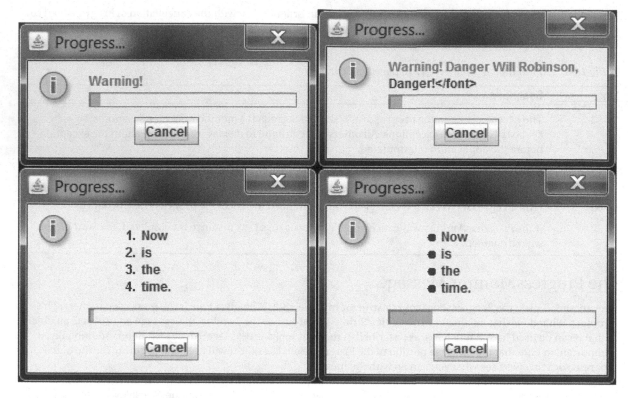

Figure 18-7. ProgressMonitor with HTML message strings

The ProgressMonitor Note

In the ProgressMonitor constructor in Table 18-2, you can see that, in addition to the message parameter, a note parameter is also defined. What's the difference between the message and note parameters? As you just saw, the message parameter is an object that is represented as a JLabel, so you can use HTML tags to control how it is displayed (within limits). Additionally, it is static for the life of the ProgressMonitor. The note argument is a string that is used to initialize a note attribute. If a value of None (the Jython equivalent to the Java null value) is specified in the constructor, the value of the note attribute shouldn't change.

On the other hand, you can use the note field on the ProgressMonitor to provide information related to the progress that is being made. According to the Javadoc, you only need to call the setNote(...) method to update this portion of the ProgressMonitor. Figure 18-8 shows the output of the ProgressMonitor5.py script, which uses the note field to provide a numeric percentage indicating the progress.

Figure 18-8. ProgressMonitor with a note attribute from ProgressMonitor5.py

Does anything about this catch your eye? When I first saw this, I was more than a little surprised by the fact that bottom of the Cancel button was encroaching on the bottom edge of the dialog box. After a bit of testing, I realized what was happening. It appears that the progress monitor's size is based on the initial parameter values. If an empty note string is provided in the ProgressMonitor constructor, then no vertical space is allocated to hold the string when it is changed. How do you fix this? One simple fix is to provide a note string containing one or more blanks. Figure 18-9 shows the output of this same script when the note is initialized with a single blank. I don't know about you, but I think that this looks significantly better.

Figure 18-9. *ProgressMonitor with note initialized with ' '*

Can the note string contain HTML text? Yes it can, but again, I caution you to be careful about the kind of text that you use. It is important to remember that the ProgressMonitor class hierarchy, as shown in Listing 18-11, is based on an object and not a JComponent. So, you don't have the same kind of control over it that you do with normal Swing components, which means that you can't resize it after it is instantiated.

The ProgressMonitor parentComponent

Up to now, you have passed None as the value for the parentComponent argument. What role is this parameter supposed to play? Is there any reason for providing something other than None? The ProgressMonitor6.py script attempts to answer this question. In all of the other ProgressMonitor scripts, None was specified as the parentComponent value. This script references the application by using the self.frame value. Now, regardless of where the frame is positioned on the screen, when you press the Start button, the ProgressMonitor will be positioned with respect to the parentComponent window. This parameter provides the only control over how the ProgressMonitor appears on the screen.

Other ProgressMonitor Properties

One difference that exists between ProgressMonitor objects and other dialog boxes is that there is a delay between when the object is created and when it appears on the screen. Why is that? It's possible for there to be no reason for the ProgressMonitor to be displayed. Certain properties of the ProgressMonitor determine when and if a ProgressMonitor object should be displayed.

If you again take a look at the classInfo function introduced in Chapter 4, as shown in Listing 18-16, you'll see that there are some attributes defined in the ProgressMonitor class that aren't listed in the Javadoc.

Listing 18-16. ProgressMonitor Attributes

```
wsadmin>from javax.swing import ProgressMonitor
wsadmin>
wsadmin>classInfo( ProgressMonitor, attr = '' )
javax.swing.ProgressMonitor
  canceled, maximum, millisToDecideToPopup, millisToPopup
  minimum, note, progress
| java.lang.Object
*   class
| javax.accessibility.Accessible
*   accessibleContext
wsadmin>
```

Table 18-4 identifies and describes these attributes. This should help you understand any delay in the appearance of the ProgressMonitor dialog. What happens is that when a progress value is set, the millisToDecideToPopup value determines how long the ProgressMonitor instance waits before trying to determine if the ProgressMonitor should be visible. If the estimated time to completion is less than the millisToPopup value, the ProgressMonitor dialog will not be displayed. After millisToPopup milliseconds, the dialog will appear. Once the progress value reaches the maximum value, the ProgressMonitor is hidden.

Table 18-4. *ProgressMonitor Attributes, Explained*

Attribute Name	Description
canceled	Boolean value indicating if the Cancel button has been used.
maximum	Integer value initialized by constructor; accessible via getter and setter methods.
millisToDecideToPopup	Integer value defaulting to 500 (0.5 sec); accessible via getter and setter methods.
millisToPopup	Integer value defaulting to 2000 (2 sec); accessible via getter and setter methods.
minimum	Integer value initialized by constructor; accessible via getter and setter methods.
note	String value initialized by constructor; accessible via getter and setter methods. **Note:** If this is initialized to None, any changes made via setNote() are ignored.
progress	Write-only integer value modified via the setProgress() setter method. Values are limited by the values of minimum and maximum. **Note:** When a progress is set to the maximum, the ProgressMonitor is hidden.

One question that keeps coming up with respect to ProgressMonitor dialog boxes relates to the fact that the dialog box is hidden when the process value is set to the maximum value. Generally, developers wonder whether there is any way to get the dialog box to stay visible once the maximum value is set. Unfortunately not. However, you can pass the setProgress(...) method a value in the range from minimum to maximum - 1. Unfortunately, if the range is small (e.g., 0 .. 10), a value of maximum - 1 might leave a visible gap at the upper end of the progress bar. In this case, you might want to consider using some kind of multiplier so that the value of maximum - 1 won't be discernable.

Another possible annoyance related to doing this exists. Once the dialog is hidden, if you use the setProgress(...) method to cause it to reappear, it will not be located where the user left it. It will be located based on the original position, relative to the value of the parentComponent attribute. So, if the user moves the ProgressMonitor dialog box, the dialog box will appear to jump from where it is back to its original screen location.

ProgressMonitorInputStream Objects

There is another class, much like `ProgressMonitor`, that can use a `ProgressMonitor` object to determine the progress while data is read from an `InputStream`. As with `ProgressMonitor` objects, the `ProgressMonitorInputStream`[14] processing (reading data from the `InputStream`) should be performed by a separate (`SwingWorker`) type of task.

Unfortunately, space and time limitations don't allow me to provide more detail about this particular class.

Summary

This chapter covered monitoring and communicating progress to the user with a variety of techniques. The really nice thing that this shows you is how much control application developers have over the way they convey progress to their users. It's important to understand the implications and consequence of each choice you make, so keep this in mind. In next chapter, you'll learn about internal frames, which allow you to create even more interesting applications.

---

[14]See http://docs.oracle.com/javase/8/docs/api/javax/swing/ProgressMonitorInputStream.html.

Internal Frames

Up to this point, the applications you've seen have been able to create and use individual windows. Almost every sample has used a single JFrame to display information and interact with the users. Now you're going to look at using internal frames. First you will take a quick look at a collection of inner frames, because there are times when applications can use a variety of views in order to convey different information to the users. The chapter begins by comparing internal frames to the JFrame used in the previous applications. Then you'll build an application that uses internal frames that display information in a variety of ways.

Looking at Inner Frames

Figure 19-1 shows the output of a simple application that displays three inner frames.

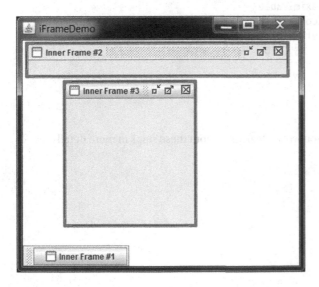

Figure 19-1. *Simple application with three inner frames*

Listing 19-1 shows the code required to produce this kind of simple inner frame. As you can see, even though very little code is required, it is quite functional.[1] The script, which you can find in the code\Chap_19\iFrameDemo.py file, shows that each of the inner frames can be moved, resized, closed, iconified, restored, and even maximized within the available space.

Listing 19-1. iFrameDemo Class Within iFrameDemo.py

```
 8|class iFrameDemo( java.lang.Runnable ) :
 9|   def run( self ) :
10|       screenSize = Toolkit.getDefaultToolkit().getScreenSize()
11|       w = screenSize.width  >> 1          # 1/2 screen width
12|       h = screenSize.height >> 1          # 1/2 screen height
13|       x = ( screenSize.width  - w ) >> 1
14|       y = ( screenSize.height - h ) >> 1
15|       frame = JFrame(
16|           'iFrameDemo',
17|           bounds = ( x, y, w, h ),         # location & size
18|           defaultCloseOperation = JFrame.EXIT_ON_CLOSE
19|       )
20|       desktop = JDesktopPane()
21|       for i in range( 3 ) :
22|           inner = JInternalFrame(
23|               'Inner Frame #%d' % ( i + 1 ),
24|               1,                            # Resizeable
25|               1,                            # Closeable
26|               1,                            # Maximizable
27|               1,                            # Iconifiable
28|               visible = 1,                  # setVisible( 1 )
29|               bounds = ( i * 25 + 25, i * 25 + 25, 250, 250 )
30|           )
31|           desktop.add( inner )
32|       frame.setContentPane( desktop )
33|       frame.setVisible( 1 )
```

Table 19-1 describes each of the steps in Listing 19-1. You will be learning about these steps in more detail throughout this chapter.

---

[1] Please note, however, that the iFrameDemo.py script output requires user manipulation to look like the image seen in Figure 19-1. This is discussed further in section 19-2.

Table 19-1. *iFrameDemo Class, Explained*

Lines	Description
10	Determines the size of the current screen.
11	Makes the width of the application use half the physical width of the screen.
12	Makes the height of the application use half the physical height of the screen.
13-14	Computes the upper-left corner of the application to center the application window.
15-19	Instantiates the frame using the specified parameters.
20	Creates a JDesktopPane onto which the InternalFrames will be added.
21-31	Creates three InternalFrames, one at a time, and adds them to the desktop. **Note:** The bounds keyword argument is used to size and position the inner frame on the JDesktopPane.
32	Replaces the frame ContentPane with the populated desktop.
33	Makes the application frame visible.

Before you investigate the JDesktopPane[2] class shown in Listing 19-1, it's a good idea to learn more about layers and about the JLayeredPane[3] on which this class is based.

Layers

Let's take a quick look at a simple script that demonstrates layered components using a trivial component—the JLabel object. Figure 19-2 shows a group of seven overlapping colored labels. Note how the text is centered across the top of each label, and how the labels are stacked to make all of the text visible.

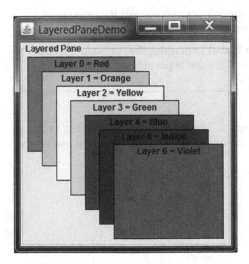

Figure 19-2. *Layered labels*

---

[2]http://docs.oracle.com/javase/8/docs/api/javax/swing/JDesktopPane.html.
[3]http://docs.oracle.com/javase/8/docs/api/javax/swing/JLayeredPane.html.

Listing 19-2 shows the relevant part of the LayeredPaneDemo class from the LayeredPaneDemo.py script.

Listing 19-2. LayeredPaneDemo Class, Part 1

```
11|class LayeredPaneDemo( java.lang.Runnable ) :
12|    def run( self ) :
  |        ...
18|        frame.setContentPane( self.createLayeredPane() )
19|        frame.pack()
20|        frame.setVisible( 1 )
21|    def createColoredLabel( self, text, color ) :
22|        return JLabel(
23|            text,
24|            opaque = 1,
25|            size = ( 150, 130 ),
26|            background = color,
27|            foreground = Color.black,
28|            verticalAlignment = JLabel.TOP,
29|            horizontalAlignment = JLabel.CENTER,
30|            border = BorderFactory.createLineBorder( Color.black )
31|        )
```

Unfortunately, this class is too long to fit onto one page, so it has to be split into pieces. Table 19-2 describes the portion of the LayeredPaneDemo shown in Listing 19-2.

Table 19-2. Comments About the LayeredPaneDemo Class, Part 1

Lines	Description
12-20	This portion of the run() method should be familiar to you by now. The only new part is where the default ContentPane is replaced by the result of calling the createLayeredPane() in line 18.
21-31	The createColoredLabel(...) method creates and returns a JLabel containing the specified text and using the specified color. Each label object is roughly square, and the text is positioned in the center of the top, with a black border.

The remainder of the LayeredPaneDemo class, the createLayeredPane(...) method, is shown in Listing 19-3. The purpose of this method is to create and return a layered pane object populated with a collection of colored labels.

Listing 19-3. LayeredPaneDemo Class, Part 2

```
32|    def createLayeredPane( self ) :
33|        colors = [
34|            ( 'Red'   , Color.red    ),
35|            ( 'Orange', Color.orange ),
36|            ( 'Yellow', Color.yellow ),
37|            ( 'Green' , Color.green  ),
38|            ( 'Blue'  , Color.blue   ),
39|            ( 'Indigo', Color(  75, 0, 130 ) ),
40|            ( 'Violet', Color( 143, 0, 255 ) )
41|        ]
```

```
42|           result = JLayeredPane(
43|               border = BorderFactory.createTitledBorder(
44|                   'Layered Pane'
45|               ),
46|               preferredSize = Dimension( 290, 280 )
47|           )
48|           position, level = Point( 10, 20 ), 0
49|           for name, color in colors :
50|               label = self.createColoredLabel(
51|                   'Layer %d = %s' % ( level, name ),
52|                   color
53|               )
54|               label.setLocation( position )
55|               position.x += 20
56|               position.y += 20
57|               result.add( label, level, 0 )
58|               level += 1
59|           return result
```

Table 19-3 describes the statements found in this method.

Table 19-3. *Comments About the LayeredPaneDemo Class, Part 2*

Lines	Description
32-59	The createLayeredPane(...) method is used to create, populate, and return a JLayeredPane object instance.
33-41	The colors array holds information about the text and colors to be used to create each of the label objects.
42-47	Creates the JLayeredPane object with the specified preferred size and a title.
48	Each label will be positioned in an overlaid fashion, at a different layer on the pane, starting with these values.
49-58	Loops over the available colors (defined in 33-41), creating and positioning the labels accordingly.
57	This statement adds the current label to the layered pane at the specified layer and proper position. I will discuss this method in more detail shortly.
58	Increments the level variable used to indicate the layer number of the next label.
59	Returns the populated JLayeredPane object instance.

Position Within the Layer

You might wonder what the third parameter on the add(...) method (line 57 in Listing 19-3) is used for.
It identifies the position, within the layer, of the component being added. Figure 19-3 shows what happens when you
don't include the position parameter. Notice how in Figure 19-2, the top portion of each label (including the text)
was visible.

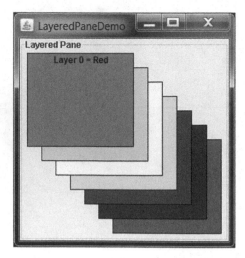

Figure 19-3. *Layered Labels without the position parameter specified*

As you can see, the layers are now stacked in reverse order, with the red label on top. If you add a `print` statement after the `add()` method statement and display the value of level (the intended level of the component being added) and the result of calling the `getLayer(...)` method for the label component on the layered panel, you'll see that an unintended `add(...)` method is being invoked and you aren't specifying the level, as expected. Listing 19-4 shows the proposed statement changes.

Listing 19-4. Changes to the `createLayeredPane()` Method

```
             ...
57|          result.add( label, level, 0 )
58|          print level, result.getLayer( label )
             ...
```

The output of the `getLayer(...)` method call for each label will show that every label is, in fact, being added to layer zero. With the three argument `add(...)` method calls, the output of the `getLayer(...)` method call will show the expected layer value.

So, what is the position supposed to do and when does it come into play? It is used when multiple components are at the same layer. It is used to determine the relationship of components on the same level. The position value should be an integer from -1 to N - 1, where N is the number of components in layer. The larger the value (the closer to N) of the position, the deeper the component.

The exception to this is -1, which is considered the same as N - 1, which means that it will be the deepest component on the layer. That's why you specify a value of zero on the `add(...)` method when you add a component to a layer. This will position the newest component as the uppermost position within the layer (closest to the user).

The JDesktopPane Class

Now that you've seen how layers work, you'll be better able to understand the `JDesktopPane` class. It is generally best to have internal frames added to a `JDesktopPane` instance in order to show and manipulate them. If you look back at Figure 19-1, you should notice familiar `JFrame` icons manipulating the internal frames. It should be clear how different these are from something as simple as a label.

There was another reason for discussing the JLayeredPane before moving onto the JDesktopPane, and that is the add(...) method as shown in Listing 19-1, line 31. If you take another look at Figure 19-1, you'll see that the internal frames have been moved around so that they don't overlap. This is because the initial output of the iFrameDemo script has the layering in an unexpected order. Unexpected until you understand which of the add(...) methods should have been used. The single argument add(...) method is used in Listing 19-1. If, on the other hand, you had used the three argument version, as shown in line 57 of Listing 19-3, the first internal frame (Inner Frame #3) would have been completely visible. Figure 19-4 shows the ordering of the internal frames when using the single and multiple argument add(...) methods.[4] As a user of GUI applications, which output would you prefer?

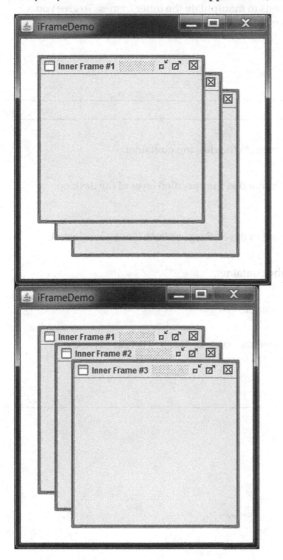

Figure 19-4. iFrameDemo using single (top) and multiple (bottom) argument add(...) methods

---

[4]The three argument add(...) method call can be seen as a comment in the iFrameDemo.py sample script. The Javadoc for which is http://docs.oracle.com/javase/8/docs/api/java/awt/Container.html#add%28java.awt.Component, %20java.lang.Object,%20int%29.

Another thing to note about these sample scripts is that when the inner frames are created, their position needs to be specified so that all of the inner frames aren't stacked on top of each other, thereby hiding the frames underneath.

One thing that you haven't learned about in much detail yet is the JDesktopPane instance onto which all of these inner frames are added. In fact, I have only mentioned its add(...) method. There have to be more, don't there? Of course there are more. In fact, there are far too many to discuss in this chapter. In fact, the sample scripts in this chapter don't use anything but the add(...) method. That doesn't mean that they aren't useful. I just don't have the space or time required to do each of them justice.

More complex scripts are likely to use the JDesktopPane methods to manipulate the inner frames. To give you a little idea what some of the methods can do, I've listed a few of the most useful in Table 19-4. Remember that this is only a partial list.

Table 19-4. *Some Useful* JDesktopPane *Methods*

Returned Value	Method Signature and Role
JInternalFrame[]	getAllFrames() Returns all JInternalFrames currently present in the desktop container.
JInternalFrame[]	getAllFramesInLayer(int layer) Returns all JInternalFrames currently contained at the specified layer of the desktop object.
JInternalFrame	getSelectedFrame() Returns the currently active JInternalFrame in the desktop, or None if none is selected.
void	remove(int index) Removes the specified component from the container.
void	removeAll() Removes all the components from the container.
JinternalFrame	selectFrame(boolean forward) Selects the next component in the container if the value of forward is true (1) or the previous component if the forward value is false (0).
void	setSelectedFrame(JInternalFrame f) Makes the specified JInternalFrame active.

JFrame or JInternalFrame?

When trying to decide how to implement an application, the similarity of the JFrame and JInternalFrame[5] classes might lead you to think that you can start with one and easily switch to the other should the need arise. Unfortunately, it's not quite as simple as that. It's better to pick one from the start and stick with it. It's possible that you could pick one way and soon realize that the other technique would have been better. If you haven't invested too much time or effort, it might be better to start over at that point. Here are some questions to consider to help you decide which approach is more advantageous for your needs.

- How contained and well defined is your application? Does it make more sense for you to see one, or multiple kinds or views of data at the same time? If you only need to see one view, then a single frame, possibly with something like tabbed panes might make more sense.

- How much data sharing will you need to do for the different portions of your application? If each aspect of your application is separate and distinct, there might be some advantage to seeing multiple views or pieces of data. If this is the case, multiple internal frames may be a better approach.

- Do multiple instances of the same kind of view make better sense, or is a single perspective sufficient? Might multiple views add complexity or confusion? If multiple, simultaneous views are advantageous, using multiple internal frames might be the best approach. However, try to consider the additional complexity that might be required by this choice.

One of the really powerful things about using Jython to produce or prototype your graphical application is how easy it is to create a proof of concept. This allows you to start your development and improve your knowledge about what exactly you want your program to do. This might help you decide which approach is best—a single frame or multiple internal frames.

The JInternalFrame Class

One way to determine the difference between the JInternalFrame and JFrame classes is by comparing the methods available to each. A quick glance shows that the JFrame class has about 30 methods and the JInternalFrame class has about 80. This would appear to be a huge difference, which in some ways, it is. Looking a bit closer at the methods, you'll see that the JInternalFrame class has a large number of methods (46) that are identified as protected, but the JFrame class has only eight. Additionally, the JInternalFrame class has some deprecated methods.

JFrame and JInternalFrame Methods

While on the topic of graphical applications, consider what it would take to create a small application that showed the JFrame and JInternalFrame methods side-by-side and determined whether the protected and deprecated methods should be viewable. Figure 19-5 shows an image from this simple application. The menu selections allow you to hide the deprecated and protected methods.

---

[5]See http://docs.oracle.com/javase/8/docs/api/javax/swing/JInternalFrame.html.

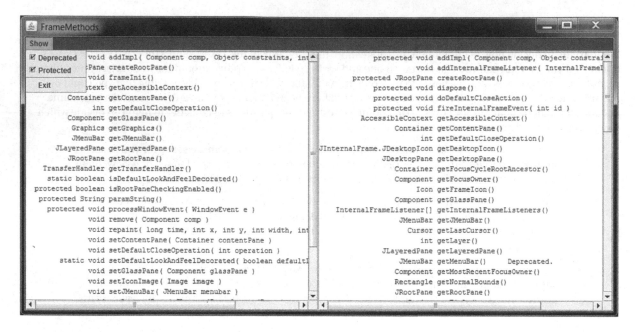

Figure 19-5. *FrameMethod application images*

To create this fairly simple application, you first have to figure out where the data exists and in what format. Based on this, you need to figure out how to get the data into your application. For simplicity's sake, I created two text files, one for each class, and one line for each method. Each line has three fields:

- The optional modifier and return type of the method

- The method signature (the method name and parameter list)

- The method abstract

The fields are separated by the | delimiter. So, the application needs to load the text from the file and process each line. Listing 19-5 contains some utility methods from the FrameMethods.py script.[6] The textFile(...) method returns a string containing the file contents and the parse(...) method formats each line to contain only the first two fields from the file, with all of the method names aligned on the first character in the method name.

Listing 19-5. FrameMethods.py Utility Methods

```
25|    def parse( self, text ) :
26|        data = [ line.split( ' | ' ) for line in text.splitlines() ]
27|        width = max(
28|            [ len( result ) for result, sign, desc in data ]
29|        )
```

---

[6]See ...\code\Chap_19\FrameMethods.py in the sample directories.

```
30|        return '\n'.join(
31|            [
32|                '%*s %s' % ( width, result, sign )
33|                for result, sign, desc in data
34|            ]
35|        )
  |    ...
111|    def textFile( self, filename ) :
112|        result = ''
113|        try :
114|            f = open( filename )
115|            result = f.read()
116|            f.close()
117|        except :
118|            Type, value = sys.exc_info()[ :2 ]
119|            result = '%s\n%s' % ( Type, value )
120|        return result
```

Listings 19-6 and 19-17 show the run(...) method from the FrameMethods class, which is used to create the application frame, define the layout, load the files, and populate the panes and the application menu. The contents and structure of this method should be quite familiar to you by now, so I won't bother describing it in detail.

Listing 19-6 shows the run(...) method of the FrameMethods.py script. In it, you can see how the frame is composed of two JTextArea sections (lines 47-53 and lines 58-64), each of which is contained in a JScrollPane (lines 54 and 65). Each text area is populated from one of the text files used by this script.

Listing 19-6. FrameMethods run() Method

```
15|class FrameMethods( java.lang.Runnable ) :
  |    ...
36|    def run( self ) :
37|        frame = JFrame(
38|            'FrameMethods',
39|            size = ( 1000, 500 ),
40|            locationRelativeTo = None,
41|            layout = GridLayout( 0, 2 ),
42|            defaultCloseOperation = JFrame.EXIT_ON_CLOSE
43|        )
44|        self.one = self.parse(
45|            self.textFile( 'JFrame Methods.txt' )
46|        )
47|        self.left = JTextArea(
48|            self.one,
49|            20,
50|            40,
51|            editable = 0,
52|            font = Font( 'Courier' , Font.PLAIN, 12 )
53|        )
```

```
54|          frame.add( JScrollPane( self.left ) )
55|          self.two = self.parse(
56|              self.textFile( 'JInternalFrame Methods.txt' )
57|          )
58|          self.right = JTextArea(
59|              self.two,
60|              20,
61|              40,
62|              editable = 0,
63|              font = Font( 'Courier' , Font.PLAIN, 12 )
64|          )
65|          frame.add( JScrollPane( self.right ) )
66|          frame.setJMenuBar( self.makeMenu() )
67|          frame.setVisible( 1 )
```

In case you are interested, the instance variables one and two are used by the event handler methods to determine the text that will be displayed in each text area. Listing 19-7 shows the makeMenu() method from the same script. As you can see, this method creates, populates, and returns the menu bar and its entries, which have the associated actionPerformed event handling methods assigned as the showItems() method.

Listing 19-7. FrameMethods makeMenu() Method

```
68|    def makeMenu( self ) :
69|        menuBar = JMenuBar(
70|            background = Color.blue,
71|            foreground = Color.white
72|        )
73|        showMenu = JMenu(
74|            'Show',
75|            background = Color.blue,
76|            foreground = Color.white
77|        )
78|        self.deprecated =  JCheckBoxMenuItem(
79|            'Deprecated',
80|            1,
81|            actionPerformed = self.showItems
82|        )
83|        showMenu.add( self.deprecated )
84|        self.protected =  JCheckBoxMenuItem(
85|            'Protected',
86|            1,
87|            actionPerformed = self.showItems
88|        )
89|        showMenu.add( self.protected )
90|        showMenu.addSeparator()
91|        showMenu.add(
92|            JMenuItem(
93|                'Exit',
94|                actionPerformed = self.exit
95|            )
96|        )
97|        menuBar.add( showMenu )
98|        return menuBar
```

Listing 19-8 shows the showItems(...) method used as the menu item ActionListener event handler. It, in turn, may use the findNot(...) method to filter the data, removing all lines containing the specified text (either "deprecated" or "protected").

Listing 19-8. The showItems() and findNot() Methods

```
18|     def findNot( self, data, text ) :
19|         return '\n'.join(
20|             [
21|                     line for line in data.splitlines()
22|                     if line.lower().find( text ) < 0
23|             ]
24|         )
  |     ...
99|     def showItems( self, event ) :
100|        item = event.getActionCommand()
101|        one = self.one
102|        two = self.two
103|        if not self.deprecated.isSelected() :
104|            one = self.findNot( one, 'deprecated' )
105|            two = self.findNot( two, 'deprecated' )
106|        if not self.protected.isSelected() :
107|            one = self.findNot( one, 'protected' )
108|            two = self.findNot( two, 'protected' )
109|        self.left.setText( one )
110|        self.right.setText( two )
```

I'll admit that I created this application quickly. It was one of those "rapid prototyping" opportunities that took about two hours, all told. Most of that time was spent creating the input files. It only required about 30 minutes to create the actual application, once I had the data in place. Not bad for a quick "proof of concept," wouldn't you say? The really neat part was that it is more than adequate, as is, to deal with the menu selection events. At first, I wasn't sure how rapidly the application would update after a menu selection was made. Watching it in action, though, I was pleasantly surprised and am very happy with the responsiveness.

Does that mean that this is the best way to go? Absolutely not. That's one of the great things about being able to create a quick proof of concept script like this. It can help you understand the problem better, as well as give you some ideas about improvements and additional features. For example, based on this example, I can imagine a more useful application that:

- Adds menu items to identify the classes to be compared, such as allows users to specify input sources (URL or filename).

- Uses jsoup (Chapter 15) to retrieve and process the Javadoc URLs.

- Uses the JList class (Chapter 9) to allow a method to be selected. If the same method signature exists in the other list, highlights it as well.

- Adds selection logic to highlight the corresponding method in the other pane, if one exists.

In fact, the more I think about it, this might be a really good enhancement to the javadocInfo script in Chapter 15. What do you think? However, since we're discussing internal frames maybe that would be a good way to do it... It's a thought.

More JFrame and JInternalFrame Differences

One reason for looking at the differences between the JFrame and JInternalFrame classes is to understand the extent. Besides looking at their methods, you might also wonder about the differences in their class hierarchies. Listing 19-9 shows the output of the classInfo function, which was introduced in Chapter 4. It emphasizes that even though the class names are similar, they are very different. One of the most important differences was pointed out in Chapter 1, where the JFrame class was identified as a top-level container.

Listing 19-9. JFrame and JInternalFrame Class Hierarchies

```
wsadmin>from javax.swing import JFrame, JInternalFrame
wsadmin>
wsadmin>classInfo( JFrame )
javax.swing.JFrame
| java.awt.Frame
| | java.awt.Window
| | | java.awt.Container
| | | | java.awt.Component
| | | | | java.lang.Object
| | | | | java.awt.image.ImageObserver
| | | | | java.awt.MenuContainer
| | | | | java.io.Serializable
| | | javax.accessibility.Accessible
| | java.awt.MenuContainer
| javax.swing.WindowConstants
| javax.accessibility.Accessible
| javax.swing.RootPaneContainer
wsadmin>
wsadmin>classInfo( JInternalFrame )
javax.swing.JInternalFrame
| javax.swing.JComponent
| | java.awt.Container
| | | java.awt.Component
| | | | java.lang.Object
| | | | java.awt.image.ImageObserver
| | | | java.awt.MenuContainer
| | | | java.io.Serializable
| | java.io.Serializable
| javax.accessibility.Accessible
| javax.swing.WindowConstants
| javax.swing.RootPaneContainer
wsadmin>
```

The differences between these two classes are significant, even though the function they provide is quite similar in nature. One area that differs significantly is the type of events recognized by each class.

JInternalFrame Events

In order to work well with internal fames, you need to understand the events that can occur in order to decide how your application should react when these events occur. The Javadoc for the JInternalFrame class identifies the InternalFrameListener[7] class as the base class for dealing with these kinds of events. Since it is an identified as an interface, it is probably better idea to consider using the InternalFrameAdapter[8] class as a base class.

What would it take to create an application that uses internal frames to help you better understand internal frame events? You can use one perpetual internal frame to display details about the internal frame events when they occur.[9] All of the others can be simple internal frames that can be created, minimized, restored, maximized, and closed.

The perpetual inner frame should contain a scrollable text area. This would allow your application to display the details and information about the events as they occur. Taking a quick look back to Listing 19-1, you can make some decisions about what arguments should be used to create this special internal frame. It would probably make the application much more complex if you allowed zero or multiple instances of this special internal frame to exist. So let's start simply by allowing only one perpetual instance in your application.

Listing 19-10 shows the first attempt of implementing a logging internal frame class. As you can see, it's really simple and straightforward. In fact, there really shouldn't be anything surprising about it.

Listing 19-10. The eventLogger Class, First Attempt from iFrameEvents1.py

```
10|class eventLogger( JInternalFrame ) :
11|    def __init__ ( self ) :
12|        JInternalFrame.__init__(
13|            self,
14|            'eventLogger',
15|            1,                  # Resizeable  - yes
16|            0,                  # Closeable   - no
17|            0,                  # Maximizable - no
18|            1,                  # Iconifiable - yes
19|            visible = 1,
20|            bounds = ( 0, 0, 250, 250 )
21|        )
22|        self.textArea = JTextArea(
23|            20,                # rows
24|            40,                # columns
25|            editable = 0       # read-only
26|        )
27|        self.add( JScrollPane( self.textArea ) )
```

---

[7]See http://docs.oracle.com/javase/8/docs/api/javax/swing/event/InternalFrameListener.html.
[8]See http://docs.oracle.com/javase/8/docs/api/javax/swing/event/InternalFrameAdapter.html.
[9]See http://docs.oracle.com/javase/8/docs/api/javax/swing/event/InternalFrameEvent.html.

When instantiated, this class creates an internal frame, positions it, defines its size, and adds a scrollable pane containing a read-only text area to it. Wow, that was easy. Figure 19-6 shows the top-left portion of an application showing this internal frame.

Figure 19-6. `iFrameEvents1.py` *initial display*

That's nice, but how is it supposed to log an `InternalFrameEvent`? How is the application supposed to create any other internal frames?

The first issue is easy enough to solve. You can have the `eventLogger` class instantiate an `InternalFrameAdapter` instance and provide a getter method to access it. This means that when any `InternalFrameEvent` occurs, the event handler will be able to access the event logger frame and add text to it.

The second issue is solved by adding a simple menu that allows you to create more internal frames.

Most of the revised script is in `code\Chap_19\iFrameEvents2.py` and is shown in the following listings. Listing 19-11 shows the utility methods for this class, which should look quite familiar by now.

Listing 19-11. Beginning of the `iFrameEvents` Class from `iFrameEvents2.py`

```
56|class iFrameEvents2( java.lang.Runnable ) :
57|    def addIframe( self, event ) :
58|        desktop = self.desktop
59|        self.iFrameCount += 1
60|        i = self.iFrameCount % 10
61|        inner = JInternalFrame(
62|            'Inner Frame #%d' % self.iFrameCount,
63|            1,                          # Resizeable
64|            1,                          # Closeable
65|            1,                          # Maximizable
66|            1,                          # Iconifiable
67|            bounds = ( i * 20 + 20, i * 20 + 20, 200, 200 )
68|        )
69|        inner.addInternalFrameListener( self.logger.getListener() )
70|        inner.setVisible( 1 )
71|        desktop.add( inner, i, 0 )
72|    def exit( self, event ) :
73|        sys.exit()
74|    def menuBar( self ) :
```

```
75|          result = JMenuBar()
76|          newMenu = result.add( JMenu( 'New' ) )
77|          newMenu.add(
78|              JMenuItem(
79|                  'InnerFrame',
80|                  actionPerformed = self.addIframe
81|              )
82|          )
83|          newMenu.addSeparator()
84|          newMenu.add(
85|              JMenuItem(
86|                  'Exit',
87|                  actionPerformed = self.exit
88|              )
89|          )
90|          return result
```

The addIframe(...) method, shown in lines 57-71, is called by the menu entry event handler to create a new internal frame. It is important to note that this method depends on the self.logger instance attribute value (see line 69), which is initialized in the run() method.

Listing 19-12 shows the run() method, which:

- Creates the initial application frame of the initial size and location
- Creates and adds the menu bar
- Creates a desktop instance to hold the internal frames
- Creates the special internal frame, which is an instance of the eventLogger class
- Adds the special eventLogger instance to the desktop
- Replaces the initial frame ContentPane with the desktop
- Makes the application visible

Listing 19-12. The run() Method from the iFrameEvents Class from iFrameEvents2.py

```
91|     def run( self ) :
92|         screenSize = Toolkit.getDefaultToolkit().getScreenSize()
93|         w = screenSize.width  >> 1          # 1/2 screen width
94|         h = screenSize.height >> 1          # 1/2 screen height
95|         x = ( screenSize.width  - w ) >> 1
96|         y = ( screenSize.height - h ) >> 1
97|         frame = JFrame(
98|             'iFrameEvents2',
99|             bounds = ( x, y, w, h ),        # location & size
100|            defaultCloseOperation = JFrame.EXIT_ON_CLOSE
101|         )
102|         frame.setJMenuBar( self.menuBar() )
103|         self.desktop = desktop = JDesktopPane()
104|         self.logger = eventLogger()
105|         desktop.add( self.logger, 0, 0 )
106|         frame.setContentPane( desktop )
107|         self.iFrameCount = 0
108|         frame.setVisible( 1 )
```

The event listener that is added to each internal frame was instantiated by the run() method and is an instance of the eventLogger class, as shown in Listing 19-13. In fact, I added a getter for the eventAdapter instance, as shown in lines 54 and 55.

Listing 19-13. The eventLogger Class from iFrameEvents2.py

```
34|class eventLogger( JInternalFrame ) :
35|    def __init__( self ) :
36|        JInternalFrame.__init__(
37|            self,
38|            'eventLogger',
39|            1,                    # Resizeable  - yes
40|            0,                    # Closeable   - no
41|            0,                    # Maximizable - no
42|            1,                    # Iconifiable - yes
43|            visible = 1,
44|            bounds = ( 0, 0, 250, 250 )
45|        )
46|        self.textArea = JTextArea(
47|            '',                   # Inital text
48|            20,                   # rows
49|            40,                   # columns
50|            editable = 0    # read-only
51|        )
52|        self.eventListener = eventAdapter( self.textArea )
53|        self.add( JScrollPane( self.textArea ) )
54|    def getListener( self ) :
55|        return self.eventListener
```

Listing 19-14 shows the eventAdapter class that is used by the eventLogger class. It is important to note how the constructor, in lines 16-18, requires the text area to be updated by the messages that this class needs to log. The log(...) utility method, found on lines 19-26, uses a regular expression (RegExp) to extract the name for the kind of event being logged and updates the specified text area with a line identifying the title of the internal frame for which the event occurred, as well as the kind of event.

■ **Note**   Notice how all of the event handler methods are trivial calls to the log() method, which then does all of the real work.

Listing 19-14. The eventAdapter Class from iFrameEvents2.py

```
15|class eventAdapter( event.InternalFrameAdapter ) :
16|    def __init__( self, textArea ) :
17|        self.textArea = textArea
18|        self.regexp = re.compile( '\[INTERNAL_FRAME_(\w+)]' )
19|    def log( self, event ) :
20|        title = event.getInternalFrame().getTitle()
21|        mo = re.search( self.regexp, event.toString() )
22|        if mo :
23|            Type = mo.group( 1 ).capitalize()
```

```
24|        else :
25|            Type = 'unknown'
26|        self.textArea.append( '\n%s : %s' % ( title, Type ) )
27|    def internalFrameActivated( self, ife ) : self.log( ife )
28|    def internalFrameClosed( self, ife ) : self.log( ife )
29|    def internalFrameClosing( self, ife ) : self.log( ife )
30|    def internalFrameDeactivated( self, ife ) : self.log( ife )
31|    def internalFrameDeiconified( self, ife ) : self.log( ife )
32|    def internalFrameIconified( self, ife ) : self.log( ife )
33|    def internalFrameOpened( self, ife ) :  self.log( ife )
```

I'll let you play with the sample application to get a feel for the kinds of events that are generated and the order in which they can occur.

More JInternalFrame Topics

Unfortunately, internal frames, and the manipulation thereof, are not simple or easy. There are lots of things to deal with. For example, you can use the simple iFrameEvents2.py script to get a better idea.

1. Start the script.

2. Choose New ➤ InnerFrame to create Inner Frame #1.

3. Use the minimize icon on Inner Frame #1 to iconify it.

4. Resize the application to hide the iconified inner frame.

How are you supposed to access the iconified inner frame without making the application larger? This is a simple example of one of the many kinds of things that you need to consider when you are dealing with inner frames. It may also help you understand the need for some of the JDesktopPane methods listed in Table 19-4.

Building an Application from Scratch

This section shows what it takes to build an application that uses the JInternalFrame class. Rather than showing the end result, the section iterates with fairly simple steps to create the script from absolutely nothing, to the point where you'll have a better understanding of what it takes to put these Swing components together into some semblance of a complete application.

Where should you start? Let's look for something, hopefully simple, that you can use to make an interesting application. From the WebSphere Application Server online documentation, you can find a simple script written in Jacl that can be used to change the console timeout value.[10] This value determines the length of time (in minutes) that the administrator console will remain active without user input.

Since the script in the documentation is written in Jacl, you'll begin by taking a look at it. In the code directory for this chapter, you can find the consoleTimeout_00.jacl script (see code\Chap_19\consoleTimeout_00.jacl). It is slightly different from the online documentation. It is different in that it allows users to specify the new timeout value on the wsadmin command line. The script in the documentation requires you to edit the script file and replace the two instances of <timeout value> with the desired timeout value (in minutes).

---

[10]See http://publib.boulder.ibm.com/infocenter/wasinfo/v7r0/index.jsp?topic=/com.ibm.websphere.nd.doc/info/ae/isc/cons_sessionto.html.

Figure 19-7 shows an example invocation of this wsadmin script, which presumes that the current working directory contains the WebSphere Application Server wsadmin.sh script.

./wsadmin.sh -f consoleTimeout.jacl 30

Figure 19-7. *Using the consoleTimeout_00.jacl script*

Simple Non-GUI Jython Version of the consoleTimeout Script

I don't know about you, but I find it a challenge to write and modify Jacl scripts.[11] So, let's start by converting this Jacl script to a roughly equivalent Jython script. Listings 19-14 and 19-15 show the consoleTimeout routine from this converted script. During the conversion, a little usability enhancement was added to display the current timeout value if no command-line parameters are provided. Additionally, if too many parameters are specified, some usage information is displayed.

Listing 19-15. The consoleTimeout Routine from consoleTimeout_01.py, Part 1

```
23|def consoleTimeout_01( cmdName = 'consoleTimeout_01' ) :
24|    argc = len( sys.argv )              # Number of args
25|    if argc > 1 :                       # Too many?
26|        Usage( cmdName )                #    show Usage info
27|    value = None
28|    if argc == 1 :
29|        value = sys.argv[ 0 ]
30|        if not re.search( re.compile( '^\d+$' ), value ) :
31|            print nonNumeric % locals()
32|            Usage( cmdName )
33|    dep = AdminConfig.getid( '/Deployment:isclite/' )
34|    if not dep :
35|        print noISCLite % locals()
36|        Usage( cmdName )
37|    appDep    = AdminConfig.list( 'ApplicationDeployment', dep )
38|    appConfig = AdminConfig.list( 'ApplicationConfig', appDep )
39|    if not appConfig :
40|        appConfig = AdminConfig.create(
41|            'ApplicationConfig',
42|            appDep,
43|            []
44|        )
45|    sesMgmt = AdminConfig.list( 'SessionManager', appDep )
46|    if not sesMgmt :
47|        sesMgmt = AdminConfig.create(
48|            'SessionManager',
49|            appConfig,
50|            []
51|        )
```

---

[11]I'll admit it, it took me much longer than it should have to figure out how to modify the consoleTimeout.jacl script to accept and use command-line parameters. I am not proficient with Jacl since I use it so infrequently.

This script should be pretty straightforward to those with a modicum of wsadmin scripting experience. It verifies that the user-supplied valid numeric input then uses some calls to the wsadmin scripting objects to locate the session manager configuration object so that its tuning parameters can be checked. Listing 19-16 deals with creating tuning parameters in order to set the invalidationTimeout attribute value. One interesting thing about this simple script is the fact that almost 60 lines are needed to provide this simple functionality.

■ **Note**   In case you are interested, you can look at the complete source code to see that the lines that aren't shown in these listings are comments, initialization statements, and a Usage(...) method, which displays appropriate information about how the script can and should be used.

Listing 19-16. The consoleTimeout Routine from consoleTimeout_01.py, Part 2

```
52|    tuningParams = AdminConfig.showAttribute(
53|        sesMgmt,
54|        'tuningParams'
55|    )
56|    if value :
57|        if not tuningParams :
58|            AdminConfig.create(
59|                'TuningParams',
60|                sesMgmt,
61|                [[ 'invalidationTimeout', value ]]
62|            )
63|        else :
64|            AdminConfig.modify(
65|                tuningParams,
66|                [[ 'invalidationTimeout', value ]]
67|            )
68|    else :
69|        if not tuningParams :
70|            print noTPobj % locals()
71|        else :
72|            timeout = AdminConfig.showAttribute(
73|                tuningParams,
74|                'invalidationTimeout'
75|            )
76|            print currentVal % locals()
77|    if AdminConfig.hasChanges() :
78|        print saveConfig % locals()
79|        AdminConfig.save()
```

First GUI Jython Version of the consoleTimeout Script

The first Jython Swing version of this script is shown in Listings 19-16 and 19-17. Remember that first impressions can be deceiving. Even though there appear to be many more statements in the Swing version (consoleTimeout_02.py), that's simply because of the number of statements displayed on multiple lines so that they fit in the space available in the listings in this publication.

Listing 19-17 contains most of the run(...) method from the ConsoleTimeout class in this script. Note that very little effort was put into any complex layout of the Swing components. If you make the frame wider, I think that you'll agree that it doesn't look as nice as it could.

Listing 19-17. The ConsoleTimeout Class run(...) Method from consoleTimeout_02.py

```
 9|class consoleTimeout_02( java.lang.Runnable ) :
10|    def run( self ) :
11|        frame = JFrame(
12|            'consoleTimeout_02',
13|            layout = FlowLayout(),
14|            size = ( 180, 120 ),
15|            locationRelativeTo = None,
16|            defaultCloseOperation = JFrame.EXIT_ON_CLOSE
17|        )
18|        dep = AdminConfig.getid( '/Deployment:isclite/' )
  |        ...
48|        if not self.tuningParms :
49|            timeout = ''
50|            messageText = "tuningParams object doesn't exist."
51|        else :
52|            timeout = AdminConfig.showAttribute(
53|                self.tuningParms,
54|                'invalidationTimeout'
55|            )
56|            messageText = ''
57|        frame.add( JLabel( 'Timeout:' ) )
58|        self.text = frame.add(
59|            JTextField(
60|                3,
61|                text = timeout,
62|                actionPerformed = self.update
63|            )
64|        )
65|        frame.add( JLabel( 'minutes' ) )
66|        self.message = frame.add( JLabel( messageText ) )
  |        ...
76|        frame.setVisible( 1 )
```

Listing 19-18 contains the update(...) method from the same ConsoleTimeout class, which is almost identical to the previous code. It is important to remember that this method is an event handler.

Listing 19-18. The ConsoleTimeout Class update(...) Method from consoleTimeout_02.py

```
77|    def update( self, event ) :
78|        value = self.text.getText()
79|        if not re.search( re.compile( '^\d+$' ), value ) :
80|            text = 'Invalid numeric value: "%s"' % value
81|        else :
82|            if not self.tuningParms :
83|                try :
84|                    AdminConfig.create(
85|                        'TuningParams',
86|                        self.sesMgmt,
87|                        [[ 'invalidationTimeout', value ]]
88|                    )
```

```
89|                        AdminConfig.save()
90|                        text = 'The TuningParams object has ' + \
91|                                'been created successfully'
92|                    except :
93|                        text = 'A problem was encountered while ' + \
94|                                'creating the TuningParams object.'
95|                else :
96|                    try :
97|                        AdminConfig.modify(
98|                            self.tuningParms,
99|                            [[ 'invalidationTimeout', value ]]
100|                        )
101|                        AdminConfig.save()
102|                        text = 'Update successful.'
103|                    except :
104|                        text = 'A problem was encountered while ' + \
105|                                'updating the TuningParams object.'
106|            self.message.setText( text )
```

It's important to realize that this version of the script does a very bad thing. What is that, you ask? Well, take a look at the update(...) method again. It is the event handler code that verifies the user-specified input and attempts to modify the invalidation timeout attribute for the administration console application.

The big mistake is the fact that the event handler routine contains calls to wsadmin scripting object (AdminConfig) methods. These kinds of calls should always be done on a separate (SwingWorker) thread. Why? It's because they are likely to require a non-trivial amount of time (the first call took about five seconds) to complete the requested action and return. In the meantime, the application can't respond to any user events. That's why it is not a good way to implement GUI scripts.

What does this look like when you run the script? Figure 19-8 shows a sample image created by this script. Go ahead and test it out yourself. See what happens when you enter a value and press Enter. Is there any kind of indication on the GUI that something is happening? Nope, at least not until the calls to the AdminConfig objects are complete and control returns to the application. Is this how you want your GUI applications to work and interact with your users? Absolutely not; this kind of behavior is unacceptable.

Figure 19-8. Output from consoleTimeout_02.py

Adding SwingWorker Instance to the Mix

Listing 19-19 shows how easy it is to take the statements from the update(...) method shown in consoleTimeout_02.py (that's Listing 19-18) and put them into an separate SwingWorker class. It also shows how simple the event handler update(...) method then becomes (see lines 122 and 122).

Listing 19-19. The WSAStask Class from consoleTimeout_03.py

```
10|class WSAStask( SwingWorker ) :
11|    def __init__( self, app ) :
12|        self.app = app                       # application reference
13|        self.messageText = ''
14|        SwingWorker.__init__( self )
15|    def doInBackground( self ) :
16|        problem = 'A problem was encountered while %s ' + \
17|                    'the TuningParams object.'
18|        messageText = self.messageText
19|        self.app.textField.setEnabled( 0 )
20|        self.app.message.setText(
21|            '<html>working...' + ( ' ' * 20 )
22|        )
23|        value = self.app.textField.getText()    # JTextField value
24|        if not re.search( re.compile( '^\d+$' ), value ) :
25|            messageText = 'Invalid numeric value: "%s"' % value
26|        else :
27|            if not self.app.tuningParms :
28|                try :
29|                    AdminConfig.create(
30|                        'TuningParams',
31|                        self.app.sesMgmt,
32|                        [[ 'invalidationTimeout', value ]]
33|                    )
34|                    AdminConfig.save()
35|                    messageText = 'The TuningParams object' + \
36|                                    'has been created successfully'
37|                except :
38|                    messageText = problem % 'creating'
39|            else :
40|                try :
41|                    AdminConfig.modify(
42|                        self.app.tuningParms,
43|                        [[ 'invalidationTimeout', value ]]
44|                    )
45|                    AdminConfig.save()
46|                    messageText = 'Update complete.'
47|                except :
48|                    messageText = problem % 'updating'
49|    def done( self ) :
50|        self.app.textField.setEnabled( 1 )
51|        self.app.message.setText( self.messageText )
52|class consoleTimeout_03( java.lang.Runnable ) :
  |    ...
121|    def update( self, event ) :
122|        WSAStask( self ).execute()
```

One thing that you should notice when this SwingWorker thread is performing an update is the fact that application text input field is disabled. This kind of attention to detail adds significantly to the user experience and should be considered essential when you are developing graphical applications.

Additionally, a status message is displayed to show that the thread is executing. It is only when this separate processing is complete that the text input field is enabled and an updated status message is displayed.

Adding Menu Items

As you've previously seen, you can add significant usability to your applications with simple menu items. Figure 19-9 shows the impact of making some small changes to this script.

Figure 19-9. *Images from consoleTimeout_04.py*

Listing 19-20 shows the new and modified code from the application class in this updated script. The menuBar() method creates and populates the application menu bar. Three new methods were added to respond to each of the new menu actions. And that is pretty much it. All in all, this is a good return on investment for about 50 lines of code. I think that you'll agree that the additional user value is significant.

In case you're wondering, the about(...) and notice(...) method adds some nice functionality. The former serves the same kind of role normally performed by a usage message that a non-graphical application uses to tell users how the program should be used, and the latter is useful as a valuable disclaimer message.

Listing 19-20. New and Modified Code from consoleTimeout_04.py

```
 87|class consoleTimeout_04( java.lang.Runnable ) :
   |    ...
110|    def run( self ) :
   |        ...
119|        frame.setJMenuBar( self.menuBar() )
   |        ...
178|        frame.setVisible( 1 )
179|    def Exit( self, event ) :
180|        sys.exit( 0 )
181|    def about( self, event ) :
182|        text = __doc__.replace( '<', '&lt;'
183|        ).replace( '>', '&gt;'
184|        ).replace( ' ', ' '
185|        ).replace( '\n', '<br>' )
```

```
186|          JOptionPane.showMessageDialog(
187|            self.frame,
188|            JLabel(
189|              '<html>' + text,
190|              font = monoFont
191|            ),
192|            'About',
193|            JOptionPane.PLAIN_MESSAGE
194|          )
195|    def notice( self, event ) :
196|        JOptionPane.showMessageDialog(
197|            self.frame,
198|            disclaimer,
199|            'Notice',
200|            JOptionPane.WARNING_MESSAGE
201|        )
202|    def update( self, event ) :
203|        WSAStask( self ).execute()
```

Changing from JFrame to JInternalFrame

For the next iteration, you'll see how to convert the script to use internal frames. Begin by taking a look at the revised consoleTimeout class from the revised consoleTimeout_05.py script. Listing 19-21 shows the important methods from this class. As you saw earlier, internal frames need to be added to an instance of the JDesktopPane class. Overall, it shouldn't be terribly new to you. You may, however, wonder about the call to the setSelected(...) method on line 186.

This isn't an error. Table 19-3 shows that the JDesktopPane class has a similar method called setSelectedFrame(...). This is a method from the JInternalFrame class, and the parameter is a boolean value indicating that the specified object instance is being selected (in which case, a value that is recognized as true should be specified). What happens if you comment out this line in the script and execute it?

The internal frame doesn't obtain the focus, which means that the current timeout value isn't obtained and the input field remains empty. At least until you put focus on the internal frame, such as by clicking somewhere on it. Then you see that the input field is populated with the current timeout value.

Listing 19-21. Revised consoleTimeout Class from consoleTimeout_05.py, Part 1

```
167|class consoleTimeout_05( java.lang.Runnable ) :
168|    def run( self ) :
169|        self.frame = frame = JFrame(
170|            'consoleTimeout_05',
171|            size = ( 428, 474 ),
172|            locationRelativeTo = None,
173|            defaultCloseOperation = JFrame.EXIT_ON_CLOSE
174|        )
175|        frame.setJMenuBar( self.MenuBar() )
176|        desktop = JDesktopPane()
177|        if globals().has_key( 'AdminConfig' ) :
178|            self.timeout = self.initialTimeout()
179|            self.inner = TextField( self )  # JTextField only
180|            desktop.add( self.inner )
```

```
181|          else :
182|              self.inner = self.noWSAS()        # WebSphere not found
183|              desktop.add( self.inner )
184|          frame.add( desktop )
185|          frame.setVisible( 1 )
186|          self.inner.setSelected( 1 )
```

The initialTimeout() method (see line 178) isn't shown because it contains the same steps that you've seen before to obtain the initial value, if one exists. The most important change in this script is shown in Listing 19-22. It contains the class used by all of the subsequent internal frame instances for this application. The first time you look at it, however, you may wonder why it is descended from InternalFrameListener and not from InternalFrameAdapter. That way, you wouldn't need to have empty methods (ones like internalFrameClosed(...) that consist of a single pass statement).

Listing 19-22. InternalFrame Class from consoleTimeout_05.py, Part 1

```
90|class InternalFrame( JInternalFrame, InternalFrameListener ) :
91|    def __init__( self,
92|        title,
93|        outer,
94|        size,
95|        location = None,
96|        layout = None
97|    ) :
98|        if location == None :
99|            location = Point( 0, 0 )
100|        if layout == None :
101|            layout = FlowLayout()
102|        JInternalFrame.__init__(
103|            self,
104|            title,
105|            0,                  # resizeable = false
106|            0,                  # closable  = false
107|            size = size,
108|            internalFrameListener = self,
109|            layout = layout
110|        )
111|        self.setLocation( location )   # keyword parm doesn't exist
112|        self.outer = outer             # application object
113|    def internalFrameActivated( self, e ) :
114|        self.outer.inner = e.getInternalFrame()
115|    def internalFrameClosed( self, e ) :
116|        pass
117|    def internalFrameClosing( self, e ) :
118|        pass
119|    def internalFrameDeactivated( self, e ) :
120|        self.outer.inner.message.setText( '' )
121|    def internalFrameDeiconified( self, e ) :
122|        pass
123|    def internalFrameIconified( self, e ) :
124|        pass
```

```
125|     def internalFrameOpened( self, e ) :
126|         pass
127|     def getValue( self ) :
128|         print 'InternalFrame.getValue() - not yet implemented'
129|         return None
130|     def setValue( self, value ) :
131|         print 'InternalFrame.setValue() - not yet implemented'
132|     def working( self ) :
133|         print 'InternalFrame.working() - not yet implemented'
134|     def finished( self ) :
135|         print 'InternalFrame.finished() - not yet implemented'
```

Listing 19-23 shows what happens when you try to base an InternalFrame class on the JInternalFrame and the InternalFrameAdapter classes. Jython complains about this issue. Why doesn't it complain about basing a class on JInternalFrame and the InternalFrameListener classes? This is allowed because the InternalFrameListener is actually an interface, not a class that can be instantiated.

Listing 19-23. Multiple Inheritance Issue

```
wsadmin>from javax.swing        import JInternalFrame
wsadmin>from javax.swing.event import InternalFrameAdapter
wsadmin>
wsadmin>class InternalFrame( JInternalFrame, InternalFrameAdapter ) :
wsadmin>    def __init__( self, title ) :
wsadmin>        JInternalFrame.__init__( self, title )
wsadmin>
WASX7015E: Exception running command: ""; exception information:
 com.ibm.bsf.BSFException: exception from Jython:
Traceback (innermost last):
  File "<input>", line 1, in ?
TypeError: no multiple inheritance for Java classes:
 javax.swing.event.InternalFrameAdapter and javax.swing.JInternalFrame

wsadmin>
```

Listing 19-24 shows the TextField class from the consoleTimeout_05.py script. In it, you can see that the constructor (in lines 137-154) is responsible for populating the internal frame and providing the input components. Additionally, it includes instruction for the methods that are needed by this object. It is important to note that the internalFrameActivated(...) method, which is invoked when the object instance is activated, is responsible for updating the application attribute value that identifies the active internal frame, obtains the current timeout value from the application, and calls the object setValue(...) method to initialize the timeout value for this object instance.

Listing 19-24. TextField Class from consoleTimeout_05.py

```
136|class TextField( InternalFrame ) :
137|    def __init__( self, outer ) :
138|        InternalFrame.__init__(
139|            self,
140|            'TextField',
141|            outer,
142|            size = ( 180, 85 ),
143|            location = Point( 5, 5 )
144|        )
```

```
145|            self.add( JLabel( 'Timeout (minutes):' ) )
146|            self.text = self.add(
147|                JTextField(
148|                    3,
149|                    actionPerformed = outer.update
150|                )
151|            )
152|            self.message = self.add( JLabel() )
153|            self.setVisible( 1 )
154|            self.text.requestFocusInWindow()
155|        def internalFrameActivated( self, e ) :
156|            self.outer.inner = e.getInternalFrame()
157|            self.setValue( self.outer.timeout )
158|        def getValue( self ) :
159|            return self.text.getText()
160|        def setValue( self, value ) :
161|            self.value = value
162|            self.text.setText( value )
163|        def working( self ) :
164|            self.text.setEnabled( 0 )
165|        def finished( self ) :
166|            self.text.setEnabled( 1 )
```

All this is possible because of the framework provided by the InternalFrame class on which it is based. There are some important things to note about this class and how it fits into the application. One of these is the way in which this constructor begins by calling its base class constructor to initialize itself. One of the important steps performed by the base class constructor (InternalFrame.__init__) call, shown on lines 138-144, is the fact that it saves a reference to the application frame in an instance attribute called self.outer (see lines 90-110 in Listing 19-22).

What purpose does this application instance variable serve? It allows each inner frame to easily obtain access to this reference so that the event handlers can manipulate the appropriate fields. How does it do this? Take a look at the internalFrameActivated(...) method in lines 155-157. When an internal frame is activated, the application variable called self.outer is used to update the self.inner application variable, which identifies the active inner frame. By defining and updating this variable, the utility routines can easily access the "current" or "active" internal frame values with simple statements. All you have to do is ensure that every internal frame class implements these values the same way.

For example, this reference (self.inner) allows the object instance to specify the application update(...) method as the ActionListener event handler for the text field on this inner frame. This application update(...) method, as shown in Listing 19-25, is extremely simple. As an event handler routine, it should be simple.

Listing 19-25. The update(...) Method from consoleTimeout_05.py

```
272|    def update( self, event ) :
273|        self.timeout = self.inner.getValue()
274|        WSAStask( self ).execute()
```

There are, however, some subtle changes needed in the WSAStask class in this script that is instantiated to create a separate thread to modify the timeout value. Listing 19-26 shows this modified WSAStask class from the consoleTimeout_05.py script. The important changes are all related to the fact that this class needs to work with the active internal frame that initiated the creation of the task.

Take a look at line 51 where a local variable, frame, is used to hold a reference to the active inner frame. This reference is then used to invoke the appropriate working() method (line 52), the appropriate getValue() method (line 53), the appropriate message.setText(...) method (lines 54-56 and 89), and the appropriate finished() method (line 88).

The rest of this chapter shows how easily you can create other classes to take advantage of this design simplification.

Listing 19-26. WSAStask Class from `consoleTimeout_05.py`

```
46|class WSAStask( SwingWorker ) :
47|    def __init__( self, app ) :
48|        self.app = app                      # application reference
49|        self.messageText = ''
50|        SwingWorker.__init__( self )
51|    def doInBackground( self ) :
52|        messageText = self.messageText
53|        frame = self.app.inner              # Active Inner Frame
54|        frame.working()
55|        value = frame.getValue()
56|        frame.message.setText(
57|            '<html>working...' + ( ' ' * 20 )
58|        )
59|        if not re.search( re.compile( '^\d+$' ), value ) :
60|            messageText = 'Invalid numeric value: "%s"' % value
61|        else :
62|            TPobj   = 'TuningParams'
63|            success = 'The %s object was created successfully.'
64|            problem = 'A problem was encountered %s the %s object.'
65|            if not self.app.tuningParms :
66|                try :
67|                    self.tuningParms = AdminConfig.create(
68|                        TPobj,
69|                        self.app.sesMgmt,
70|                        [[ 'invalidationTimeout', value ]]
71|                    )
72|                    AdminConfig.save()
73|                    messageText = success % TPobj
74|                except :
75|                    messageText = problem % ( 'creating', TPobj )
76|            else :
77|                try :
78|                    AdminConfig.modify(
79|                        self.app.tuningParms,
80|                        [[ 'invalidationTimeout', value ]]
81|                    )
82|                    AdminConfig.save()
83|                    messageText = 'Update complete.'
84|                except :
85|                    messageText = problem % ( 'updating', TPobj )
86|    def done( self ) :
87|        frame = self.app.inner
88|        frame.finished()
89|        frame.message.setText( self.messageText )
```

What does this mean as far as the application's appearance is concerned? Figure 19-10 shows part of the application output created by this script. The remainder of this chapter deals with iterations of this script that will fill in the blanks as far as this application output is concerned.

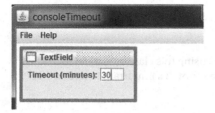

Figure 19-10. Output from consoleTimeout_05.py

Adding a Second Internal Frame Class

Until now, it really looks like a lot of code is required to create a fairly simple application with one internal frame. Was it worth it? In order to answer that question, take a look at what is required to add a second, different, internal frame. Listing 19-27 shows is the code required to define another class—the TextandButton class, which is based on the TextField class shown in Listing 19-24. It is almost trivial due to the fact that all of the class methods, other than the constructor, are in fact identical to those defined in the base TextField class. Isn't inheritance wonderful? You bet it is!

Listing 19-27. The TextandButton Class from consoleTimeout_06.py

```
168|class TextandButton( TextField ) :
169|    def __init__( self, outer ) :
170|        InternalFrame.__init__(
171|            self,
172|            'TextField and Button',
173|            outer,
174|            size = ( 180, 125 ),
175|            location = Point( 5, 95 )
176|        )
177|        self.add( JLabel( 'Timeout: (minutes)' ) )
178|        self.text = self.add(
179|            JTextField(
180|                3,
181|                actionPerformed = outer.update
182|            )
183|        )
184|        self.button = self.add(
185|            JButton(
186|                'Update',
187|                actionPerformed = outer.update
188|            )
189|        )
```

```
190|          self.message = self.add( JLabel() )
191|          self.setVisible( 1 )
192|          self.text.requestFocusInWindow()
193|class consoleTimeout_06( java.lang.Runnable ) :
194|    def run( self ) :
   |...
207|              desktop.add( TextandButton( self ) )
```

This listing also shows, in line 207, the code needed to instantiate an object using this class and add it to the application desktop. Figure 19-11 shows the initial output of this iteration of the script. It's important to notice that you now have two internal frames, only one of which is active.

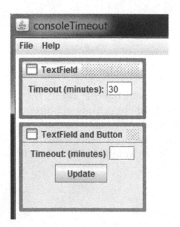

Figure 19-11. *Output from* `consoleTimeout_06.py`

Adding a Third Internal Frame Class

Let's see what it takes to add a very different internal frame classes to this application. Listings 19-28, 19-29, and 19-30 show another class based on the `TextField` class that adds a group of `RadioButtons` for commonly used timeout values. In addition, an "other" `RadioButton` is defined that allows the users to specify an uncommon value using an associated text field.

Note, however, that this class demonstrates a solution to an issue that may not be obvious without explanation. In Listing 19-28, line 228, you can see that the `self.setting` variable is defined and initialized in the class constructor. As the comment indicates, this value is used in the `stateChange(...)` method (found in Listing 19-30) and the `setValue(...)` method (shown in Listing 19-29). The purpose of this variable is to deal with a possible race condition that might occur. It is possible that the `stateChange(...)` method will be invoked before the `setValue(...)` method has completed. If this occurs, the state of the text field may be indeterminate, so the `stateChange(...)` method exits without making any changes if the value of `self.setting` is non-zero.

This is the kind of thing that can occur in event-driven applications. So you should be aware of this possibility and be on the lookout for it. You may want to see what happens to the script without this and other issues related to interrupt-driven applications.

This is a good time for me to bring up an "oops" moment. At this point, while testing the current script, I found a significant flaw. You can see what happens with the previous version of the script—`consoleTimeout_06.py`. I haven't gone back to correct either of the previous iterations, just to give you a chance to see the flaw and compare the current version of the script to see how it handles things better.

What's the error? It's most obvious in the previous script because of the presence of multiple inner frames. Enter an invalid numeric value in the text input field and press Enter. A message is displayed indicating that the value is bad. So far, so good. Now put focus on the other inner frame and see what happens. The bad value is displayed as the current value in the selected inner frame. Is this that you want to happen? I don't think so. This is exactly the kind of thing that you need to consider when using inner frames that can gain and lose focus at unexpected times.

So, how do you fix it? Well, you have to make some changes to a few of the existing methods. The biggest change needs to be made in the setValue(...) methods so that only valid values are saved. Note that the setValue(...) method only exists in the TextField class. The TextAndButton class reuses the base method, thereby limiting and simplifying the necessary changes.

It is important to note, however, that the new RadioButtons class has to implement this method because of the different data components in this new inner frame. The presence of the "other" radio button associated with a text input field means that you also have to change the update(...) method to properly deal with invalid input values.

Take a look at the resulting changes, focusing first on the new RadioButtons class. Listing 19-28 shows the constructors (__init__()) and getValue(...) methods. Notice how these are more complicated because they use RadioButtons and a text input field to display the current value.

One thing that is all too easy to overlook with Jython Swing code is how easily event handler methods can be assigned. Take another look at the class constructor, specifically line 210. This line uses a keyword argument to identify the ChangeListener event handler to each RadioButton object as the stateChange(...) method. The code for this method is shown in Listing 19-30.

Listing 19-28. RadioButtons Class from consoleTimeout_07.py, Part 1

```
205|class RadioButtons( TextField ) :
206|    def __init__( self, outer ) :
207|        InternalFrame.__init__(
   |            ...
213|        )
214|        self.add( JLabel( 'Timeout (minutes):' ) )
215|        buttons = {}
216|        self.bg = ButtonGroup()
217|        for name in '0,15,30,60,Other'.split( ',' ) :
218|            button = JRadioButton(
219|                name,
220|                itemStateChanged = self.stateChange
221|            )
222|            self.bg.add( button )
223|            self.add( button )
224|            buttons[ name ] = button
225|        self.r00  = buttons[ '0'   ]
226|        self.r15  = buttons[ '15'  ]
227|        self.r30  = buttons[ '30'  ]
228|        self.r60  = buttons[ '60'  ]
229|        self.rot  = buttons[ 'Other' ]
230|        self.text = self.add(
231|            JTextField(
232|                '',
233|                3,
234|                actionPerformed = outer.update
235|            )
236|        )
```

```
237|          self.message = self.add( JLabel() )
238|          self.setting = 0              # see stateChange() and setValue()
239|          self.setVisible( 1 )
240|     def getValue( self ) :
241|          if self.r00.isSelected() :
242|              result = '0'
243|          elif self.r15.isSelected() :
244|              result = '15'
245|          elif self.r30.isSelected() :
246|              result = '30'
247|          elif self.r60.isSelected() :
248|              result = '60'
249|          elif self.rot.isSelected() :
250|              result = self.text.getText()
251|              try :
252|                  int( result )
253|              except :
254|                  messageText = badNumber % result
255|                  self.message.setText( messageText )
256|          else :
257|              result = None
258|          return result
```

Listing 19-29 shows the setValue(...) method, which is also a bit more complex because it deals with multiple components to set the console timeout value.

Listing 19-29. setValue(...) Method in the RadioButtons Class from consoleTimeout_07.py

```
259|     def setValue( self, value ) :
260|          self.setting = 1
261|          if value == '0' :
262|              self.r00.setSelected( 1 )
263|              self.r00.requestFocusInWindow()
264|              self.text.setText( '' )
265|              self.text.setEnabled( 0 )
266|          elif value == '15' :
267|              self.r15.setSelected( 1 )
268|              self.r15.requestFocusInWindow()
269|              self.text.setText( '' )
270|              self.text.setEnabled( 0 )
271|          elif value == '30' :
272|              self.r30.setSelected( 1 )
273|              self.r30.requestFocusInWindow()
274|              self.text.setText( '' )
275|              self.text.setEnabled( 0 )
276|          elif value == '60' :
277|              self.r60.setSelected( 1 )
278|              self.r60.requestFocusInWindow()
279|              self.text.setText( '' )
280|              self.text.setEnabled( 0 )
```

```
281|        else :
282|            self.rot.setSelected( 1 )
283|            self.text.setText( value )
284|            self.text.setEnabled( 1 )
285|            self.text.requestFocusInWindow()
286|        self.value = value
287|        self.setting = 0
```

You may note that this setValue(...) method doesn't bother to include code to check for an invalid value in the text field. How can you get away with this? Isn't this an oversight? Not really, because the update(...) method already includes that kind of code, so you're covered.

Listing 19-30 shows the rest of the methods from this class. Note how easily you can enable and disable all of the RadioButton components using a simple loop that iterates over the list of RadioButton components.

Note also line 312, where the RadioButtons inner frame is instantiated and added to the desktop frame.

Listing 19-30. Utility Methods for the RadioButtons Class from consoleTimeout_07.py

```
288|    def working( self ) :
289|        for obj in [
290|            self.r00, self.r15, self.r30,
291|            self.r60, self.rot, self.text
292|        ] :
293|            obj.setEnabled( 0 )
294|    def finished( self ) :
295|        for obj in [
296|            self.r00, self.r15, self.r30,
297|            self.r60, self.rot
298|        ] :
299|            obj.setEnabled( 1 )
300|        self.text.setEnabled( self.rot.isSelected() )
301|    def stateChange( self, event ) :
302|        item = event.getItem()
303|        if not self.setting :
304|            if item.getText() == 'Other' :
305|                self.text.setEnabled( item.isSelected() )
306|            else :
307|                self.text.setEnabled( 0 )
308|                self.text.setText( '' )
309|                value = self.getValue()
310|                if value :
311|                    self.outer.update( event )
312|class consoleTimeout_07( java.lang.Runnable ) :
313|    def run( self ) :
   |        ...
327|            desktop.add( RadioButtons( self ) )
```

I think that the functionality added by just over 100 lines of code in this class is pretty impressive. I hope that you agree. The most important point about this is that defining the way in which the classes interact and use the framework makes each additional class significantly easier to implement.

What does this look like as far as the application output is concerned? Well, take a look at Figure 19-12, which should help you understand the component configuration.

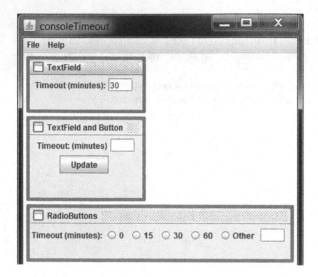

Figure 19-12. *Output from consoleTimeout_07.py*

Filling in the Blanks

Rather than continue showing every simple InternalFrame class definition, I'll cut to the chase[12] and simply show the end result of adding a few more internal frame descendant classes. The complete source is found in the consoleTimeout_08.py script file. Figure 19-13 shows the initial appearance of the final result of the application.

---

[12]See http://en.wikipedia.org/wiki/Cut_to_the_chase.

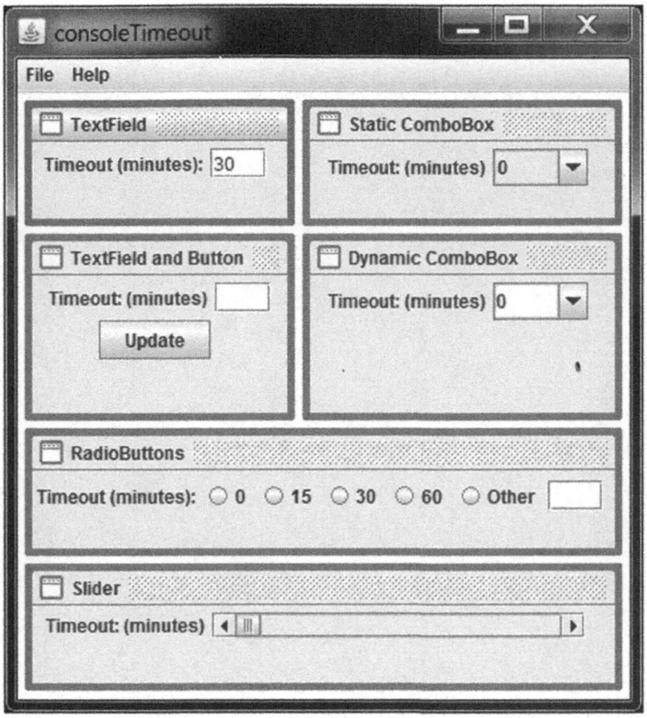

Figure 19-13. *Output from* `consoleTimeout_08.py`

Remember that this is merely a sample use of internal frames. Your applications are much more likely to have a variety of internal frame types, depending on your requirement. This sample is simply provided to demonstrate some of the ways in which an application that uses internal frames can deal with issues.

Summary

Internal frames can make your applications dynamic and interesting. There is a tradeoff in that events may contribute to increased complexity, especially when the frames need to share data in some way. This should have been quite obvious in the chapter example, even though only one data value needed to be shared between the inner frames. You get to decide if the increased complexity is worth the investment of time and effort. In the next chapter, you'll use the same iterative approach to build an application that interacts with the WebSphere scripting object to create an application that can be used to more easily display the help text for the objects and their methods.

CHAPTER 20

■ ■ ■

Building a Graphical Help Application

In Chapter 15, you learned how to retrieve information from a web page and use Swing objects to find and display only the details in which you were interested. Now you're going to use the same kind of techniques to build an application that allows you to more easily find and manipulate the Help text that is available for the wsadmin scripting objects.

In Chapter 7 of the book titled *WebSphere Application Server Administration Using Jython,*[1,2] you learned about the wsadmin scripting objects. It describes how to use these objects and explained how to use their help(...) methods to obtain information about the methods that each object provides. Unfortunately, the interactive sessions and sample scripts provided in that book aren't as useful as they could be if an interactive graphical application were available. In this chapter, you'll remedy that situation.

Showing the Help Text

To begin, consider what you need to display the output returned by a call to the Help.help() method. You'll need to keep these issues in mind:

- You should display the text in a scrollable pane

- If you want the text displayed correctly, don't use a proportional font

Only a tiny amount of effort is required to produce the first iteration, the main class of which is shown in Listing 20-1. One of the things that I hadn't remembered was that the Help text contains a number of tab characters (see '\t') to align the text. To simplify things, the text of the call to the help() method is immediately passed to the string's expandtabs() method, which is provided by Jython (see line 19).

Listing 20-1. WSAShelp_01.py Help.help() in a Scrollable Pane

```
 9|class WSAShelp( java.lang.Runnable ) :
10|    def run( self ) :
11|        frame = JFrame(
12|            'WSAShelp',
13|            locationRelativeTo = None,
14|            defaultCloseOperation = JFrame.EXIT_ON_CLOSE
15|        )
```

---

[1]See http://www.ibmpressbooks.com/store/websphere-application-server-administration-using-jython-9780137009527.
[2]Hereafter referred to as "the WAuJ book" for simplicity's sake.

```
16|          frame.add(
17|            JScrollPane(
18|              JTextArea(
19|                  Help.help().expandtabs(),
20|                  20,
21|                  80,
22|                  font = Font( 'Courier' , Font.PLAIN, 12 )
23|              )
24|            )
25|          )
26|          frame.pack()
27|          size = frame.getSize()
28|          loc = frame.getLocation()
29|          loc.x -= ( size.width  >> 1 )
30|          loc.y -= ( size.height >> 1 )
31|          frame.setLocation( loc )
32|          frame.setVisible( 1 )
```

The other statements that may cause you some pause are found in lines 27-31. When the frame in constructed (lines 11-15), the locationRelativeTo keyword argument places the upper-left corner of the frame in the center of the screen. Lines 27-31 adjust the frame to the left by half the frame width (line 29) and up by half the frame height (line 30) to center the frame in the screen. Figure 20-1 shows the simple result of the WSAShelp_01.py script.

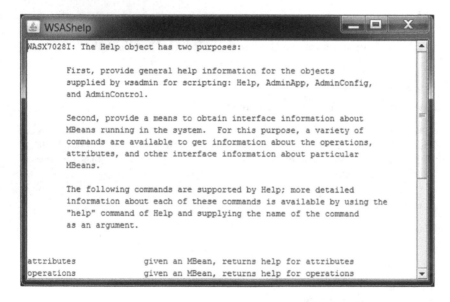

Figure 20-1. WSAShelp_01.py sample output

Using a Tabbed Pane

This next iteration uses tabbed panes to display the help text of the five wsadmin scripting objects (Help, AdminApp, AdminConfig, AdminControl, and AdminTask). Listing 20-2 demonstrates how a simple list (lines 28-34) can be used to easily identify the name of the tab and the associated scripting object about which help should be displayed.

Listing 20-2. Modifications to the WSAShelp Class in WSAShelp_02.py

```
11|class WSAShelp( java.lang.Runnable ) :
  |    ...
28|        objs = [
29|            ( 'Help'        , Help         ),
30|            ( 'AdminApp'    , AdminApp     ),
31|            ( 'AdminConfig' , AdminConfig  ),
32|            ( 'AdminControl', AdminControl ),
33|            ( 'AdminTask'   , AdminTask    )
34|        ]
35|        tabs = JTabbedPane()
36|        for name, obj in objs :
37|            tabs.addTab(
38|                name,
39|                JScrollPane(
40|                    JTextArea(
41|                        obj.help().expandtabs(),
42|                        20,
43|                        90,
44|                        font = Font( 'Courier' , Font.PLAIN, 12 )
45|                    )
46|                )
47|            )
48|        frame.add( tabs )
  |    ...
```

Figure 20-2 shows sample output of the tabs produced by this script. Using this script helps you not only verify the way that it looks and responds, but it's also a good place to stop and think about what you can and should do next.

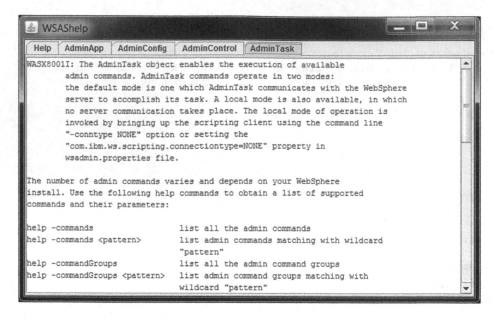

Figure 20-2. *WSAShelp_02.py sample output*

What can you learn from this script? The first thing is that the text area should be read-only, which is a trivial change. The next is that I wondered how difficult it would be to replace the textArea with a split pane. The top portion could display the general help for the scripting object and the bottom portion could scroll the method help. You'll see what that looks like before you have to decide if you want to continue down that path or use a different approach.

Adding Split Panes

In order to split the scripting object help text, you need to determine where the general description ends and the list of methods begins. To do that, you will use a regular expression (RegExp). This topic is discussed in the WAuJ book in Chapter 7. For all of the scripting objects (except the AdminTask object), you can use a relatively simple RegExp to determine where the method names start in the help text. The AdminTask help is a different beast entirely, so you have to deal with that in a different way. Let's start by dealing with the four scripting objects for which a relatively simple regular expression pattern works.

Listing 20-3 shows a simple script that demonstrates using a RegExp to determine the length of the description section for the majority of scripting objects.

Listing 20-3. The desc.py Script

```
1|import re
2|pat = re.compile( r'^(\w+)(?:\s+.*)$', re.MULTILINE )
3|objs = [
4|    ( 'Help'       , Help        ),
5|    ( 'AdminApp'    , AdminApp     ),
6|    ( 'AdminConfig' , AdminConfig  ),
7|    ( 'AdminControl', AdminControl )
8|]
9|print '    Object   | #Lines | 1st method'
10|print '-------------+--------+--------------------'
```

```
11|for name, obj in objs :
12|    text = obj.help()
13|    mo = re.search( pat, text )
14|    desc = text[ :mo.start( 1 ) ].strip().splitlines()
15|    method = text[ mo.start( 1 ) : mo.end( 1 ) ]
16|    print '%-12s | %6d | %s' % ( name, len( desc ), method )
```

Figure 20-3 shows the output of the desc.py script in Listing 20-3. The WSAShelp_03.py script incorporates this technique to process these scripting objects so that their tabs will contain a split pane.

```
    Object    | #Lines | 1st method
------------+--------+--------------------
Help        |     16 | attributes
AdminApp    |     15 | deleteUserAndGroupEntries
AdminConfig |     19 | attributes
AdminControl|     21 | completeObjectName
```

Figure 20-3. *Output generated by desc.py*

Figure 20-4 shows the next version of this WSAShelp script, which uses this technique. In this version of the script, you can see that all of the tabs, except for the AdminTask tab, show a vertical split pane. The scripting object description is above the divider, and the information about the scripting object methods is below. The divider even has one touch expand icons (the little triangles) that can be used to expand or collapse the corresponding top or bottom pane, all with a single click. This is starting to look pretty neat. The complete WSAShelp_03.py script can be found in the code\Chap_20 directory.

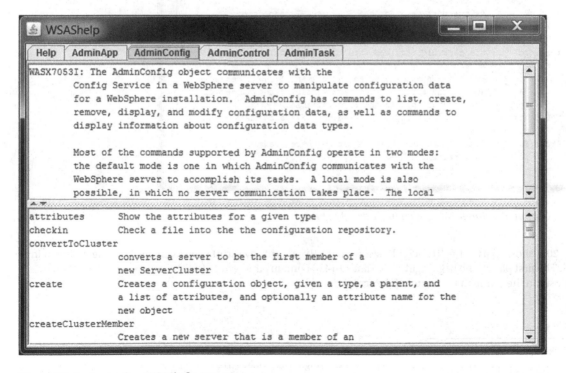

Figure 20-4. *Image from WSAShelp_03.py*

Text Highlighting

Looking at the output of WSAShelp_03.py made me wonder how difficult it would be to add text highlighting to the application. You could use this to locate specific text on a page. Before you change the WSAShelp script, let's see what is required to do this.

First, you need to realize that the JTextArea class doesn't provide a way to do this kind of thing. It, along with JTextField and JPasswordField, are subclasses of the abstract JTextComponent class,[3] which allows only a single kind of attribute for the entire component. This means that all of the data in the component must have the same font and color.

What you want to do is use a JTextComponent that allows multiple attributes for the contents. This means that you need to use JEditorPane or JTextPane[4] to hold and display the application's text.

To decide if you want to add this capability to your WSAShelp script, start simply by creating a simple script that allows you to improve your understanding of what might be required to use this capability well.

Figure 20-5 shows the output of Highlight.py; its complete source is found in the code\Chap_20 directory. The image shows the text of the Help.wsadmin() method, displayed in a read-only JTextPane that is within a ScrollPane. Beneath the text pane is a label and an input field that can be used to enter the highlighted text. The scroll pane above the input field shows an image after the word "the" has been entered,[5] and the scroll pane was scrolled down to display a number of highlighted occurrences of the word.

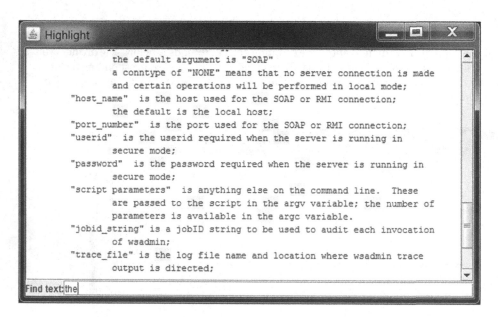

Figure 20-5. *Output of a simple script showing text highlighting*

Listing 20-4 shows part of the Highlight class from the Highlight.py script used to create the images shown in Figure 20-5. The first part of the Highlight class (lines 16-26) contains the center(...) method, which is called in line 51, to position the frame in the center of the screen.

---

[3]See http://docs.oracle.com/javase/8/docs/api/javax/swing/text/JTextComponent.html.
[4]See http://docs.oracle.com/javase/8/docs/api/javax/swing/JTextPane.html.
[5]Remember that the JTextField ActionListener is called when the user presses Enter.

Lines 32-34 instantiate an instance of the static `DefaultHighlightPainter` class.[6] This allows the application to specify the color to be used to highlight portions of the `JTextPane`.

Lines 35-40 instantiate the `JTextPane`, make it read-only, define the preferred size, initialize the text, set the font, and provides the default highlighter to be used.[7]

Line 41 is needed so that when the application becomes visible, the start of the text pane area is seen. If this statement is commented out or removed, the end of the text will be shown instead. Line 42 is where the text pane is added to the application frame within a scroll pane.

Lines 43-49 should look familiar to you. This is where the label and text input field are defined and added to a panel, which is then added to the bottom of the application frame. Of particular note is the keyword assignment on line 46, which identifies the `ActionListener` event handler that is invoked when the user presses Enter while the keyboard focus is on this component.

Listing 20-4. Portions of the `Highlight.py` Script

```
15|class Highlight( java.lang.Runnable ) :
  |     ...
27|    def run( self ) :
28|        frame = JFrame(
29|            'Highlight',
30|            defaultCloseOperation = JFrame.EXIT_ON_CLOSE
31|        )
32|        self.painter = DefaultHighlighter.DefaultHighlightPainter(
33|            Color.YELLOW
34|        )
35|        pane = self.tPane = JTextPane(
  |            ...
40|        )
41|        pane.moveCaretPosition( 0 )
42|        frame.add( JScrollPane( pane ), 'Center' )
43|        info = JPanel( BorderLayout() )
44|        info.add( JLabel( 'Find text:' ), 'West' )
45|        tf = JTextField(
46|            actionPerformed = self.search
47|        )
48|        info.add( tf, 'Center' )
49|        frame.add( info, 'South' )
50|        frame.pack()
51|        self.center( frame )
52|        frame.setVisible( 1 )
53|        tf.requestFocusInWindow()
```

Listing 20-5 shows the `search(...)` method from the `Highlight.py` script. This is where the actual highlighting works occurs. It begins by retrieving the contents of the input (`JTextField`) and removing any existing highlights. The advantage of doing it this way is that if the user enters an empty string, pressing the Enter key will remove any existing highlights.

---

[6] See http://docs.oracle.com/javase/8/docs/api/javax/swing/text/DefaultHighlighter.DefaultHighlightPainter.html.
[7] See http://docs.oracle.com/javase/8/docs/api/javax/swing/text/DefaultHighlighter.html.

Lines 54-70 are where the searching and adding of highlights to the text pane occurs. The string find(...) method, as shown in lines 62 and 70, return the offset or position in the text string of the data for being located. If no match is found, an offset of -1 is returned. So, if a non-negative offset is returned, it identifies the location of the first character of the data string in the text string being searched. The actual work of creating the highlighter occurs in lines 64-68 and identifies the painter to be used to highlight the text in which the user is interested.

Listing 20-5. The search(...) Method from the Highlight.py Script

```
54|    def search( self, event ) :
55|        data    = event.getSource().getText()
56|        hiliter = self.tPane.getHighlighter()
57|        hiliter.removeAllHighlights()
58|        if data :
59|            doc   = self.tPane.getDocument()
60|            text  = doc.getText( 0, doc.getLength() )
61|            start = 0
62|            here  = text.find( data, start )
63|            while here > -1 :
64|                hiliter.addHighlight(
65|                    here,
66|                    here + len( data ),
67|                    self.painter
68|                )
69|                start = here + len( data )
70|                here  = text.find( data, start )
```

Adding Text Highlighting to WSAShelp Application

Overall, that appears to be pretty simple and straightforward, right? Is there anything that you need to consider or be concerned about in order to add this capability to the existing WSAShelp application?

One issue that comes to mind is how the user specifies the text to be highlighted. Do you want to add an input field below the tabbed pane or consider something else? Might you want to add some menu options that allow you to highlight the text?

How should the highlighting work? As you can see in the Highlight.py script, the DefaultHighlighter class instance is associated with the abstract JTextComponent class using the setHighlighter(...) method or using the Jython keyword assignment syntax, as shown in line 45 of Listing 20-4. It isn't clear whether one of these class instances can, or should be, shared among JTextPane instances. This isn't good practice, so I, for one, will avoid doing this. What does this mean for your application? Well, for each of the text pane instances that you want to highlight, you need a highlighter instance.

How should the application deal with highlighted text when the user changes the selected tab? That's going to make things interesting, isn't it?

You can start by adding a ChangeListener to the TabbedPane. What does that take? As is frequently the case, it's much easier than I originally thought it would be. Listing 20-6 shows the trivial changes that you need to make to the WSAShelp_03.py script in order to determine and display the name of the selected tab. The WSAShelp_04.py script includes these minor modifications.

Listing 20-6. Changes Need to Identify Tab Selection from `WSAShelp_04.py`

```
 |          ...
39|          tabs = JTabbedPane( stateChanged = self.tabPicked )
 |          ...
89|      def tabPicked( self, event ) :
90|          pane = event.getSource()
91|          print pane.getTitleAt( pane.getSelectedIndex() )
```

With this `ChangeListener` method, you can easily access the name of the selected tab. If you add a dictionary to the application class that is indexed by tab name, with each entry being a tab-specific highlighter instance, the change listener method can use this information to highlight the tab-specific text. Let's hold off on this decision for a moment while you learn about some complications.

Tabbed Highlighting Complications

What is the application supposed to do when the user selects a tab that contains a split pane? If you want the text in each pane to be highlighted, that is going to require a separate highlighter for each panel, isn't it? Well, as you saw with the `Highlight.py` application, you can use the `DefaultHighlighter` for the text pane. Can't you use this same technique for each of the panes on each of the tabs in the application? If you do, the change listener event handler can process each of the panes on the tab to reset and populate the highlights to be displayed when the tab is selected. This would probably work best if you had a single, shared "find" input field.

During the development and testing of this iteration, it became apparent how quickly things can get complicated. What do I mean? Well, consider this for a few moments. In the change listener, you can easily determine which tab was selected. You can also tell what the tab contains. Unfortunately, it will either be a `JScrollPane` or a `JSplitPane`. The `JSplitPane` will have two parts, each of which will contain a `JScrollPane`. So far, so good. Now comes some of the "fun" (challenging) part. Given a `JScrollPane`, you can access the actual `JTextPane` component by calling the `getViewport().getView()` methods from the `JScrollPane` component. I'm sure you can see the circuitous kind of path that needs to be followed to access the `JTextPane` in which you're interested.

For a change listener method called when the tab contains a `JScrollPane` and not a `JSplitPane`, the methods shown in Figure 20-6 need to be called just to get access to the `JTextPane` contained within the `JScrollPane`, on the specified tab. To simplify the code as you'll as improve its performance, you'll create a dictionary indexed by the tab name, with references to each of the `JTextPanes` contained on the specified tab.

```
pane  = event.getSource()
index = pane.getSelectedIndex()
comp  = pane.getComponentAt( index )
tPane = comp.getViewport().getView()
```

Figure 20-6. *Calls needed to find a JTextPane in a JScrollPane*

Based on this observation, changes you're made to produce the `WSAShelp_05.py` script. Figure 20-7 shows an image from this application after "`default`" is highlighted on the `AdminConfig` tabs.

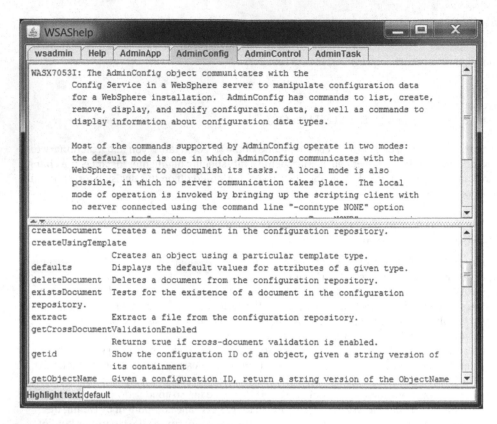

Figure 20-7. WSAShelp_05.py *sample output*

To create this iteration of the application required about 50 more lines of code, most of which can be seen in Listing 20-7. The highlight(...) method is called by the change listener event handler (the tabPicked(...) method), which is invoked when the user selects a new tab. Additionally, it is called by the action listener event handler (the lookFor(...) method) when the user presses Enter while the keyboard focus is on the JTextField at the bottom of the window.

Listing 20-7. New and Changed Methods in WSAShelp_05.py

```
35|    def hilight( self, tPane, text ) :
36|        hiliter = tPane.getHighlighter()
37|        hiliter.removeAllHighlights()
38|        if text :
39|            doc   = tPane.getDocument()
40|            info  = doc.getText( 0, doc.getLength() )
41|            start = 0
42|            here  = info.find( text, start )
43|            while here > -1 :
44|                hiliter.addHighlight(
45|                    here,
46|                    here + len( text ),
47|                    self.painter
48|                )
```

```
49|                    start = here + len( text )
50|                    here  = info.find( text, start )
51|    def lookFor( self, event ) :
52|        text  = event.getSource().getText()
53|        index = self.tabs.getSelectedIndex()
54|        name  = self.tabs.getTitleAt( index )
55|        for tPane in self.tPanes[ name ] :
56|            self.hilight( tPane, text )
  |    ...
134|    def tabPicked( self, event ) :
135|        pane  = event.getSource()
136|        index = pane.getSelectedIndex()
137|        name  = pane.getTitleAt( index )
138|        try :
139|            for tPane in self.tPanes[ name ] :
140|                self.hilight( tPane, self.textField.getText() )
141|        except :
142|            pass
```

■ **Note** You may wonder why you need a try/except clause in the change listener method. It is there because this method is invoked when the first tab is added to the JTabbedPane container. When this occurs, the data structure (the self.tPanes dictionary) hasn't been initialized, so the specified reference (self.tPanes[name]) is invalid. Other than that, the changes are pretty straightforward and make the application more useful, at least in my opinion.

Displaying Methods in a Table

I don't know about you, but every time that I look at the method (and scripting objects) sections (the bottom split pane sections), I wonder how difficult it would be to display this part in a table within a scroll pane. The big question related to this change is how it affects the highlighting.

Let's approach these challenges one at a time. You can start by creating a table for the bottom part of the split panes. Then, you can take a look at the cell rendering portion to see if you can easily resolve the highlighting issue.

So how should you go about building a table containing the method name in one column and the method abstract/description in another? Let's start by using a simple application that does this and only this. Then, you can determine what changes, if any, need to be made before incorporating this into your application.

Figure 20-8 shows the method names and descriptions that you're extracted from the output of calling the Help.help() method.

Method	Description / Abstract
attributes	given an MBean, returns help for attributes
operations	given an MBean, returns help for operations
constructors	given an MBean, returns help for constructors
description	given an MBean, returns help for description
notifications	given an MBean, returns help for notifications
classname	given an MBean, returns help for classname
all	given an MBean, returns help for all the above
help	returns this help text
AdminControl	returns general help text for the AdminControl object
AdminConfig	returns general help text for the AdminConfig object
AdminApp	returns general help text for the AdminApp object
AdminTask	returns general help text for the AdminTask object
wsadmin	returns general help text for the wsadmin script launcher
message	given a message id, returns explanation and user action message

Figure 20-8. *Proof of concept for displaying method info in a table*

Listing 20-8 shows the majority of the statements from the MethodTable1.py proof of concept (PoC) script used to produce the output shown in Figure 20-8. Since it is a PoC script, it's simple. As you can see, the run(...) method is very simple. It uses the parseMethodHelp(...) method to extract the method names and descriptions from the specified help text in order to populate the table.

Listing 20-8. run(...) Method of MethodTable Class from MethodTable1.py Script

```
10|class MethodTable1( java.lang.Runnable ) :
  |    ...
22|    def run( self ) :
23|        frame = JFrame(
24|            'MethodTable1',
25|            defaultCloseOperation = JFrame.EXIT_ON_CLOSE
26|        )
27|        helpText = Help.help().expandtabs()
28|        headings = [ 'Method', 'Description / Abstract' ]
29|        data = self.parseMethodHelp( helpText )
30|        table = JTable(
31|            data,
32|            headings,
33|            font = Font( 'Courier' , Font.PLAIN, 12 )
34|        )
35|        frame.add( JScrollPane( table ), 'Center' )
36|        frame.pack()
37|        self.center( frame )
38|        frame.setVisible( 1 )
```

The parseMethodHelp(...) method, shown in Listing 20-9, is where all of the real work takes place. It uses a regular expression (RegExp) to locate each method name in the specified input string.

Listing 20-9. `parseMethodHelp(...)` Method of the `MethodTable` Class from the `MethodTable1.py` Script

```
39|    def parseMethodHelp( self, helpText ) :
40|        def fix( text ) :
41|            text = text.replace( '\n', ' ' ).strip()
42|            return re.sub( ' +', ' ', text )
43|        methRE = re.compile( r'^(\w+)(?:\s+.*)$', re.MULTILINE )
44|        result = []
45|        mo   = methRE.search( helpText )
46|        name = None
47|        while mo :
48|            start, finish = mo.span( 1 )
49|            if name :
50|                result.append(
51|                    [
52|                        name,
53|                        fix( helpText[ prev : start ] )
54|                    ]
55|                )
56|            name = helpText[ start : finish ]
57|            prev = finish + 1
58|            mo = methRE.search( helpText, finish )
59|        if name :
60|            result.append( [ name, fix( helpText[ prev: ] ) ] )
61|        return result
```

The remainder of the text up to the next method name is considered the associated description. The result of this method is an array, with one row for each method, and two columns. The first column of the table contains the method name and the second column the entire description string. In order to do this, the fix routine, shown in lines 40-42 of Listing 20-9, replaces the newline characters ('\n') with a space. Then, all of the leading, trailing, and multiple adjacent spaces are removed.

Highlighting Text Within the Table

One of the nice things about using a JTextPane component to hold the text to be displayed is that you can use the DefaultHighlighter as you'll as the DefaultHighlightPainter class instances to locate and highlight text of interest to the user. Unfortunately, these classes aren't available on the contents of the JTable instance. So, what can you do? The default renderer for the table cells uses a JLabel instance to format the cell contents.

The neat thing about this is that a JLabel can use HTML tags to format the cell contents. This means that all you have to do to highlight a portion of a cell is surround it with the appropriate HTML tags. To do that, make the changes shown in Listing 20-10.

Listing 20-10. Changes to the Highlight Table Text from `MethodTable2.py`

```
10|class MethodTable2( java.lang.Runnable ) :
  |    ...
22|    def run( self ) :
  |        ...
29|        data = self.parseMethodHelp( helpText )
30|        for r in range( len( data ) ) :
31|            for c in range( len( data[ r ] ) ) :
```

```
32|                        data[ r ][ c ] = self.hiliteText(
33|                            data[ r ][ c ],
34|                             'help'
35|                        )
36|          table = JTable(
37|              data,
38|              headings,
39|              font = Font( 'Courier' , Font.PLAIN, 12 )
40|          )
  |    ...
45|      def hiliteText( self, text, findWord ) :
46|          return '<html>' + text.replace(
47|              findWord,
48|              '<font bgcolor=yellow>%s</font>' % findWord
49|          )
```

Figure 20-9 shows the sample output generated by this script. By default, the word "help" is highlighted.

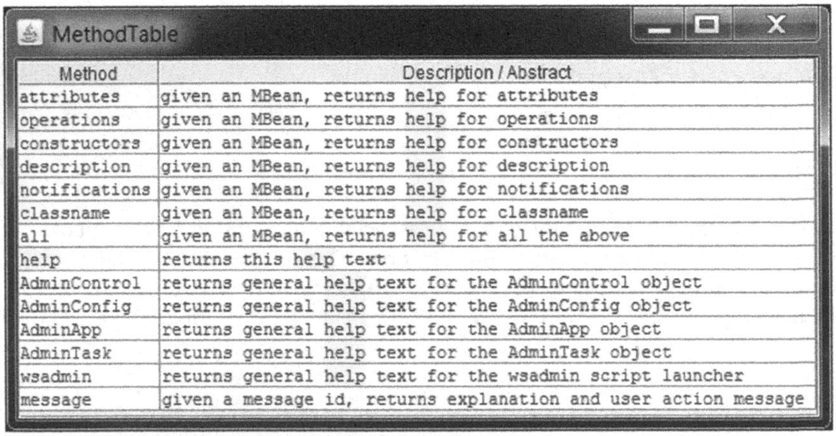

Figure 20-9. *PoC for displaying highlighted table text*

Using Tables in the Help Application

Are there any problems with adding this to the help application? If you take a few moments to test the MethodTable scripts, you are likely to see a noticeable delay during the application startup. Unfortunately, this is the kind of thing that users find particularly annoying. As discussed earlier, whenever you encounter an operation that could take a long time, it should execute on a separate thread. Since the operation in question involves the creation of the attribute and description table, it should be executed on a separate thread.

These choices might cause you to ask yourself some questions. For example, what should you display on the bottom part of the split pane until the table thread completes? An easy and reasonable approach is to display a simple message indicating that results will be available shortly. So, you'll just use a JLabel instance with a message.

You might also wonder which attributes the tables should use. You don't want the user to attempt to make any changes to the table data, so the table cells should be read-only. Additionally, you know that the data type for each cell should be a java.lang.String. Add a table model class (methodTableModel) that descends from the DefaultTableModel class.

Listing 20-11. The methodTableModel Class from WSAShelp_06.py

```
26|class methodTableModel( DefaultTableModel ) :
27|    def __init__( self, data, headings ) :
28|        DefaultTableModel.__init__( self, data, headings )
29|    def isCellEditable( self, row, col ) :
30|        return 0
31|    def getColumnClass( self, col ) :
32|        return String
```

Listing 20-11 shows just how simple this kind of descendent class can be. Unfortunately, you also need to add code to adjust the table column widths. Without it, the table will give each column as close to 50% of the table width as it can. With the information that you want to display, this isn't a great distribution of the available space. So, WSAShelp_06.py also includes the setColumnWidths(...) method shown in Listing 20-12 to try to adjust the column widths.

Listing 20-12. The setColumnWidths(...) Method from WSAShelp_06.py

```
76|    def setColumnWidths( self, table ) :
77|        header = table.getTableHeader()
78|        tcm = table.getColumnModel()          # Table Column Model
79|        data = table.getModel()               # To access table data
80|        margin = tcm.getColumnMargin()        # gap betyouen columns
81|        rows = data.getRowCount()             # Number of rows
82|        cols = tcm.getColumnCount()           # Number of cols
83|        for i in range( cols ) :              # For col 0..N
84|            col = tcm.getColumn( i )          # TableColumn: col i
85|            idx = col.getModelIndex()         # model index: col i
86|            render = col.getHeaderRenderer()# header renderer
87|            if render :
88|                comp = render.getTableCellRendererComponent(
89|                    table,
90|                    col.getHeaderValue(),
91|                    0,
92|                    0,
93|                    -1,
94|                    i
95|                )
96|                cWidth = comp.getPreferredSize().width
97|            else :
98|                cWidth = -1
99|            for row in range( rows ) :
100|                val = str( data.getValueAt( row, idx ) )
101|                r = table.getCellRenderer( row, i )
102|                comp = r.getTableCellRendererComponent(
103|                    table,
104|                    val,                       # formatted value
105|                    0,                         # not selected
106|                    0,                         # not in focus
107|                    row,                       # row num
108|                    i                          # col num
109|                )
```

```
110|                    cWidth = max(
111|                        cWidth,
112|                        comp.getPreferredSize().width
113|                    )
114|                if cWidth > 0 :
115|                    col.setPreferredWidth( cWidth + margin )
```

Figure 20-10 shows a sample image from the WSAShelp_06.py script. As you can see, some of the tabs can't display complete information that is available to both columns. When this occurs, the contents have ellipses (. . .) appended to the truncated values.

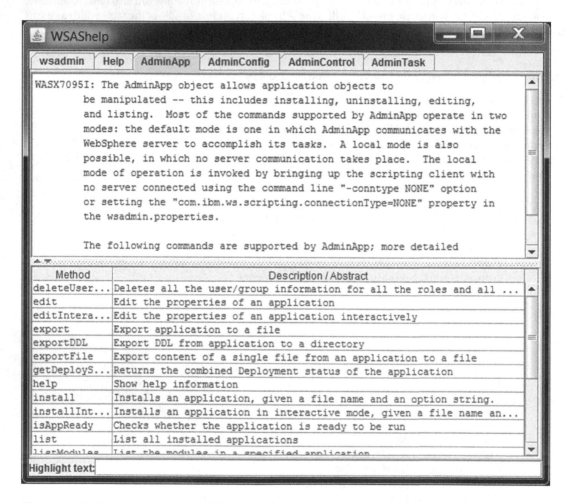

Figure 20-10. *Sample output from WSAShelp_06.py*

Grab and drag the separator bar between the column headings and see what happens when you change the column widths. Is that responsive enough for you? I don't notice any delay at all and am quite pleased.

Fixing the Table Appearance

Many people would find the ellipses a distraction and an annoyance. How do you fix this? The first thing to do is to remember how the cell data is represented. In Chapter 12, you learned about cell renderers. Fortunately, all of the table cells contain simple strings. So you only need to provide a renderer for this data type.

The challenge, though, is how you deal with the cell data that doesn't fit in the available space. First, you need to be able to figure out:

- How much space is available

- How you want to display the data

- How you split the data to fit in the available space

The program uses a monospace font, which makes sense when you're displaying the help text that is normally seen in an interactive wsadmin session.

Another choice that makes life a little easier is to use a JTable to display the method information. How does it make things easier? If you take another look back at Chapter 12, you'll see that the default cell renderer for a JTable will use a JLabel to display a cell. You can then use HTML to format the cell contents. This allows you to specify
 (the HTML line break tag) where you want the break to occur. Unfortunately, if you are going to use multiple lines of text to display the cell text, you also have top deal with the row height to allow multiple lines.

An additional challenge involves how you intend to split any long method names. Blanks aren't allowed as part of a method name, so you have to decide if you want to split the method name between arbitrary letters or use a little additional effort and recognize that method names use a camelcase[8] naming convention. Personally, I prefer to split the method names between the camelcase words. You need to use a JLabel method, specifically the getFontMetrics(...) method, to determine how much of the data will fit in the available width. Listings 20-13 and 20-14 show the table cell renderer class from WSAShelp_07.py. Unfortunately, it doesn't fit on one page so has to be shown in two pieces.

Listing 20-13. The methRenderer Class from WSAShelp_07.py Part 1

```
27|class methRenderer( DefaultTableCellRenderer ) :
28|    def __init__( self ) :
29|        self.fm = JLabel().getFontMetrics( monoFont )
30|        self.widths = [ 0, 0 ]
31|        self.hiText = ''
32|    def getTableCellRendererComponent(
33|        self,
34|        table,              # JTable  - table containing value
35|        value,              # Object  - value being rendered
36|        isSelected,         # boolean - Is value selected?
37|        hasFocus,           # boolean - Does this cell have focus?
38|        row,                # int     - Row # ( 0 .. N-1 )
39|        col                 # int     - Col # ( 0 .. N-1 )
40|    ) :
41|        def camelWords( name ) :
42|            prev, result = 0, []
43|            for i in range( len( name ) ) :
44|                ch = name[ i ]
```

---

[8]See http://en.wikipedia.org/wiki/CamelCase.

```
45|                    if ch == ch.upper() or ch == '_' :
46|                        result.append( name[ prev:i ] )
47|                        prev = i
48|                result.append( name[ prev: ] )
49|                return result
50|            DTCR = DefaultTableCellRenderer
51|            comp = DTCR.getTableCellRendererComponent(
52|                self, table, value, isSelected, hasFocus, row, col
53|            )
54|            pWidth = self.widths[ col ]    # Preferred column width
```

The first portion of the class, shown in Listing 20-13, shows the class constructor in lines 28-31 as well as the initial portion of the getTableCellRendererComponent(...) method. Note that this method includes the local camelWords(...) method on lines 41-49. It is only used in the next segment of code (on line 62) where the contents of column 0 are being processed.

It takes advantage of the similarity of splitting method names and the method abstract text. If the text doesn't fit into the available width, the data is reformatted using HTML to use multiple lines. Since the renderer is the class that uses HTML to format the data, it is also the right place to add HTML to highlight any text that the user requests.

If you look closely at the renderer class in Listing 20-14, you might notice a couple of methods that are unique to this renderer (they don't exist in the base class). These are the setHiText(...), and setWidths(...) methods on lines 92-95. These were added to provide the class instance with the information that it needs to format the text to fit in the available width, as well as add the appropriate highlighting, as needed. Is this a perfect answer? Probably not, but it is certainly good enough, especially for this application.

Listing 20-14. The methRenderer Class from WSAShelp_07.py Part 2

```
55|            if pWidth :                        # Has it been set?
56|                hiHTML = '<font bgcolor=yellow>%s</font>'
57|                pWidth -= 3
58|                if self.fm.stringWidth( value ) > pWidth :
59|                    if col :
60|                        pad, words = ' ', value.split( ' ' )
61|                    else :
62|                        pad, words = '', camelWords( value )
63|                    result, curr = '<html>', ''
64|                    for word in words :
65|                        width = self.fm.stringWidth(
66|                            curr + pad + word
67|                        )
68|                        if width > pWidth :
69|                            result += curr + '<br>'
70|                            curr = ''
71|                        if curr :
72|                            curr += pad + word
73|                        else :
74|                            curr = word
75|                    result += curr
```

```
76|                    if self.hiText :
77|                        if result.count( self.hiText ) > 0 :
78|                            result = result.replace(
79|                                self.hiText,
80|                                hiHTML % self.hiText
81|                                )
82|                    comp.setText( result )
83|                else :
84|                    if self.hiText :
85|                        if value.count( self.hiText ) > 0 :
86|                            value = value.replace(
87|                                self.hiText,
88|                                hiHTML % self.hiText
89|                                )
90|                    comp.setText( '<html>' + value )
91|        return comp
92|    def setHiText( self, text ) :
93|        self.hiText = text
94|    def setWidths( self, width0, width1 ) :
95|        self.widths = [ width0, width1 ]
```

How and when would the setWidths(...) method need to be called? Think about it for a few moments. When does the table need to be displayed? The first time would be when the tab on which a table exists is selected. Another time would be when the application frame was resized (maximized). If you take a look at the WSAShelp_07.py script, and search for calls to this routine, you will find calls to this routine in these two event handlers.

Take a few moments to test this script and see what happens when you resize the frame. Personally, I like the way it responds to the resize requests; I hope that you agree.

Selecting Table Cells

Now that you have the scripting object methods in a nice little table at the bottom of each split pane, what's next? You can now progress to one of the goals that I had for this application. I wanted to be able to select the tab for a specific scripting object, scroll down to show the name of the method in which I was interested, and select the method. Wouldn't it be neat if selecting the method in the table showed the help for the selected method? What is needed to do this? Listing 20-15 shows the class that was added to provide this capability to the WSAShelp_08.py script.

Listing 20-15. ListSelectionListener from WSAShelp_08.py

```
30|class cellSelector( ListSelectionListener ) :
31|    def __init__( self, table, WASobj ) :
32|        self.table = table
33|        self.WASobj = WASobj
34|        self.objName = WASobj.help()[ :40 ].split( ' ' )[ 2 ]
35|    def valueChanged( self, event ) :
36|        if not event.getValueIsAdjusting() :
37|            table = self.table
38|            row = table.getSelectedRow()
39|            if row > -1 :
40|                method = table.getModel().getValueAt( row, 0 )
```

```
41|                    title = '%s.help( "%s" )' % (
42|                        self.objName,
43|                        method
44|                    )
45|                    text = self.WASobj.help( method )
46|                    text = JTextArea(
47|                        text,
48|                        20,
49|                        80,
50|                        font = monoFont
51|                    )
52|                    dialog = JDialog(
53|                        None,                   # owner
54|                        title,                  # title
55|                        1,                      # modal = true
56|                        layout = BorderLayout(),
57|                        locationRelativeTo = None
58|                    )
59|                    dialog.add(
60|                        JScrollPane(
61|                            text
62|                        ),
63|                        BorderLayout.CENTER
64|                    )
65|                    dialog.pack()
66|                    dialog.setVisible( 1 )
```

The class constructor may require a bit of explanation though. The reason for providing the table as an argument to the constructor will be explained shortly. The reason for having the WASobj (AdminApp, AdminConfig, and so on), specified makes things for the valueChanged(...) method much simpler, because given the scripting object, and the name of the method in question, all the routine needs to do is invoke the help(...) method, as see on line 45. This leaves you with the expression on line 34. What is it doing?

Listing 20-16 shows how the constructor expression works. Basically, it depends on the fact that the first line of the help text for each of these scripting objects uses the same format. The message number is followed by a sentence that starts with "The", followed by the name of the scripting object. The expression on line 34 of Listing 20-15 simply uses this fact to save the name of the specified scripting object.

Listing 20-16. Extracting an Object Name from its Help Text

```
wsadmin>for obj in [ AdminApp, AdminConfig, AdminControl, Help ] :
wsadmin>    print obj.help()[ :40 ]
wsadmin>
WASX7095I: The AdminApp object allows ap
WASX7053I: The AdminConfig object commun
WASX7027I: The AdminControl object enabl
WASX7028I: The Help object has two purpo
wsadmin>
```

Instances of the cellSelector listener class shown in Listing 20-15 are added when the table is created in the tableTask instance, specifically in the done(...) method. Listing 20-17 shows how the selection listener is added to table using its selection model. The fact that the selection listener instance is added to the selection model, and not the table itself, is the main reason that the table instance is passed on the cellSelector constructor. The code in the valueChanged(...) event handler method, as shown in Listing 20-15, uses the table to identify the user-selected method, so that the appropriate help text can be displayed.

Listing 20-17. Adding Selection Listener Instance from WSAShelp_08.py

```
178|         table.getSelectionModel().addListSelectionListener(
179|           cellSelector(
180|               table,
181|               self.WASobj
182|           )
183|         )
```

What do these changes allow you to do? Figure 20-11 shows a sample dialog box that is displayed when some of the scripting object table rows are selected. Note how the title of the dialog box identifies the scripting object and method for which help is being displayed.

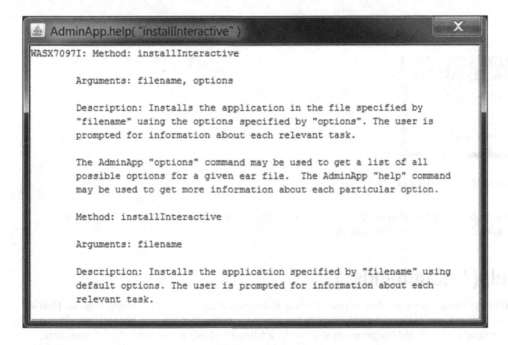

Figure 20-11. *Sample image from* WSAShelp_08.py *script*

■ **Note**   To make things simpler for the application, modal dialog boxes are used. Additionally, the text is displayed in a scroll pane, just in case it's larger than the available space.

Adding a Menu

One of the things that I wasn't too happy about with the previous scripts was how the "Highlight text" label and input field were always showing on the bottom of the frame. Another alternative is to use menu items for this and other kinds of actions. Let's start simple and replace the label and input field with a "Show" menu that allows the user to specify text to be highlighted. You can also provide some information about the script with some "Help" menu items. What does this do to the application? Figure 20-12 has some images from the WSAShelp_09.py script, showing the initial look of the menu and the associated drop-down menus. Additionally, you see an image showing the input dialog box that is displayed when the user selects the Show ➤ Highlight Text menu item.

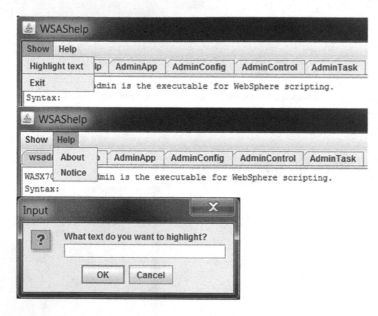

Figure 20-12. *Sample images from WSAShelp_09.py script*

The complete application can be found in the code\Chap_20\WSAShelp_09.py file and requires only about 80 additional lines of code to add this non-trivial functionality.

AdminTask.help('-commands')

In the WAuJ book two different scripts were used to format all of the help text for the wsadmin scripting objects. That's because the AdminTask scripting object is significantly different from the other scripting objects. In fact it provides a framework for WebSphere developers to add scripting capabilities by adding methods to the AdminTask framework, instead of forcing changes to be made to the existing objects.

When I began to consider adding the ability of displaying AdminTask help information to the WSAShelp scripts, I first considered adding some kind of listener to the AdminTask pane that would allow the user to select either the "help -commands", or "help -commandGroups" portions of that pane. Unfortunately, this would not be an obvious solution to the problem. How would you convey this information to the user? Maybe by using some kind of special highlighting, possibly even using something like the convention used by browsers to indicate that text is, in fact, a link to additional information. I quickly discarded this approach after taking another look at the menu items that had just been added to the WSAShelp_09.py script. This appeared to be a much more obvious solution to the problem.

Unfortunately, trying to display information about the available AdminTask commands brings challenges of its own. For example, depending on the version of the WebSphere Application Server product being used, there can be a huge list of available AdminTask commands from which to choose. The following sections address some of the questions that come to mind.

How Do We Find and Identify Existing Commands?

The obvious answer to this question is to take a look at the output produced by the AdminTask.help('-commands') method call. How much text is generated by this call? As mentioned earlier, it depends. To give you an idea, you can run a quick test. Listing 20-18 shows that for a WebSphere version 7.0, network deployment installation, almost 1,200 lines of text are generated.

Listing 20-18. Lines of Text from the AdminTask.help('-commands') Output

```
wsadmin>print len( AdminTask.help( '-commands' ).splitlines() )
1190
wsadmin>
```

WebSphere version 8.0 has more than 1,250 lines and WebSphere version 8.5 has more than 1,400.

The time to process this output is not something that you would want to do in a simple event handler. That would be likely to cause a noticeable and unacceptable delay in the application. As you've read, you should consider doing this processing on a separate (SwingWorker) thread.

Showing the User that Something Is Happening

Since the processing of the AdminTask.help('-commands') command output may cause a non-trivial delay, you need to consider how you communicate this fact to the user. One thing that came to mind was that you can initialize the Show ➤ AdminTask ➤ -commands menu item as disabled, at least until the processing is complete and the data exists in a usable form.

If you proceed with this decision, the SwingWorker class that you're going to use has to know the menu item that needs to be enabled once processing completes. Additionally, it needs to know how to make the results of its processing available to the application.

It seems pretty obvious that the result of the processing of this text should be an array or list of AdminTask command names. Don't you think?

Alright, what's it going to take to have a separate SwingWorker thread to process the output of the AdminTask.help('-commands') call? Listing 20-19 shows that it doesn't take much effort. The doInBackground(...) method makes the call and processes each line of the resulting text. It can use a simple regular expression to identify the method names and each one that is found is added to the list. Then, all the done(...) method needs to do is enable the specified menu item.

Listing 20-19. ATcommandTask Class from WSAShelp_10.py

```
176|class ATcommandTask( SwingWorker ) :
177|    def __init__( self, List, menuItem ) :
178|        SwingWorker.__init__( self )
179|        self.commands = List
180|        self.menuItem = menuItem
181|    def doInBackground( self ) :
182|        data = AdminTask.help( '-commands' ).splitlines()
183|        for line in data[ 1: ] :
184|            mo = re.match( '([a-zA-Z_2]+) -', line )
```

```
185|            if mo :
186|                self.commands.append( mo.group( 1 ) )
187|    def done( self ) :
188|        self.menuItem.setEnabled( 1 )
```

Now that you have this long list of commands or methods, how do you make things easy for your users? Scrolling through a list of 1,000 plus names is not exactly user friendly.

Do you remember what you did back in Chapter 15, with the javadocInfo script? You added an input field that allowed the user to filter the list of items to be displayed.[9] You can do the same thing here. If I'm looking for the AdminTask methods that have something to do with a particular topic, it can be somewhat daunting to look through 1,000 plus command names. By adding a filtering mechanism, you can greatly diminish the number of commands through which the user has to look.

Figure 20-13 shows some sample images from the WSAShelp_10.py script. The first shows what happens to the application when the "Show" menu item has been selected. The second shows what happens when the AdminTask menu item has been selected. The third shows the initial view of the dialog box. One thing that you should notice is the size of the scrollbar thumb, which gives you an indication of the size of the list. Finally, you see what happens to the number of commands that contain "Lis". I think that you'll agree that this technique vastly improves the user experience when dealing with this huge list of AdminTask commands.

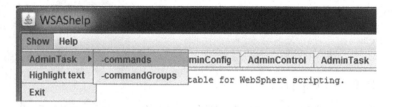

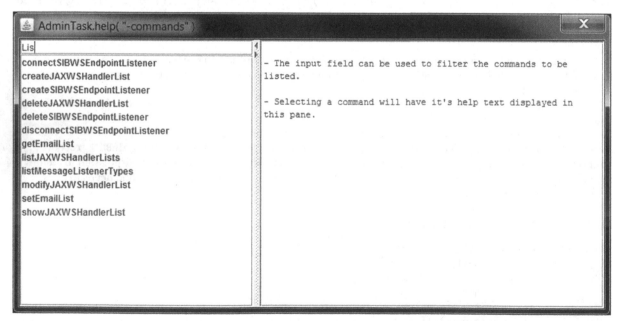

Figure 20-13. Sample images from WSAShelp_10.py script

---

[9]The filtering was first added to javadocInfo_06.py, which is discussed in the section entitled "Filtering the List."

One thing that you may notice about the WSAShelp_10.py script output is what happens when you select Show ➤ AdminTask ➤ -commandGroups menu item. A placeholder dialog box is displayed, indicating that work remains to be done.

AdminTask.help('-commandGroups')

Now you get to figure out how to deal with the "-commandGroups" menu item. When you were working with the "-commands" menu item, it made sense to generate a list of the available AdminTask commands. With this selection, that makes less sense. Since each commandGroup is supposed to represent a group of similar commands, doesn't it make more sense to display this as a tree, with each node of the tree representing one of the command groups? That way, to see the commands within a group, you would only have to expand the group by selecting (double-clicking) on a group name.

Like the ATcommandTask class seen in Listing 20-19 it seems reasonable to expect that you're going to need another SwingWorker descendent class to process the AdminTask.help('-commandGroups') output to build the application dialog box.

The first thing that this class will need to do is to extract the commandGroup names from the AdminTask.help('-commandGroups') output. To figure out how to do this, first take a look at what this output looks like. Listing 20-20 shows the first few lines of output produced by this command.

Listing 20-20. The AdminTask.help('-commandGroups') Output

```
wsadmin>print AdminTask.help( '-commandGroups' )
WASX8005I: Available admin command groups:

AdminAgentNode - Admin Agent Managed Node related tasks
AdminAgentSecurityCommands - Commands used to configure security ...
AdminReports - Admin configuration reports
AdministrativeJobs - This command group contains all the job mana...
AppManagementCommands - Application management commands.
AuditAuthorizationCommands - Audit Authorization Table Commands
...
```

This format allows for easy identification and processing of the command group names. When a group name is identified (AdminAgentNode), then a subsequent AdminTask.help(...) method call can be used to identify the associated commands, if any, that exist within the group. For example, the output seen in Listing 20-21 shows the help text for two different command groups, only one of which (AdminReports) has associated commands. The format used by these command group help text messages make processing of them easy as well.

Listing 20-21. AdminTask.help(...) Using commandGroup Names

```
wsadmin>print AdminTask.help( 'AdminAgentNode' )
WASX8007I: Detailed help for command group: AdminAgentNode

Description: Admin Agent Managed Node related tasks

Commands:

wsadmin>print AdminTask.help( 'AdminReports' )
WASX8007I: Detailed help for command group: AdminReports

Description: Admin configuration reports
```

```
Commands:
reportConfigInconsistencies - Checks the configuation repository ...
reportConfiguredPorts - Generates a report of the ports configure...

wsadmin>
```

Listing 20-22 shows the SwingWorker descendent class used to process the AdminTask.help('-commandGroups') text, to identify the names of the command groups and the associated AdminTask commands. This class is from the WSAShelp_11.py script. It may be interesting to note that the constructor requires only one parameter, that is, the variable used to identify the menu item to be enabled when processing is complete.

Listing 20-22. ATgroupsTask Class from WSAShelp_11.py

```
196|class ATgroupsTask( SwingWorker ) :
197|    def __init__( self, menuItem ) :
198|        SwingWorker.__init__( self )
199|        self.menuItem = menuItem
200|    def doInBackground( self ) :
201|        try :
202|            data = AdminTask.help(
203|                '-commandGroups'
204|            ).expandtabs().splitlines()
205|            self.root = DefaultMutableTreeNode(
206|                'command groups'
207|            )
208|            empty = []
209|            for line in data[ 1: ] :
210|                mo = re.match( '([a-zA-Z ]+) -', line )
211|                if mo :
212|                    groupName = mo.group( 1 )
213|                    group = None
214|                    text = AdminTask.help( groupName )
215|                    cmds = text.find( 'Commands:' )
216|                    if cmds > 0 :
217|                        for line in text[cmds+9:].splitlines() :
218|                            mo = re.match('([a-zA-Z_2]+) -', line)
219|                            if mo :
220|                                if not group :
221|                                    group = DefaultMutableTreeNode(
222|                                        groupName
223|                                    )
224|                                group.add(
225|                                    DefaultMutableTreeNode(
226|                                        mo.group( 1 )
227|                                    )
228|                                )
229|                        if group :
230|                            self.root.add( group )
231|                        else :
232|                            empty.append( groupName )
```

```
233|        except :
234|            print '\nError: %s\nvalue: %s' % sys.exc_info()[ :2 ]
235|    def done( self ) :
236|        self.menuItem.setEnabled( 1 )
```

Notice that this class constructor didn't include a parameter for the result like you saw in the `ATcommandTask` class, in Listing 20-19. This was done simply to show another approach. Are there problems with this approach? To answer that question, let's take a look at the code used to instantiate this class and access the resulting data (a `DefaultMutableTreeNode`[10]) for the root node. Listing 20-23 shows the other places in the code that instantiate and execute the `ATgroupsTask`, as well as retrieve the result of its processing.

Listing 20-23. Use of ATgroupsTask class in WSAShelp_11.py

```
    |        ...
464|        self.ATgroupsTree = None
465|        self.groups = ATgroupsTask( groupMI )
466|        self.groups.execute()
    |        ...
623|    def showCmdGroups( self, event ) :
    |        ...
631|        left = JPanel( layout = BorderLayout() )
632|        left.add(
633|            JScrollPane(
634|                JTree(
635|                    self.groups.root,
636|                    rootVisible = 0,
637|                    valueChanged = self.pickATgroup
638|                )
639|            ),
640|            BorderLayout.CENTER
641|        )
    |        ...
```

■ **Note** It's important to note that in order to access the result of the `ATgroupsTask` processing, you need to have a variable for referencing the object. That is why `WSAShelp_11.py` includes the `self.groups` variable.

It might not be immediately obvious that the `showCmdGroups(...)` method uses the `self.groups` variable to reference the root node for the tree. The event listener routine is called when the Show ➤ AdminTask ➤ -commandGroups menu item is selected.

What does this mean as far as the JTree instance is concerned? To understand this, you should consider when and how often this routine is called. Each time the user invokes this routine, a new JTree instance is created. For a tiny application such as this, it might not make much of a difference, but it is better to understand the implications of your decisions as far as potential performance impact is concerned.

---

[10]See http://docs.oracle.com/javase/8/docs/api/javax/swing/tree/DefaultMutableTreeNode.html.

Another ATgroupsTask Implementation

If you want to have the JTree populated by the ATgroupsTask process, what do you need to do? First, you have to realize what is required in order for the ATgroupsTask instance to modify the data of a JTree parameter passed to it. The JTree documentation[11] shows that no method exists to replace the tree root (no setRoot(...) method exists). Why is this?

You have to remember that the JTree class, like many other Swing classes (the JTable), has the data managed by an associated model. In the case of the JTree class, the data exists in, and is maintained by, the associated TreeModel[12] instance, which in all likelihood would be a DefaultTreeModel[13] object instance. The DefaultTreeModel class is where the setRoot(...) method resides. So, what do you need to change in the ATgroupsTask? Not much. You need to add a parameter for the constructor to hold the JTree object to be updated. It then adds a statement in the done(...) method that gets the tree model instance and uses its setRoot(...) method to replace the tree data. Another encouraging thing about this approach is that it also simplifies the event handler, instead of creating a new JTree.

Figure 20-14 shows the output after selecting the commandGroups menu item and then double-clicking the AutoGen Commands entry. Note that if you only select a table entry, it isn't expanded to display the child nodes.

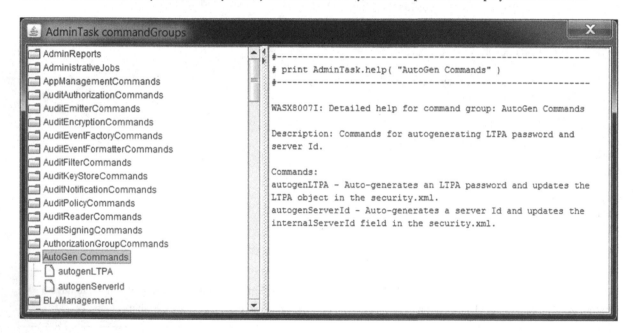

Figure 20-14. Sample image from WSAShelp_12.py script

---

[11]See http://docs.oracle.com/javase/8/docs/api/javax/swing/JTree.html.

[12]See http://docs.oracle.com/javase/8/docs/api/javax/swing/tree/TreeModel.html.

[13]See http://docs.oracle.com/javase/8/docs/api/javax/swing/tree/DefaultTreeModel.html.

Step It Up: Displaying the "Steps" Help Text

I was going to finish this application, as well as the chapter, with the previous iteration of the script. But I demonstrated it to a friend who asked me some very good questions. What about the "steps" that some of the AdminTask commands have? Is there any way to view the help for these steps?

I told him that I would think about it and see what I could do. To begin, I had to see how many of the AdminTask commands had steps, as well as to see what it would take to display this information with a minimum impact to the existing script.

It didn't take much effort to write a script to locate and display the names of the AdminTask commands that had any steps. It also displayed a little detail about the information that was processed. For example, when I ran this script (steps.py) in a WebSphere V 7 environment, it showed that 42 of the 1,162 commands have one or more steps (3.61%). That's why I had forgotten all about this aspect of some AdminTask commands—only a small number have the "Steps" section populated.

How Should You Do It?

Realizing that steps exist doesn't explain how to display the help text for a step. To understand that, you need only take a look at the AdminTask help text, as shown in Listing 20-24.

Listing 20-24. The Part of AdminTask.help() Text About Steps

```
help commandName stepName      display detailed information for
                               the specified step belonging to the
                               specified command
```

This answers the question, "how do you get the help text for a command step?" But it doesn't answer the more challenging question, "how do you modify the WSAShelp_12.py script to allow the user to see this help text?"

Should You Add a Menu?

One thought is to add a menu to the command window that would allow the users to get the help for a specific step. When the command help text is being processed, if no steps exist, then the menu could be disabled or you could decide not to add the menu. Each step could be listed on the menu, thereby allowing the users to select the step for which help could be displayed in a modal dialog box. The good news is that you know how to do these things and you've seen them done. However, it's not clear whether this is the best approach available. Let's see what other options exist before you make a decision.

Should You Add Another Split Pane?

Another alternative that comes to mind to detect when steps exist and then use a split pane with the general command help description at the top, and a table with one row for each of the steps at the bottom. Again, this is something that you know how to do since this technique is shown on the middle tabs of the application. The bad news is that it would seem to be a significant amount of work and code for very infrequent use. Since less than 5% of the AdminTask commands have steps, it is not clear that this approach is worth the time and effort to implement.

Can You Make Parts of the Text Pane Selectable?

Another alternative is to allow the users to click on any of the visible step names. This is a little different and might be interesting to implement. Unfortunately, since you haven't done this yet, it's not clear how much time and effort, not to mention code, is required to do this.

And Now for Something Completely Different...

One of the things that got my attention while I was thinking about how best to approach this task was the fact that all of the previous options require extra effort on the part of the user to decide which of the steps they want to investigate. If they want to view multiple steps, multiple actions are required (select a menu item, look at the modal dialog box, close it, and repeat as necessary). Is there an easier way?

That's when I wondered about the possibility of displaying the help text for any and all steps in the same scrollable text pane containing the help text for the command. Another advantage to this approach is the fact that it requires about a dozen lines of code to be added in two places (the `pickATcmd(...)` and the `pickATgroup(...)` methods).

This iteration of the script is available in the `code\Chap_20` directory, and is named `WSAShelp_13.py`. Figure 20-15 shows the "Steps" section of the help text for the `createCluster` command, and the beginning of the help text for the first of the associated steps.

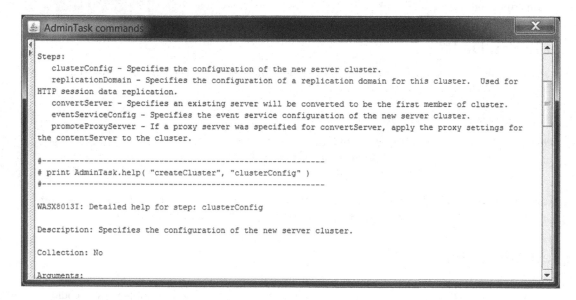

Figure 20-15. *The help text for the `clusterConfig` step*

One of the important things about this iteration is that the first approach that came to mind wasn't the easiest or best approach for this particular situation. In fact, I considered multiple approaches and started to investigate what changes would be required for each approach before the "simple" answer came to me. Sometimes, it's not the first idea that comes to mind that ends up being the best approach.

Summary

All in all, this is now a pretty decent example of the iterative development of a non-trivial graphical application that uses a large variety of Swing capabilities. Even though it isn't perfect, it's a good tutorial on one way that Jython Swing applications can be developed. It is also a good example of how you might want to decide which approach is the most appropriate for you and your users' needs. Don't be afraid to stop and think about the options and which ones are going to make the application most useful for your users. It's also good to remember that you can do a quick proof of concept for potential enhancements for your application.

In the next chapter, you'll look at a different application and use an iterative improvement to add functionality as you improve the application. This application will be used to display details related to the security configuration report about a WebSphere environment.

CHAPTER 21

■ ■ ■

A Security Configuration
Report Application

Not too long ago, someone asked me how difficult it would be to generate a security configuration report, similar to what is available from the WebSphere administration console. This chapter explores the creation of such an application to display the security report in a user-friendly way, all the while using the techniques that you've learned so far. This will allow the users to interact with the information in a way that provides a better understanding of the security-related configuration information for a WebSphere Application Server.

Generating the Administration Console Report

To get started, you are going to generate a static HTML security report for the environment. Then you will learn how, using iterative steps, to create an application that uses a GUI to display this security information in a user friendly way. To begin, an administrator must use the administration console to generate the report. This requires the administrator to be logged into the administration console using an appropriate security role. To generate the report, follow these steps (see Figure 21-1):

1. Select/expand the Security section on the left frame.

2. Select the Global Security link.

3. Click on the Security Configuration Report button.

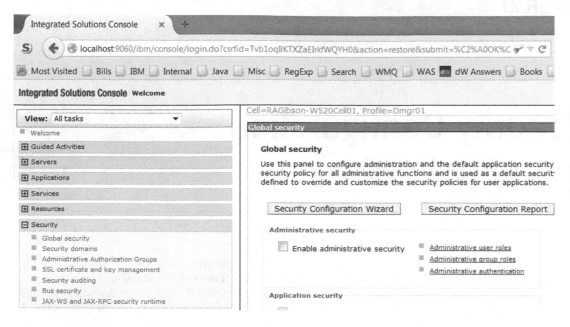

Figure 21-1. *Generating a security configuration report*

This causes a browser page to be displayed containing the security report. Figure 21-2 shows the top of one such configuration report browser page.

Console Name	Security Configuration Name	Value
Security Settings		
Active authentication mechanism	activeAuthMechanism	LTPA_1
User account repository	activeUserRegistry	WIMUser
Allow basic authentication	allowBasicAuth	true
Application security	appEnabled	false
Authentication cache timeout	cacheTimeout	600 seco
Default SSL settings	defaultSSLSettings	SSLConfi
Dynamically update run time when SSL configuration changes occur	dynamicallyUpdateSSLConfig	true
Administrative security	enabled	true
Restrict access to resource authentication data	enforceFineGrainedJCASecurity	false
Java 2 security	enforceJava2Security	false
Warn if applications are granted custom permissions	issuePermissionWarning	true
Use realm-qualified user names	useDomainQualifiedUserNames	false
Use the local security server	useLocalSecurityServer	true
Authentication mechanisms and expiration		

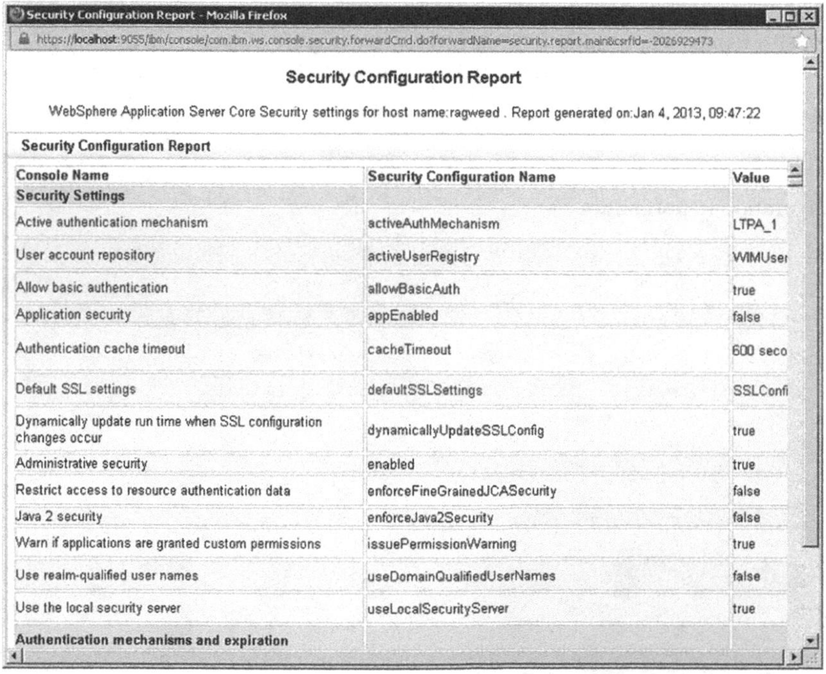

Figure 21-2. *Sample Security Configuration Report output*

Do you see any problem with this? My biggest complaint about this report is that it is very static. About the only thing that you can do with it is to use the text-searching capability of the browser to locate specific text. These steps were tested on three different versions of the WebSphere Application Server product and are the same for versions 7.0, 8.0, and 8.5, which is good. It makes it easier to describe it here. The biggest challenge that I encountered in verifying these steps in this version is the fact that I had to see which, if any, of the deployment managers were active, start those that weren't currently active, log into the administration console, and check the steps.

The next challenge was consuming the report data. The browser page produced when the report button is selected is, in a word, huge. The good news, however, is that it is in a table format, with each section having its own header row shaded in a different color. The report is so big because there are about two dozen sections and some of the sections are quite large. In fact, some of the sections have more than 300 rows of information. In case you are interested, I've included the script that I used to determine this information—reportSectionSize.py—in the code\Chap_21 directory.

The Scripting Report Method

Since you're interested in accessing this information using an wsadmin script, you need to determine whether there is a command or scripting object method that allows you access to this information. You can even use the WSAShelp.py script from the previous chapter to locate it.

Choose the Show ➤ Highlight Text menu and move through the various tabs. You'll see that there isn't a method with a name or abstract that contains the word "report." Use the Show ➤ AdminTask ➤ -commands filtering mechanism to verify that the only commands that include "eport" (the "r" is omitted to avoid case-sensitive returns) are those shown in Figure 21-3.

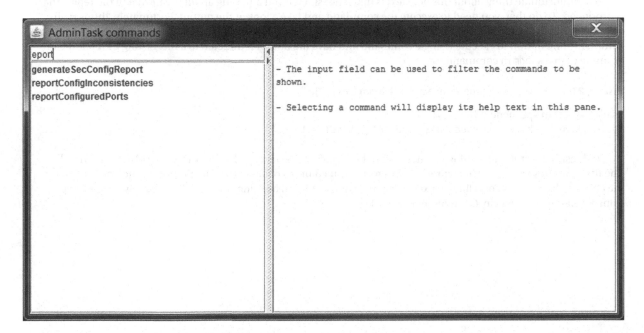

Figure 21-3. *AdminTask commands containing "eport"*

Select the first option—generateSecConfigReport—and click on the top one-touch expansion icon on the divider. You'll see an image similar to Figure 21-4.

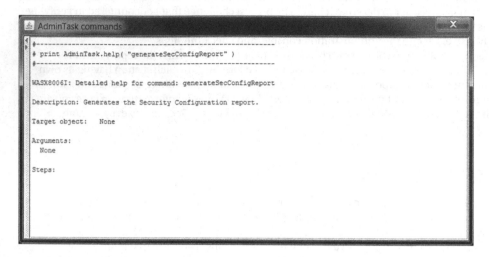

```
 AdminTask commands                                                    x

 #--------------------------------------------------------------
 # print AdminTask.help( "generateSecConfigReport" )
 #--------------------------------------------------------------

 WASX8006I: Detailed help for command: generateSecConfigReport

 Description: Generates the Security Configuration report.

 Target object:   None

 Arguments:
   None

 Steps:
```

Figure 21-4. *AdminTask commands containing "eport"*

The unfortunate thing about this help text is that it doesn't tell you anything about the format of the report that is produced. To do that, you need to execute the command and take a look at the output. Fortunately, this is really easy to do with the wsadmin command. Because of the number of lines generated, I suggest that you use the wsadmin -c command-line option to execute a single command and have the output redirected to a file. Listing 21-1 shows an example of this wsadmin command.[1]

Listing 21-1. Sending the generateSecConfigReport to a File

```
wsadmin -conntype none -lang jython -c \
"print AdminTask.generateSecConfigReport()" >SecCfgRpt.txt
```

It doesn't take too much effort to understand the format of the data produced by this AdminTask command. The first few lines are shown in Figure 21-5. There are four columns of data on each line, and semicolons (;) delimit the column data. The second line of text corresponds to the column headings on the table (the rows containing Console Name and Security Configuration Name).

---

[1]The -lang jython command-line option is needed only if you haven't changed the default scripting language in the appropriat wsadmin.properties file. The -conntype none option tells wsadmin to execute in local mode, so no connection is attempted to a possibly inactive application server. It is important to remember that the command should appear on a single line. The backslash\isn't actually part of the command and should not be entered.

```
DOMAIN ; Cell ; resourceName ; resourceType ;
Console Name ; Security Configuration Name ; Value ; Console Path Name ;
_Security Settings ;    ;    ;    ;
Active authentication mechanism ; activeAuthMechanism ; LTPA_1 ; …
```

Figure 21-5. *Example security report output*

Each section heading row has a leading underscore (_) in front of the section heading (such as _Security Settings). The rows that follow contain the values for each row in the table.[2]

First Attempt

Let's see what it takes to process this information using the data format that was just discussed, and see how it looks. Listing 21-2 shows the first (arguably quick and dirty) attempt at doing this.

Listing 21-2. SecConfigReport_01.py—Quick and Dirty Attempt

```
 7|class SecConfigReport_01( java.lang.Runnable ) :
 8|    def run( self ) :
 9|        frame = JFrame(
10|            'SecConfigReport_01',
11|            size = ( 300, 300 ),
12|            locationRelativeTo = None,
13|            defaultCloseOperation = JFrame.EXIT_ON_CLOSE
14|        )
15|        data = []
16|        text = AdminTask.generateSecConfigReport()
17|        for line in text.splitlines()[ 2: ] :
18|            data.append(
19|                [ info.strip() for info in line.split( ';' ) ]
20|            )
21|        frame.add(
22|            JScrollPane(
23|                JTable( data, ';;;;'.split( ';' ) )
24|            )
25|        )
26|        frame.pack()
27|        frame.setVisible( 1 )
```

Figure 21-6 shows the output that is produced when this script is executed. The good news is that you don't have to invest too much time or effort into this application. The bad news is that this lack of effort shows.

---

[2]In fact, this information is how the reportSectionSize.py script processes the data to determine the number and sizes of the report sections.

_Security Setti...				
Active authenti...	activeAuthMec...	LTPA_1	Security > Glo...	
User account ...	activeUserRe...	WIMUserRegi...	Security > Glo...	
Allow basic a...	allowBasicAuth	true	Security > Glo...	
Application se...	appEnabled	false	Security > Glo...	
Authentication...	cacheTimeout	600 seconds	Security > Glo...	
Default SSL s...	defaultSSLSet...	SSLConfig_1	Security > SS...	
Dynamically u...	dynamicallyU...	true	Security > SS...	
Administrative...	enabled	true	Security > Glo...	
Restrict acces...	enforceFineGr...	false	Security > Glo...	
Java 2 security	enforceJava2...	false	Security > Glo...	
Warn if applic...	issuePermiss...	true	Security > Glo...	
Use realm-qu...	useDomainQ...	false	Security > Glo...	
Use the local ...	useLocalSec...	true	Security > Glo...	
_Authenticatio...			Security > Glo...	
Authentication...	authConfig	system.KRB5	Security > Glo...	
Authentication...	authContextl...	com.ibm.ISec...	Security > Glo...	
Authentication...	authValidation...	system.KRB5	Security > Glo...	
Enable deleg...	enabledGssC...	true	Security > Glo...	
Kerberos conf...	krb5Config		Security > Glo...	
Kerberos keyt...	krb5Keytab		Security > Glo...	
Kerberos real...	krb5Realm		Security > Glo...	
Kerberos serv...	krb5Spn	WAS/${HOST}	Security > Glo...	
Simple authe...	simpleAuthCo...	system.KRB5	Security > Glo...	
Trim Kerbero...	trimUserName	true	Security > Glo...	

Figure 21-6. *Output of SecConfigReport_01.py*

From this output, you can see that each cell in the last column is empty. That's a little strange, isn't it? Based on this information, I took another, closer look at the text returned by the AdminTask command and found that every line ends with a semicolon, followed by a space (that's ";"). So, you can take this into account and remove this extraneous delimiting data in your subsequent attempts.

The other thing that this first attempt shows is that the time needed to process the text, although it wasn't insignificant, wasn't exactly terrible, at least on the machine that I was using. You will need to decide if the data processing should be performed on a separate thread, and if so, what the application should display while this processing is occurring.

Second Attempt, Ignoring the Last Delimiter

This next attempt focuses on fixing those immediately obvious shortcomings. This requires two changes to the code. Listing 21-3 shows these modifications.

Listing 21-3. SecConfigReport_02.py—Modified Lines

```
   |         ...
 17|         for line in text.splitlines()[ 2: ] :
 18|             data.append(
 19|                 [
 20|                     info.strip() for info in
 21|                     line[ :-2 ].split( ';' )
 22|                 ]
 23|             )
```

```
24|        frame.add(
25|            JScrollPane(
26|                JTable( data, ';;;'.split( ';' ) )
27|            )
28|        )
  |        ...
```

1. Instead of splitting each line of text using the semicolon delimiter, you simply need to ignore the last two characters of each line. To understand this change, compare line 19 in Listing 21-2 with lines 19-22 in Listing 21-3. The only reason that this list is shown on multiple lines in Listing 21-3 is to fit better within the book's margins.

2. Since you are removing and ignoring the last delimiter from each line, you also need to remove one of the semicolons in the second parameter of the JTable instantiation. This is so the empty header array has the same number of columns as the data array parameter.

Figure 21-7 shows the resulting output of this application. Notice the empty last column that you saw in the first attempt is now gone.

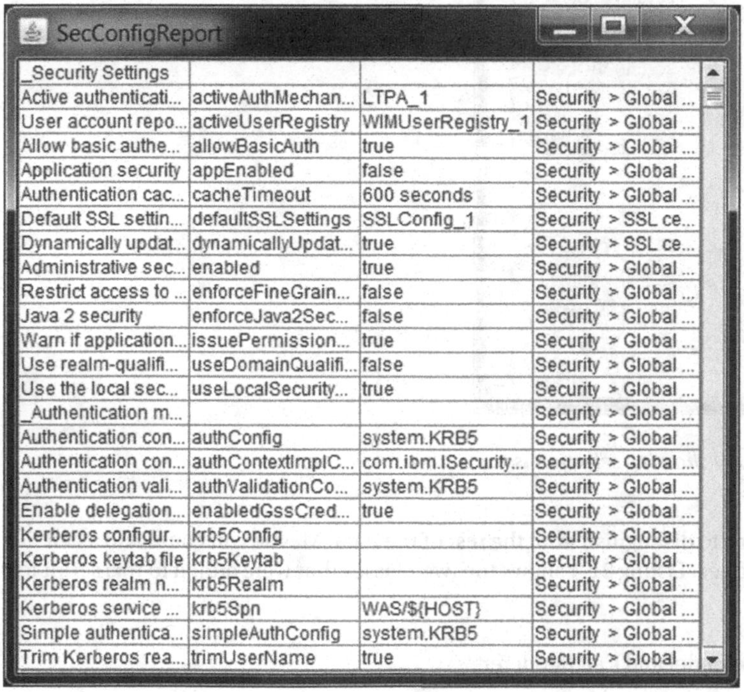

Figure 21-7. Initial output of SecConfigReport_02.py

Adding a Table Model and Cell Renderer

If you test the application, it shouldn't take long to figure out that, as discussed in Chapter 12, the default values used by the JTable class may not be best fit for this application. For example, is there any reason that you would want the user to be able to modify any of the table cells? Not if you want to create an application that can display security configuration settings.

Another default setting that doesn't work well here is the fact that the user can select multiple non-contiguous rows. Figure 21-8 shows this multiple selection issue at work.

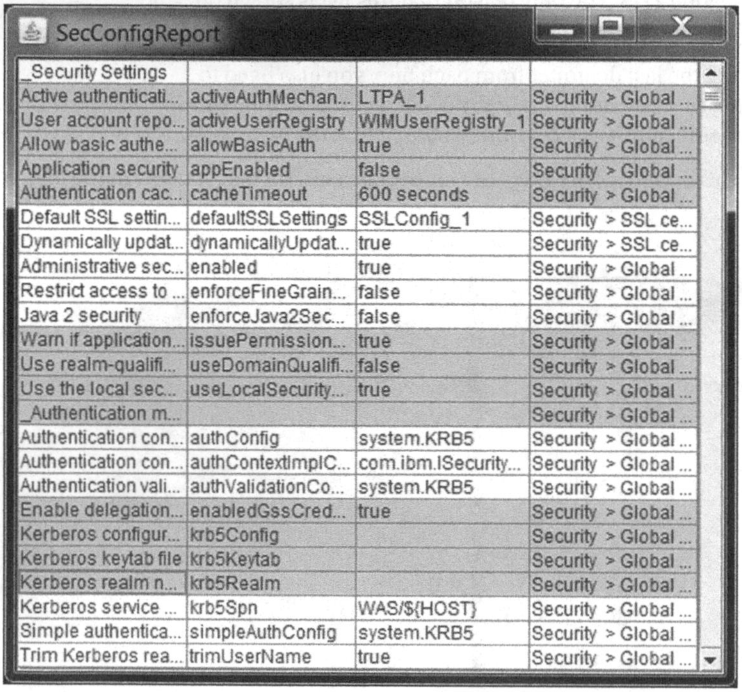

Figure 21-8. *Output of SecConfigReport_02.py showing selection issue*

It's also not great that the sections are hard to distinguish from the rest of the data. Maybe you could add a cell renderer to make these rows easier to find and see. Listing 21-4 shows the two classes that were added to this script for the table model and cell renderer instances.

Listing 21-4. SecConfigReport_03.py—TableModel and Cell Renderer

```
12|class reportTableModel( DefaultTableModel ) :
13|    def __init__( self, data, headings ) :
14|        DefaultTableModel.__init__( self, data, headings )
15|    def isCellEditable( self, row, col ) :
16|        return 0
17|    def getColumnClass( self, col ) :
18|        return String
```

```
19|class reportRenderer( DefaultTableCellRenderer ) :
20|    def getTableCellRendererComponent(
21|        self,
22|        table,                # JTable  - table containing value
23|        value,                # Object  - value being rendered
24|        isSelected,           # boolean - Is value selected?
25|        hasFocus,             # boolean - Does this cell have focus?
26|        row,                  # int     - Row # ( 0 .. N-1 )
27|        col                   # int     - Col # ( 0 .. N-1 )
28|    ) :
29|        DTCR = DefaultTableCellRenderer
30|        comp = DTCR.getTableCellRendererComponent(
31|            self, table, value, isSelected, hasFocus, row, col
32|        )
33|        if value :
34|            if table.getValueAt( row, 0 ).startswith( '_' ) :
35|                if col == 0 :
36|                    value = value[ 1: ]
37|                comp.setText( '<html><b>%s</b>' % value )
38|        return comp
```

Figure 21-9 shows the effects of these changes. This is a real improvement. I'm not sure if displaying the section row data in bold is good enough, but it does make it easier to locate these rows, doesn't it?

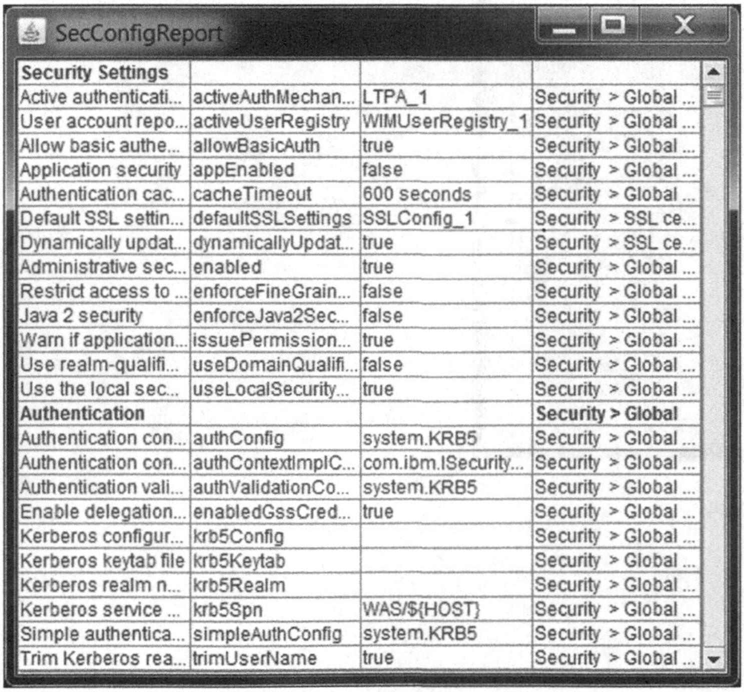

Figure 21-9. *Output of SecConfigReport_03.py*

Using Color Instead of a Bold Font

Wait a minute, since you're using HTML to make the section rows bold, why don't you just use HTML to add color instead? Listing 21-5 shows the changes made to SecConfigReport_04.py to do just this.

Listing 21-5. SecConfigReport_04.py—HTML Coloring

```
33|        html = '<html><font bgcolor=blue color=white>%s</font>'
34|        if value :
35|            if table.getValueAt( row, 0 ).startswith( '_' ) :
36|                if col == 0 :
37|                    value = value[ 1: ]
38|                comp.setText( html % value )
```

This should solve the problem, right? Well, not quite. Figure 21-10 shows that for empty cells the HTML coloring has no effect.

Security Settings			
Active authenticati...	activeAuthMechan...	LTPA_1	Security > Global ...
User account repo...	activeUserRegistry	WIMUserRegistry_1	Security > Global ...
Allow basic authe...	allowBasicAuth	true	Security > Global ...
Application security	appEnabled	false	Security > Global ...
Authentication cac...	cacheTimeout	600 seconds	Security > Global ...
Default SSL settin...	defaultSSLSettings	SSLConfig_1	Security > SSL ce...
Dynamically updat...	dynamicallyUpdat...	true	Security > SSL ce...
Administrative sec...	enabled	true	Security > Global ...
Restrict access to ...	enforceFineGrain...	false	Security > Global ...
Java 2 security	enforceJava2Sec...	false	Security > Global ...
Warn if application...	issuePermission...	true	Security > Global ...
Use realm-qualifi...	useDomainQualifi...	false	Security > Global ...
Use the local sec...	useLocalSecurity...	true	Security > Global ...
Authentication			Security > Global
Authentication con...	authConfig	system.KRB5	Security > Global ...
Authentication con...	authContextImplC...	com.ibm.ISecurity...	Security > Global ...
Authentication vali...	authValidationCo...	system.KRB5	Security > Global ...
Enable delegation...	enabledGssCred...	true	Security > Global ...
Kerberos configur...	krb5Config		Security > Global ...
Kerberos keytab file	krb5Keytab		Security > Global ...
Kerberos realm n...	krb5Realm		Security > Global ...
Kerberos service ...	krb5Spn	WAS/${HOST}	Security > Global ...
Simple authentica...	simpleAuthConfig	system.KRB5	Security > Global ...
Trim Kerberos rea...	trimUserName	true	Security > Global ...

Figure 21-10. Output of SecConfigReport_04.py

You can solve this problem by remembering that the JLabel component that's used by the renderer also has color properties. Don't forget that the component is reused for every cell of the same type, so if you are going to change the cell color for section row cells, you also have to do so for every other cell in the table. Listing 21-6 shows the cell renderer class from SecConfigReport_05.py.

Listing 21-6. SecConfigReport_05.py—Revised Cell Renderer

```
20|class reportRenderer( DefaultTableCellRenderer ) :
21|    def __init__( self ) :
22|        self.bg = self.fg = None
23|    def getTableCellRendererComponent(
24|        self,
25|        table,                 # JTable  - table containing value
26|        value,                 # Object  - value being rendered
27|        isSelected,            # boolean - Is value selected?
28|        hasFocus,              # boolean - Does this cell have focus?
29|        row,                   # int     - Row # ( 0 .. N-1 )
30|        col                    # int     - Col # ( 0 .. N-1 )
31|    ) :
32|        DTCR = DefaultTableCellRenderer
33|        comp = DTCR.getTableCellRendererComponent(
34|            self, table, value, isSelected, hasFocus, row, col
35|        )
36|        if self.bg == self.fg :
37|            self.bg = comp.getBackground()
38|            self.fg = comp.getForeground()
39|        if value :
40|            if table.getValueAt( row, 0 ).startswith( '_' ) :
41|                comp.setBackground( Color.blue )
42|                comp.setForeground( Color.white )
43|                if col == 0 :
44|                    value = value[ 1: ]
45|                comp.setText( '<html><b>%s</b>' % value )
46|            else :
47|                comp.setBackground( self.bg )
48|                comp.setForeground( self.fg )
49|        return comp
```

What does this do for the application output? Figure 21-11 shows that this significantly improves the application's output.

Security Settings			
Active authenticati...	activeAuthMechan...	LTPA_1	Security > Global ...
User account repo...	activeUserRegistry	WIMUserRegistry_1	Security > Global ...
Allow basic authe...	allowBasicAuth	true	Security > Global ...
Application security	appEnabled	false	Security > Global ...
Authentication cac...	cacheTimeout	600 seconds	Security > Global ...
Default SSL settin...	defaultSSLSettings	SSLConfig_1	Security > SSL ce...
Dynamically updat...	dynamicallyUpdat...	true	Security > SSL ce...
Administrative sec...	enabled	true	Security > Global ...
Restrict access to ...	enforceFineGrain...	false	Security > Global ...
Java 2 security	enforceJava2Sec...	false	Security > Global ...
Warn if application...	issuePermission...	true	Security > Global ...
Use realm-qualifi...	useDomainQualifi...	false	Security > Global ...
Use the local sec...	useLocalSecurity...	true	Security > Global ...
Authentication			Security > Global
Authentication con...	authConfig	system.KRB5	Security > Global ...
Authentication con...	authContextImplC...	com.ibm.ISecurity...	Security > Global ...
Authentication vali...	authValidationCo...	system.KRB5	Security > Global ...
Enable delegation...	enabledGssCred...	true	Security > Global ...
Kerberos configur...	krb5Config		Security > Global ...
Kerberos keytab file	krb5Keytab		Security > Global ...
Kerberos realm n...	krb5Realm		Security > Global ...
Kerberos service ...	krb5Spn	WAS/${HOST}	Security > Global ...
Simple authentica...	simpleAuthConfig	system.KRB5	Security > Global ...
Trim Kerberos rea...	trimUserName	true	Security > Global ...

Figure 21-11. *Output of SecConfigReport_05.py*

Adjusting Column Widths

If you take another look at any of the preceding figures that show the output from any of the scripts, you should notice that even though all of the tables are within scroll panes, only vertical scrollbars are visible. Why do you think that is? Taking a closer look at the tables should give you a hint. The width of the table is fixed, and by default, each column is allocated the same amount of horizontal space. When a value can't be displayed in the available column space, the value is truncated and ellipses appear.

Unfortunately, the table doesn't have any column headings, so you can't adjust the width of individual columns. You can only maximize the application and hope that the screen on which the application is being displayed is wide enough to allow all of the available information. This isn't a good choice for developers. What you need to do is figure how to deal with this and make some changes to the application so that the users can see all of the information that exists.

In Chapter 20, you learned that you can use the renderer to deal with cells where the data was too wide for the available space. Let's take a closer look at the data that exists in each column to see if you can do the same kind of thing with this application. You can write a quick script to tell you about the maximum number of characters in each column. Note that the last column has a number of entries that contain the arrow, or greater than, symbol >. While you're finding the width of each column, you can also count the maximum number of arrows in each column. Listing 21-7 shows the processReport routine from the columnInfo1.py script; you can find it in the code\Chap_21 directory.

Listing 21-7. The processReport Routine from the columnInfo1.py Script

```
 1|def columnInfo1() :
 2|    widths  = [ 0 ] * 5
 3|    arrows  = [ 0 ] * 5
 4|    report = AdminTask.generateSecConfigReport()
 5|    for line in report.splitlines()[ 2: ] :
 6|        col = 0
 7|        for cell in line.split( ';' ) :
 8|            widths[ col ] = max(
 9|                len( cell.strip() ),
10|                widths[ col ]
11|            )
12|            arrows[ col ] = max(
13|                cell.count( '>' ),
14|                arrows[ col ]
15|            )
16|            col += 1
17|    print ' widths:', widths
18|    print ' arrows:', arrows
```

Figure 21-12 shows the results of using this script on the three most current versions of WebSphere Application Server.

```
* WebSphere version 7.0
  widths: [70, 56, 131, 128, 0]
  arrows: [0, 0, 0, 4, 0]

* WebSphere version 8.0
  widths: [83, 56, 131, 128, 0]
  arrows: [0, 0, 0, 4, 0]

* WebSphere version 8.5
  widths: [83, 55, 131, 128, 0]
  arrows: [0, 0, 0, 4, 0]
```

Figure 21-12. *Output of the columnInfo1.py script*

If you are going to have the cell renderer process the cell data and possibly use HTML to display the cell contents on multiple lines, any routine that determines the preferred column width should use the same kind of processing to more accurately determine the widest line in the column cells. Looking at the results in Figure 21-12, you'll want to take a closer look at the contents of third and fourth columns to reduce the width requirements for these columns.

Column Widths and Row Heights

The next iteration of the script, SecConfigReport_06.py, adds a routine to process the data to determine the maximum width of each column. It also sets the height of each row based on the space required to display the data in the available column width. Listings 21-8 and 21-9 show the setColumnWidths() method.

Listing 21-8. Part 1 of the setColumnWidths(...) Method from SecConfigReport_06.py

```
88|    def setColumnWidths( self, table ) :
89|        tcm    = table.getColumnModel() # Table Column Model
90|        model  = table.getModel()       # access the table data
91|        margin = tcm.getColumnMargin()  # gap between columns
92|        rows = model.getRowCount()      # How many rows    exist?
93|        cols = tcm.getColumnCount()     # How many columns exist?
94|        labels = [
95|            JLabel( font = plainFont ),
96|            JLabel( font = boldFont  )
97|        ]
98|        print '               Now Min Pre Max'
99|        print '---------------+---+---+---+---'
100|        metrics = [ fmPlain, fmBold ]
101|        tWidth = 0                      # Table width
102|        section = 0                     # is this row a section?
103|        sections = 0                    # Number of sections
104|        for i in range( cols ) :        # i == column index
105|            col = tcm.getColumn( i )
106|            idx = col.getModelIndex()
107|            cWidth = 0                  # Initial column width
108|            for row in range( rows ) :
109|                v0 = model.getValueAt( row, 0 )
110|                if v0.startswith( '_' ) :
111|                    section = 1
112|                    sections += 1
113|                else :
114|                    section = 0
115|                comp = labels[ section ]
116|                fm   = metrics[ section ]       # FontMetric
117|                r = table.getCellRenderer( row, i )
118|                v = model.getValueAt( row, idx )
119|                if v.startswith( '_' ) :
120|                    v = v[ 1: ]
121|                comp.setText( v )
122|                cWidth = max(
123|                    cWidth,
124|                    comp.getPreferredSize().width
125|                )
```

One thing that might catch your eye when you look at Listing 21-8 is the code on lines 111 and 112. What's the difference between the section and sections variables? The former is used to indicate when the current row is a section header. So its value will be 0 or 1 to indicate this. If you search for occurrences of this variable, you will see where it is used as an index to both the labels and metrics arrays (lines 115 and 116). The sections variable is used to count the total number of sections processed in the report.

Listing 21-9. Part 2 of the setColumnWidths(...) Method from SecConfigReport_06.py

```
126|            if cWidth > 0 :
127|                col.setMinWidth( 128 + margin )
128|                col.setPreferredWidth( 128 + margin )
129|                col.setMaxWidth( cWidth + margin )
130|                print 'Col: %d  widths |%3d|%3d|%3d|%d' % (
131|                    i,
132|                    col.getWidth(),
133|                    col.getMinWidth(),
134|                    col.getPreferredWidth(),
135|                    col.getMaxWidth()
136|                )
137|            tWidth += col.getPreferredWidth()
138|        print '---------------+---+---+---+---'
139|        h0 = table.getRowHeight()
140|        print 'rowHeight:', h0
141|        sections /= cols
142|        print '#Sections:', sections
143|        for row in range( rows ) :
144|            lines = 1
145|            for i in range( cols ) :
146|                col = tcm.getColumn( i )
147|                pre = col.getPreferredWidth()
148|                idx = col.getModelIndex()
149|                val = model.getValueAt( row, idx )
150|                if not i :
151|                    section = val.startswith( '_' )
152|                fm    = metrics[ section ]        # FontMetric
153|                lines = max(
154|                    lines, int(
155|                        round( fm.stringWidth( val ) / pre ) + 1
156|                    )
157|                )
158|            table.setRowHeight( row, lines * h0 )
159|        table.setPreferredScrollableViewportSize(
160|            Dimension(
161|                tWidth,
162|                sections * table.getRowHeight()
163|            )
164|        )
```

Figure 21-13 shows the output of SecConfigReport_06.py. Comparing this image with the one in Figure 21-11, you can see that the most significant difference is the heights of the individual rows.

Figure 21-13. *Output of SecConfigReport_06.py*

Adding a Frame Resize Listener

The next iteration of the script adds code to display the cell data (the width and height). Additionally, a new event handler routine determines how the information is displayed when the frame is resized. Listing 21-10 contains the source for this event handler.

Listing 21-10. The frameResized Method from SecConfigReport_07.py

```
82|    def frameResized( self, ce ) :
83|        try :
84|            table   = self.table
85|            model   = table.getModel()        # Access the table data
86|            width   = table.getParent().getExtentSize().getWidth()
87|            pWidth = int( width ) >> 2
88|            tcm     = table.getColumnModel() # Table Column Model
89|            margin = tcm.getColumnMargin()   # gap between columns
90|            cols    = tcm.getColumnCount()
91|            for c in range( cols ) :
92|                col = tcm.getColumn( c )
93|                w = min( col.getMaxWidth, pWidth )
94|                col.setWidth( w )
95|                col.setPreferredWidth( w )
96|            height = table.getRowHeight()
97|            for row in range( model.getRowCount() ) :
98|                table.setRowHeight( row, height )
99|            table.repaint()
100|        except :
101|            print '\nError: %s\nvalue: %s' % sys.exc_info()[ :2 ]
```

What does this mean as far as the application output is concerned? Figure 21-14 shows the initial, default rendering of the table and Figure 21-15 shows how the text changes when the frame, and therefore the table, are widened.

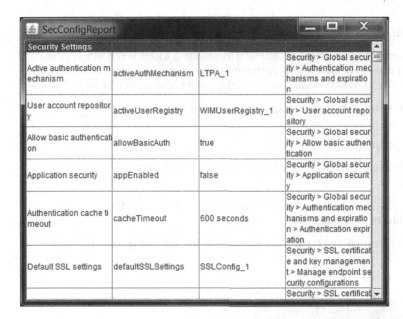

Figure 21-14. *Narrow output of* SecConfigReport_07.py

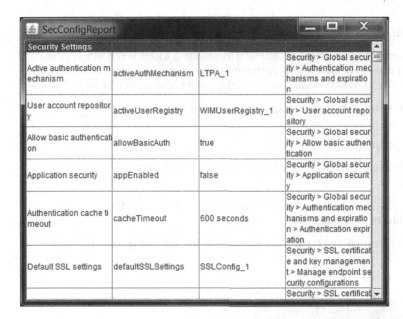

Figure 21-15. *Wider output of* SecConfigReport_07.py

Notice how the cell contents are wrapped (especially in the first and last columns). Figure 21-15 shows what happens to the cell contents when the frame is widened. It is important that you notice how the row heights are adjusted based on how much vertical space is required to display the text.

Fixing the Row Selection Colors

Unfortunately there is a problem with this iteration of the script. If you test it by selecting a row, you'll witness the problem. There is no visual indication that a row has been selected. Fortunately, the changes required to fix this issue are localized to the table cell renderer code. The most significant changes in the reportRenderer class are these:

- The constructor initializes some arrays to hold the background colors for both selected and unselected rows.

- The getTableCellRendererComponent(...) method now:

  - Saves the background and foreground colors for selected and unselected rows when they are first encountered.

  - Decides which background and foreground color to use based on whether a row is selected and whether it is one of the header rows.

Figure 21-16 shows the sample output of the modified code. It can be found in the SecConfigReport_08.py script file.

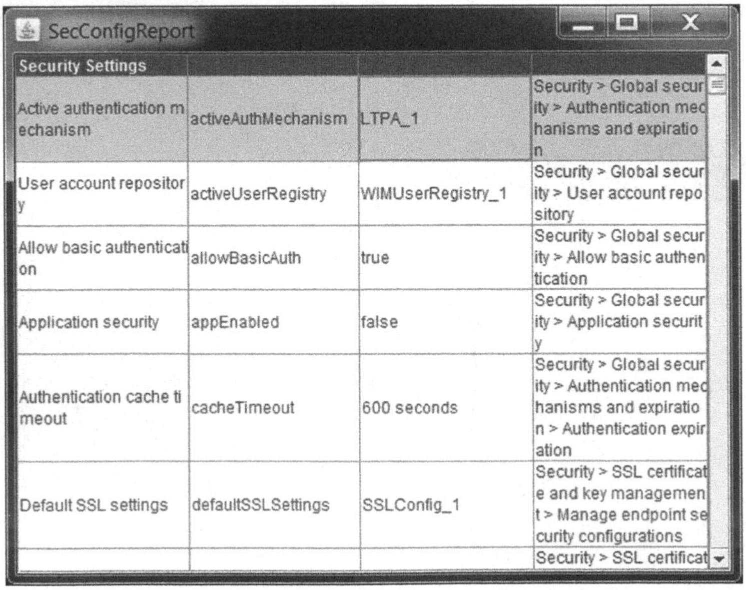

Figure 21-16. *Output of SecConfigReport_08.py*

Which Rows Are Visible?

The next iteration of the script, shown in SecConfigReport_09.py, adds a descendent of the ChangeListener class to monitor changes in the viewport (which is a kind of JViewport[3]), which is the parent of the JTable containing the application information.[4] When the user views a different part of the table, the change listener event handler is called and it prints some information about which rows of the table are visible. Listing 21-11 shows the rowFinder class from this iteration of the script.

Listing 21-11. The rowFinder Class from SecConfigReport_09.py

```
88|class rowFinder( ChangeListener ) :
89|    def __init__( self, table ) :
90|        self.table = table
91|    def stateChanged( self, ce ) :
92|        vPort = ce.getSource()
93|        table = self.table
94|        rect  = vPort.getViewRect()
95|        first = table.rowAtPoint(
96|            Point( 0, rect.y )
97|        )
98|        last  = table.rowAtPoint(
99|            Point( 0, rect.y + rect.height - 1 )
100|        )
101|        print 'rows: %d..%d  isValid: %d' % (
102|            first,
103|            last,
104|            vPort.isValid()
105|        )
```

I was hoping that the result of calling the isValid() method could be used to determine which rows are visible. Unfortunately, the result returned from this method wasn't quite what I expected. When it returns true, you can easily determine which rows are visible using code similar to Listing 21-11. However, the first and last rows that are visible include partial rows. So you can't use the result of this method to easily determine which complete table rows are visible. To do that requires additional computation.

If you look again at the output in Figure 21-17, you'll see that the routine is invoked multiple times. For most of these the result of the isValid() method is false. Eventually it will return a value of true, which is when you can determine which rows are partially visible. If you look back at Figure 21-16, you can see that rows 0 through 6 are fully visible, but only a little bit of row 7 is shown.

[3]See http://docs.oracle.com/javase/7/docs/api/javax/swing/JViewport.html.
[4]You can display the value returned by vPort.getClass(),which tells you that the variable refers to an instance of javax.swing. JViewport.

```
rows: 0..23  isValid: 0
rows: 0..23  isValid: 0
rows: 0..7  isValid: 0
rows: 0..23  isValid: 0
rows: 0..23  isValid: 0
rows: 0..7  isValid: 0
rows: 0..7  isValid: 0
rows: 0..7  isValid: 0
rows: 0..7  isValid: 1
```

Figure 21-17. Sample output of the rowFinder stateChanged(...) method

Table Alignment in the Viewport

The previous iteration shows that sometimes you try something and realize that it isn't going to work out as well as you had hoped. That's one of the really wonderful things about software. Unlike something like woodworking, software is infinitely malleable. You can change it and then change it right back if you don't like the change! In this next iteration, SecConfigReport_10.py, you'll remove the rowFinder class and add the upDownAction class shown in Listing 21-12.

Listing 21-12. Part 1 of the upDownAction Class from SecConfigReport_10.py

```
25|class upDownAction( AbstractAction ) :
26|    def __init__( self, table, keyName ) :
27|        self.table   = table
28|        ks           = KeyStroke.getKeyStroke( keyName )
29|        self.up      = keyName.find( 'UP' ) > -1
30|        self.action  = action = table.getInputMap(
31|            JComponent.WHEN_ANCESTOR_OF_FOCUSED_COMPONENT
32|        ).get( ks )
33|        self.original = table.getActionMap().get( action )
34|        self.table.getActionMap().put( action, self )
  |    ...
181|        keys = 'UP,DOWN,PAGE_UP,PAGE_DOWN,ctrl END'.split( ',' )
182|        for key in keys :
183|            upDownAction( table, key )
```

Don't be confused by the indentation in Listing 21-12. The last three lines (181-183) are not part of the upDownAction class constructor. They are, in fact, from the run(...) method of the SecConfigReport class. However, it is much easier to include them in this listing than it is to create one just for those three lines. Additionally, since these lines are the only reference to this class, it makes sense to show them here to allow for a more complete understanding of how the class is instantiated.

What does this class do? The hint can be found in lines 181-183. It is here that the class is used. Note how the class constructor uses the table instance and the name of a keystroke. In lines 26-34, you can see how the class constructor uses the table to determine the action currently associated with the specified keystroke. This action is saved in an instance variable (called self.original) and replaces it with the action being constructed.

Listing 21-13 shows the remainder of the upDownAction class, specifically the actionPerformed(...) method, which is invoked when a key-related event is generated. When the user presses any of these keys, the newly constructed Action instance is invoked. It uses the original keystroke action, and then adjusts the viewport to better align the table within the available space.

Without this alignment, the top and/or bottom of the viewport may be somewhere in the middle of the row. So, the top of the viewport could be bisecting the row, and the bottom of the viewport might be showing a similar fraction of the row at the bottom. The role of the upDownAction class is to adjust the viewport to align with the bottom of the last visible row when the keystroke used is moving down. When the direction is up, the alignment of the viewport will be with the top row visible row.

Why is this necessary? The simple answer is that when the table rows have variable heights, the default movement actions don't align the table rows nicely in the viewport. So, this is all related to the fact that the information you want to display doesn't fit well in the available horizontal space.

Listing 21-13. Part 2 of the upDownAction Class from SecConfigReport_10.py

```
35|    def actionPerformed( self, actionEvent ) :
36|        table = self.table
37|        self.original.actionPerformed( actionEvent )
38|        if self.action == 'selectLastRow' :
39|            self.original.actionPerformed( actionEvent )
40|        vPort = table.getParent()
41|        rect  = vPort.getViewRect()
42|        row = table.getSelectedRow()
43|        if row > -1 :
44|            cRect = table.getCellRect( row, 0, 1 )
45|            rBot  = rect.y + rect.height     # Bottom of viewPort
46|            cBot  = cRect.y + cRect.height # Bottom of cell
47|            if rect.y <= cRect.y and rBot >= cBot :
48|                return
49|        if self.up :
50|            first = table.rowAtPoint( Point( 0, rect.y ) )
51|            cell  = table.getCellRect( first, 0, 1 )
52|            diff  = rect.y - cell.y
53|        else :
54|            if row > -1 :
55|                cell  = table.getCellRect( row, 0, 1 )
56|            else :
57|                last  = table.rowAtPoint(
58|                    Point(
59|                        0,
60|                        rect.y + rect.height - 1
61|                    )
62|                )
```

```
63|              cell  = table.getCellRect( last, 0, 1 )
64|          bot  = rect.y + rect.height
65|          end  = cell.y + cell.height
66|          diff = end - bot
67|        point = vPort.getViewPosition()
68|        vPort.setViewPosition(
69|          Point( point.x, point.y + diff )
70|        )
```

Table Row Filtering

In this next iteration, called SecConfigReport_11.py, you add menu items and row filtering. What's row filtering? Well, you've already seen that the application can identify which rows are section heading rows.

When I was first thinking about this application, I wondered whether there was any easy way to make only specific sections of the report visible. I thought that maybe I could have each section on a CardLayout[5] (see Chapter 5) or on a JTabbedPane.[6] The problem with using a tabbed pane is that there are too many sections. An application with two dozen tabs wouldn't look very good, would it? If you used a CardLayout, you would need some way to specify which section should be displayed.

That's when I remembered row filtering. Row filtering enables your application to decide which table rows to display. What does that mean for the output?

Figure 21-18 shows some sample output of this iteration of the application. The first image shows the initial application display. Here you can see the new Show and Help menu items. The second image shows that the Show menu has three sub-menu items, called Collapse All, Expand All, and Exit. The last image shows the result of selecting Collapse All—the row filtering hides the non-section heading table rows.

---

[5]See http://docs.oracle.com/javase/7/docs/api/java/awt/CardLayout.html.
[6]See http://docs.oracle.com/javase/7/docs/api/javax/swing/JTabbedPane.html.

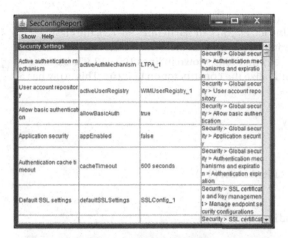

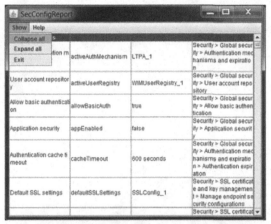

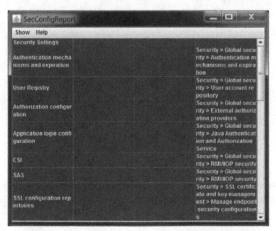

Figure 21-18. *Output of SecConfigReport_11.py*

Listing 21-14 shows the changes to SecConfigReport_11.py to make this happen. One of the interesting things is how simple the descendent of the abstract RowFilter class[7] is. In fact, as you can see in lines 98-100, the class needs only three lines. However, in order to do this, you need to add two methods to the table model class called reportTable Model—specifically the setVisible() and isVisible() methods shown in lines 109-112. These methods use a new class attribute—the self.visible array—to initialize the constructor on line 104. This array has a Boolean value indicating whether the corresponding row is visible.

Listing 21-14. Row Filtering Changes in SecConfigReport_11.py

```
 98|class sectionFilter( RowFilter ) :
 99|    def include( self, entry ) :
100|        return entry.getModel().isVisible( entry.getIdentifier() )
101|class reportTableModel( DefaultTableModel ) :
102|    def __init__( self, data, headings ) :
103|        DefaultTableModel.__init__( self, data, headings )
104|        self.visible = [ 1 ] * len( data )
   |    ...
109|    def isVisible( self, row ) :
110|        return self.visible[ row ]
111|    def setVisible( self, row, trueFalse ) :
112|        self.visible[ row ] = trueFalse
   |    ...
189|    def collapse( self, event ) :
190|        table = self.table
191|        model = table.getModel()
192|        for row in range( model.getRowCount() ) :
193|            model.setVisible(
194|                row,
195|                model.getValueAt( row, 0 ).startswith( '_' )
196|            )
197|        table.getRowSorter().setRowFilter(
198|            sectionFilter()
199|        )
   |    ...
202|    def expand( self, event ) :
203|        table = self.table
204|        model = table.getModel()
205|        for row in range( model.getRowCount() ) :
206|            model.setVisible( row, 1 )
207|        table.getRowSorter().setRowFilter(
208|            sectionFilter()
209|        )
```

The initial implementations of the event handler routines invoked by the menu items collapse the sections by setting the non-section rows visible entry to 0 (false) and expand the sections by setting every row's visible entry to 1 (true).

---

[7]See http://docs.oracle.com/javase/7/docs/api/javax/swing/RowFilter.html.

Finding Text

The next iteration, called SecConfigReport_12.py, adds another menu item so the users can specify text to be found and highlighted. This works in conjunction with row filtering so that the user can collapse all rows, find the text of interest, and make those rows visible as well. Figure 21-19 shows the sample output of this new feature.

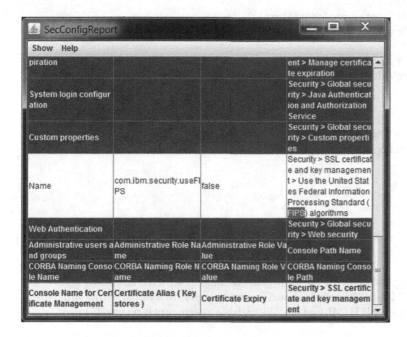

Figure 21-19. *Output of SecConfigReport_12.py*

The output shown in Figure 21-19 was produced using the following steps:

1. Choose Show ➤ Collapse All to hide all of the non-section heading rows.

2. Choose Show ➤ Find. Type FIPS in the input field and press the Enter key.

3. Press Ctrl-End to reposition the view to the bottom of the table.[8]

Listings 21-15 and 21-16 show the majority of the code changes required to add this capability to the script. One choice that made this change particularly easy was to add the findText attribute to the reportTableModel class. With this attribute and some getter and setter methods (getFindText(...) and setFindText(...)), the row filter class (sectionFilter) can easily determine what, if any, text needs to be located in the row to ensure that it will be displayed.

---

[8]Note that a different color scheme indicates when a section row is selected (as you can see on the last row of the table).

Listing 21-15. Part 1 of the Changes Made to SecConfigReport_12.py

```
 45|hilightHTML = '<font bgcolor="green" color="yellow">%s</font>'
   |...
 99|class sectionFilter( RowFilter ) :
100|    def include( self, entry ) :
101|        model    = entry.getModel()
102|        result   = model.isVisible( entry.getIdentifier() )
103|        findText = model.getFindText()
104|        if findText :
105|            for col in range( entry.getValueCount() ) :
106|                if entry.getStringValue( col ).find( findText ) > -
107|                    result = 1
108|                    break
109|        return result
110|class reportTableModel( DefaultTableModel ) :
111|    def __init__( self, data, headings ) :
   |        ...
114|        self.findText = None
   |    ...
121|    def getFindText( self ) :
122|        return self.findText
123|    def setFindText( self, text ) :
124|        self.findText = text
```

The table cell renderer, shown in Listing 21-16 can use the same getter method to see if the text needs to be matched and highlighted in the cell. The hilightHTML variable shown on line 189 refers to a global format string that is used to highlight the specified text using a simple HTML font tag. The variable assignment is on line 45 in Listing 21-15.

Listing 21-16. Part 2 of the Changes Made to SecConfigReport_12.py

```
127|class reportRenderer( DefaultTableCellRenderer ) :
   |        ...
181|            result = result.replace(
182|                '>', '&gt;'
183|            ).replace( '\n', '<br>' )
184|            findText = table.getModel().getFindText()
185|            if findText :
186|                if result.find( findText ) > -1 :
187|                    result = result.replace(
188|                        findText,
189|                        hilightHTML % findText
190|                    )
191|            value = '<html>' + result.replace( ' ', ' ' )
   |...
```

```
194|class SecConfigReport_12( java.lang.Runnable ) :
   |...
232|    def Find( self, event ) :
233|        result = JOptionPane.showInputDialog(
234|            self.frame,                    # parentComponent
235|            'Text to be found:'            # message text
236|        )
237|        self.table.getModel().setFindText( result )
238|        self.table.getRowSorter().setRowFilter(
239|            sectionFilter()
240|        )
```

This code simply locates instances of the user-specified text and replaces that text with the HTML that highlights the text for the user.

Section Visibility

If you use this iteration for a short time, you will find that being able to collapse and expand all sections is nice, but not quite good enough. Wouldn't it be great if you could show or hide individual sections simply by double-clicking on the section row?

Figure 21-20 shows a sample image from the latest iteration of the application, SecConfigReport_13.py. In it, you can see that all sections have been collapsed, and the view has been scrolled about half way down the table until the section named Management Scope is visible at the top of the viewport. The image shows the output after finding the rows containing scopeName; three additional rows are now visible.

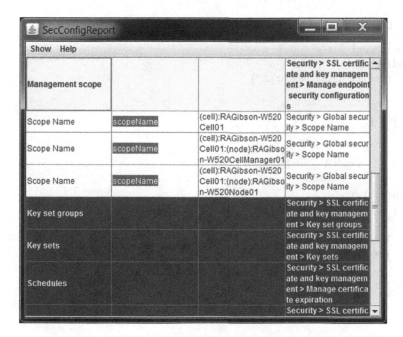

Figure 21-20. Output of SecConfigReport_13.py

411

Listings 21-16 through 21-20 show the code changes that provide this capability. Most of the changes are to the reportTableModel class in order to add attributes and methods to identify the sections in the table.

Let's start by taking a look at the modified sectionFilter class, which is shown in Listing 21-17. The only changes made here are on lines 101 through 103. The role of this method is to return true (1) when the row specified by the entry argument should be visible. In previous versions of this class, the row would be visible only if the whole section was visible or if the user specified some text that exists in the current row.

Listing 21-17. Modified sectionFilter Class from SecConfigReport_13.py

```
 98|class sectionFilter( RowFilter ) :
 99|    def include( self, entry ) :
100|        model   = entry.getModel()
101|        row     = entry.getIdentifier()
102|        section = model.getSectionNumber( row )
103|        result  = model.isRowVisible( row ) or
   |                      model.isSectionVisible( section )
104|        findText = model.getFindText()
105|        if findText :
106|            for col in range( entry.getValueCount() ) :
107|                if entry.getStringValue( col ).find( findText ) > -1 :
108|                    result = 1
109|                    break
110|        return result
```

Changes to the include(...) method (see line 103) assume that one section is visible. You can see this by collapsing all of the sections (choose Show ➤ Collapse All) and then double-clicking on one of the visible section headings.

Listing 21-18. The reportTableModel Class from SecConfigReport_13.py

```
111|class reportTableModel( DefaultTableModel ) :
112|    def __init__( self, data, headings ) :
113|        DefaultTableModel.__init__( self, data, headings )
114|        L = len( data )
115|        self.visible  = [ 1 ] * L
116|        self.sectionNumber = [ 0 ] * L
117|        self.sections = 0
118|        section = -1
119|        for i in range( L ) :
120|            row = data[ i ]
121|            if row[ 0 ].startswith( '_' ) :
122|                self.sections += 1
123|                section  += 1
124|            self.sectionNumber[ i ] = section
125|        self.sectionVisible = [ 1 ] * self.sections
126|        self.findText = None
127|    def getColumnClass( self, col ) :
128|        return String
129|    def getFindText( self ) :
130|        return self.findText
131|    def getSectionCount( self ) :
132|        return self.sections
```

```
133|    def getSectionNumber( self, row ) :
134|        try :
135|            result = self.sectionNumber[ row ]
136|        except :
137|            result = -1
138|        return result
139|    def isCellEditable( self, row, col ) :
140|        return 0
141|    def isSectionVisible( self, sectionNum ) :
142|        try :
143|            result = self.sectionVisible[ sectionNum ]
144|        except :
145|            result = 0
146|        return result
147|    def isRowVisible( self, row ) :
148|        return self.visible[ row ]
149|    def setFindText( self, text ) :
150|        self.findText = text
151|    def setSectionVisible( self, sectionNum, trueFalse ) :
152|        self.sectionVisible[ sectionNum ] = trueFalse
153|    def setRowVisible( self, row, trueFalse ) :
154|        self.visible[ row ] = trueFalse
```

The changes to the sectionFilter class are not the only ones you need to make; you also have to make some significant changes to the reportTableModel class. This revised class is shown in Listing 21-18. You should be able to see that most of the changes to this class deal with identifying sections and being able to determine the section number for each row in the data.

You also need to add a mouse listener event handler in the application class (SecConfigReport) to detect when the user double-clicks on the table. The mouseClicked event handler method shown in Listing 21-19 is added to each row of the table. It is important to note, however, that it only changes the visibility of a section by checking that the row that was double-clicked is a section heading (see line 241).

Listing 21-19. The clicker(...) Method in SecConfigReport_13.py

```
217|class SecConfigReport_13( java.lang.Runnable ) :
   |    ...
234|    def clicker( self, event ) :
235|        if event.getClickCount() == 2 :
236|            table = event.getSource()
237|            model = table.getModel()
238|            view  = row = table.getSelectedRow()
239|            if view > -1 :
240|                row = table.convertRowIndexToModel( view )
241|                if model.getValueAt( row, 0 ).startswith( '_' ) :
242|                    sNum = model.getSectionNumber( row )
243|                    model.setSectionVisible(
244|                        sNum,
245|                        not model.isSectionVisible( sNum )
246|                    )
```

```
247|                    else :
248|                        sNum = -1
249|                else :
250|                    sNum = -1
251|                table.getRowSorter().setRowFilter(
252|                    sectionFilter()
253|                )
```

The other significant changes are made to the Find(...) method so that it takes the table model section attributes and methods into account. The modified Find(...) method is shown in Listing 21-20.

Listing 21-20. Modified Find(...) Method from SecConfigReport_13.py

```
279|    def Find( self, event ) :
280|        table  = self.table
281|        cols   = table.getColumnModel().getColumnCount()
282|        model  = table.getModel()
283|        result = JOptionPane.showInputDialog(
284|            self.frame,                    # parentComponent
285|            'Text to be found:'            # message text
286|        )
287|        model.setFindText( result )
288|        for row in range( model.getRowCount() ) :
289|            visible = model.getValueAt(
290|                row,
291|                0
292|            ).startswith( '_' )
293|            if result and not visible :
294|                for col in range( cols ) :
295|                    val = model.getValueAt( row, col )
296|                    if val.find( result ) > -1 :
297|                        visible = 1
298|                        break
299|            model.setRowVisible( row, visible )
300|        table.getRowSorter().setRowFilter(
301|            sectionFilter()
302|        )
```

Does It Work?

One thing that you should have learned by this point is that you always need to test your applications to verify that they act as you expect. To see if the double-click event handler is doing its job, you can use the Show ➤ Collapse All menu selections, and then double-click the visible section heading rows to see if the associated rows become visible. This test appears to validate the expectations. What else can you test? Does it work correctly when you double-click a section heading row after expanding the rows? See Figure 21-21.

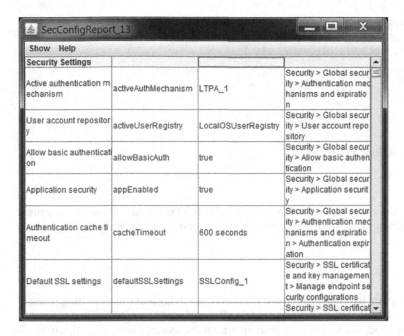

Figure 21-21. Testing SecConfigReport_13.py

Unfortunately, no, it doesn't. What's going on? Why doesn't it work correctly? Take another look at the include(...) method in the sectionFilter class in Listing 21-17. Under what conditions will a row be visible? Line 103 shows that in order for a row to be hidden, both isRowVisible(...) and isSectionVisible(...) must return false.

What happens to the mouseClicked event handler method when a section heading row is the target of the event? Which of these model properties is affected? Only the sectionVisible property is affected, so the visible property of each row in the section is unaffected. That's the problem right there. To fix this, the event handler has to change the visible property for each row in the section.

Listing 21-21 shows the modified clicker(...) method event handler. Note how the target row is verified as a section header row. Its new visibility is determined (line 243), set (line 244), and then used to assign the visibility of each row within the section (lines 245 through 249).

Listing 21-21. Modified clicker() Method from SecConfigReport_14.py

```
234|     def clicker( self, event ) :
235|         if event.getClickCount() == 2 :
236|             table = event.getSource()
237|             model = table.getModel()
238|             view  = row = table.getSelectedRow()
239|             if view > -1 :
240|                 row = table.convertRowIndexToModel( view )
241|                 if model.getValueAt( row, 0 ).startswith( '_' ) :
242|                     sNum = model.getSectionNumber( row )
243|                     vis  = not model.isSectionVisible( sNum )
244|                     model.setSectionVisible( sNum, vis )
```

```
245|                        for row in range( row + 1, model.getRowCount() ) :
246|                            if model.getSectionNumber( row ) == sNum :
247|                                model.setRowVisible( row, vis )
248|                            else :
249|                                break
250|                else :
251|                    sNum = -1
252|            else :
253|                sNum = -1
254|            table.getRowSorter().setRowFilter(
255|                sectionFilter()
256|            )
```

Please keep in mind that the event handler code should be done quickly. You don't want the routine to delay the update. If you test this version of the application, you'll see that the event handler doesn't take too long to complete.

Progress Indicator

In relation to the possibility of a delay in the event handler, I wondered also about the delay that was occurring when the script begins to execute. A bit of testing shows that there is a non-trivial amount of time required to execute the AdminTask.generateSecConfigReport() method. See for yourself. Start an interactive wsadmin session[9] and, when the command prompt is displayed, execute the generateSecConfigReport() method.[10] Take note of how long it takes to complete.

Based on this improved understanding of what was occurring, I tried a few things to display some kind of progress indicator to show the user that something was happening. Unfortunately, I didn't have much luck. My attempt to use a SwingWorker task to perform the AdminTask method call and display an indeterminate progress bar in a dialog box didn't work for some reason. I decided to use a different approach.

Listing 21-22 shows the changes made to this next iteration of the script. As you can see in lines 66-70, a trivial SwingWorker class performs the call to the AdminTask method on a background thread and makes the result available via a simple getter method.

Listing 21-22. Modified run(...) Method from SecConfigReport_15.py

```
66|class reportTask( SwingWorker ) :
67|    def doInBackground( self ) :
68|        self.results = AdminTask.generateSecConfigReport(
  |            ).splitlines()[ 2: ]
69|    def getResults( self ) :
70|        return self.results
  |...
```

```
9wsadmin -conntype none -lang jython
10text = AdminTask.generateSecConfigReport()
```

```
229|class SecConfigReport_15( java.lang.Runnable ) :
   |...
364|    def run( self ) :
365|        try :
366|            task = reportTask()
367|            task.execute()
368|            chars = r'-\|/'
369|            char  = 0
370|            while not task.isDone() :
371|                print '\b%s\b' % chars[ char ],
372|                sleep( 0.25 )
373|                char = ( char + 1 ) % len( chars )
374|            print '\b \b',
375|            info = task.getResults()
376|        except :
377|            print '\nError: %s\nvalue: %s' % sys.exc_info()[ :2 ]
378|            sys.exit()
   |...
```

Lines 366 and 367 show how this task instance is created and executed. You need to save a reference to the task instance object in order to call its getResults() method once the task is complete.[11] Lines 368-373 display a trivial character-oriented indicator to show that the AdminTask method call has not yet completed. Once the task is complete, its results are retrieved, and the application can get on with its purpose.

Is this application perfect? Absolutely not. As indicated earlier, it is merely a proof of concept (PoC). If you wanted to enhance it and use it in a more permanent arrangement, you could base those decisions on what you can see and do with this script. You could also use it to test possible enhancements or improvements.

Summary

The purpose of this chapter is twofold. First it is intended to show how easily you can turn a report into an interactive graphical user application. It is also intended to show that by taking small steps you can more easily verify that each iteration of the script works as it should. If it isn't, you can more easily determine the source of the problem and correct it.wsadmin

---

[11]Note the use of the isDone() method on line 370, which is used to determination when the background task is complete.

CHAPTER 22

■ ■ ■

WASports: A WebSphere Port Application

One of the first topics that grabbed my imagination when I started thinking about graphical wsadmin scripts was the possibility of displaying and managing all of the TCP/IP port numbers being used by a WebSphere Application Server cell. Trying to use the administration console to view the port numbers being used by all of the servers in a cell can be frustrating and tedious. I wanted an iterative graphical application that can be used to quickly and easily understand which application servers exist in the cell, and use a tree structure to show the hierarchical relationship between these servers. Additionally I wanted to be able to show the port numbers being used by each of these servers. This chapter shows how to build this application using the same type of iterative approach used previously.

Using the Administration Console

What does it take to use the Administration console to view the port numbers currently being used by a managed application server? The following steps are needed to view and change just one TCP/IP port number for an existing application server using the administrative console.

1. If the Deployment Manager is active, skip to Step 3.

2. Use the startManager command to start the Deployment Manager.

3. Use a browser to access the Administration console associated with the Deployment Manager. Enter the appropriate username and password to view the desired information.

4. Select and expand the Servers section in the left frame.

5. Select and expand the Server Types section.

6. Select the WebSphere Application Servers link.

7. Select the appropriate server link (such as server1).

8. Expand the Ports section under the Communications heading.

9. Use the Details button or the Ports link to show a table of the named endpoints and the associated port number values used by the specified application server.

10. Select the desired endpoint name to be modified, such as BOOTSTRAP_ADDRESS.

11. Modify the Port input field to identify the new port number value.

12. Select the Apply or OK button.

13. Select the Save link to update the master configuration.

14. After all the required changes have been made, stop and restart the server to use the modified port numbers.

Figure 22-1 shows a simple example of a table of the port numbers being used by a single application server. This corresponds to the kind of table that is the result of performing Step 8.

⊟ Ports

Port Name	Port
BOOTSTRAP_ADDRESS	2810
SOAP_CONNECTOR_ADDRESS	8881
ORB_LISTENER_ADDRESS	9102
SAS_SSL_SERVERAUTH_LISTENER_ADDRESS	9409
CSIV2_SSL_SERVERAUTH_LISTENER_ADDRESS	9408
CSIV2_SSL_MUTUALAUTH_LISTENER_ADDRESS	9407
WC_adminhost	9062
WC_defaulthost	9081
DCS_UNICAST_ADDRESS	9354
WC_adminhost_secure	9045
WC_defaulthost_secure	9444
SIP_DEFAULTHOST	5063
SIP_DEFAULTHOST_SECURE	5062
SIB_ENDPOINT_ADDRESS	7278
SIB_ENDPOINT_SECURE_ADDRESS	7287
SIB_MQ_ENDPOINT_ADDRESS	5559
SIB_MQ_ENDPOINT_SECURE_ADDRESS	5579
IPC_CONNECTOR_ADDRESS	9634

Figure 22-1. *Sample list of application server port settings*

If you view and modify the port numbers being used by the Deployment Manager or the node agents, you need to start by selecting and expanding the System Administration section instead of performing Steps 4 and 5. All this is used to show the number of steps needed to view and modify the port numbers being used by an application server using the administration console.

The AdminTask.listServerPorts( ) Method

Using the WAShelp.py script from Chapter 20, you can search for any scripting object methods that identify the ports being used by a server. Figure 22-2 shows what happens when you search for AdminTask methods containing the word "Ports" anywhere in the method name.

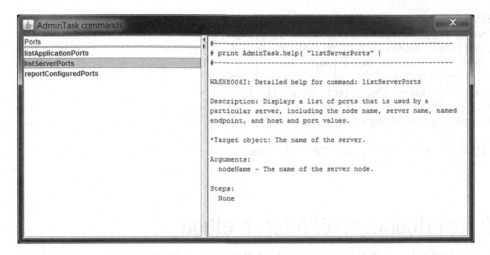

Figure 22-2. AdminTask methods with "Ports" in the name

The listServerPorts(...) method looks really promising. Let's see what it produces for the dmgr server.[1] The result is a string list identifying the port numbers configured for the specified application server. Unfortunately, the result of calling this method isn't as useful as you might hope it would be. Listing 22-1 shows some sample output from this method. Imagine the processing required to use this information. Few people would think the processing required to parse this output worth the effort. This is especially true since the information is more easily available using other techniques.

Listing 22-1. Sample AdminTask.listServerPorts(...) Output

```
wsadmin>print AdminTask.listServerPorts( 'dmgr' )
[[IPC_CONNECTOR_ADDRESS [[[host ${LOCALHOST_NAME}] [node RAGibson
-W520CellManager01] [server dmgr] [port 9632] ]]] ]
[[CSIV2_SSL_SERVERAUTH_LISTENER_ADDRESS [[[host RAGibson-W520.ral
eigh.ibm.com] [node RAGibson-W520CellManager01] [server dmgr] [po
rt 9403] ]]] ]
[[WC_adminhost [[[host *] [node RAGibson-W520CellManager01] [serv
er dmgr] [port 9060] ]]] ]
[[DataPowerMgr_inbound_secure [[[host *] [node RAGibson-W520CellM
anager01] [server dmgr] [port 5555] ]]] ]
[[DCS_UNICAST_ADDRESS [[[host *] [node RAGibson-W520CellManager01
] [server dmgr] [port 9352] ]]] ]
[[BOOTSTRAP_ADDRESS [[[host RAGibson-W520.raleigh.ibm.com] [node
RAGibson-W520CellManager01] [server dmgr] [port 9809] ]]] ]
[[SAS_SSL_SERVERAUTH_LISTENER_ADDRESS [[[host RAGibson-W520.ralei
gh.ibm.com] [node RAGibson-W520CellManager01] [server dmgr] [port
 9401] ]]] ]
```

---

[1]Note that if the server name is not unique, a qualifying -nodename parameter must be specified.

```
[[SOAP_CONNECTOR_ADDRESS [[[host RAGibson-W520.raleigh.ibm.com] [
node RAGibson-W520CellManager01] [server dmgr] [port 8879] ]]] ]
[[CELL_DISCOVERY_ADDRESS [[[host RAGibson-W520.raleigh.ibm.com] [
node RAGibson-W520CellManager01] [server dmgr] [port 7277] ]]] ]
[[ORB_LISTENER_ADDRESS [[[host RAGibson-W520.raleigh.ibm.com] [no
de RAGibson-W520CellManager01] [server dmgr] [port 9100] ]]] ]
[[CSIV2_SSL_MUTUALAUTH_LISTENER_ADDRESS [[[host RAGibson-W520.ral
eigh.ibm.com] [node RAGibson-W520CellManager01] [server dmgr] [po
rt 9402] ]]] ]
[[WC_adminhost_secure [[[host *] [node RAGibson-W520CellManager01
] [server dmgr] [port 9043] ]]] ]
wsadmin>
```

The AdminTask.reportConfiguredPorts() Method

The other interesting AdminTask method listed by the WAShelp script is the reportConfiguredPorts(...) method. Figure 22-3 shows the help text for this method.

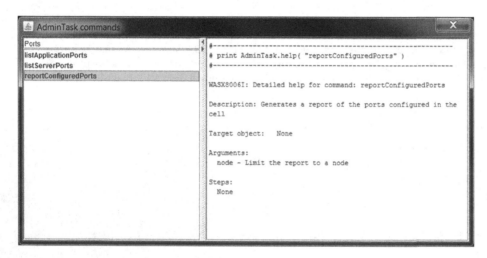

Figure 22-3. *Help text for AdminTask.reportConfiguredPorts(...) method*

The description of this method is quite promising. The real question though is what kind of output is generated by this method? Listing 22-2 shows the initial output generated by a call to the AdminTask.reportConfiguredPorts(...) method.

Listing 22-2. Initial Output of reportConfiguredPorts(...) Method Call

```
wsadmin>print AdminTask.reportConfiguredPorts()
Ports configured in cell RAGibson-W520Cell01

Node RAGibson-W520CellManager01 / Server dmgr
    RAGibson-W520.raleigh.ibm.com:7277 CELL_DISCOVERY_ADDRESS
    RAGibson-W520.raleigh.ibm.com:9809 BOOTSTRAP_ADDRESS
    ${LOCALHOST_NAME}:9632 IPC_CONNECTOR_ADDRESS
    RAGibson-W520.raleigh.ibm.com:8879 SOAP_CONNECTOR_ADDRESS
    RAGibson-W520.raleigh.ibm.com:9100 ORB_LISTENER_ADDRESS
    RAGibson-W520.raleigh.ibm.com:9401 SAS_SSL_SERVERAUTH_LIST...
    RAGibson-W520.raleigh.ibm.com:9402 CSIV2_SSL_MUTUALAUTH_LI...
    RAGibson-W520.raleigh.ibm.com:9403 CSIV2_SSL_SERVERAUTH_LI...
    *:9060 WC_adminhost
    *:9043 WC_adminhost_secure
    *:9352 DCS_UNICAST_ADDRESS
    *:5555 DataPowerMgr_inbound_secure
...
```

This certainly seems to be much easier to read and understand from the human perspective. However, some challenges remain if you intend to process this kind of result in your scripts.

Using AdminConfig Methods

In Chapter 11, you saw how easy it was to produce a tree hierarchy representing the cell.[2] Let's see what it takes to produce information about the nodes, servers, and their configured ports using a non-graphical script. Listing 22-3 shows most of the main routine needed to do just that.[3]

Listing 22-3. ListPorts Routine from the ListPorts.py Script[4]

```
42|def ListPorts() :
43|    gAV = getAttributeValue  # For line shortening purposes
44|    names = {}
45|    nodes = 0
46|    for node in AdminConfig.list( 'Node' ).splitlines() :
47|        nodes += 1
48|        names[ 'nodeName' ] = gAV( node, 'name' )
49|        names[ 'profName' ] = profileName( node )
50|        SEs = AdminConfig.list( 'ServerEntry', node )
51|        servers = 0
```

---

[2]For example, see the code\Chap_11\Tree4.py sample script.
[3]The complete script can be found in the code\Chap_22\ListPorts.py file.
[4]Remember that many of the scripts listed in the book are written to fit within the available horizontal space.

```
52|        for se in SEs.splitlines() :
53|            servers += 1
54|            names[ 'servName' ] = gAV( se, 'serverName' )
55|            names[ 'hosts' ] = ', '.join( getHostnames( se ) )
56|            print formatString % names
57|            data = []
58|            NEPs = AdminConfig.list( 'NamedEndPoint', se )
59|            for nep in NEPs.splitlines() :
60|                name = gAV( nep, 'endPointName' )
61|                epId = gAV( nep, 'endPoint' )
62|                port = gAV( epId, 'port' )
63|                data.append( ( port, name ) )
64|            data.sort( lambda a, b : cmp( a[ 1 ], b[ 1 ] ) )
65|            for port, name in data :
66|                print '%5d | %s' % ( port, name )
67|            print
```

What does the output of this script look like? Listing 22-4 shows the initial portion of the output generated when this script was executed using a WebSphere Application Server V 7.0 environment on my local machine.

Listing 22-4. Sample Output of the ListPorts.py Script

```
Profile name: Dmgr01
Host name(s): RAGibson-W520.raleigh.ibm.com
   Node name: RAGibson-W520CellManager01
 Server name: dmgr

Port | EndPoint Name
------+--------------
9809 | BOOTSTRAP_ADDRESS
7277 | CELL_DISCOVERY_ADDRESS
9402 | CSIV2_SSL_MUTUALAUTH_LISTENER_ADDRESS
9403 | CSIV2_SSL_SERVERAUTH_LISTENER_ADDRESS
9352 | DCS_UNICAST_ADDRESS
5555 | DataPowerMgr_inbound_secure
9632 | IPC_CONNECTOR_ADDRESS
9100 | ORB_LISTENER_ADDRESS
9401 | SAS_SSL_SERVERAUTH_LISTENER_ADDRESS
8879 | SOAP_CONNECTOR_ADDRESS
9060 | WC_adminhost
9043 | WC_adminhost_secure
```

The output produced by this simple script has some nice properties including the ease of reading and understanding the information. It also corresponds closely with the way in which information is displayed on the Administration console, as shown in Figure 22-1.

Step 0: Creating a WASports Application

Let's start by creating a simple empty frame application. I choose to call this step 0 because using an existing script template is so trivial. The code in Listing 22-5 should be very familiar to you by now, so I won't bother to elaborate. The only part that might not be familiar to you is in lines 18 and 19, where a JDesktopPane instance is created and used as the frame content pane. This is discussed in more detail in Chapter 19.

Listing 22-5. WASports Class from the WASports_00.py Script

```
 6|class WASports_00( java.lang.Runnable ) :
 7|    def run( self ) :
 8|        screenSize = Toolkit.getDefaultToolkit().getScreenSize()
 9|        w = screenSize.width  >> 1        # Use 1/2 screen width
10|        h = screenSize.height >> 1        # and 1/2 screen height
11|        x = ( screenSize.width  - w ) >> 1 # Top left corner
12|        y = ( screenSize.height - h ) >> 1
13|        frame = self.frame = JFrame(
14|            'WASports_00',
15|            bounds = ( x, y, w, h ),
16|            defaultCloseOperation = JFrame.EXIT_ON_CLOSE
17|        )
18|        desktop = JDesktopPane()
19|        frame.setContentPane( desktop )
20|        frame.setVisible( 1 )
```

Step 1: Adding an Empty Internal Frame

Next you need to add a little code to create an empty internal frame to the application desktop. Listing 22-6 shows how this is done in the next iteration of the WASports script (in WASports_01.py).

Listing 22-6. Defining and Using an InternalFrame Class

```
 9|class InternalFrame( JInternalFrame ) :
10|    def __init__( self, title, size, location, closable = 0 ) :
11|        JInternalFrame.__init__(
12|            self,
13|            title,
14|            resizable   = 1,
15|            closable    = closable,
16|            maximizable = 1,
17|            iconifiable = 1,
18|            size        = size
19|        )
20|        self.setLocation( location )
21|        self.setVisible( 1 )
```

```
22|class WASports_01( java.lang.Runnable ) :
23|    def run( self ) :
  |        ...
34|        desktop = JDesktopPane()
35|        internal = InternalFrame(
36|            'InternalFrame',
37|            size = Dimension( w >> 1, h >> 1 ),
38|            location = Point( 5, 5 )
39|        )
40|        desktop.add( internal )
41|        frame.setContentPane( desktop )
42|        frame.setVisible( 1 )
```

Step 2: Adding an Empty JSplitPane to the Internal Frame

Next you need to add an empty split pane to the internal frame. Listing 22-7 shows how easily this can be done. The code from this listing is from the WASports_02.py script file. The statement in line 30 is used to position the divider in the middle of the internal frame.

Listing 22-7. JSplitPane Code Added to WASports_02.py

```
11|class InternalFrame( JInternalFrame ) :
12|    def __init__( self, title, size, location, closable = 0 ) :
  |        ...
22|        self.setLocation( location )
23|        pane = self.add(
24|            JSplitPane(
25|                JSplitPane.HORIZONTAL_SPLIT,
26|                JLabel( 'Left' ),
27|                JLabel( 'Right' )
28|            )
29|        )
30|        pane.setDividerLocation( size.width >> 1 )
31|        self.setVisible( 1 )
```

The JLabel instances in this example are simple placeholders for other kinds of Swing components.

Step 3: Adding a Cell Hierarchy Tree to the JSplitPane

Listing 22-8 shows that very little new code is needed in the WASports_03.py script file in order to create a cell hierarchy tree on the left portion of the split pane. The cellTree(...) method (lines 40-54) contains code very similar to Listing 22-3.

Listing 22-8. JTree Code Added to WASports_03.py

```
15|class InternalFrame( JInternalFrame ) :
16|    def __init__( self, title, size, location, closable = 0 ) :
  |        ...
26|        self.setLocation( location )
27|        tree = self.cellTree()
28|        tree.getSelectionModel().setSelectionMode(
29|            TreeSelectionModel.SINGLE_TREE_SELECTION
30|        )
31|        pane = self.add(
32|            JSplitPane(
33|                JSplitPane.HORIZONTAL_SPLIT,
34|                JScrollPane( tree ),
35|                JLabel( 'Right' )
36|            )
37|        )
38|        pane.setDividerLocation( size.width >> 1 )
39|        self.setVisible( 1 )
40|    def cellTree( self ) :
41|        cell = AdminConfig.list( 'Cell' )
42|        root = DefaultMutableTreeNode( self.getName( cell ) )
43|        for node in AdminConfig.list( 'Node' ).splitlines() :
44|            here = DefaultMutableTreeNode(
45|                self.getName( node )
46|            )
47|            servers = AdminConfig.list( 'Server', node )
48|            for server in servers.splitlines() :
49|                leaf = DefaultMutableTreeNode(
50|                    self.getName( server )
51|                )
52|                here.add( leaf )
53|            root.add( here )
54|        return JTree( root )
55|    def getName( self, configId ) :
56|        return AdminConfig.showAttribute( configId, 'name' )
```

It's probably about time to see some sample output of this iteration of the WASports script. Figure 22-4 shows that the WASports application is starting to take shape. The application frame and internal frame can be moved, resized, and so on, as the user desires. It also limits the number of tree nodes that may be selected at one time.

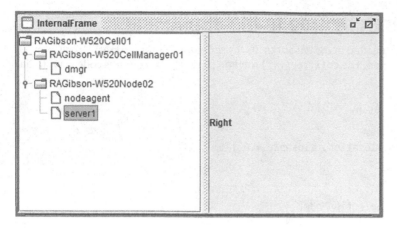

Figure 22-4. *Sample output of the WASports_03.py script*

Step 4: Updating the Right Pane

The next step is to update the other side of the split pane based on the user selections of the tree nodes. This requires a bit more work. In fact, if you simply look at the "lines of code" (ignoring comments and blank lines), this version of the WASports script is about half as large as the previous one. However, it still isn't too much of a difference because it only requires about 125 lines of code to provide this kind of functionality. What "big changes" are needed to do this? Listing 22-9 shows the cellTSL class that is used by the script to react to tree selection events.

Listing 22-9. The cellTSL Class from WASports_04.py[5]

```
16|class cellTSL( TreeSelectionListener ) :
17|    def __init__( self, tree, pane, name2cfgId ) :
18|        self.tree = tree
19|        self.pane = pane
20|        self.name2cfgId = name2cfgId
21|    def valueChanged( self, tse ) :
22|        format = (
23|            '<html>  node: %s<br/>' +
24|            'isLeaf: %s<br/>parent: %s'
25|        )
26|        pane = self.pane
27|        node = self.tree.getLastSelectedPathComponent()
28|        if node :
29|            text = format % (
30|                node,
31|                [ 'No', 'Yes' ][ node.isLeaf() ],
32|                node.getParent()
33|            )
```

---

[5]Where TSL is an acronym for TreeSelectionListener.

```
34|            if node.isLeaf() :
35|                key = ( str( node.getParent() ), str( node ) )
36|            else :
37|                key = node.toString()
38|            if self.name2cfgId.has_key( key ) :
39|                text += '<br/><br/>%s' % self.name2cfgId[ key ]
40|            else :
41|                text += '<br/><br/> key missing: %s' % key
42|        else :
43|            text = 'Nothing selected'
44|        pane.setText( text )
```

When a cellTSL object is instantiated, the caller must provide references to:

- The JTree instance being monitored

- The pane being updated

- A dictionary containing information to be used to update the pane

The first two parameters are likely to be obvious, but the last is less likely to be so. This dictionary is used in lines 38 and 39 simply to demonstrate how the selection can be used to retrieve the associated configuration ID from the dictionary. For this example, this configuration ID is part of the information that is displayed in the right pane when a tree node is selected.

Listing 22-10. Tree and Split Pane Creation Code from WASports_04.py

```
  |        ...
56|        self.setLocation( location )
57|        tree, self.name2cfgId = self.cellTree()
58|        tree.getSelectionModel().setSelectionMode(
59|            TreeSelectionModel.SINGLE_TREE_SELECTION
60|        )
61|        self.status = JLabel( 'Right' )
62|        tree.addTreeSelectionListener(
63|            cellTSL(
64|                tree,
65|                self.status,
66|                self.name2cfgId
67|            )
68|        )
69|        pane = self.add(
70|            JSplitPane(
71|                JSplitPane.HORIZONTAL_SPLIT,
72|                JScrollPane( tree ),
73|                JScrollPane( self.status )
74|            )
75|        )
```

Listing 22-10 shows the modification to the WASports_04.py script to instantiate the TreeSelectionListener for the cell hierarchy tree. It's important to note that the constructor call requires a dictionary as the third argument. Listing 22-11 shows the modifications that were made to the cellTree() method in order to build and return this dictionary. It is important to note that the dictionary index is simple for non-leaf tree nodes (the root and all of the nodes corresponding to WebSphere node names). It is only the leaf nodes that use a tuple as an index. Why is this? Because the leaf nodes correspond to the individual application servers in the cell, the names of which do not have to be unique. The server names only have to be unique within a node. The dictionary entries for the individual servers use a tuple composed of the node name and the server name (see line 93).

Listing 22-11. Modified cellTree() Method

```
78|     def cellTree( self ) :
79|         cell = AdminConfig.list( 'Cell' )
80|         cellName = self.getName( cell )
81|         root = DefaultMutableTreeNode( cellName )
82|         result = { cellName : cell }
83|         for node in AdminConfig.list( 'Node' ).splitlines() :
84|             nodeName = self.getName( node )
85|             here = DefaultMutableTreeNode(
86|                 nodeName
87|             )
88|             result[ nodeName ] = node
89|             servers = AdminConfig.list( 'Server', node )
90|             for server in servers.splitlines() :
91|                 name = self.getName( server )
92|                 leaf = DefaultMutableTreeNode( name )
93|                 result[ ( nodeName, name ) ] = server
94|                 here.add( leaf )
95|             root.add( here )
96|         return JTree( root ), result
```

What does this mean for the application? Figure 22-5 shows how the right pane is updated based on user selections on the tree in the left pane. The second image shows the result of selecting a server. Note how the bottom line of the right pane is the configuration ID for the selected server.

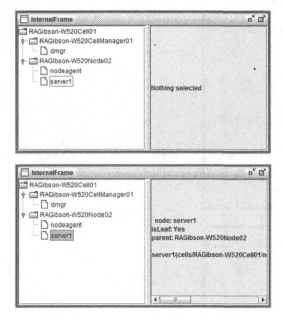

Figure 22-5. *Sample output of the* WASports_04.py *script*

Step 5: Displaying Cell and Node Details

A reasonable next step is to see what you can do to improve the information displayed in the right panel when the cell and node (non-leaf) tree items are selected. Figure 22-6 has some sample output from the next iteration of this script. It shows the different kinds of information displayed depending on the various types of tree nodes that can be selected. The first shows what is displayed when the cell node is selected, the second shows the slightly different information displayed when a WebSphere node is selected, and the last shows a minimum amount of information when a server entry is selected.

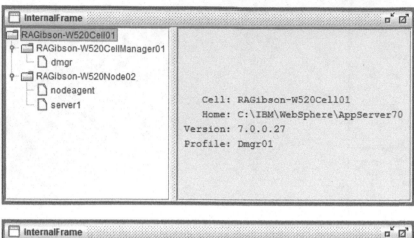

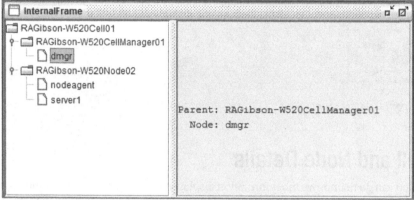

Figure 22-6. *Sample output of the WASports_05.py script*

Utility Routines

At first glance, it might appear simple to determine the values being displayed in the images in Figure 22-6. Unfortunately, it takes a bit more effort and code than you might imagine. For example, Listing 22-12 includes the utility routines needed to obtain some of this information.

Listing 22-12. Part 1 of the WASports_05.py Utility Routines

```
39|def findScopedTypes( Type, value, scope = None, attr = None ) :
40|    if not attr :
41|        attr = 'name'
42|    return [
43|        x for x in AdminConfig.list( Type, scope ).splitlines()
44|        if getAttributeValue( x, attr ) == value
45|    ]
```

```
46|def getAttributeValue( cfgId, attr  ) :
47|    return AdminConfig.showAttribute( cfgId, attr )
48|def getIPaddresses( hostnames ) :
49|    result = []
50|    for hostname in hostnames :
51|        try :
52|            addr = gethostbyname( hostname )
53|            if addr not in result :
54|                result.extend( addr.split( ',' ) )
55|        except :
56|            pass
57|    return result
58|def getHostnames( nodeName, serverName ) :
59|    exclude = [
60|        '*',
61|        'localhost',
62|        '${LOCALHOST_NAME}',
63|        '232.133.104.73',
64|        'ff01::1'
65|    ]
66|    result = []
67|    node   = findScopedTypes( 'Node', nodeName )[ 0 ]
68|    server = findScopedTypes(
69|        'ServerEntry',
70|        serverName,
71|        node,
72|        'serverName'
73|    )[ 0 ]
74|    NEPs = AdminConfig.list( 'NamedEndPoint', server )
75|    for nep in NEPs.splitlines() :
76|        epId = getAttributeValue( nep, 'endPoint' )
77|        host = getAttributeValue( epId, 'host' )
78|        if host not in exclude :
79|            result.append( host )
80|            exclude.append( host )
81|    return result
```

Table 22-1 describes each of the routines found in Listing 22-12. It is interesting to see how much of these routines use WebSphere specific objects and attribute values.

Table 22-1. Part 1 of the WASports_05.py Utility Routines, Explained

Lines	Description
39–45	The findScopedTypes(...) routine is used to return a list of configuration IDs for configuration objects of the specified Type that have a particular attribute value.
46–47	The getAttributeValue(...) routine is simply a technique used to shorten lines that would normally call the Adminconfig.showAttribute(...) method.
48–57	The getIPaddresses(...) routine returns a list IP addresses for the specified hostname.
58–81	The getHostnames(...) routine returns a list of unique hostnames referenced by the endPoint configuration objects on the specified server. **Note:** Since server names are only guaranteed to be unique within a node, the node name also needs to be provided.

Listing 22-13 contains some additional utility routines, all of which have names beginning with "WAS" to indicate how specific they are to WebSphere Application Server product information. In fact, most of them use the WebSphere product variables in order to determine the value to be returned.

Listing 22-13. Part 2 of the WASports_05.py Utility Routines

```
82|def WASversion( id ) :
83|    if AdminConfig.getObjectType( id ) == 'Cell' :
84|        nodeName = System.getProperty( 'local.node' )
85|    else :
86|        nodeName = getAttributeValue( id, 'name' )
87|    return AdminTask.getNodeBaseProductVersion(
88|        '[-nodeName %s]' % nodeName
89|    )
90|def WASprofileName( id ) :
91|    result = WASvarLookup( id, 'USER_INSTALL_ROOT' )
92|    if result :
93|        result = result.split( os.sep )[ -1 ]
94|    return result
95|def WAShome( id ) :
96|    return WASvarLookup( id, 'WAS_INSTALL_ROOT' )
97|def WASvarLookup( id, name ) :
98|    VSE = AdminConfig.list( 'VariableSubstitutionEntry', id )
99|    for var in VSE.splitlines () :
100|        if getAttributeValue( var, 'symbolicName' ) == name :
101|            result = getAttributeValue( var, 'value' )
102|            break
103|    else :
104|        result = None
105|    return result
```

Table 22-2 provides a description of each of these routines.

Table 22-2. *Part 2 of the WASports_05.py Utility Routines, Explained*

Lines	Description
82–89	The WASversion(...) routine is called when a tree node that corresponds to the cell or a WebSphere node is selected. A string is returned that identifies the product version of the cell or WebSphere node.
90–94	The WASprofileName(...) routine determines and returns the name of the WebSphere profile associated with the specified configuration ID.
95–96	The WAShome(...) routine determines and returns the WebSphere installation directory.
97–105	The WASvarLookup(...) routine determines the value of the specified WebSphere environment variable.

New Classes for WASports_05

Listing 22-14 shows the revised and simplified cellTSL class that includes the actions to be taken when tree selection events occur. The most significant change is related to the last parameter specified on the constructor, which has changed from a dictionary to a cellInfo object.

Listing 22-14. The WASports_05.py Revised cellTSL Class

```
106|class cellTSL( TreeSelectionListener ) :
107|    def __init__( self, tree, pane, data ) :
108|        self.tree = tree
109|        self.pane = pane
110|        self.data = data
111|    def valueChanged( self, tse ) :
112|        pane = self.pane
113|        node = self.tree.getLastSelectedPathComponent()
114|        if node :
115|            if node.isLeaf() :
116|                text = leafFormatString % (
117|                    node.getParent(),
118|                    node
119|                )
120|            else :
121|                text = self.data.getInfoValue( node.toString() )
122|        else :
123|            text = '<html><br/><b>Nothing selected<b/>'
124|        pane.setText( text )
```

Listing 22-15 shows the cellInfo class that is instantiated by the cellTree method (not shown) and that's used by the TreeSelectionListener class shown in Listing 22-14.

Listing 22-15. The WASports_05.py Inner cellInfo Class

```
209|    class cellInfo :
210|        def __init__( self ) :
211|            self.names = {}        # Dict[ name ] -> configId
212|            self.info  = {}        # Dict[ name ] -> node info
213|        def getNames( self ) :
214|            return self.names
215|        def setNames( self, names ) :
216|            self.names = names
217|        def addInfoValue( self, index, value ) :
218|            self.info[ index ] = '<html>' + (
219|                value.replace( '&', '&amp;' ).replace( '<',
220|                '&lt;' ).replace( '>', '&gt;' ).replace( ' ',
221|                ' ' ).replace( '\n', '<br/>' )
222|            )
223|        def getInfoValue( self, index ) :
224|            return self.info[ index ]
```

Step 6: Displaying Server Port Number Information

The next logical step is to add code to display information about the selected server in the right side of the split pane. Let's take a quick look at the result of these changes. Figure 22-7 shows the initial attempt of displaying the table of port numbers and their associated named endpoints. Even though it isn't perfect, it does show that you're going in the right direction.

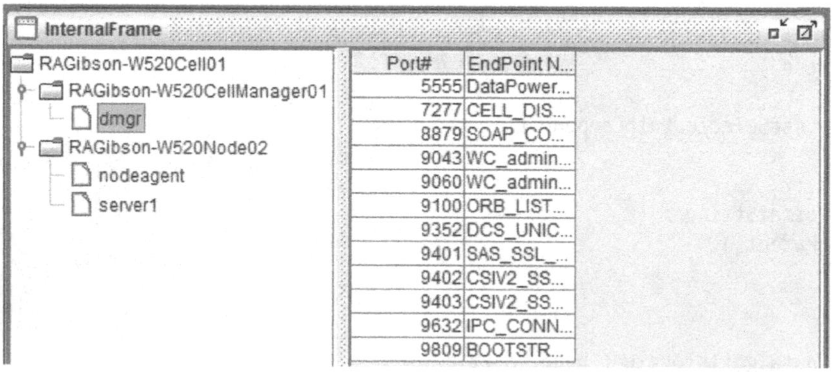

Figure 22-7. Sample output of the WASports_06.py script

To add this functionality to this iteration of the script, start by recognizing the possible value of the firstNamedConfigType(...) routine, shown in Listing 22-16. It can be used to simplify calls elsewhere in the script. It will return the first configuration ID matching the specified values or None.

Listing 22-16. New Utility Routine for WASports_06.py

```
53|def firstNamedConfigType(
54|    Type, value, scope = None, attr = None
55|) :
56|    items = findScopedTypes( Type, value, scope, attr )
57|    if len( items ) :
58|        result = items[ 0 ]
59|    else :
60|        result = None
61|    return result
```

Listing 22-17 shows the modified TreeSelectionListener class this is now used to display the appropriate information about the selected tree item, including the JTable instance that is returned by the call to the getPortTable(...) method that starts on line 135.

Listing 22-17. Modified cellTSL (TreeSelectionListener) Class

```
122|class cellTSL( TreeSelectionListener ) :
123|    def __init__( self, tree, pane, data ) :
124|        self.tree = tree
125|        self.pane = pane        # Reference to splitpane
126|        self.data = data
127|    def valueChanged( self, tse ) :
128|        pane = self.pane
129|        loc  = pane.getDividerLocation()
130|        node = self.tree.getLastSelectedPathComponent()
131|        if node :
132|            if node.isLeaf() :
133|                pane.setRightComponent (
134|                    JScrollPane(
135|                        self.data.getPortTable(
136|                            (
137|                                str( node.getParent() ),
138|                                str( node )
139|                            )
140|                        )
141|                    )
142|                )
143|            else :
144|                pane.setRightComponent (
145|                    JScrollPane(
146|                        JLabel(
147|                            self.data.getInfoValue( str( node ) ),
148|                            font = MONOFONT
149|                        )
150|                    )
151|                )
```

```
152|        else :
153|            pane.setRightComponent (
154|                JScrollPane(
155|                    JLabel(
156|                        '<html><br/><b>Nothing selected<b/>',
157|                        font = MONOFONT
158|                    )
159|                )
160|            )
161|        pane.setDividerLocation( loc )
```

A new PortLookupTask class, shown in Listing 22-18, was created to perform the necessary calls to the AdminConfig scripting object in order to create a JTable instance of the port numbers and associated named endpoints (shown on lines 267- 270). When the task finishes, the data object, which is an instance of the cellInfo class, is populated with the appropriate server port table data.

Listing 22-18. Part 1 of the New PortLookupTask Class

```
246|class PortLookupTask( SwingWorker ) :
247|    lock = threading.Lock()
248|    def __init__(
249|        self,
250|        nodeName,
251|        serverName,
252|        data
253|    ) :
254|        self.nodeName = nodeName
255|        self.servName = serverName
256|        self.data     = data
257|        SwingWorker.__init__( self )
258|    def doInBackground( self ) :
259|        self.lock.acquire()
260|        try :
261|            pDict = self.getPorts( self.nodeName, self.servName )
262|            ports = pDict.keys()
263|            ports.sort( lambda x,y: cmp( int( x ), int( y ) ) )
264|            result = []
265|            for port in ports :
266|                result.append( [ port, pDict[ port ] ] )
267|            table = JTable(
268|                PortTableModel( result ),
269|                autoResizeMode = JTable.AUTO_RESIZE_OFF
270|            )
271|            table.getTableHeader().setReorderingAllowed( 0 )
272|            self.data.addPortTable(
273|                ( self.nodeName, self.servName ),
274|                table
275|            )
276|        except :
277|            print '\nError: %s\nvalue: %s' % sys.exc_info()[ :2 ]
278|        self.lock.release()
```

The remainder of this class is shown in Listing 22-19. Remember that the doInBackground(...) method will call the done(...) method when it is complete. In this case, this method doesn't have to do any additional processing so it only contains the pass statement. The method is left as a placeholder to remind you to consider if additional actions need to be performed.

Listing 22-19. Part 2 of the New PortLookupTask Class

```
279|    def done( self ) :
280|        pass
281|    def getPorts( self, nodeName, serverName ) :
282|        scope = firstNamedConfigType( 'Node', nodeName )
283|        serverEntry = firstNamedConfigType(
284|            'ServerEntry',
285|            serverName,
286|            scope,
287|            'serverName'
288|        )
289|        result = {}
290|        if serverEntry :
291|            nEPs = AdminConfig.list(
292|                'NamedEndPoint',
293|                serverEntry
294|            )
295|            for namedEndPoint in nEPs.splitlines() :
296|                Name = getAttributeValue(
297|                    namedEndPoint,
298|                    'endPointName'
299|                )
300|                epId = getAttributeValue(
301|                    namedEndPoint,
302|                    'endPoint'
303|                )
304|                port = getAttributeValue( epId, 'port' )
305|                result[ port ] = Name
306|        return result
```

Listing 22-20 shows the PortTableModel class used to hold the data for each server in the cell. This table model class isn't quite complete, but it is a reasonable start. It identifies the data type for each of the two columns, it identifies only the first column (column 0) as editable, and it includes range checking on the user-supplied port number values.

Listing 22-20. New PortTableModel Class for Holding Port Table Data

```
307|class PortTableModel( DefaultTableModel ) :
308|    headings = 'Port#,EndPoint Name'.split( ',' )
309|    def __init__( self, data ) :
310|        for row in range( len( data ) ) :
311|            data[ row ] = [
312|                int( data[ row ][ 0 ] ), data[ row ][ 1 ]
313|            ]
314|        DefaultTableModel.__init__( self, data, self.headings )
```

```
315|     def getColumnClass( self, col ) :
316|         if col == 0 :
317|             return Integer
318|         else :
319|             return String
320|     def isCellEditable( self, row, col ) :
321|         return col == 0
322|     def setValueAt( self, value, row, col ) :
323|         if 0 <= value <= 65535 :
324|             index = ( self, row )
325|             DefaultTableModel.setValueAt( self, value, row, col )
326|         else :
327|             DefaultTableModel.setValueAt(
328|                 self,
329|                 self.getValueAt( row, col ),
330|                 row,
331|                 col
332|             )
333|         self.fireTableCellUpdated( row, col )
```

Step 7: Computing Table Column Widths

Next, you'll see that by adding a small amount of code, you can improve the appearance of the application. Figure 22-8 shows the result of adding a routine to determine the preferred widths of the table columns.

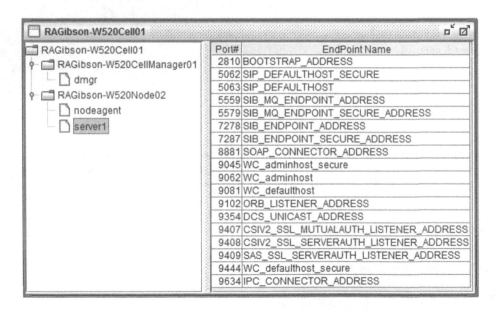

Figure 22-8. Sample output of the WASports_07.py script

Listing 22-21 shows the setColumnWidths(...) method that was added to the PortLookupTask class. It is brief because it knows about the table contents. For example, rather than looking for the widest value in column 1, the preferred width for this column is determined using the largest allowed value (65535) for this column.

Listing 22-21. The setColumnWidths(...) Method Added to WASports_07.py

```
311|    def setColumnWidths( self, table ) :
312|        tcm    = table.getColumnModel()      # Table Column Model
313|        data   = table.getModel()            # To access table data
314|        margin = tcm.getColumnMargin()       # gap between columns
315|        render = table.getCellRenderer( 0, 0 )
316|        comp = render.getTableCellRendererComponent(
317|            table,                       # table being processed
318|            '65535',                     # max port number
319|            0,                           # not selected
320|            0,                           # not in focus
321|            0,                           # row num
322|            0                            # col num
323|        )
324|        cWidth = comp.getPreferredSize().width
325|        col = tcm.getColumn( 0 )
326|        col.setPreferredWidth( cWidth + margin )
327|        cWidth = -1
328|        for row in range( data.getRowCount() ) :
329|            render = table.getCellRenderer( row, 1 )
330|            comp = render.getTableCellRendererComponent(
331|                table,
332|                data.getValueAt( row, 1 ),   # cell value
333|                0,                           # not selected
334|                0,                           # not in focus
335|                row,                         # row num
336|                1                            # col num
337|            )
338|            cWidth = max(
339|                cWidth,
340|                comp.getPreferredSize().width
341|            )
342|        col = tcm.getColumn( 1 )
343|        col.setPreferredWidth( cWidth + margin )
```

441

Step 8: Adding Menu Items

What do the changes in this iteration do to the application? Figure 22-9 shows the results of these changes. You can see the menu items that were added.

Figure 22-9. *Sample menu items from the WASports_08.py script*

Listing 22-22 shows the new MenuBar(...) method that was added to the WASports class to create the menu and specify the corresponding event-handling routines for each menu item. One thing that is important to notice is the fact that the Changes menu entry is initialized as disabled (as you can see from the first image in Figure 22-9). This iteration of the script doesn't include code to enable this menu entry, so you won't be able to see the Save and Discard menu items until a future iteration of the script.

Listing 22-22. New MenuBar(...) Method in the WASports Class from WASports_08.py

```
457|    def MenuBar( self ) :
458|        menu = JMenuBar()
459|        self.ChangesMI = JMenu( 'Changes', enabled = 0 )
460|        self.ChangesMI.add(
461|            JMenuItem(
462|                'Save',
463|                actionPerformed = self.save
464|            )
465|        )
466|        self.ChangesMI.add(
467|            JMenuItem(
468|                'Discard',
469|                actionPerformed = self.discard
470|            )
471|        )
472|        jmFile = JMenu( 'File' )
473|        jmFile.add( self.ChangesMI )
474|        jmFile.add(
475|            JMenuItem(
476|                'Exit',
477|                actionPerformed = self.Exit
478|            )
479|        )
480|        menu.add( jmFile )
481|        jmHelp = JMenu( 'Help' )
```

```
482|        jmHelp.add(
483|            JMenuItem(
484|                'About',
485|                actionPerformed = self.about
486|            )
487|        )
488|        jmHelp.add(
489|            JMenuItem(
490|                'Notice',
491|                actionPerformed = self.notice
492|            )
493|        )
494|        menu.add( jmHelp )
495|        return menu
```

Listing 22-23 shows the initial implementations of the event handler methods for the new menu items. One important thing to note is the reference by the about(...) method to the aboutTask.getResult() method. A new AboutTask class was also added to this iteration of the script in order to process the script docstring[6] and create an HTML string that displays nicely. The reason a separate thread task was used is to allow the application to perform the string conversion processing off the main thread, without causing the entire application to pause.

Listing 22-23. The New Event Handlers Added to WASports_08.py

```
496|    def about( self, e ) :
497|        JOptionPane.showMessageDialog(
498|            self.frame,
499|            JLabel(
500|                self.aboutTask.getResult(),
501|                font = MONOFONT
502|            ),
503|            'About',
504|            JOptionPane.PLAIN_MESSAGE
505|        )
506|    def notice( self, e ) :
507|        JOptionPane.showMessageDialog(
508|            self.frame,
509|            Disclaimer,
510|            'Notice',
511|            JOptionPane.WARNING_MESSAGE
512|        )
513|    def save( self, e ) :
514|        print 'save() - Not yet implemented'
515|    def discard( self, e ) :
516|        AdminConfig.reset()
517|    def Exit( self, e ) :
518|        sys.exit()
```

---

[6]See https://www.python.org/dev/peps/pep-0257/.

Step 9: Implementing Save and Discard

Now that some menu items are in place, it is reasonable to implement the event handlers and associated code to allow these menu items to be used. Figure 22-10 shows that when a port number value changes, the Changes menu item is enabled, which allows the user to save or discard the changes. Additionally, a dialog box is displayed when the user tries to exit the application without saving or tries to discard their changes.

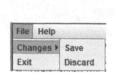

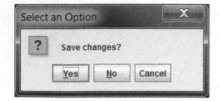

Figure 22-10. *Sample menu items from the WASports_08.py script*

Listing 22-24 shows the appCleanup(...) routine that displays a confirm dialog box when the user tries to exit the application when unsaved changes exist. If the user doesn't want to discard the changes, control is returned to the caller, which is responsible for resuming operation.

Listing 22-24. The appCleanup() Routine Checks for Unsaved Changes from WASports_09.py

```
79|def appCleanup( app ) :
80|    if AdminConfig.hasChanges() :
81|        answer = JOptionPane.showConfirmDialog(
82|            app, 'Save changes?'
83|        )
84|        if answer == JOptionPane.YES_OPTION :
85|            AdminConfig.save()
86|        elif answer in [
87|            JOptionPane.CLOSED_OPTION,
88|            JOptionPane.CANCEL_OPTION
89|        ] :
90|            return
91|        else :
92|            AdminConfig.reset()
93|            print '\nConfiguration changes discarded.'
94|    System.gc()                # call Java Garbage Collector
95|    time.sleep( 0.5 )          # Slight delay for garbage pickup
96|    sys.exit( 0 )
```

Listing 22-25 shows the new SaveTask and DiscardTask classes, which are used to perform the potentially long-running AdminConfig.save() or AdminConfig.reset() as a background task. In addition, the DiscardTask is responsible for updating the port number values in the tables on which the changes were made.

Listing 22-25. The SaveTask and DiscardTask Classes from WASports_09.py

```
311|class SaveTask( SwingWorker ) :
312|    def __init__( self, cellData ) :
313|        self.cellData = cellData
314|    def doInBackground( self ) :
315|        try :
316|            original = self.cellData.clearOriginals()
317|            AdminConfig.save()
318|        except :
319|            print '\nError: %s\nvalue: %s' % sys.exc_info()[ :2 ]
320|class DiscardTask( SwingWorker ) :
321|    def __init__( self, cellData ) :
322|        self.cellData = cellData
323|    def doInBackground( self ) :
324|        try :
325|            original = self.cellData.getOriginal()
326|            tables = []
327|            for index in original.keys() :
328|                table, row = index
329|                table.getModel().resetPortValue(
330|                    row,
331|                    original[ index ]
332|                )
333|                if table not in tables :
334|                    tables.append( table )
335|            for table in tables :
336|                table.repaint()
337|            AdminConfig.reset()
338|        except :
339|            print '\nError: %s\nvalue: %s' % sys.exc_info()[ :2 ]
```

Listing 22-26 required changes in order to perform the actual AdminConfig.modify(...) method (see line 470), which uses the AdminConfig scripting object to change the specified port number for the indicated named endpoint on the user-selected application server. It is also responsible for calling the cellInfo addOriginal(...) method that's used to save the original value should the Discard menu entry be called.

Listing 22-26. Part 1 of the Modified PortTableModel Class from WASports_09.py

```
444|class PortTableModel( DefaultTableModel ) :
445|    headings = 'Port#,EndPoint Name'.split( ',' )
446|    def __init__( self, data ) :
447|        self.table      = None
448|        self.nodeName   = None
449|        self.serverName = None
450|        self.epIdDict   = None
451|        self.app        = None
452|        for row in range( len( data ) ) :
453|            data[ row ][ 0 ] = int( data[ row ][ 0 ] )
454|        DefaultTableModel.__init__( self, data, self.headings )
```

445

```
455|    def getColumnClass( self, col ) :
456|        if col == 0 :
457|            return Integer
458|        else :
459|            return String
460|    def isCellEditable( self, row, col ) :
461|        return col == 0
462|    def resetPortValue( self, row, value ) :
463|        DefaultTableModel.setValueAt( self, value, row, 0 )
464|        self.fireTableCellUpdated( row, 0 )
```

Listing 22-27 shows the remainder of the PortTableModel class. You are encouraged to search in the script file to see which of these methods is referenced by the rest of the script.

Listing 22-27. Part 2 of the Modified PortTableModel Class from WASports_09.py

```
465|    def setValueAt( self, value, row, col ) :
466|        prev = self.getValueAt( row, col )
467|        if 0 <= value <= 65535 :
468|            name = self.getValueAt( row, 1 )
469|            epId = self.epIdDict[ name ]
470|            AdminConfig.modify( epId, [ [ 'port', value ],] )
471|            self.app.ChangesMI.setEnabled( 1 )
472|            DefaultTableModel.setValueAt( self, value, row, col )
473|            self.app.cellData.addOriginal( self.table, row, prev )
474|        else :
475|            DefaultTableModel.setValueAt(
476|                self,
477|                prev,
478|                row,
479|                col
480|            )
481|        self.fireTableCellUpdated( row, col )
482|    def getContext( self ) :
483|        return self.table, self.nodeName, self.serverName
484|    def setContext(
485|        self, table, nodeName, serverName, epIdDict, app
486|    ) :
487|        self.table      = table
488|        self.nodeName   = nodeName
489|        self.serverName = serverName
490|        self.epIdDict   = epIdDict
491|        self.app        = app
```

Listing 22-28 shows the changes that need to be made to the cellInfo class to allow the original port number values to be saved when the user modifies a value.

Listing 22-28. The Modified (Inner) `cellInfo` Class

```
492|class WASports_09( java.lang.Runnable ) :
493|    class cellInfo :
   |        ...
500|        def addOriginal( self, table, row, value ) :
501|            self.lock.acquire()
502|            index = ( table, row )
503|            if not self.before.has_key( index ) :
504|                self.before[ index ] = value
505|            self.lock.release()
506|        def getOriginal( self ) :
507|            self.lock.acquire()
508|            result = self.before
509|            self.lock.release()
510|            return result
511|        def clearOriginals( self ) :
512|            self.lock.acquire()
513|            self.before = {}
514|            self.lock.release()
```

Listing 22-29 defines a `WindowAdapter` descendent for the application. The event handler method in this class is invoked when the user clicks on the application close icon (the [X] in the upper-right corner of the application).

Listing 22-29. The `WindowAdapter` Class Handles the `windowClosed` Events from `WASports_09.py`

```
650|class windowAdapter( WindowAdapter ) :
651|    def windowClosed( self, e ) :
652|        frame = e.getWindow()
653|        appCleanup( frame )
654|        frame.setVisible( 1 )      # User chose cancel or close
```

Step 10: Implementing the Export Functionality

Now you get to some new and interesting[7] stuff that is unrelated to Swing, but directly related to non-trivial applications that need to be developed. Take a few moments to consider how you might implement an Export capability. It is important to realize that one of the most important questions you should ask is, "What data format should be used?" A number of potential alternatives may come to mind, some being more useful than others.

When I first started thinking about this topic, I considered using XML files to hold the information. This also makes a lot of sense when dealing with WebSphere Application Server configuration files because so many of them use the XML format.

My initial investigations into using the simplest XML module (`xml.dom.minidom`) didn't fare well. I tried using a trivial example to test the validity of this as far as the needs of this program were concerned. Listing 22-30 shows a simple interactive `wsadmin` session and the inability of the `xml.dom.minidom` module to perform the simplest of XML parsing.

---

[7]Remember that old curse, "may you live in interesting times?" See `http://en.wikipedia.org/wiki/May_you_live_in_interesting_times`.

Listing 22-30. Testing the `xml.dom.minidom`

```
wsadmin>from xml.dom.minidom import parse
wsadmin>
wsadmin>try :
wsadmin>    dom = parse( '7ODM.xml' )
wsadmin>except :
wsadmin>    print '\nError: %s\nvalue: %s' % sys.exc_info()[ :2 ]
wsadmin>
Failed to get environment, environ will be empty: ...

Error: exceptions.AttributeError
value: feed
wsadmin>
```

Does this mean that you can't use XML to represent the data that the application needs to save (export) or load (import)? Not at all. The `xml.dom.minidom` module is part of the optional libraries that are provided by `wsadmin` scripts.[8] Just because they are present doesn't mean that you have to use them.

What other XML modules and libraries exist? It is important, especially at times like these, to remember that other libraries exist as part of Java J2EE.[9] There are a number of free online resources that explain how to work with XML in Java.[10] I spent some time reading the J2EE tutorial,[11] specifically Chapter 2, "Understanding XML." There is also a number of very good publications that discuss XML processing with Java. Unfortunately, the Jython version of those would be a whole separate book, so I'll provide some examples that correspond very closely to the kind of Java examples available elsewhere.

Using the Document Object Model API

The kinds of XML processes discussed in this section use the Document Object Model (DOM) Application Programming Interface (API) and the Simple API for XML (SAX). Of these two, the DOM is much simpler and easier to write and therefore to read and understand. Let's start with it.

Listing 22-31 shows the important part of a simple script that demonstrates how to read an XML file and then process the data structure that is created when the input file is successfully parsed. It is so simple to read and parse an XML file that it can be performed in a single statement (see lines 22-25). The traverse routine on lines 6-19 uses recursion to traverse the data structure that's produced.

Listing 22-31. Simple DOM Routines from `xmlDOM.py`

```
 6|def traverse( node, indent = 0 ) :
 7|    prefix = '%*s' % ( indent, '' )
 8|    while node :
 9|        if node.getNodeType() == Node.ELEMENT_NODE :
10|            print '%s<%s>' % ( prefix, node.getNodeName() )
11|            traverse( node.getFirstChild(), indent + 2 )
12|            print '%s</%s>' % ( prefix, node.getNodeName() )
```

---

[8]For example, `%WAS_HOME%\optionalLibraries\jython\Lib\xml\dom\minidom.py`.
[9]*I admit that I tend to use the J2EE Reference because WebSphere is an Application Server.*
[10]See `http://docs.oracle.com/javaee/1.4/tutorial/information/faq.html`.
[11]See `http://docs.oracle.com/javaee/1.4/tutorial/doc/index.html` or `http://docs.oracle.com/javaee/1.4/tutorial/doc/J2EETutorial.pdf`.

```
13|         elif node.getNodeType() == Node.TEXT_NODE :
14|             value = node.getNodeValue()
15|             if value :
16|                 value = value.strip()
17|                 if value :
18|                     print '%s"%s"' % ( prefix, value )
19|         node = node.getNextSibling()
20|def dom( filename ):
21|    try :
22|        doc  = DocumentBuilderFactory.newInstance(
23|        ).newDocumentBuilder().parse(
24|            File( filename )
25|        )
26|        root = doc.getDocumentElement()
27|        root.normalize()
28|        traverse( root )
29|    except :
30|        print '\nError: %s\nvalue: %s' % sys.exc_info()[ :2 ]
```

This example demonstrates one of the greatest drawbacks of the DOM, and that is the fact that parsing an XML file using the DOM API requires the entire contents of the file to be loaded into memory. For the current application, this might not be too much of a restriction if you are working with the information pertaining to a single WebSphere Application Server cell. However, some cells can be quite large, so this might be a limiting factor. Additionally, I can imagine the application being expanded to work with multiple cells, which could significantly increase the memory requirements of the application.

Using the Simple API for XML (SAX)

Just how simple is the Simple API for XML? It's really not too bad at all. It is possible to have a single statement that parses an XML file using the SAX API, but I'm not going to be that mean to myself or others.[12] Listing 22-32 shows a trivial routine from the xmlSAX.py script file that shows how to instantiate a SAX parser and use it to parse a user-specified XML input file.

■ **Note**   One of the import differences between these two examples is that this script validates the XML during the processing. So, in addition to the XML input, a Document Type Definition (DTD) file defines the tags that can exist in a valid XML file, how they should be used, and their relationship to one another. Unfortunately, details describing and explaining DTDs are beyond the scope of this book.

---

[12]Just because it is possible to write a one line statement to perform this task does *not* mean that you should.

449

Listing 22-32. The readFileSAX Routine from xmlSAX.py

```
61|def readFileSAX( filename ) :
62|    try :
63|        FIS    = FileInputStream( File( filename ) )
64|        ISR    = InputStreamReader( FIS, ENCODING )
65|        src    = InputSource( ISR, encoding = ENCODING )
66|        factory = SAXParserFactory.newInstance()
67|        factory.setValidating( 1 )
68|        parser  = factory.newSAXParser()
69|        parser.parse( src, SAXhandler() )
70|    except :
71|        print '\nError: %s\nvalue: %s' % sys.exc_info()[ :2 ]
```

Listings 22-33 and 22-34 show the SAXhandler class from the xmlSAX.py file. It is important to note that the SAXhandler methods are called by the SAX parser while the input file is being processed. This allows the script using this class to transform the input data into whatever data structure the developer chooses. Using the DOM technique results in a completely processed XML file being represented in memory using the Document Object Model. If this data structure isn't appropriate for your application needs, you need to transform the DOM to a more appropriate data structure for your specific needs.

Listing 22-33. Part 1 of the SAXhandler class from xmlSAX.py

```
10|class SAXhandler( DefaultHandler ) :
11|    def __init__( self ) :
12|        self.chars  = ''
13|        self.prefix = ''
14|        self.width  = 0
15|    def indent( self ) :
16|        self.width += 2
17|        self.prefix = '%*s' % ( self.width, '' )
18|    def dedent( self ) :
19|        self.width -= 2
20|        self.prefix = '%*s' % ( self.width, '' )
21|    def startElement( self, uri, localName, name, attributes ) :
22|        if self.chars :
23|            print '%s"%s"' % ( self.prefix, self.chars )
24|            self.chars = ''
25|        attr = [
26|            (
27|                attributes.getQName( i ),
28|                attributes.getValue( i )
29|            )
30|            for i in range( attributes.getLength() )
31|        ]
```

```
32|        if attr :
33|            print '%s<%s %s>' % (
34|                self.prefix,
35|                name,
36|                ', '.join(
37|                    [
38|                        '%s="%s"' % ( n, v ) for n, v in attr
39|                    ]
40|                )
41|            )
42|        else :
43|            print '%s<%s>' % ( self.prefix, name )
44|        self.indent()
```

Listing 22-34 shows the remainder of the SAXhandler class.

Listing 22-34. Part 2 of the SAXhandler Class from xmlSAX.py

```
45|    def endElement( self, uri, localName, name ) :
46|        if self.chars :
47|            print '%s"%s"' % ( self.prefix, self.chars )
48|            self.chars = ''
49|        self.dedent()
50|        print '%s</%s>' % ( self.prefix, name )
51|    def characters( self, ch, start, length ) :
52|        value = str( String( ch, start, length ) ).strip()
53|        if value :
54|            self.chars += value
55|    def warning( self, e ) :
56|         print 'Warning:', e.getMessage()
57|    def error( self, e ) :
58|         print 'Error:', e.getMessage()
59|    def fatalError( self, e ) :
60|         print 'Fatal error:', e.getMessage()
```

The SAX parser calls only some of the methods in the SAXhandler class directly. Specifically, the startElement(...), endElement(...), and characters(...) methods are called during normal parsing of an XML document. The warning(...), error(...), and fatalError(...) methods are called when unexpected input is encountered.

It might not be obvious why the chars attribute is used as a sort of holding buffer. Why not just display the data when the characters(...) method is called? The answer is that there is no guarantee that all of the data between a start and end tag will be processed at one time. Character sequences can be processed in multiple segments. This class buffers the character data until the next start or end tag is encountered. That is why the startElement(...) and endElement(...) methods begin by looking for buffered character data.

The Document Type Definition (DTD)

One of the useful features of the XML parsers is the support provided to validate the input being processed against the description of valid input. That is the role of the Document Type Definition (DTD). It identifies the valid tags and their order, and identifies which tags are allowed to have attributes. Given an appropriate DTD, the parser factory can have validation enabled by calling the setValidating(...) method, as shown in Listing 22-32, line 67. Then, the XML file should identify how the validation should be checked. One way to do this is to include a DOCTYPE definition that identifies whether the DTD is contained in the XML file or in an external file, as shown in Figure 22-11.

```
<!DOCTYPE WASports SYSTEM "WASports.dtd">
```

Figure 22-11. *DOCTYPE definition identifying an external DTD file*

Initial WASports DTD

Using the information contained in the cellInfo class, you can describe the format of an XML file using the DTD shown in Listing 22-35.[13] If you aren't familiar with the syntax of the DTD file, information is available in a number of places on the Internet[14] and in publications about XML.

Listing 22-35. Initial WASports.dtd

```
 1|<!ELEMENT WASports   (cell)>
 2|<!ATTLIST WASports   version CDATA #REQUIRED>
 3|<!ELEMENT cell       (name,WAShome,WASversion,profile,node+)>
 4|<!ELEMENT node       (name,WAShome,WASversion,profile,
  |hostname+,ipaddr,server+)>
 5|<!ELEMENT server     (name,endpoint+)>
 6|<!ELEMENT name       (#PCDATA)>
 7|<!ELEMENT WAShome    (#PCDATA)>
 8|<!ELEMENT WASversion (#PCDATA)>
 9|<!ELEMENT profile    (#PCDATA)>
10|<!ELEMENT hostname   (#PCDATA)>
11|<!ELEMENT ipaddr     (#PCDATA)>
12|<!ELEMENT endpoint   (name,port)>
13|<!ELEMENT port       (#PCDATA)>
```

Table 22-3 describes the DTD in Figure 22-11, line by line. Using the description and the WASports_10.py application, you should be able to better understand the correlation between the application output and the DTD format.

---

[13]Note that line 4 is too long to fit in the available space and is continued on the next line.
[14]For example, see http://www.w3schools.com/dtd/dtd_intro.asp.

Table 22-3. `WASports.dtd`, *Explained*

Lines	Description
1	The root tag is WASports and it has only one cell tag.
2	The WASports tag has a required attribute called version.
3	The cell tag requires a name, WAShome, WASversion, profile, and one or more node tags.
4	The node tag requires a name, WAShome, WASversion, profile, one or more hostnames, one ip_addr and one or more server tags.
5	Each server tag requires one name and one or more endpoint tags.
12	Each endpoint tag requires a name and port tag.
6–13	The tags identified as having (#PCDATA) require some character data.

The ExportTask Class

You need to make some changes to the application menu structure, in order to provide the user with a way to specify that an export should occur. Creating the menu is simple enough that it doesn't need to be shown here. However, the event handler that is called requires a bit more explanation, so the Export(...) method is shown in Listing 22-36.

Listing 22-36. Export(...) Method from WASports_10.py

```
788|     def Export( self, event ) :
789|         title = 'Export (Save) cell details'
790|         fc = JFileChooser(
791|             currentDirectory = File( '.' ),
792|             dialogTitle = title,
793|             fileFilter  = XMLfiles()
794|         )
795|         if fc.showOpenDialog(
796|             self.frame
797|         ) == JFileChooser.APPROVE_OPTION :
798|             f = fc.getSelectedFile()
799|             fileName = fc.getSelectedFile().getAbsolutePath()
800|             if not fileName.endswith( '.xml' ) :
801|                 fileName += '.xml'
802|             msg = 'Overwrite existing file (%s)?'
803|             if os.path.isfile( fileName ) :
804|                 response = JOptionPane.showConfirmDialog(
805|                     None,
806|                     msg % os.path.basename( fileName ),
807|                     'Confirm Overwrite',
808|                     JOptionPane.OK_CANCEL_OPTION,
809|                     JOptionPane.QUESTION_MESSAGE
810|                 )
811|                 if response == JOptionPane.CANCEL_OPTION :
812|                     return
813|             ExportTask( fileName, self.cellData ).execute()
```

This method uses the JFileChooser and FileFilter classes discussed in detail in Chapter 17. It limits the kinds of files displayed by the JFileChooser to those having an .xml extension. If the user selects an existing file, it also verifies that the user wants to replace the existing file using a simple confirmation dialog window. The most important part of this method is when it instantiates and begins execution of an ExportTask thread to actually create the specified file (line 813). Listing 22-37 shows the first of three parts of the ExportTask class.

Listing 22-37. Part 1 of the ExportTask Class from WASports_10.py

```
356|class ExportTask( SwingWorker ) :
357|    def __init__( self, fileName, cellData ) :
358|        self.fileName = fileName
359|        self.cellData = cellData
360|    def doInBackground( self ) :
361|        try :
362|            fos = FileOutputStream( self.fileName )
363|            streamResult = StreamResult(
364|                OutputStreamWriter( fos, 'ISO-8859-1' )
365|            )
366|            trans = SAXTransformerFactory.newInstance()
367|            trans.setAttribute( 'indent-number', 4 )
368|            tHand = trans.newTransformerHandler()
369|            serializer = tHand.getTransformer()
370|            serializer.setOutputProperty(
371|                OutputKeys.ENCODING, 'ISO-8859-1'
372|            )
373|            serializer.setOutputProperty(
374|                OutputKeys.DOCTYPE_SYSTEM, 'WASports.dtd'
375|            )
376|            serializer.setOutputProperty(
377|                OutputKeys.INDENT, 'yes'
378|            )
379|            tHand.setResult( streamResult )
380|            tHand.startDocument()
381|            atts = AttributesImpl()
382|            atts.addAttribute(
383|                '', '', 'version', 'CDATA', __version__
384|            )
385|            tHand.startElement( '', '', 'WASports', atts )
386|            atts.clear()
387|            tHand.startElement( '', '', 'cell', atts )
388|            data = self.cellData
389|            root = data.tree.getModel().getRoot()
390|            cellName = root.toString()
391|            self.addTagAndText( tHand, 'name', cellName )
392|            info = data.getInfoDict( cellName )
393|            self.addTagAndText(
394|                tHand, 'WAShome', info[ 'WAShome' ]
395|            )
396|            self.addTagAndText(
397|                tHand, 'WASversion', info[ 'WASversion' ]
398|            )
```

```
399|            self.addTagAndText(
400|                tHand, 'profile', info[ 'profile' ]
401|                )
```

Listing 22-38 shows the next part of the ExportTask class. Again, you can see that a non-trivial class can't easily be forced to fit onto one or even two pages of this book.

Listing 22-38. Part 2 of the ExportTask Class from WASports_10.py

```
402|            nodes = root.children()
403|            while nodes.hasMoreElements() :
404|                node = nodes.nextElement()
405|                nodeName = node.toString()
406|                info = data.getInfoDict( nodeName )
407|                tHand.startElement( '', '', 'node', atts )
408|                self.addTagAndText( tHand, 'name', nodeName )
409|                self.addTagAndText(
410|                    tHand, 'WAShome', info[ 'WAShome' ]
411|                    )
412|                self.addTagAndText(
413|                    tHand, 'WASversion', info[ 'WASversion' ]
414|                    )
415|                self.addTagAndText(
416|                    tHand, 'profile', info[ 'profile' ]
417|                    )
418|                self.addTagAndText(
419|                    tHand, 'hostname', info[ 'hostnames' ]
420|                    )
421|                self.addTagAndText(
422|                    tHand, 'ip_addr', info[ 'ipaddr' ]
423|                    )
424|                servers = node.children()
425|                while servers.hasMoreElements() :
426|                    server = servers.nextElement()
427|                    serverName = server.toString()
428|                    tHand.startElement(
429|                        '', '', 'server', atts
430|                        )
431|                    self.addTagAndText(
432|                        tHand, 'name', serverName
433|                        )
434|                    table = data.getPortTable(
435|                        ( nodeName, serverName )
436|                        )
437|                    model = table.getModel()
438|                    for row in range( model.getRowCount() ) :
439|                        tHand.startElement(
440|                            '', '', 'endpoint', atts
441|                            )
442|                        name = model.getValueAt( row, 1 )
```

Listing 22-39 shows the remainder of the ExportTask class. Unfortunately, breaking a listing like this across multiple pages can make it difficult to read. Therefore, you are encouraged to use your favorite text editor and view the script source file.

Listing 22-39. Part 3 of the ExportTask Class from WASports_10.py

```
443|                        self.addTagAndText(
444|                            tHand, 'name', name
445|                        )
446|                        port = str(
447|                            model.getValueAt( row, 0 )
448|                        )
449|                        self.addTagAndText(
450|                            tHand, 'port', port
451|                        )
452|                        tHand.endElement(
453|                            '', '', 'endpoint'
454|                        )
455|                    tHand.endElement( '', '', 'server' )
456|                tHand.endElement( '', '', 'node' )
457|            tHand.endElement( '', '', 'cell' )
458|            tHand.endElement( '', '', 'WASports' )
459|            tHand.endDocument()
460|        except :
461|            msgText = '\nExportTask() Error: %s\nvalue: %s'
462|            print msgText % sys.exc_info()[ :2 ]
463|    def addTagAndText( self, handler, tagName, text ) :
464|        handler.startElement(
465|            '', '', tagName, AttributesImpl()
466|        )
467|        handler.characters(
468|            String( text ).toCharArray(), 0, len( text )
469|        )
470|        handler.endElement( '', '', tagName )
```

The ExportTask shown in Listings 22-37 through 22-39 is described in detail in Table 22-4. The important point to note about the ExportTask class is that every XML tag calls the startElement(...) method, the required nested elements, and the endElement(...) method in order to create a properly formed XML document.

Table 22-4. *ExportTask Class, Explained*

Lines	Description
357–359	Class constructor used to save the specified filename and `cellInfo` structure containing the information to be exported.
362–365	The output file stream is instantiated.
366–367	A `SAXTransformerFactory` instance is created with the specified indentation (for readability).
368–379	A transformer handler instance is created with the specified properties (such as encoding). It is also associated with the output stream created earlier.
380	The `startDocument(...)` method begins to create the XML document being produced.
381–385	The `WASports` tag is created with the required `version` attribute.
386	Since no other tags in the document have attributes, the `atts` variable is cleared so it can be reused on other tags.
387	The only instance of the cell tag is started.
388–401	The tags required to be present in the cell tag hierarchy are created using the `addTagAndText(...)` utility method.
402–456	Each node in the cell has its required tags and all of the associated server entries are created.
457–459	Note how each `startElement` has a matching `endElement` after all the contained tags have been created.
460–462	An exception clause is invoked when an error is encountered. Unfortunately, it is a trivial error handler.
463–470	The `addTagAndText(...)` utility method simplifies the creation of tags like `<tagName>text value</tagName>`.

Step 11: Implementing the Import Functionality

One of the most challenging aspects of the iterative development of non-trivial applications such as `WASports` is that you can reach a point where significant changes are required for the next iteration. Step 11 is where these changes are recognized. How do I know that? Let's take some time to consider the implications associated with being able to import application information. To make it more interesting, you'll do so by using a few question and answers to get things started.

Table 22-5. *Important Questions and Answers*

Q: What should occur when a WASports file is imported?

A: A new internal frame should be created similar in nature to the one that is created when the application starts.

Q: How will an imported frame differ from an existing one?

A: These frames can be closed, and if changes are made, a save needs to be performed using the export functionality, instead of changing the current configuration.

Q: Do changes to existing classes and data structures need to be made?

A: Yes; for example, the internal cellInfo class needs to be made global so that both local cell data and imported cell data can use the same class. Additionally, the setColumnWidths(...) method should be moved from within the PortLookupTask class to the global scope so that it can also be called by the ImportTask class. Additionally, the names dictionary in the cellInfo class can't refer to an actual configuration ID because you don't want any of the changes made to imported data to be made in the local configuration. So, for the imported data, a pseudo-configId will be created instead.

Q: What kinds of things needed to be "fixed" because of improved understanding and how should they be handled?

A: During this iteration, it became clear that the internal form of the JOption dialog boxes should have been used instead of the default external form (that is, the JOptionPane.showInternalConfirmDialog(...) method instead of the JOptionPane.showConfirmDialog(...) method). Additionally, using an ip_addr tag for the ipaddr entry in the cellInfo class added unnecessary complexity. So the DTD and code was changed to use an ipaddr tag instead.

The ImportTask Class

The changes required to add the Import functionality are similar to the changes needed to add the Export functionality discussed previously. The Import(...) event handler method[15] isn't shown here, but can be found in the WASports_11.py script file.[16] It too uses a JFileChooser instance to allow the user to identify the XML file to be imported. Once the input file is identified, an ImportTask instance is created to perform the input processing on a separate thread. Listing 22-40 shows the ImportTask class used by this iteration of the WASports script.

Listing 22-40. Part 1 of the ImportTask Class from WASports_11.py

```
780|class ImportTask( SwingWorker ) :
   |    ...
992|    def __init__( self, app, menuItem, fileName ) :
993|        self.app      = app
994|        self.menuItem = menuItem
995|        self.fileName = fileName
996|        self.handler  = ImportTask.SAXhandler( app )
997|        menuItem.setEnabled( 0 )
998|        self.msgText  = ''
```

---

[15]Note the use of capitalization to differentiate this method name from the import keyword.
[16]The complete source can be found in ...\code\Chap_22\WASports_11.py.

```
 999|     def doInBackground( self ) :
1000|         try :
1001|             FIS     = FileInputStream( File( self.fileName ) )
1002|             ISR     = InputStreamReader( FIS, ENCODING )
1003|             src     = InputSource( ISR, encoding = ENCODING )
1004|             factory = SAXParserFactory.newInstance()
1005|             factory.setValidating( 1 )
1006|             parser  = factory.newSAXParser()
1007|             parser.parse( src, self.handler )
1008|             FIS.close()
1009|         except :
1010|             msgText = 'Error: %s\nvalue: %s'
1011|             self.msgText = msgText % sys.exc_info()[ :2 ]
1012|     def done( self ) :
1013|         localFrame = self.app.localFrame
1014|         desktop    = self.app.frame.getContentPane()
1015|         errors     = self.handler.errors
1016|         if self.msgText or errors :
1017|             if self.msgText :
1018|                 msg = self.msgText + '\n'
1019|             else :
1020|                 msg = ''
1021|             for error in self.handler.errors :
1022|                 msg += ( '\n' + error )
1023|             if msg.startswith( '\n' ) :
1024|                 msg = msg[ 1: ]
1025|             JOptionPane.showInternalMessageDialog(
1026|                 desktop,
1027|                 msg,
1028|                 'Import failed',
1029|                 JOptionPane.ERROR_MESSAGE,
1030|                 None
1031|             )
```

Listing 22-41 continues the ImportTask class started in the previous listing.

Listing 22-41. Part 2 of the ImportTask Class from WASports_11.py

```
1032|         else :
1033|             cellData = self.handler.getResults()
1034|             tree = cellData.getTree()
1035|             root = tree.getModel().getRoot()
1036|             name = root.toString()
1037|             if localFrame :
1038|                 size  = localFrame.getSize()
1039|                 w, h  = size.width, size.height
1040|                 count = len( self.app.frames )
1041|                 num   = ( count - 1 ) % 8
1042|                 loc   = Point(
1043|                     num * 27 + 32,
1044|                     num * 27 + 32
1045|                 )
```

459

```
1046|              else :
1047|                  print '\nWarning: no localFrame'
1048|                  size      = self.app.frame.getSize()
1049|                  w, h      = size.width >> 1, size.height >> 1
1050|                  count     = 0
1051|                  loc       = Point( 32, 32 )
1052|              internal      = InternalFrame(
1053|                  title     = '%d : %s' % ( count, name ),
1054|                  size      = Dimension( w , h ),
1055|                  location  = loc,
1056|                  cellData  = cellData,
1057|                  app       = self.app,
1058|                  closable  = 1
1059|              )
1060|              self.app.frames.append(
1061|                  ( internal, self.fileName )
1062|              )
1063|              desktop.add( internal, None, 0 )
1064|              internal.setSelected( 1 )
1065|              node = tree.getModel().getRoot()
1066|              tree.expandPath( TreePath( node.getPath() ) )
1067|          self.menuItem.setEnabled( 1 )
```

It is interesting to see how much of this code deals with potential problems. This is one of the temptations that exist with rapid prototyping and the iterative development of applications. There is a tendency to leave out error checking and diagnostic or informational messages.

Unfortunately, this choice has its consequences, which are, by definition, self-inflicted and often painful. When you don't include error checking and diagnostic messages as you're developing your application, it's much more difficult to determine the source of any problems that crop up.[17]

Most of the code in Listings 22-40 and 22-41 should look familiar. For example, compare the doInBackground(...) method (lines 1001-1008) with the code in Listing 22-27. Both prepare the input stream using the appropriate encoding and instantiate a validating SAXParserFactory instance. They also both use this parser to process the specified input stream using a SAXhandler instance that has been customized for the application.

In this case, the SAXhandler class isn't shown, but is very similar, at least in structure, to the one in Listing 22-33. The biggest difference is that instead of displaying the buffered character strings, they are saved in a cellInfo dictionary indexed by the associated tag name (the cell name is in an entry indexed by cellName).

The code is simplified by the fact that the parser validates the input against the DTD and calls one of the error-related routines if an error condition is detected (the warning(...), error(...), or fatalError(...) methods).

At the appropriate points in the parsing process (when the node startElement event is detected), all of the details required by the preceding hierarchy level (in this case, between the cell tag and the node tag) have been saved and can now be used to add a new tree element.

When the end of the XML document is encountered and no error conditions have been detected, the done(...) method process shown in Listing 22-40 uses the result of the processing to create a new inner frame instance and display it on the application desktop.

---

[17]Personal note: I learned the hard way that SwingWorker threads can fail silently (exceptions aren't displayed), so it is good to consider using try/except blocks in these kinds of threads.

What's Left?

At this point, the script is a realistic demonstration of the kinds of things that you can do to create a reasonable graphical interactive wsadmin application. Of course, there are features that you could add to make the application even more useful. The next sections discuss what you would need to do to add functionality to the script.

Text Highlighting

What would it take to add text highlighting to the application? It depends on what you want to highlight. For example, if you want to highlight the port table rows that contain specific text or specific port number values, you need to use a TableCellRenderer (see Chapter 12) to control how each cell should be rendered. Be careful, though; it is easy to forget that the isSelected argument of the getTableCellRendererComponent(...) method should be involved with determining how the table cell should be rendered.

Another possibility is to allow the user to highlight those table rows for active ports. However, remember to take into account the hostname or IP address of the local machine when determining whether imported port table rows should be highlighted.

There is also the possibility of adding multiple or combined highlighting conditions at the same time (both active and highlighted because of matching endpoint names or port numbers).

Maybe you want to allow the user to dynamically select the colors to be used for highlighting. If so, how would you allow the user to save this kind of preference information?

Table Sorting

It would be somewhat helpful to be able to sort and reorder the port tables. It isn't too difficult to implement,[18] but the potential value is more difficult to judge. This is true because it is hard to guess how valuable being able to reorder the data will be to the users of your application.

Comparing Configurations

One interesting possibility to consider is related to the prospect of using this kind of application to compare two (or possibly more) configurations. What kinds of comparisons would you like to make? You could use an application like this to identify port conflicts and differences.

Wouldn't it be useful if the application could export the current port details and then import the previous configuration details and highlight the differences? Would you want it to be able to copy the port numbers from an imported XML file and use this information to change the values used in the local configuration? This kind of thing might be very useful if you wanted the environments to use identical port numbers.

Report Generation

Another potentially useful feature would be the capability to generate reports about the port numbers being used in one or more WebSphere environments. How might you want these reports organized? How important would it be for the data in these reports to be aggregates or filtering of the available data?

---

[18]See http://docs.oracle.com/javase/tutorial/uiswing/components/table.html#sorting.

Summary

What next step makes the most sense to you? It depends on your specific needs. Can you use this application as it is? Maybe, maybe not; it depends on your needs. Consider using an application like this to view and manage all of the port numbers being used by your environment. Which would you prefer—to use an application like this or to use the WebSphere administration console to identify and manage the port numbers in your environment?

I think that you'll agree that this kind of application has real potential for making the administration of your WebSphere Application Server environment much simpler.

I hope that this book helps you on your journey of creating useful graphical `wsadmin` scripting applications.

Index

■ F

FileFilter class, 454
findScopedTypes(...) routine, 434
firstNamedConfigType(...) routine, 436
FlowLayout Manager, 37
FormattingVisitor() method, 248
frame.add() method, 23
frame.getBounds() method, 221
Frame resize method, 400

■ G

generateSecConfigReport, 388
getAttributeValue(...) routine, 434
getContentPane() method, 18, 300
getFontMetrics(...) method, 371
getHeaders class, 246
getHostnames(...) routine, 434
getIPaddresses(...) routine, 434
getMonths() method, 93
getPortTable(...) method, 437
getPreferredSize() method, 36
getTableCellEditorComponent(...) method, 171
getTableCellRendererComponent(...) method, 184, 372
getViewport().getView() methods, 363
getWeekdays() method, 93
Global security application
    content pane, 17
    glass pane, 16–17
    JLabel, 15
    layered pane, 17
    optional MenuBar, 17
Glue components, 56
GraphicsConfiguration object, 267
    ScreenLoc class, 268
    ScreenPos class, 268
GraphicsEnvironment class, 266
GraphicsEnvironment session, 266
GridLayout Manager
    addButtons() method, 59
    addComponents() method, 61
    application, 58, 60
    buttonPress() method, 59
    displayConstraints() function, 61
    event.getActionCommand() method, 59
    GridBagConstraints class, 61–62
    layoutContainer() method, 60
    pane.getLayout() method, 60
    run() method, 59
GroupLayout Manager, 62

■ H

headerTask class, 247, 256
Help.help() method, 355
Help.wsadmin() method, 360
Hypertext markup language (HTML)
    FormattingVisitor() method, 248
    getHeaders class, 246
    getHeader scripts, 249
    getLinks routine, 232
    headerTask class, 247
    head(...) method, 248
    HTML label, 243
    HTML text modification, 244
    javadocInfo_03 sample output, 241
    Java "HTML" classes, 231
    JToggleButton, 245
    rendering HTML, 242
    textTask class, 241

■ I

IBM website, 233
Import(...) event handler method, 458
ImportTask class, 458
Inner cellInfo class, 436
InputMethodListener class, 114–115
InputVerifier method, 227
Interactive scripts
    deprecation message, 11
    equivalent Java application, 10
    Welcome.py script file, 9
Internal frames
    iFrameDemo class, 317–319
    JDesktopPane class, 322–324
    JInternalFrame classes (see JInternalFrame classes)
    layers
        labels, 319
        LayeredPaneDemo class, 320–321
        positioning, 321–322
    scratch
        application output, 347
        consoleTimeout script (see consoleTimeout script)
        InternalFrame class, 343–344
        menu items, 341–342
        multiple inheritance issue, 344
        RadioButton class, 349–351
        result, 352
        revised consoleTimeout class, 342
        setSelected() method, 342
        setValue(...) method, 350–351

■ K